Charles M. G.

The Pure Theory of
International
Trade and
Investment

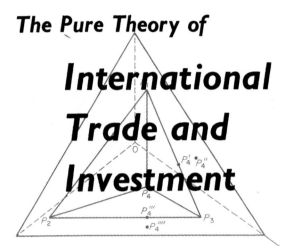

MURRAY C. KEMP
School of Economics
University of New South Wales
Australia

Prentice–Hall Inc, · *Englewood Cliffs, N.J.*

13-742544-9
Library of Congress Card Catalog Number: 74-84455

Current Printing (last number)

10 9 8 7 6 5 4 3 2 1

PRENTICE-HALL INTERNATIONAL, INC., *London*
PRENTICE-HALL OF AUSTRALIA PTY., LTD., *Sydney*
PRENTICE-HALL OF CANADA, LTD., *Toronto*
PRENTICE-HALL OF INDIA PRIVATE LTD., *New Delhi*
PRENTICE-HALL OF JAPAN, INC., *Tokyo*

Printed in the United States of America

Preface

In the present volume I have sought to provide graduate students and advanced undergraduates with a fairly rigorous account of the barter theory of international trade and investment. I hope to supplement it later with a companion volume dealing with the monetary aspects of international economics.

The treatment is, I think, systematic and moderately comprehensive. There are nevertheless three important omissions. At first I had hoped to include a couple of chapters on preferential trading relationships (including, as special cases, customs unions and free trade associations). However I have not been able to compress an adequate discussion into fifty pages; and, in any case, I hope to publish soon an extensive treatment in book form. There is lacking also an adequate analysis of the gains from trade and investment. Within its frame of reference the discussion in Chaps. 12 and 13 is fairly complete; but the point of view adopted in those chapters is uncompromisingly static. Until a late stage in the preparation of the manuscript I had planned to include two companion chapters entitled, respectively, "The Gain from Trade and Investment Dynamically Considered" and "Optimal Trade and Investment Dynamically Considered." In those chapters I had hoped to discuss the implications for welfare of factor endowments and technologies which systematically change over time, and to examine the problem of formulating an optimal commercial policy over time. In the end, however, the plan was abandoned, partly out of a growing

iii

dissatisfaction with the existing literature and partly because my own approaches produced nothing of sufficient simplicity or elegance to justify inclusion in a textbook. To remind the reader of their limitations the initial headings for Chaps. 12 and 13 have been retained. Finally, the reader will look in vain for a discussion of transport costs. My reason for omitting this important and neglected topic is simply that I have not been able to develop an exposition which is sufficiently simple and at the same time faces up to the central issues.[1]

The present volume overlaps the barter sections of my *Pure Theory of International Trade* (Prentice-Hall, Inc., 1964). However the overlap is incomplete. On the one hand, some topics are now treated much more adequately. Thus the earlier comparative statistical treatment of the relationships between growth and trade is now supplemented by a fully developed dynamic analysis (Chaps. 10 and 11); and the implications of international factor mobility are much more completely worked out. On the other hand, some topics treated earlier are now omitted altogether or dealt with only by implication. In the former category are costs of transport, already mentioned, and trade warfare. In the latter category are the static gains from international investment to which in 1964 two chapters were devoted. Since 1964 I have come to see that in a *barter world* international borrowing and lending can be viewed as the purchase and sale of a raw material (capital services) and that therefore the gains from international investment can be handled with the standard gains-from-trade apparatus.

All books are joint products; but some are more joint than others. It is a profound happiness to acknowledge my indebtedness to three former colleagues at the University of New South Wales: Ken-ichi Inada, Takashi Negishi and Leon W. Wegge. To each I owe the resolution of a major difficulty. I am indebted also to good friends with whom I have regularly corresponded over the years. With Henry Y. Wan, Jr. and Ronald W. Jones in particular, the cumulative balance of trade in ideas has gone heavily against me; and much the same is true of my "commerce of the pen" with John Chipman, James R. Melvin, Paul Samuelson and Yasuo Uekawa. I am especially grateful to Professor Jones for his ready permission to include (in Chap. 5) the substance of a joint article of ours; and to Professor Wegge for agreeing to bury in a textbook the jointly-written appendix to Chap. 1.

---

[1] Professor George Hadley and I have provided a treatment of transport costs which satisfies the second criterion but not the first. See George Hadley and Murray C. Kemp, "Equilibrium and Efficiency in International Trade," *Metroeconomica*, XVIII, No. 2 (May-August 1966), 125–141. The reader may also refer to Horst Herberg, "Zur Möglichkeit der Einbeziehung von Transportkosten in die reine Theorie des internationalen Handels," *Jahrbüchern für Nationalökonomie und Statistik*, Band 181, Heft 6 (1968), 549–66.

Most of the book was written at the University of New South Wales which has for many years provided me with the perfect environment for theoretical speculation—peace and quiet. Some of the ideas in Chap. 9, however, were developed during my stay in 1968 at the Institute for International Economic Studies of the University of Stockholm.

Murray C. Kemp

Contents

Introduction 1

Part **I**

**BARTER TRADE BETWEEN
FULLY EMPLOYED
BARTER ECONOMIES**

1. A Simple Closed Economy 5

1. The Formal Model, *5* / 2. The Fundamental Duality Relations, *13* / 3. Other Properties of the Model, *19* / 4. Taxation and Relative Factor Rewards, *21* / Problems, *26* / References, *28* / Appendix*, *30*.

2. A Simple Open Economy 52

1. The Implications of Technical Improvements, *53* / 2. The Implications of a Change in the Terms of Trade, *60* / 3. The Implications of a Tariff, *64* / 4. Some Implications of an Excise Tax, *67* / Problems, *68* / References, *69*.

3. A Trading World 71

1. A model of a Trading World, *71* / 2. Properties of Trading Equilibria— The Heckscher-Ohlin Theorem, *74* / 3. Properties of Trading Equilibria— The Equalization of Factor Rewards, *77* / 4. Properties of Trading Equilibria—Stability, *83* / Problems, *87* / References, *90* / Appendix*, *92*.

4. **A Trading World—Comparative Statics** 95

1. Tariff Changes, *95* / 2. Demand Shifts, *98* / 3. International Transfers, *102* / 4. Economic Expansion, *104* / Problems, *113* / References, *116*.

5.* **Variable Factor Supply and the Theory of International Trade** 119

1. The Formal Model—Revised Version, *120* / 2. The Relationships Between Commodity Prices, Factor Prices, and Outputs, *122* / 3. The Offer Curve, *127* / 4. Geometric Illustrations, *129* / Problems, *132* / References, *133*.

6.* **Non-Traded Commodities** 134

1. Basic Relationships, *135* / 2. The Offer Curve, *138* / 3. The Terms of Trade, The Balance of Payments and Unilateral Transfers, *141* / 4. Tariff Changes, *142* / 5. Changes in Factor Endowments, *144*, / 6. Final Comments, *146* / Problems, *146* / References, *147*.

7.* **Intermediate Goods** 148

Problems, *152* / References, *153*.

8.* **Variable Returns to Scale** 154

1. Theoretical Background, *158* / 2. The Stolper-Samielson Theorem, *161* / 3. The Samuelson-Rybczynski Theorem, *164* / 4. The Relation between Equilibrium Outputs and Commodity Prices, *166* / 5. The Offer Curve, *167* / 6. International Equilibrium, *169* / 7. The Stability of International Equilibrium, *169* / 8. Variable Returns and the Equalization of Relative Factor Rewards, *173* / 9. Other Cases Briefly Considered, *174* / Problems, *178* / References, *179*.

9. **The International Migration of Factors of Production** 181

1. Formal Extensions of the Model and Some Preliminary Results, *182* / 2. Market Stability, *192* / 3. Tariff Changes, *196* / 4. Tax Changes, *203* / 5. The Migration of Labor, *206* / 6. Final Remarks *210* / Problems, *211* / References, *212*.

Part **II**

**TRADE AND INVESTMENT
IN A CONTEXT
OF GROWTH**

10. **International Trade and Economic Growth** 215

1. Short-run Equilibrium, *216* / 2. Long-run Equilibrium, *219* / Problems, *236* / References, *236*.

11.   Trade, International Investment and Growth   237

1. The Model, *237* / 2. Existence and Stability of Short-run Equilibrium, *240* / 3. Existence and Stability of Long-run Equilibrium, *243* / 4. Long-run Trade and Investment, *246* / 5. Comparative Dynamics, *248* / 6. Cautionary Remarks, *248* / References, *249*.

Part **III**

THE APPRAISAL OF
INTERNATIONAL TRADE
AND INVESTMENT

**12.   The Gain From Trade and Investment
Statically Considered**   253

1. Statement and Proof of the Theorem, *254* / 2. Extension of the Proof to Cover Imported Raw Materials, *260* / 3. The Accommodation of Unilateral Transfers, *261* / 4. Welfare and the Terms of Trade, *262* / 5. A Footnote to the Preceding Sections, *265* / 6. Restricted Trade is Superior to No Trade, *267* / 7. Welfare and the Terms of Trade Again, *268* / 8. Increasing Returns to Scale, *270* / 9. Increasing Returns with Distorting Externalities, *273* / 10. The Gains from Trade for Tax-Ridden Economies, *275* / 11. The Gains from Trade for Economies Suffering from other Domestic Distortions, *278* / 12. Welfare and Technical Improvements, *282* / 13. Final Comments, *285* / Problems, *286* / References, *287*.

**13.   Optimal Trade and Investment
Statically Considered**   290

1. World Prices Given, *290* / 2. World Prices Variable, *296* / 3. Sub-Optimal Tariff Policy, *310* / Problems, *313* / References, *315* / Appendices*, *318*.

Part **IV**

THE INTRODUCTION
OF MONEY AND
OTHER SECURITIES

**14.   The Rate of Exchange, the Terms of Trade,
and the Balance of Payments**   331

1. The Introduction of Fiat Currencies—Pegged Rate of Exchange, *332* / 2. The Short-run Effects of Devaluation, *335* / 3. The Long-run Effects of Devaluation *339* / 4. Related Comparative Statical Problems, *340* / 5. The Analysis of Floating Exchange Rates, *344* / 6. The Introduction of Bonds and the Rate of Interest, *345* / Problems, *348* / References, *349* / Appendix on Price Elasticities, *352*.

Introduction

This introductory chapter contains a few general hints for the reader. They will prove less useful than the apothecary's "Three times a day, after meals" and may be disregarded without dire consequences.

It is not necessary that the pages be read from first to last, consecutively. On a first (or nth) reading it is possible to skip whole chapters without loss of continuity. Indeed it is recommended that certain starred sections and chapters be reserved for a second or later reading, not because they are more or less difficult than other sections but because they are side excursions at best only loosely connected to later developments.

The exposition is essentially algebraic, in spite of the fact that for the most part attention is restricted to the simple two-commodities/two-factors/two-countries case, for which geometry and the English language combine to form a more-or-less adequate vehicle of analysis. The reason is that algebraic analyses point most clearly to their own generalizations and mutations. In spite of the liberal use of diagrams, therefore, the reader is advised to persevere with each section until he has mastered the essential algebra.

To each chapter is appended a list of problems, and a list of references. Some of the problems are mere finger exercises; for the most part, however, they cover topics which are of intrinsic interest but which are not handled in the text. They are designed to confirm the reader's understanding of the text. He should at least look at the problems attached to each chapter, and in the case of the early, foundation-laying chapters (Chaps. 1–3) he is urged to work his way through *all* of the problems.

To some entries in the bibliographies I have attached a dagger. Articles and books distinguished in this way contain what, in my view, are the major original contributions to the subject. The daggers separate the pioneers, who broke the trails, from those who merely provided (possibly much-needed) syntheses, elaborations of special cases, minor or obvious extensions, or new garb. To know one's creditors is a virtue; it is suggested therefore that readers prepared to sample in the bibliographies might begin with the daggers.[1]

Equations are numbered by the chapter in which they first appear, and by their order of appearance in that chapter. Equation (2.5), for example, is the fifth new and numbered equation in Chap. 2.

REFERENCES

[1] Caves, Richard E., *Trade and Economic Structure: Models and Methods*. Cambridge, Mass.: Harvard University Press, 1960.

[2] Chipman, John S., "A Survey of the Theory of International Trade," *Econometrica*, XXXIII, No. 3 (July 1965), 477–519; XXXIII, No. 4 (October 1965), 685–760; and XXXIV, No. 1 (January 1966), 18–76.

[3] Viner, Jacob, *Studies in the Theory of International Trade*, London: George Allen and Unwin Ltd., n.d.

[1] Readers interested in the development over time of the theory of international trade may consult Caves [1], Chipman [2], and Viner [3].

part I

Barter Trade between Fully Employed Barter Economies

chapter I

A Simple Closed Economy

On the well-tried (but not infallible) pedagogic principle of proceeding from the particular to the general, the present chapter is devoted to the consideration of a completely closed economy. On the same principle, it is assumed that the economy is perfectly competitive, that in each industry returns to scale are constant, that both production and consumption are free of external economies and diseconomies, and that all productive factors are in completely inelastic supply. For the most part, we shall be engaged in the construction of a formal model of such an economy and in deriving a few of its more important properties. Towards the end of the chapter, however, the model will be put to work in solving a simple problem of comparative statics.

1. THE FORMAL MODEL

We consider a country which produces two commodities, in quantities X_1 and X_2, with the aid of two homogeneous primary factors of production, say labor and capital, in quantities L and K, respectively. K_i is the amount of capital employed in the ith industry, L_i is the amount of labor employed in the ith industry. The ith production relationship is written

$$X_i = F_i(K_i, L_i) \qquad i = 1, 2$$

It is assumed that both factors are indispensible, in the sense that

$$F_i(0, L_i) = F_i(K_i, 0) = 0 \qquad i = 1, 2$$

It is assumed also that F_i is homogeneous of the first degree[1] in K_i and L_i, so that the average product of labor depends only on the capital:labor ratio, $k_i \equiv K_i/L_i$, and total output may be expressed as the product of a scale factor (L_i) and a function f_i of k_i:[2]

$$X_i = L_i f_i(k_i) \equiv L_i F_i\left(\frac{K_i}{L_i}, 1\right) \qquad i = 1, 2 \tag{1.1}$$

The marginal product of capital in terms of the ith commodity is then

$$f_i'(k_i) \equiv \frac{df_i}{dk_i} \equiv \frac{\partial}{\partial K_i} F_i(K_i, L_i) \qquad i = 1, 2$$

The corresponding marginal product of labor is

$$f_i(k_i) - k_i f_i'(k_i) \equiv \frac{\partial}{\partial L_i} F_i(K_i, L_i) \qquad i = 1, 2$$

Notice that the marginal product also depends on factor proportions only. All marginal products are assumed to be positive but diminishing, so that

$$f_i'(k_i) > 0 \quad \text{if} \quad k_i > 0$$
$$f_i''(k_i) < 0$$

It will be assumed also that

$$\lim_{k_i \to 0} f_i(k_i) = 0$$

$$\lim_{k_i \to \infty} f_i(k_i) = \infty$$

$$\lim_{k_i \to 0} f_i'(k_i) = \infty$$

$$\lim_{k_i \to \infty} f_i'(k_i) = 0$$

---

[1] Here and elsewhere I adopt the disreputable but convenient practice of allowing the capitalized symbols, X_1, X_2, L and K, to stand both for names and for quantities.

[2] Let $X = F(K, L)$ be positively homogeneous of degree one in K and L. Then

$$\lambda X = F(\lambda K, \lambda L) \qquad \lambda > 0$$

In particular, let $\lambda = 1/L$. Then, say,

$$\frac{X}{L} = F(k, 1) = f(k)$$

Then the graph of $f_i(k_i)$ is as depicted in Fig. 1.1:

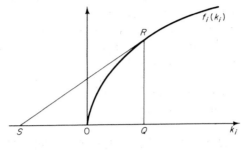

FIGURE 1.1

Under competitive conditions, with no technical external economies or diseconomies *and with something of each commodity produced*, the value of the marginal product of a factor must be equal to the reward of that factor and therefore the same in each industry. If we denote by p_i the price of the ith commodity, by r the rental per unit of capital, and by w the wage rate, each in terms of some arbitrary unit of account, the required equalities may be written as

$$r = p_i f'_i$$
$$w = p_i(f_i - k_i f'_i) \qquad i = 1, 2 \tag{1.2}$$

It follows that the ratio of factor rewards is equal to

$$\omega \equiv \frac{w}{r} = \frac{f_i}{f'_i} - k_i \qquad i = 1, 2 \tag{1.3}$$

Suppose that $k_i = OQ$ in Fig. 1.1. Then

$$\omega = \frac{f_i}{f'_i} - k_i = \frac{RQ}{\dfrac{RQ}{SQ}} - OQ = SO$$

In view of the restrictions placed on $f_i(k_i)$, Eqs. (1.3) determine k_i uniquely in terms of ω, with

$$\frac{dk_i}{d\omega} = -\frac{(f'_i)^2}{f_i f''_i} > 0 \tag{1.4}$$

The relationship between k_i and ω is illustrated by Fig. 1.2. The R_i-curve shows, for the ith industry, the relationship between the factor ratio in that industry and the ratio of factor rewards (which in turn is equal to the ratio of marginal products), and slopes upwards from left to right in accordance with Eqs. (1.4).[3] To any assigned ratio of factor rewards, say ω', there corresponds a pair of cost-minimizing factor ratios, k_1' and k_2'. If the ratio of factor rewards is raised, say to ω'', both industries are induced to economize in the employment of labor and a new pair of cost-minimizing factor ratios, k_1'' and k_2'', is established, with $k_i'' > k_i'$. Given ω, and therefore k_i, one can calculate the relative unit costs or supply prices of the two commodities. Thus if we denote by p^s the relative supply price of the second commodity in terms of the first, we have, in easy steps,

$$p^s(\omega) = \frac{\text{average cost of producing the second commodity}}{\text{average cost of producing the first commodity}}$$

$$= \frac{wL_2 + rK_2}{L_2 f_2} \bigg/ \frac{wL_1 + rK_1}{L_1 f_1}$$

$$= \frac{\omega + k_1(\omega)}{f_2[k_2(\omega)]} \bigg/ \frac{\omega + k_2(\omega)}{f_1[k_1(\omega)]} \tag{1.5}$$

Differentiating logarithmically with respect to ω, and making use of Eqs. (1.3)

$$\frac{\omega}{p^s} \cdot \frac{dp^s}{d\omega} = - \frac{\omega}{\omega + k_1} + \frac{\omega}{\omega + k_2} \tag{1.6}$$

where $\omega/(\omega + k_i)$ is the share of labor in the ith industry. Thus $p^s(\omega)$ is positively sloped if $k_1(\omega) > k_2(\omega)$, negatively sloped if $k_2(\omega) > k_1(\omega)$. The

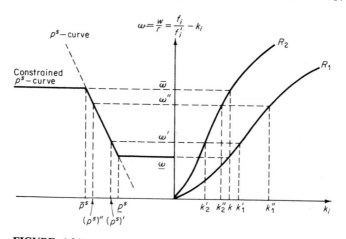

FIGURE 1.2(a)

[3] The elasticity of the R_i-curve is equal to the "elasticity of substitution" of factors in the ith production function. See Prob. 1.7.

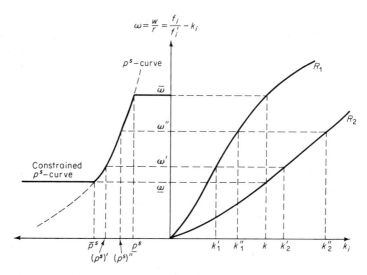

FIGURE 1.2(b)

dotted p^s-curve of Fig. 1.2(a) illustrates the case in which $k_1(\omega) > k_2(\omega)$; the p^s-curve of Fig. 1.2(b) illustrates the case in which $k_2(\omega) > k_1(\omega)$; and the (non-monotonic) p^s-curve of Fig. 1.2(c) illustrates the more complicated possibility that $k_1(\omega) - k_2(\omega)$ is positive for some ω, negative for others. In this latter case the same p^s may correspond to several different values of ω. Thus $p^s(\omega') = p^s(\omega'') = p^s(\omega''')$. It follows that in this case an increase in the value of ω may raise, lower, or leave unchanged the value of p^s, depending on the magnitude of the change.

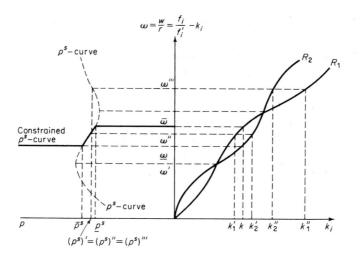

FIGURE 1.2(c)

The relative supply price p^s is defined for all observable values of ω. However, not all positive values of ω are observable. To see this, we note that under competitive conditions, with production functions of the type depicted in Fig. 1.1, both factors of production must be fully employed; that is,

$$L_1 + L_2 = L$$
$$k_1 L_1 + k_2 L_2 = K \tag{1.7}$$

where L and K are constants, in keeping with our *pro tempore* assumption that both factors of production are in inelastic supply. For arbitrary ω [and $k_i(\omega)$], however, we cannot be sure that Eqs. (1.7) will yield nonnegative L_1 and L_2. The point may be illustrated in terms of Fig. 1.2. Let $k = K/L$ be the overall factor endowment ratio, and let

$$\bar{\omega} = \max \{\omega_1, \omega_2\}$$
$$\underline{\omega} = \min \{\omega_1, \omega_2\} \tag{1.8}$$

where ω_i is defined by $k = k_i(\omega_i)$. Thus $\underline{\omega}$ and $\bar{\omega}$ are found successively by reading up from k until the two R_i-curves are encountered. Then any ω greater than $\bar{\omega}$ or less than $\underline{\omega}$ will induce the two industries to adopt factor ratios both lying on the same side of k and therefore incompatible with the full employment of both factors. Under competitive conditions, therefore, one would observe only those ω lying between $\underline{\omega}$ and $\bar{\omega}$:

$$\underline{\omega} \leq \omega \leq \bar{\omega}$$

It follows that the *constrained* p^s-curve (the heavy curve in the left hand quadrant of Fig. 1.2) becomes perfectly elastic at $\underline{\omega}$ and $\bar{\omega}$. Let us define $\underline{p}^s \equiv \min \{p^s(\underline{\omega}), p^s(\bar{\omega})\}$ and $\bar{p}^s \equiv \max \{p^s(\underline{\omega}), p^s(\bar{\omega})\}$ and suppose that the market price ratio, $p \equiv p_2/p_1$, lies at or below $\underline{p}^s$. Clearly the country must be completely specialized in the production of the first commodity, with $\omega = \underline{\omega}$ or $\omega = \bar{\omega}$. Similarly, if $p \geq \bar{p}^s$ the country must be completely specialized in the production of the second commodity, with $\omega = \underline{\omega}$ or $\omega = \bar{\omega}$. In whichever industry is idle both marginal products are zero. To accommodate the possibility of complete specialization it is necessary to rewrite Eqs. (1.2) less restrictively as

$$r \geq p_i f_i'$$
$$w \geq p_i (f_i - k_i f_i') \qquad i = 1, 2$$

with strict equality for $i = 1$ and/or 2.

Before proceeding it is convenient to collect the elements of our model described so far. We begin with the two production relations, written now as

$$y_i = l_i f_i(k_i) \qquad i = 1, 2 \tag{1.9}$$

where $y_i \equiv X_i/L$ is the per capita output of the ith commodity and $l_i \equiv L_i/L$ is the proportion of the labor force employed in the ith industry. Our full employment equations are rewritten as

$$l_1 + l_2 = 1$$
$$k_1 l_1 + k_2 l_2 = k \tag{1.10}$$

The "marginal conditions" become

$$r \geqq p_i f'_i, \qquad\qquad k_i(r - p_i f'_i) = 0$$
$$w \geqq p_i(f_i - k_i f'_i), \qquad l_i[w - p_i(f_i - k_i f'_i)] = 0 \tag{1.11}$$

$$\omega = \frac{f_i}{f'_i} - k_i \qquad i = 1 \text{ and/or } 2 \tag{1.11'}$$

in acknowledgement of the fact that either a factor's reward is equated to the value of its marginal product in a particular industry, or that industry is idle. Finally, expression is given to the possibility of complete specialization:

$$l_i \geqq 0 \quad \text{with} \quad \begin{cases} l_1 = 0 & \text{if } p > \bar{p}^s \\ l_2 = 0 & \text{if } p < \underline{p}^s \end{cases} \tag{1.12}$$

with $\underline{p}^s$ and $\bar{p}^s$ defined recursively by

$$\omega_i = \frac{f_i(k)}{f'_i(k)} - k \qquad i = 1, 2 \tag{1.13}$$

$$\bar{\omega} \equiv \max\{\omega_1, \omega_2\}$$
$$\underline{\omega} \equiv \min\{\omega_1, \omega_2\} \tag{1.14}$$

$$\bar{p}^s = \max\{p^s(\underline{\omega}), p^s(\bar{\omega})\} = \max\left\{\frac{f'_1[k_1(\underline{\omega})]}{f'_2[k_2(\underline{\omega})]}, \frac{f'_1[k_1(\bar{\omega})]}{f'_2[k_2(\bar{\omega})]}\right\}$$

$$\underline{p}^s = \min\{p^s(\underline{\omega}), p^s(\bar{\omega})\} = \min\left\{\frac{f'_1[k_1(\underline{\omega})]}{f'_2[k_2(\underline{\omega})]}, \frac{f'_1[k_1(\bar{\omega})]}{f'_2[k_2(\bar{\omega})]}\right\} \tag{1.15}$$

If commodity prices are known we can expect to solve Eqs. (1.9)–(1.15) for y_i, k_i, l_i, w, r, $\underline{p}$, $\bar{p}^s$, $\underline{\omega}$, $\bar{\omega}$ and ω_i.

To pin down commodity prices we must fill in the demand side of our system. Given commodity prices, we are able to calculate both factor rewards. Given factor rewards and the distribution of the community's assets, both total income and its distribution are determined. Thus if we are given commodity prices we are in principle able to calculate all the determinants of individual (and therefore total) commodity demands and are justified in writing

$$d_i = d_i(p_1, p_2) \qquad i = 1, 2$$

where d_i is the demand per capita for the ith commodity. The familiar equilibrium conditions, that either the demand for each commodity equal the supply or the price be zero, may therefore be written[4]

$$d_i(p_1, p_2) \leq y_i, \qquad p_i[d_i(p_1, p_2) - y_i] = 0 \qquad (1.16)$$

In fact the restrictions we have placed on f_i rule out the possibility of $d_i < y_i$ with $p_i = 0$. We therefore may write, quite simply,

$$d_i(p_1, p_2) - y_i = 0 \qquad (1.17)$$

In fact not both of these demand-supply relationships provide independent restrictions on the variables: Either may be derived from the other with the aid of the budget restraint.[5] Thus we have 15 independent restrictions on the 16 variables y_i, k_i, l_i, w, r, $\underline{p}^s$, $\bar{p}^s$, $\underline{\omega}$, $\bar{\omega}$, ω_i, and p_i. Note, however, that all functions are homogeneous of degree zero in the two nominal prices, p_1 and p_2. The equations and inequations may be rewritten, therefore, in terms of the price ratio $p = p_2/p_1$. This done, we are left with the same number of variables as restrictions.

That completes the construction of our model of a simple "two-by-two" economy (two factors, two products) in which factor supplies are completely inelastic.

[4] The functions d_1 and d_2 fail to give expression to the possibility that demand may depend on the distribution of income between the two categories of factor owners, capitalists and labourers. This omission can be easily remedied (see the worked exercise at the end of this chapter). But in the present context this mite of realism seems not worth the analytical complications which accompany it.

[5] The requirement that consumers' budgets be balanced, in the aggregate, may be expressed as

$$p_1 d_1 + p_2 d_2 = p_1 y_1 + p_2 y_2$$

By Eq. (1.17), however, $d_2 = y_2$; hence $d_1 = y_1$.

Drawing on the several one-to-one relationships in the model, it is possible to envisage the final determination of p in terms of a simple demand-supply diagram. To any hypothetical p there corresponds a ω, which can be read off the constrained p^s-curve. This ω determines the k_i and, through the full employment equations, the l_i. Given k_i and l_i we may then calculate y_i. By varying p we may generate the "supply function" $y_i = y_i(p)$ illustrated by Fig. 1.3. Given the y_i and p we may also calculate real income and, therefore,

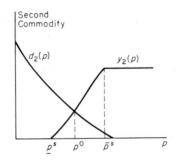

FIGURE 1.3

demand d_2. By varying p we may generate the "demand function" $d_2 = d_2(p)$, also illustrated by Fig. 1.3. Any price p^0 which equates $y_2(p)$ and $d_2(p)$ is an equilibrium price.

In Chap. 3 our model will be extended to accommodate trading relations with other countries. Before exploring more complex worlds, however, it is essential that we become familiar with the more important properties of models of the general type just constructed, and that we acquire some facility in the formal manipulation of them. That will be the objective of the next two sections.

2. THE FUNDAMENTAL DUALITY RELATIONS

Let us consider the subsystem consisting of Eqs. (1.9)–(1.11), on the assumption that neither industry is idle. That subsystem comprises eight equations in the ten variables y_i, k_i, l_i, p_i, w, and r, and describes the "production side" of the economy. The system may be solved, we suppose, for any eight variables in terms of the other two. In particular, we may treat the p_i as known parameters and solve for the remaining variables. Going a step further, we then may calculate the effect on the equilibrium values of those variables of autonomous changes in the p_i, and in K and L. In the present section we shall be especially interested in the response of outputs to changes in the factor endowment, and in the response of factor rewards to changes in commodity prices.

The Samuelson–Rybczynski Theorem

We first explore the implications of a change in the factor endowment at constant prices. Specifically, we consider a small increase in the stock of capital K. Let us begin by recalling from Eqs. (1.2) that the factor ratios k_i depend only on the parameters p_i and not at all on K (or L).[6] In other words, factor intensities are insensitive to changes in the factor endowment. If, however, k_1 and k_2 are constant and unequal, the extra capital can be absorbed only by an expansion of the relatively capital-intensive industry (the industry with the higher k_i) and a contraction of the relatively labor-intensive industry.

This is a striking result, of which we shall later make much use. It is easily verified mathematically. From Eqs. (1.9),

$$\frac{dX_i}{dK} = \frac{dy_i}{dk} = f_i \frac{dl_i}{dk} \qquad i = 1, 2 \tag{1.18}$$

and, from Eqs. (1.10),

$$\frac{dl_i}{dk} = \frac{(-1)^i}{k_2 - k_1} \qquad i = 1, 2 \tag{1.19}$$

Substituting from Eqs. (1.19) into Eqs. (1.18),

$$\frac{dX_i}{dK} = (-1)^i \frac{f_i}{k_2 - k_1} \qquad i = 1, 2 \tag{1.20a}$$

In similar fashion

$$\frac{dX_1}{dL} = y_1 - k \frac{dy_1}{dk} = \frac{k_2 f_1}{k_2 - k_1}$$

$$\frac{dX_2}{dL} = y_2 - k \frac{dy_2}{dk} = -\frac{k_1 f_2}{k_2 - k_1} \tag{1.20b}$$

Thus *an increase in the endowment of any factor results in an expansion of whichever industry is relatively intensive in its use of that factor, and in a decline in the output of the other industry.*

Given this result, it is not surprising, perhaps, that the output of the

---

[6] This is not quite literally true. Equations (1.2) may possess multiple solutions. The full employment equations then "select" from these solutions that *one* which is compatible with our assumption that neither industry is idle.

expanding industry must grow in greater proportion than the factor endowment. This expectation may be verified by rewriting Eqs. (1.20) in elasticity form. Thus

$$\frac{d \log X_1}{d \log K} = \frac{K}{X_1} \cdot \frac{dX_1}{dK} = -\frac{k_1 + \dfrac{K_2}{L_1}}{k_2 - k_1} \tag{1.20a'}$$

$$\frac{d \log X_2}{d \log K} = \frac{K}{X_2} \cdot \frac{dX_2}{dK} = \frac{k_2 + \dfrac{K_1}{L_2}}{k_2 - k_1}$$

and

$$\frac{d \log X_1}{d \log L} = \frac{L}{X_1} \cdot \frac{dX_1}{dL} = \frac{k_2}{l_1(k_2 - k_1)} \tag{1.20b'}$$

$$\frac{d \log X_2}{d \log L} = \frac{L}{X_2} \cdot \frac{dX_2}{dL} = -\frac{k_1}{l_2(k_2 - k_1)}$$

so that $d \log X_1/d \log K$ and $d \log X_2/d \log L$ are greater than one if $k_1 > k_2$, and $d \log X_1/d \log L$ and $d \log X_2/d \log K$ are greater than one if $k_2 > k_1$. Finally, it is easy to show that the elasticity of *relative* output with respect to the *relative* factor endowment is greater than one in absolute value. Thus

$$\frac{d \log \dfrac{X_1}{X_2}}{d \log \dfrac{K}{L}} = \frac{d \log \dfrac{X_1}{X_2}}{d \log K} \quad \text{[from the homogeneity of } F_i\text{]}$$

$$= \frac{d \log X_1}{d \log K} - \frac{d \log X_2}{d \log K}$$

$$\left.\begin{aligned} &= \frac{k_1 + \text{pos. number}}{k_1 - k_2} \\ &= -\frac{k_2 + \text{pos. number}}{k_2 - k_1} \end{aligned}\right\} \quad \text{[from Eqs. (1.20')]}$$

so that the elasticity is greater than one if $k_1 > k_2$ and less than minus one if $k_2 > k_1$.

The above analysis lends itself to a simple geometric illustration based on the familiar Edgeworth–Bowley box diagram. The dimensions of the box are initially $\bar{L}$ and $\bar{K}$ (see Fig. 1.4). The box contains two systems of isoquants (not shown); the system pertaining to the first commodity has origin O_1, that pertaining to the second commodity has origin O_2. The locus of tangencies, or "contract locus," is the curved line O_1PO_2. The initial production point, P, lies of course on the contract locus. The slopes of the

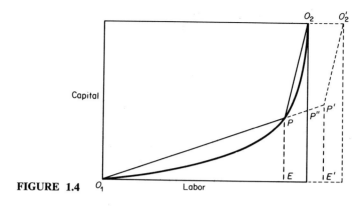

FIGURE 1.4

two rays, O_1P and O_2P, are equal to the factor ratios, k_1 and k_2, respectively. In the particular case illustrated, $k_1 < k_2$. Now if the supply of labor increases, the labor dimension of the box expands and the two origins become O_1 and O_2'. We know that factor proportions depend only on the p_i, which are constant. It follows that the new production point, say P', must lie on O_1P extended, at the intersection with $O_2'P'$ (drawn parallel to O_2P). That O_1P' is greater than O_1P means that the output of the first commodity has increased; that $O_2'P'$ is shorter than O_2P means that the output of the second has fallen off. That the output of the first commodity grows in greater proportion than the labor endowment may be seen by noting (a) that the relative increase in the output of the first industry is $PP'/O_1P = EE'/O_1E$, and the relative increase in the labor endowment O_2O_2'/AO_2, and (b) that $EE' > O_2O_2'$ and $O_1E < AO_2$. Finally, we note a possibility which is of no interest in the present, closed-economy context but which will play an important role in later discussion. If the supply of labor continues to grow, production eventually will be completely specialized on the first or relatively labor-intensive commodity: Nothing at all will be produced of the second or relatively capital-intensive commodity. Any further addition to the labor force will promote a further expansion of the labor-intensive industry. But the additional labor will be absorbed by increasing the ratio in which labor is combined with capital. The upshot will be a decline in the marginal product (and real wage) of labor and an increase in the marginal product (and real reward) of capital.

The Stopler–Samuelson Theorem

As a second exercise we explore the implications for factor rewards of changes in commodity prices.

We know already [from Eq. (1.6)] that, if something is produced of both commodities, an increase in the ith commodity price will give rise to an increase or decrease in the wage:rental ratio as the ith industry is, respectively, relatively labor-intensive or relatively capital-intensive. Here, however, we are interested in the effect of commodity price changes on individual factor rewards. For this purpose we need refer only to Eqs. (1.2). Differentiating totally, first with respect to p_1 and then with respect to p_2, and solving, we obtain

$$\frac{dr}{dp_i} = \frac{(-1)^i f_i}{k_2 - k_1} \tag{1.21a}$$

and

$$\frac{dw}{dp_1} = \frac{k_2 f_1}{k_2 - k_1}$$
$$\frac{dw}{dp_2} = -\frac{k_1 f_2}{k_2 - k_1} \tag{1.21b}$$

Thus an autonomous increase in the price of any commodity results in an increase in the nominal reward of whichever factor is used relatively intensively in the production of that commodity, and in a reduction in the nominal reward of the other factor. It is possible to show, moreover, that the increase in reward is in greater proportion than the increase in price, so that we can say without risk of ambiguity that *an increase in the price of any commodity gives rise to an increase in the* real *reward of whichever factor is used relatively intensively in the production of that commodity, and to a decline in the* real *reward of the other factor*. Thus, rewriting Eqs. (1.21) in elasticity form, and using Eqs. (1.3),

$$\frac{d \log r}{d \log p_i} = (-1)^i \frac{k_i + \omega}{k_2 - k_1} \qquad i = 1, 2 \tag{1.21a'}$$

$$\frac{d \log w}{d \log p_i} = (-1)^i \frac{k_j(k_i + \omega)}{\omega(k_1 - k_2)} \qquad i, j = 1, 2; j \neq i \tag{1.21b'}$$

whence $d \log r/d \log p_1$ and $d \log w/d \log p_2$ are greater than one if $k_1 > k_2$, and $d \log r/d \log p_2$ and $d \log w/d \log p_1$ are greater than one if $k_2 > k_1$. Finally, it is easy to show that the elasticity of relative factor prices with respect to relative product prices is greater than one in absolute value. Thus, relying successively on the homogeneity of F_i and on Eqs. (1.21'),

$$\frac{d \log \omega}{d \log p} = \frac{d \log \omega}{d \log p_2}$$

$$= -\left(\frac{k_2 + \omega}{k_2 - k_1}\right)\left(\frac{k_1 + \omega}{\omega}\right) \tag{1.22a}$$

$$= \left(\frac{k_1 + \omega}{k_1 - k_2}\right)\left(\frac{k_2 + \omega}{\omega}\right) \tag{1.22b}$$

If the first industry is relatively labor-intensive $(k_2 > k_1)$, each of the bracketed expressions in Eq. (1.22a) exceeds one; if the first industry is relatively capital-intensive $(k_1 > k_2)$, each of the bracketed expressions in Eq. (1.22b) exceeds one; if, finally, k_1 and k_2 approach equality, $d \log \omega/d \log p$ approaches plus or minus infinity. Hence

$$\left| \frac{d \log \omega}{d \log p} \right| > 1 \qquad\qquad (1.23)$$

[This may be seen to follow also from Eq. (1.6) if it is recalled that $\omega/(k_i + \omega)$ is the share of labor in the ith industry and therefore a positive fraction.]

The conclusion is illustrated by Fig. 1.5. Suppose that commodity units are chosen so that in an initial equilibrium the relative commodity price is unity $(p_1 = p_2)$. Then the two unit isoquants, $I_1 I_1$ and $I_2 I_2$, are tangential to the same isocost line CC, the slope of which is (minus) the wage:rental ratio. In the case illustrated, the first industry is relatively capital-intensive. If the first commodity price increases, then in the new equilibrium factor rewards must be such that the average cost of producing the first commodity exceeds the average cost of producing the second commodity. Clearly the wage: rental ratio must fall, so that the new iso-cost lines $C'C'$ and $C''C''$ are less steep in slope than CC. The capital:labor ratio must decline in each industry; hence, from the assumption of diminishing returns, the marginal product of labor (in terms of either commodity) must fall and the marginal product of capital rise.

The graphical relationship between the ratio of factor rewards and the product price ratio will be called the "price locus." It is illustrated by Fig. 1.6 (and also by the unconstrained p^s-curves of Fig. 1.2). The two dotted

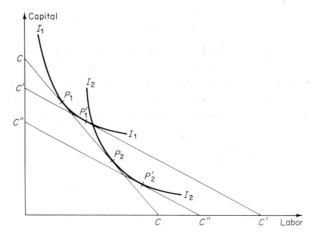

FIGURE 1.5

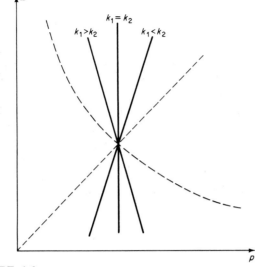

FIGURE 1.6

guiding lines in Fig. 1.6 are of unit elasticity, one elasticity positive and the other negative.

Duality

Comparison of Eqs. (1.20) and Eqs. (1.21) reveals the fundamental duality relationships of our system. If we write $g_1 \equiv w$, $g_2 \equiv r$, $V_1 = K$ and $V_2 = L$, these relationships may be written

$$\frac{dg_i}{dp_j} = \frac{dX_j}{dV_i} \qquad i, j = 1, 2 \qquad (1.24)$$

In the appendix to this chapter we shall study these relationships in greater detail and under more general assumptions. At this point we draw attention only to the close connection they establish between the theorems of Samuelson and Rybczynski and of Stolper and Samuelson.

3. OTHER PROPERTIES OF THE MODEL

Other properties of the model are merely described; proofs are left as problems.[7]

[7] See Probs. 1.1 to 1.4.

Suppose, first, that per capita production of the first commodity, y_1, were treated as a parameter of the subsystem comprising Eqs. (1.9)–(1.11). We could then solve for the amount produced of the second commodity as a function of y_1. The graphical counterpart of $y_2 = y_2(y_1)$ is called the "production possibility curve" [see Fig. 1.7(a)] and shows the various combinations of amounts of the two commodities which might be produced under competitive conditions. It happens to be true, under our present assumptions, that $y_2(y_1)$ is also the *maximum* amount of the second commodity that could be produced if at least y_1 of the first commodity is produced.

Alternatively, we might adopt the ith commodity as *numéraire*, by equating p_i to one, and then, treating the wage rate w as parameter, solve for the rental of capital r. By allowing w to assume alternative values, we obtain the "factor reward frontier" $r = r_i(w)$,[8] illustrated by Fig. 1.7(b). This locus

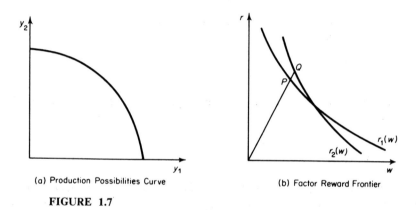

(a) Production Possibilities Curve   (b) Factor Reward Frontier

FIGURE 1.7

shows the various combinations of real factor rewards (in terms of the ith commodity) which are possible under competitive conditions with a given state of the arts. On our present assumptions $r_i(w)$ happens also to tell us the maximum reward to capital which is compatible with a given minimum real wage.

There are of course two distinct frontiers, one for each choice of *numéraire*. Both are convex. Moreover, since $\dfrac{r}{p_1}\Big/\dfrac{w}{p_1} = \dfrac{r}{p_2}\Big/\dfrac{w}{p_2}$ there is a correspondence between points, one on each locus, which lie on the same radius vector. Thus P corresponds to Q in Fig. 1.7(b).

Finally, we merely note that there is a close connection between the elasticities of the two factor reward frontiers and the competitive distribution of income. The details are banished to Problems (1.4), (1.5) and (1.7).

[8] Cf. Samuelson [13].

4. TAXATION AND RELATIVE FACTOR REWARDS

The following worked exercise is of interest in its own right. It also provides useful practice in manipulating models of the type constructed in this
chapter, and indicates some of the dangers implicit in our neglect of distributional considerations.

Suppose that an excise tax is levied on the second commodity at an *ad
valorem* rate of $100t$ per cent. What will be the effect of the raising and
spending of such a tax on the relative rewards of labor and capital? The
original statement of the problem is due to Frederic Benham.[9] Benham
failed to provide a complete solution, but he went part of the way. Assuming
that the taxed commodity is relatively "capital intensive," that is, in our
notation, that $k_2 > k_1$, he argued that[10]

> ... if in the new equilibrium the production of X_2 has expanded and that of
> X_1 contracted, the rental of capital will have risen relatively to that of labour.
> If the opposite has occurred, the rental of capital will have fallen relatively to
> that of labour. The change in the relative princes of X_2 and X_1 will have no
> direct relevance to the result. The sole criterion will be which industry has
> expanded and which contracted. For both capital and labour are employed
> in both industries, so that the earnings and the value of the marginal product
> of a unit of capital (or of labour) will be the same in both industries.
>
> Suppose that X_2 production has expanded. This implies that more labour
> than before is combined with a unit of capital in both industries. This must
> be so if supplies of capital and labour remain constant and there is sufficient
> competition to ensure that all the capital and all the labour are employed
> (unless labour becomes a free good—which would merely be an extreme case
> of a fall in the relative price of labour). But this in turn implies that the
> marginal physical productivity of capital is greater, and of labour is less, than
> it was before, in both industries. Therefore the price of labour must have
> fallen relatively to the price of capital, in order to induce the owners of capital
> to alter the proportions sufficiently to employ all the labour. The extent of
> the relative fall will depend on the extent of the change in the relative marginal
> physical productivity of capital and labour: the more imperfect a substitute
> is labour for capital, the greater will be the relative fall.

This is an admirable passage. But the analysis contained therein is defective
in at least two respects. Having argued that relative factor rewards are
unambiguously related to relative commodity outputs, Benham fails to
indicate the relationship which holds between relative commodity prices and
relative commodity outputs. Much more seriously, Benham fails to realise

---

[9] Benham [17]. See also Johnson [19].
[10] Benham [17], p. 201. I have made minor changes to make the passage conform to
my notation.

that, under his assumptions, relative factor rewards are tied *directly* to relative commodity prices, and that one does not need to consult commodity outputs to determine the response of relative factor rewards. The direct link between relative commodity prices and relative factor rewards has been established above;[11] the relationship between commodity outputs and factor rewards will be explored in Chap. 5.

Our problem therefore reduces to that of discovering the effect of a sales tax on relative commodity prices. In approaching this problem let us note that the price received by the producers of the second commodity now differs, by the amount of the tax, from the price paid by its purchasers; p_2 cannot continue to stand for both prices. Let us agree, then, that p_2 now stands for the price received by the producer and that $p_2(1 + t)$ stands for the price paid by the consumer. For the time being it will be assumed that the community's preferences may be summarized by a quasi-concave utility function[12] so that we may write

$$d_i = d_i[q, p_1, p_2(1 + t)] \qquad i = 1, 2$$

where q is income per capita. Before q can be defined it is necessary to adopt some specific assumption concerning the disposal of the proceeds of the tax. (The latter, per capita, are equal to tp_2y_2). It is convenient to assume that they are handed over to the consumer as a subsidy, so that

$$q = p_1y_1 + p_2y_2 + tp_2y_2 = p_1y_1 + p_2(1 + t)y_2 \qquad (1.25)$$

and Eq. (1.17) becomes

$$d_2[q, p_1, p_2(1 + t)] = y_2 \qquad (1.26)$$

Let us set $p_1 = 1$, so that $p_2 = p$, the relative (consumers') price of the second commodity. Differentiating Eqs. (1.25) and (1.26) totally with respect to t, and solving for dp_2/dt, we obtain[13]

$$\frac{dp_2}{dt} = -p_2 \frac{d_2(\eta_2 + m_2)}{(1 + t)d_2\eta_2 - p_2(1 + t)\dfrac{\partial y_2}{\partial p_2} + m_2\left[tp_2\dfrac{\partial y_2}{\partial p_2} + (1 + t)d_2\right]} \qquad (1.27)$$

[11] Here and in what follows I ignore the possibility that at all factor prices the two industries hire factors in the same proportions. In that singular case $k_1 = k_2 = k$, the capital:labor endowment ratio; and relative rewards are unaffected by the tax.

[12] For the conditions on individual preferences and asset holdings under which this representation is permissible, see Samuelson [24] and Eisenberg [22].

[13] In obtaining Eq. (1.27) use has been made of the result stated in Prob. 1.2.

where

$$\eta_2 \equiv \frac{p_2(1+t)}{d_2} \cdot \frac{\partial d_2}{\partial p_2(1+t)}$$

is the partial price elasticity of demand for the second commodity and

$$m_2 \equiv p_2(1+t)\frac{\partial d_2}{\partial q}$$

is the marginal propensity to consume the second commodity. The price elasticity may, however, be separated into a pure substitution elasticity, $\bar{\eta}_2$, and an income term:[14]

$$\eta_2 = \bar{\eta}_2 - m_2$$

Hence Eq. (1.27) reduces to

$$\frac{dp_2}{dt} = -p_2 \frac{d_2\bar{\eta}_2}{(1+t)d_2\bar{\eta}_2 - p_2\frac{\partial y_2}{\partial p_2}[1 + t(1 - m_2)]} \qquad (1.27')$$

and, in the special case in which $t = 0$, to

$$\frac{dp_2}{dt} = -p_2 \frac{d_2\bar{\eta}_2}{d_2\bar{\eta}_2 - p_2\frac{\partial y_2}{\partial p_2}} \qquad (1.27'')$$

It is a simple matter to show that $\partial y_2/\partial p_2$ is positive, that is, that an autonomous increase in the price of a commodity gives rise to an expansion of output. Moreover, if we ignore the limiting case of right-angled isoquants, $\bar{\eta}_2$ is negative. Thus we may conclude that the introduction of an excise tax on a particular commodity will reduce the relative price received by the producers of that commodity, hence reduce the real reward of the factor used relatively intensively in its production and enhance the real reward of the other factor. This conclusion, it may be noted, is independent of the size of the tax. Figure 1.8(a) illustrates. *PP* is the production possibility curve, p^0 is the initial, pre-tax production and consumption point, and the initial price ratio is indicated by the slope of the line p^0. The post-tax production and consumption equilibrium falls at P', with the producers' price ratio indicated by the slope of the line p' and the consumers' price ratio indicated by the slope of the line $p'(1 + t)$. The dotted lines are community indifference

[14] See Slutzky [25].

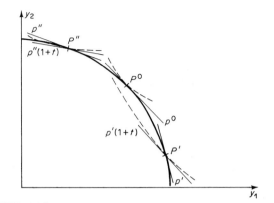

FIGURE 1.8(a)

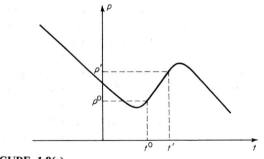

FIGURE 1.8(b)

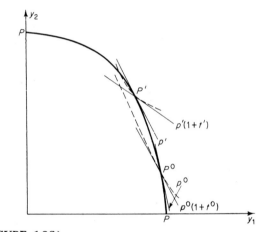

FIGURE 1.8(c)

curves. That the relative price of the taxed commodity cannot increase may be seen by supposing that the post-tax equilibrium is at P''. Such an equilibrium necessarily involves intersecting indifference curves.

If we start with a tax-ridden situation, we can no longer be sure that an increase in the rate of tax will give rise to a decrease in p_2. Thus if m_2 is sufficiently large the denominator on the right-hand side of Eq. (1.27′), and therefore dp_2/dt itself, will be positive. Figures 1.8(b) and 1.8(c) illustrate the possibility. For this paradoxical outcome, however, it is necessary that m_2 be greater than one, that is, that the untaxed commodity be inferior. This is a first sample of the paradoxes associated with inferiority in consumption. It will not be the last. In Chaps. 2–4 we shall encounter several paradoxes similar to that described, and in Chaps. 12 and 13 we shall notice several welfare paradoxes also requiring inferiority. In a two-commodity situation one may perhaps feel justified in ruling out inferiority. When many commodities are recognized, however, inferiority cannot with clear conscience be ignored.

The entire analysis, so far, has proceeded on the assumption that the community behaves like a single utility-maximizing individual so that demand is quite independent of the distribution of earned income between the two factors of production. If that assumption is relaxed, it is by no means impossible that an excise tax might raise the price received by the producers of the taxed commodity and, therefore, enhance the real reward of the factor used relatively intensively in its production, *even if initially $t = 0$ and even if inferiority is excluded.* To establish this possibility we first derive the condition under which $dp_2/dt = 0$ and then show that these conditions can be modified slightly to ensure that $dp_2/dt > 0$. We observe first that if p_2 is constant so must be the two outputs and, therefore, d_2; and conversely. Thus we may seek, as "proxy" for the conditions under which $dp_2/dt = 0$, the conditions under which $dd_2/dt = 0$, the differentiation to be performed with p_2 held constant. Let us distinguish by superscripts the marginal propensities, demand elasticities, etc., of laborers and owners of capital; and let us denote by v_L and $v_K (v_L + v_K = 1)$ the proportions of the tax proceeds received by the two classes of factor owners. Then it is not difficult to show that $dp_2/dt = dd_2/dt = 0$ if and only if

$$\sum_{i=L,K} v_i m_2^i = - \sum_{i=L,K} \frac{D_2^i}{D_2} \eta_2^i \qquad (1.28)$$

that is, if a weighted average of the two marginal propensities is equal to another weighted average of the two price elasticities of demand. Drawing on the Slutzky relations,[15]

$$\eta_2^i = \bar{\eta}_2^i - m_2^i \qquad i = L, K$$

[15] See footnote 14.

Equation (1.28) becomes

$$\Sum \left(v_i - \frac{D_2^i}{D_2} \right) m_2^i = -\Sum \frac{D_2^i}{D_2} \bar{\eta}_2^i \qquad (1.28')$$

This condition may be satisfied even in the absence of inferiority; consider, for example, the case in which $m_2^L = \frac{3}{4}$, $m_2^T = \frac{1}{4}$, $v_L = \frac{3}{4}$, $v_K = \frac{1}{4}$, $d_2^L = d_2^K$. Moreover, the equality in (1.28') may be replaced by either inequality, which establishes the possibility.

This may serve as a warning against the neglect of distributional considerations, a neglect in which, nevertheless, we shall stubbornly persist.

PROBLEMS

Properties of the Model

1.1 Consider the subsystem comprising Eqs. (1.9)–(1.11). Close the system by treating y_2 as a parameter and show that, if neither industry is idle,

$$\frac{dy_1}{dy_2} = -p$$

Obtain an expression for d^2y_1/dy_2^2 and deduce that the production frontier is concave to the origin if $k_1 \neq k_2$, otherwise a straight line.

1.2 Close the subsystem comprising Eqs. (1.9)–(1.11) by treating p as a parameter and show that

$$\frac{dy_1}{dp} + p\frac{dy_2}{dp} = 0$$

and, hence, that

(a) $$\frac{d\left(\frac{q}{p_1}\right)}{dp} = \frac{dy_1}{dp} + p\frac{dy_2}{dp} + y_2 = y_2$$

(b) $$X_1 e_1 = pX_2 e_2$$

where $e_1 \equiv (1/pX_1)[dX_1/d(1/p)]$ and $e_2 \equiv (p/X_2)(dX_2/dp)$ are the "general equilibrium" elasticities of supply of, respectively, the first and second commodities.

1.3 What will be the shape of the price locus when in each industry the factor ratio is a constant?

1.4 In a one-commodity system the factor rewards are

$$w = f'$$
$$r = f - kf'$$

Treat w as a parameter and derive expressions for dr/dw and d^2r/dw^2. Deduce that the factor reward frontier is convex to the origin and that the elasticity of the function $r(w)$ is equal to the ratio of the two factors' income shares.

1.5 Close the subsystem comprised of Eqs. (1.9)–(1.11) by treating w/p_1 as a parameter, and obtain expressions for $d(r/p_1)/d(w/p_1)$ and $d^2(r/p_1)/d(w/p_1)^2$. Is it possible to infer that, in the two-commodities case also, the factor reward frontiers are convex to the origin? And what is the connection between the elasticity $(w/r).(dr/dw)$ and the distribution of income?

1.6 Show that

$$\frac{d\log w}{d\log p_1} + \frac{d\log w}{d\log p_2} = 1$$

$$\frac{d\log r}{d\log p_1} + \frac{d\log r}{d\log p_2} = 1$$

1.7 Prove that the elasticity of the R_i-curve is equal to the "elasticity of substitution" between factors in the ith industry.

Definition: the *elasticity of substitution* is the elasticity of the factor ratio k_i with respect to changes in the marginal rate of substitution between factors as we move along an isoquant. For constant-returns-to-scale production functions the elasticity of substitution reduces to

$$\frac{\omega}{k_i} \cdot \frac{dk_i}{d\omega} = -\frac{f_i'(f_i - k_i f_i')}{k_i f_i f_i''}$$

For further details, see Allen [12], pp 340–43.

1.8 Suppose that both production functions are of the simple Cobb–Douglas form:

$$X_i = K_i^{\alpha_i} L_i^{1-\alpha_i} \qquad i = 1, 2$$

Write down the specific Cobb–Douglas form of Eqs. (1.11) and

(a) Solve for k_i in terms of p;

(b) Derive an expression for $d\log \omega/d\log p$, paying special attention to the case in which $\alpha_1 = \alpha_2$;

(c) Derive expressions for the elasticities of each of the two R_i-curves [that is, in view of Prob. (1.7), for the two elasticities of substitution];

(d) Derive expressions for the elasticities of the two factor rewards frontiers.

1.9 Suppose the terms of trade are given. Show that

$$r = p_1 \frac{dX_1}{dK} + p_2 \frac{dX_2}{dK} = p_1 \frac{dy_1}{dk} + p_2 \frac{dy_2}{dk}$$

Can the expression $\left(p_1 \dfrac{dX_1}{dL} + p_2 \dfrac{dX_2}{dL}\right)$ be similarly interpreted?

1.10 What will be the effect on outputs of a simultaneous increase in the endowments of both labor and capital, with $\rho dL = dK$? For what value of ρ will $dX_1 = 0$? For what value will $dX_2 = 0$? Examine the special case in which $p = k$.

1.11 What happens to the factor price frontiers $r_1(w)$ and $r_2(w)$ when the factor endowment changes?

1.12 Given "factor intensity reversal" [Fig. 1.2(c)], does the contract locus cut the 45°-line?

Taxation and Relative Factor Rewards

1.13 Suppose that the government levies a sales tax on the second commodity at an *ad valorem* rate of $100t$ per cent. The tax is collected in terms of the second or taxed commodity. The government keeps a fraction ρ of the tax proceeds for its own purposes and spends the balance, at retail prices, on the first commodity. Is it possible for the relative price received by the producers to turn in favor of the taxed commodity?

Appendix

1.14 Generalize Theorem 1A.5(a) by showing that if $\alpha_{ii}/\alpha_{ji} \geq \alpha_{is}/\alpha_{js}$ $(i \neq j, i \neq s, i = 1, \ldots, 4)$ then the diagonal elements of S^{-1} are greater than one.

REFERENCES

Properties of the Model

†[1] Chipman, John S., "Factor Price Equalization and the Stolper–Samuelson Theorem," unpublished. Abstract in *Econometrica*, XXXII, No. 4 (October 1964), 682–83.

†[2] Inada, Ken-ichi, "Factor Intensity and the Stolper–Samuelson Condition," *Econometrica*, to be published.

[3] Johnson, Harry, G., *International Trade and Economic Growth*. London: George Allen and Unwin Ltd., 1958.

[4] Jones, Ronald W., "The Structure of Simple General Equilibrium Models," *Journal of Political Economy*, LXXIII, No. 6 (December 1965), 557–72.

[5] Jones, Ronald W., "Duality in International Trade: A Geometrical Note," *Canadian Journal of Economics and Political Science*, XXXI, No. 3 (August 1965), 390–93.

[6] Kemp, Murray C. and Ronald W. Jones, "Variable Labor Supply and the Theory of International Trade," *Journal of Political Economy*, LXX, No. 1 (February 1962), 30–36.

[7] Kemp, Murray C. and Leon L. F. Wegge, "On the Relation between Commodity Prices and Factor Rewards," *International Economic Review*, to be published.

[8] Kemp, Murray C. and Leon L. F. Wegge, "Generalization of the Stolper–Samuelson and Samuelson–Rybczynski Theorems in Terms of Conditional Input-Output Coefficients," *International Economic Review*, to be published.

[9] Minabe, Nobuo, "The Stolper–Samuelson Theorem, the Rybczynski Effect, and the Heckscher–Ohlin Theory of Trade Pattern and Factor Price Equalization: the Case of a Many-Commodity, Many-Factor Country," *Canadian Journal of Economics and Political Science*, XXXIII, No 3 (August 1967), 401–19.

[10] Rybczynski, T. N., "Factor Endowments and Relative Commodity Prices," *Economica*, New Series, XXII, No. 4 (November 1955), 336–41.

[11] Samuelson, Paul A., "International Factor Price Equalization Once Again," *Economic Journal*, LIX, No. 234 (June 1949), 181–97.

†[12] Samuelson, Paul A., Prices of Factors and Goods in General Equilibrium," *Review of Economic Studies*, XXI, No. 1 (October 1953), 1–20.

[13] Samuelson, Paul A., "Parable and Realism in Capital Theory: the Surrogate Production Function," *Review of Economic Studies*, XXIX(3), No. 80 (June 1962), 193–206.

[14] Shephard, Ronald, *Cost and Production Functions*. London: Oxford University Press, 1953.

†[15] Stolper, Wolfgang F. and Paul A. Samuelson, "Protection and Real Wages," *Review of Economic Studies*, IX, No. 1 (November 1941), 58–73. Reprinted in *Readings in the Theory of International Trade*, eds. Howard S. Ellis and Lloyd A. Metzler, 333–57. Philadelphia: The Blakiston Company, 1949.

†[16] Uekawa, Yasuo, "On the Generalization of the Stolper–Samuelson Theorem," *Econometrica*, to be published.

Taxation and Relative Factor Rewards

[17] Benham, Frederic, "Taxation and the Relative Prices of Factors of Production," *Economica*, New Series, II, No. 2 (May 1935), 198–203.

[18] Foster, Edward and Hugo Sonnenschein, "Price Distortion and Economic Welfare," *Econometrica*, to be published.

[19] Johnson, Harry G., "The General Equilibrium Analysis of Sales Taxes: a Comment," *American Economic Review*, LXVI, No. 1 (March 1956), 151–56.

Technical Equipment

[20] Aitken, A. C., *Determinants and Matrices*, 9th ed. Edinburgh and London: Oliver and Boyd, 1956.

[21] Allen, R. G. D., *Mathematical Analysis for Economists*. London: Macmillan and Company Ltd., 1938.

[22] Eisenberg E., "Aggregation of Utility Functions," *Management Science*, VII (July 1961), 337–50.

[23] Ostrowski, Alexander, "Über die Determinanten mit überwiegender Hauptdiagonale," *Commentarii Mathematici Helvetici*, 10 (1937–38), 69–96.

[24] Samuelson, Paul A., "Social Indifference Curves," *Quarterly Journal of Economics*, LXX, No. 1 (February 1956), 1–22.

[25] Slutzky, Eugene E., "Sulla teoria del Bilancio del Consumatore," *Giornale del Economisti*, LI, No. 1 (July 1915), 1–26. Reprinted, in English translation by Olga Ragusa, as "On the Theory of the Budget of the Consumer," in *Readings in Price Theory*, pp. 27–56. Homewood, Illinois: Richard D. Irwin, Inc., for the American Economic Association, 1952.

APPENDIX*

Generalizations of the Stolper–Samuelson and Samuelson–Rybczynski Theorems

Not all theorems proved for the case of two products and two factors of production admit of straight-forward generalization; and, even where a generalization is highly plausible, the proof may be quite difficult. To illustrate these propositions we consider now the problem of extending the Stolper–Samuelson and Samuelson–Rybczynski Theorems so that they cope with any number of factors and products.

A1. A REVIEW OF THE STOLPER–SAMUELSON THEOREM

We begin by introducing a slightly revised notation and by reviewing the material of Sec. 2. The new notation is as follows:

a_{ij} = the amount of factor i used in the production of a unit of commodity j
w_i = the money reward (rental) of the ith factor of production
p_j = the money price of the jth product
V_j = the community's endowment of the jth factor of production
$\theta_i = \log w_i$
$\pi_j = \log p_j$
C_j = the unit cost of producing the jth commodity

* This appendix was written jointly with Professor Leon L. Wegge of the University of California at Davis.

In each case, the subscript runs from 1 to n. In addition we shall employ the following vector notation:

$$a_j = (a_{1j}, \ldots, a_{nj})$$

$$A = \begin{pmatrix} a_{11} & \cdots & a_{1n} \\ \cdots & \cdots & \cdots \\ a_{n1} & \cdots & a_{nn} \end{pmatrix}$$

$$w = (w_1, \ldots, w_n)$$
$$p = (p_1, \ldots, p_n)$$
$$V = (V_1, \ldots, V_n)$$
$$X = (X_1, \ldots, X_n)$$
$$\theta = (\log w_1, \ldots, \log w_n)$$
$$\pi = (\log p_1, \ldots, \log p_n)$$
$$c = (c_1, \ldots, c_n)$$

In terms of this notation, the jth production function can be written

$$1 = F_j(a_j)$$

Given w, producers select those a_{ij}'s which minimize the unit cost of product j. Thus if $\chi_j \equiv \{a_j \mid f_j(a_j) = 1\}$ then

$$c_j(w) = \min_{a_j \in \chi_j, \ i} \sum_i w_i a_{ij} \qquad (1A.1)$$

where $c_j(w)$ is homogeneous of degree one and concave. From Eq. (1A.1), $\sum_i w_i(\partial a_{ij}/\partial w_k) = 0$; hence

$$\frac{\partial c_j}{\partial w_i} = a_{ij} + \sum_k w_k \left(\frac{\partial a_{kj}}{\partial w} \right) = a_{ij}$$

Under competition, with all goods produced, therefore,

$$\sum_i w_i a_{ij}(w) = c_j(w) = p_j$$

or, in vector notation,

$$p = c(w) \qquad (1A.2)$$

with the Jacobian

$$\frac{\partial c}{\partial w} = (a_{ij}) = A \qquad (1A.3)$$

It will be more convenient however to work with the logarithms of prices. Eqs. (1A.2) and (1A.3) then become

$$\pi = \log c(e^\theta) = \psi(\theta) \qquad (1A.2')$$

and

$$\frac{\partial \psi}{\partial \theta} = \psi'(\theta) = \hat{p}^{-1}A\hat{\theta} \tag{1A.3'}$$

respectively, where $\hat{p}$ and $\hat{\theta}$ are diagonal matrices so that the (i,j)th element of ψ' is

$$\alpha_{ij} = \frac{w_i a_{ij}}{p_j} \tag{1A.4}$$

Let (α_{ij}), the matrix of distributive shares, be denoted by S. It is obvious that the column sums of S are one; that is, S is a stochastic matrix. It follows that the inverse S^{-1} also has unit column sums.[16]

Stolper and Samuelson, in their consideration of the two-by-two case, assumed that

$$\frac{a_{11}}{a_{21}} > \frac{a_{12}}{a_{22}} \quad \text{and} \quad \frac{\alpha_{11}}{\alpha_{21}} > \frac{\alpha_{12}}{\alpha_{22}} \tag{1A.5}$$

In words, the first factor is used relatively intensively in the first industry, and the second factor is used relatively intensively in the second industry. It follows from inequalities (1A.5) that A^{-1} and S^{-1} possess negative off-diagonal elements and positive diagonal elements:

$$S^{-1} = \begin{pmatrix} + & - \\ - & + \end{pmatrix} \tag{1A.6}$$

And since the column sums of S^{-1} are equal to one the diagonal elements must be greater than one. In fact (1A.5) is necessary as well as sufficient for the Stolper–Samuelson result:

$$S^{-1} = \begin{pmatrix} + & - \\ - & + \end{pmatrix} \quad \text{if and only if} \quad \frac{\alpha_{11}}{\alpha_{21}} > \frac{\alpha_{12}}{\alpha_{22}} \tag{1A.7a}$$

A2. ARBITRARY BUT EQUAL NUMBERS OF PRODUCTS AND FACTORS

In view of (1A.7a) one is tempted to seek conditions on the α_{ij} which contain (1A.5) as a special case and which are necessary and sufficient for

---

[16] Let 1 be the row vector consisting of n ones. Then if S has column sums equal to one, $1S = 1$, whence $1S^{-1} = (1S)S^{-1} = 1(SS^{-1}) = 1$. The proof is Chipman's [1].

the inverse of S^{-1} to have the sign pattern

$$S^{-1} = \begin{pmatrix} + & - & \cdots & - \\ - & + & \cdots & - \\ \cdots\cdots\cdots\cdots\cdots \\ - & - & \cdots & + \end{pmatrix} \qquad (1A.8a)$$

For then, clearly, one would be able to say that an increase in the jth product price is associated with a more than proportionate increase in the jth factor reward (and therefore with an unambiguous increase in the real reward of the jth factor) and with a decline in the (money and real) rewards of all other factors. This is in fact the path to generalization we shall follow.

Notice, however, that by simply renumbering factors *or* products, the Stolper–Samuelson Theorem can be given the equivalent form:

$$S^{-1} = \begin{pmatrix} - & + \\ + & - \end{pmatrix} \quad \text{if and only if} \quad \frac{\alpha_{11}}{\alpha_{21}} < \frac{\alpha_{12}}{\alpha_{22}} \qquad (1A.7b)$$

This formulation suggests the alternative possibility of generalizing the theorem by placing restrictions on the a_{ij} necessary and sufficient for the inverse of S^{-1} to have the sign pattern

$$S^{-1} = \begin{pmatrix} - & + & \cdots & + \\ + & - & \cdots & + \\ \cdots\cdots\cdots\cdots\cdots \\ + & + & \cdots & - \end{pmatrix} \qquad (1A.8b)$$

For $n > 2$, it is impossible by simply renumbering factors or products to reduce the sign pattern (1A.8b) to the pattern (1A.8a). The two paths to generalization are, therefore, genuine alternatives. Generalizations obtained by the two paths are equivalent only for $n \leq 2$.

As already noted, we shall confine our attention to generalizations reached by the first path. The reader interested in the destination of the second path may consult Inada [2] and Kemp and Wegge [8].

We seek first a generalization of the concept of relative factor intensity; that is, we seek to generalize (1A.5) so that it may be interpreted as requiring that the ith factor of production is used relatively intensively in the ith industry. Evidently nonsingularity of the matrix S is not enough; further restrictions are necessary. There are several ways in which the concept might be generalized,[17] but it seems most natural to say that factor i is used

---

[17] Cf. Chipman [1], Minabe [9], and Uekawa [16]. Johnson ([3] p. 30) appears to deny the possibility of generalization.

relatively intensively in the ith industry, and is associated with that industry, if and only if

$$\max_s \left\{ \frac{\alpha_{is}}{\alpha_{js}} \right\} = \frac{\alpha_{ii}}{\alpha_{ji}} \qquad j = 1, \dots, n \qquad (1A.9)$$

If (1A.9) holds for all i, so that[18]

$$\frac{\alpha_{ii}}{\alpha_{ji}} > \frac{\alpha_{is}}{\alpha_{js}} \qquad i \neq j, \quad i \neq s, \quad i = 1, \dots, n \qquad (1A.10)$$

we have the required generalization. In the special two-by-two case, (1A.10) reduces to (1A.5).

Necessary Conditions

We begin by establishing three necessary conditions for the sign pattern (1A.8a). As far as possible, only the most elementary properties of matrices and determinants will be used in the proofs. In one or two places, however, appeal will be made to Jacobi's theorem on determinants[19] and to well-known properties of Minkowski matrices.[20]

Theorem 1A.1: *If S^{-1} has the sign pattern* (1A.8a) *then every principal minor of S is positive, that is, S is a P-matrix.*

Proof: Partition S and S^{-1} so that

$$S = \begin{pmatrix} S_{11} & S_{12} \\ S_{21} & S_{22} \end{pmatrix}$$

[18] For $n > 2$ the inequalities (1A.10) may be written more compactly as

$$\frac{\alpha_{ii}}{\alpha_{ij}} > \frac{\alpha_{si}}{\alpha_{sj}} \qquad i \neq j \neq s, \quad i = 1, \dots, n$$

The "missing" relation, with $s = j$, follows from $\alpha_{ii}/\alpha_{ji} > \alpha_{is}/\alpha_{js}$ and $\alpha_{jj}/\alpha_{ij} > \alpha_{js}/\alpha_{is}$. Thus (1A.10) contains just $n(n-1)(n-2)$ independent relations.

It is worth noting also that (1A.10) holds if and only if

$$\frac{\alpha_{ii}}{\alpha_{ji}} > \frac{\alpha_{is}}{\alpha_{js}} \qquad i \neq j, \quad i \neq s, \quad i = 1, \dots, n$$

[19] Cf. Aitken [20], pp. 97ff.
[20] A matrix is called Minkowski if its diagonal elements are nonnegative and its off-diagonal elements non-positive and if all of its column (row) sums are non-negative. If all column (row) sums are strictly positive the matrix is called proper Minkowski; in all other cases it is said to be improper. The determinant of a proper Minkowski matrix is positive and the inverse of an irreducible Minkowski matrix is positive. For proofs, further properties, and for references, see Ostrowski [23].

and

$$S^{-1} = \begin{pmatrix} (S^{-1})_{11} & (S^{-1})_{12} \\ (S^{-1})_{21} & (S^{-1})_{22} \end{pmatrix}$$

where S_{11} and $(S^{-1})_{11}$ are $k \times k$. The essence of the proof consists in the demonstration that

$$|S_{11}| = \frac{|(S^{-1})_{22}|}{|S^{-1}|} \tag{1A.11}$$

Once (1A.11) is proved, we can appeal to the fact that, since S^{-1} and $(S^{-1})_{22}$ are proper Minkowski matrices, both $|S^{-1}|$ and $|(S^{-1})_{22}|$, and therefore $|S_{11}|$, are positive. The proof is then completed by noting that k can take the values $1, \ldots, n - 1$.

By easy steps,

$$
\begin{aligned}
|S^{-1}| &= \begin{vmatrix} (S^{-1})_{11} & (S^{-1})_{12} \\ (S^{-1})_{21} & S(^{-1})_{22} \end{vmatrix} \\
&= |(S^{-1})_{22}| \cdot \begin{vmatrix} (S^{-1})_{11} & (S^{-1})_{12} \\ (S^{-1})_{21} & (S^{-1})_{22} \end{vmatrix} \cdot \begin{vmatrix} I & 0 \\ -((S^{-1})_{22})^{-1}(S^{-1})_{21} & ((S^{-1})_{22})^{-1} \end{vmatrix} \\
&\qquad\qquad\qquad\qquad\qquad\qquad \text{[if } (S^{-1})_{22} \text{ is nonsingular]} \\
&= |(S^{-1})_{22}| \cdot \left| \begin{pmatrix} (S^{-1})_{11} & (S^{-1})_{12} \\ (S^{-1})_{21} & (S^{-1})_{22} \end{pmatrix} \begin{pmatrix} I & 0 \\ -((S^{-1})_{22})^{-1}(S^{-1})_{21} & ((S^{-1})_{22})^{-1} \end{pmatrix} \right| \\
&= |(S^{-1})_{22}| \cdot \begin{vmatrix} (S^{-1})_{11} - (S^{-1})_{12}((S^{-1})_{22})^{-1}(S^{-1})_{21} & (S^{-1})_{12}((S^{-1})_{22})^{-1} \\ 0 & I \end{vmatrix} \\
&= |(S^{-1})_{22}| \cdot |(S^{-1})_{11} - (S^{-1})_{12}((S^{-1})_{22})^{-1}(S^{-1})_{21}| \tag{1A.12}
\end{aligned}
$$

On the other hand,

$$\begin{pmatrix} (S^{-1})_{11} & (S^{-1})_{12} \\ (S^{-1})_{21} & (S^{-1})_{22} \end{pmatrix} \begin{pmatrix} S_{11} & S_{12} \\ S_{21} & S_{22} \end{pmatrix} = \begin{pmatrix} I & 0 \\ 0 & I \end{pmatrix}$$

hence

$$(S^{-1})_{11}S_{11} + (S^{-1})_{12}S_{21} = I \tag{1A.13a}$$

and

$$(S^{-1})_{21}S_{11} + (S^{-1})_{22}S_{21} = 0 \tag{1A.13b}$$

From Eq. (1A.13b),

$$S_{21} = -[(S^{-1})_{22}]^{-1}(S^{-1})_{21}S_{11}$$

Substituting in Eq. (1A.13a),

$$S_{11} = \{(S^{-1})_{11} - (S^{-1})_{12}[(S^{-1})_{22}]^{-1}(S^{-1})_{21}\}^{-1}$$

whence

$$|S_{11}| = |(S^{-1})_{11} - (S^{-1})_{12}[(S^{-1})_{22}]^{-1}(S^{-1})_{21}|^{-1} \qquad (1A.14)$$

Combining Eqs. (1A.12) and (1A.14), we obtain Eq. (1A.11).   Q.E.D.

Theorem 1A.2: *If S^{-1} has the sign pattern* (1A.8a), *the inequalities* (1A.10) *are satisfied.*

Proof: Suppose that S^{-1} has the required sign pattern and is therefore an irreducible Minkowski matrix. Then every principal submatrix of S^{-1} is an irreducible Minkowski matrix. Hence S, and the inverse of every principal submatrix of S^{-1}, is positive. From Jacobi's theorem on determinants, for every determinant Δ

$$\Delta_{11}\Delta_{sj} - \Delta_{1j}\Delta_{s1} = \Delta_{11,sj}\Delta$$

Hence

$$\frac{\Delta_{11}}{\Delta} \cdot \frac{(-1)^{s+j}\Delta_{sj}}{\Delta} - \frac{(-1)^{1+s}\Delta_{s1}}{\Delta} \cdot \frac{(-1)^{1+j}\Delta_{1j}}{\Delta} = \frac{(-1)^{j+s}\Delta_{11,sj}}{\Delta_{11}} \cdot \frac{\Delta_{11}}{\Delta} \qquad (1A.15)$$

Applying Eq. (1A.15) to S^{-1}, and noting that $(-1)^{s+j}\Delta_{11,sj}/\Delta_{11}$ is an element of the inverse of an $(n-1)$-dimensional principal submatrix of S^{-1} and therefore positive, we conclude that $\alpha_{11}\alpha_{js} - \alpha_{j1}\alpha_{1s} > 0$. The same argument may be applied to each principal sub-matrix of S^{-1}.   Q.E.D.

Theorem 1A.3: *If S^{-1} has the sign pattern* (1A.8a), $\alpha_{ii} > \alpha_{ii}$ $(i \neq j)$.

Proof: From Theorem 1A.2, the inequalities (1A.10) are satisfied. Hence

$$\alpha_{ii}\alpha_{sj} - \alpha_{si}\alpha_{ij} > 0 \qquad s \neq j. \quad i \neq j$$

Summing over $s \neq i$,

$$\alpha_{ii} \sum_{\substack{s=1 \\ s \neq i}}^{n} \alpha_{sj} - \alpha_{ij} \sum_{\substack{s=1 \\ s \neq i}}^{n} \alpha_{si} > 0$$

That is, since column sums are one,

$$\alpha_{ii}(1 - \alpha_{ij}) - \alpha_{ij}(1 - \alpha_{ii}) > 0$$

Hence $\alpha_{ii} > \alpha_{ij}$.   Q.E.D.

Sufficient Conditions

We turn now to two sufficiency theorems, one for the case $n = 3$, the other for the case $n = 4$. For further sufficiency theorems, covering the case $n > 4$ but less easy to interpret, the reader is referred to Kemp and Wegge [8] and Uekawa [16].

Theorem 1A.4: *For $n = 3$, the inequalities* (1A.10) *imply that S^{-1} has the sign pattern* (1A.8a).

Proof: From the inequalities (1A.10), the cofactors of the diagonal elements of S are positive and the cofactors of the off-diagonal elements are negative. It therefore suffices to show that S has a positive determinant. Now

$$|S| = \begin{vmatrix} \alpha_{11} & \alpha_{12} & \alpha_{13} \\ \alpha_{21} & \alpha_{22} & \alpha_{23} \\ \alpha_{31} & \alpha_{32} & \alpha_{33} \end{vmatrix} = \frac{1}{\alpha_{32}} \begin{vmatrix} \alpha_{11}\alpha_{32} - \alpha_{31}\alpha_{12} & \alpha_{12} & \alpha_{13} \\ \alpha_{21}\alpha_{32} - \alpha_{31}\alpha_{22} & \alpha_{22} & \alpha_{23} \\ 0 & \alpha_{32} & \alpha_{33} \end{vmatrix}$$

where the second equality is obtained by multiplying the first column of $|S|$ by α_{32} then subtracting from the first column α_{31} times the second column. From (1A.10), however, $\alpha_{11}\alpha_{32} - \alpha_{31}\alpha_{12} > 0$ and $\alpha_{21}\alpha_{32} - \alpha_{31}\alpha_{22} < 0$; moreover, the cofactors associated with these two elements are respectively positive and negative. Hence $|S| > 0$. Q.E.D.

From Theorems 1A.2 and 1A.4 we infer that for $n = 3$ the inequalities (1A.10) are both necessary and sufficient for the Stolper–Samuelson conclusions.

When $n = 4$, (1A.10) no longer ensures that the off-diagonal elements of S^{-1} are negative. Consider the counter example

$$S = \frac{1}{22} \begin{pmatrix} 8.00 & 6.20 & 7.00 & 7.00 \\ 1.00 & 1.80 & 1.00 & 1.05 \\ 6.50 & 7.00 & 8.00 & 6.00 \\ 6.50 & 7.00 & 6.00 & 7.95 \end{pmatrix}$$

The matrix satisfies (1A.10) and has unit column sums; but the first row of S^{-1} is $(22/32.78)(21.33, 22.43, -11.89, -12.77)$, whence the $(1, 2)$th element of S^{-1} is positive and larger than the $(1, 1)$th element.

There is no getting round a counterexample. However, in the example provided not only are the diagonal elements of the inverse greater than one, but at least two off-diagonals are negative in each row and the diagonal element is larger in absolute value than the negative elements in the same row. It can be shown that this is always so for four-by-four matrices satis-fying the inequalities (1A.10): An increase in the price of the ith product results in an unambiguous increase in the real reward of the associated factor (the ith); the real reward of at least two other factors must decline, but at a rate which is less than the rate of increase in the reward of the ith factor.

More formally, the following theorem can be proved.

Theorem 1A.5: *For* $n = 4$, *the inequalities* (1A.10) *imply* (a) *that the determinant and therefore all principal minors of S are positive (so that S is a P-matrix),* (b) *that the diagonal elements of* S^{-1} *are greater than one,* (c) *that in each row of* S^{-1} *there are at least two negative elements,* (d) *that in each row of* S^{-1} *the diagonal element is larger in absolute value than the negative elements but may or may not be smaller than the other positive element, if there is one.*

Proof of (a): We first prove that $|S|$ cannot vanish. Suppose the contrary, that $|S| = 0$. Then the rows of S are linearly dependent, so that there exist λ_i not all zero such that

$$\sum_i \lambda_i \alpha_{ij} = 0 \qquad j = 1, \ldots, 4 \qquad (1A.17)$$

In fact, since the α_{ij} are positive, at least two λ_i must be nonzero. Without loss it may be supposed that λ_1 and λ_2 are nonzero. Subtracting α_{12} times the first equation from α_{11} times the second, we obtain

$$\lambda_2(\alpha_{22}\alpha_{11} - \alpha_{12}\alpha_{21}) + \lambda_3(\alpha_{11}\alpha_{32} - \alpha_{12}\alpha_{31}) + \lambda_4(\alpha_{11}\alpha_{42} - \alpha_{12}\alpha_{41}) = 0$$

$$(1A.18)$$

Each bracketed expression is positive, hence at least one of λ_2, λ_3, λ_4 is positive and at least one negative. It follows that if λ_1 is positive at least two of the λ_i are positive. Suppose three are positive. Then by a procedure similar to that which produced Eq. (1A.18) we can eliminate the negative λ_i and show that one of the other three λ_i's must, after all, be negative. We conclude that if λ_i is positive there must be exactly two positive λ_i and exactly two negative λ_i. By a similar argument it can be shown that if λ_1 is negative the same distribution of signs must prevail.

Without loss we may suppose that λ_1 and λ_2 are positive, λ_3 and λ_4 negative. Let us assume first that $(\lambda_1\alpha_{13} + \lambda_4\alpha_{43})$ is positive. Now, from (1A.10),

$$\frac{\lambda_1\alpha_{11}}{\lambda_1\alpha_{13}} > \frac{\lambda_4\alpha_{41}}{\lambda_4\alpha_{43}}$$

Hence, recalling that

$$\frac{c}{d} \lesseqgtr \frac{c - \gamma}{d - \delta} \quad \text{as} \quad \frac{c}{d} \gtreqless \frac{\gamma}{\delta} \qquad (1A.19)$$

if all denominators are positive, we may write

$$\frac{\lambda_1\alpha_{11}}{\lambda_1\alpha_{13}} < \frac{\lambda_1\alpha_{11} + \lambda_4\alpha_{41}}{\lambda_1\alpha_{13} + \lambda_4\alpha_{43}}$$

$$= \frac{\lambda_2\alpha_{21} + \lambda_3\alpha_{31}}{\lambda_2\alpha_{23} + \lambda_3\alpha_{33}} \qquad \text{[from Eq. (1A.17)]}$$

$$< \frac{\lambda_3\alpha_{31}}{\lambda_3\alpha_{33}}$$

in contradiction of (1A.10). Suppose, alternatively, that $(\lambda_1\alpha_{13} + \lambda_4\alpha_{43})$ is nonpositive or, from Eq. (1A.17), that $-(\lambda_2\alpha_{23} + \lambda_3\alpha_{33})$ is nonpositive. From Eq. (1A.17) we have also

$$\begin{pmatrix} \alpha_{13} & \alpha_{43} \\ \alpha_{14} & \alpha_{44} \end{pmatrix} \begin{pmatrix} \lambda_1 \\ \lambda_4 \end{pmatrix} = \begin{pmatrix} -\lambda_2\alpha_{23} - \lambda_3\alpha_{33} \\ -\lambda_2\alpha_{24} - \lambda_3\alpha_{34} \end{pmatrix}$$

so that

$$\begin{pmatrix} \lambda_1 \\ \lambda_4 \end{pmatrix} = \frac{1}{\alpha_{13}\alpha_{44} - \alpha_{14}\alpha_{43}} \begin{pmatrix} \alpha_{44} & -\alpha_{43} \\ -\alpha_{14} & \alpha_{13} \end{pmatrix} \begin{pmatrix} -\lambda_2\alpha_{23} - \lambda_3\alpha_{33} \\ -\lambda_2\alpha_{24} - \lambda_3\alpha_{34} \end{pmatrix}$$

By assumption, $\lambda_1 > 0$ and $-(\lambda_2\alpha_{23} + \lambda_3\alpha_{33}) \leq 0$; hence

$$-\lambda_2\alpha_{24} - \lambda_3\alpha_{34} < 0 \qquad\qquad (1A.20)$$

Now, from (1A.10),

$$\frac{\lambda_2\alpha_{22}}{\lambda_2\alpha_{24}} > \frac{\lambda_3\alpha_{32}}{\lambda_3\alpha_{34}}$$

Hence

$$\frac{\lambda_2\alpha_{22}}{\lambda_2\alpha_{24}} < \frac{\lambda_2\alpha_{22} + \lambda_3\alpha_{32}}{\lambda_2\alpha_{24} + \lambda_3\alpha_{34}} \qquad \text{[from Eqs (1A.19) and (1A.20)]}$$

$$= \frac{\lambda_4\alpha_{42} + \lambda_1\alpha_{12}}{\lambda_4\alpha_{44} + \lambda_1\alpha_{14}} \qquad \text{[from Eq. (1A.17)]}$$

$$< \frac{\lambda_4\alpha_{42}}{\lambda_4\alpha_{44}}$$

in contradiction of (1A.10). We conclude that $|S|$ cannot be zero.

To complete the proof that $|S| > 0$, we define the matrix

$$S(t) \equiv \begin{pmatrix} s_1\alpha_{11} & t\alpha_{12} & t\alpha_{13} & t\alpha_{14} \\ t\alpha_{21} & s_2\alpha_{22} & t\alpha_{23} & t\alpha_{24} \\ t\alpha_{31} & t\alpha_{32} & s_3\alpha_{33} & t\alpha_{34} \\ t\alpha_{41} & t\alpha_{42} & t\alpha_{43} & s_4\alpha_{44} \end{pmatrix}$$

where

$$s_i \equiv \left(1 - t\sum_{\substack{i=1\\i\neq j}}^{4}\alpha_{ij}\right)\bigg/\alpha_{ii}$$

Evidently $|S(t)|$ is a continuous function of t, with $|S(0)| > 0$. Moreover, for $0 < t \leq 1$, $S(t)$ is a stochastic matrix satisfying the inequalities (1A.10), so that $|S(t)| \neq 0$. It follows that $|S| \equiv |S(1)| > 0$.   Q.E.D.

Proof of (b): It suffices to show that the first diagonal element is greater than one. Let the (i, j)th cofactor of S be represented by S_{ij}. Then

$$|S| \doteq \begin{vmatrix} 1 & 1 & 1 & 1 \\ \alpha_{21} & \alpha_{22} & \alpha_{23} & \alpha_{24} \\ \alpha_{31} & \alpha_{32} & \alpha_{33} & \alpha_{34} \\ \alpha_{41} & \alpha_{42} & \alpha_{43} & \alpha_{44} \end{vmatrix}$$ [Add all other rows to the first and recall that S is a stochastic matrix.]

$$= \begin{vmatrix} 1 & 0 & 0 & 0 \\ \alpha_{21} & \alpha_{22} - \alpha_{21} & \alpha_{23} - \alpha_{21} & \alpha_{24} - \alpha_{21} \\ \alpha_{31} & \alpha_{32} - \alpha_{31} & \alpha_{33} - \alpha_{31} & \alpha_{34} - \alpha_{31} \\ \alpha_{41} & \alpha_{42} - \alpha_{41} & \alpha_{43} - \alpha_{41} & \alpha_{44} - \alpha_{41} \end{vmatrix}$$ [Subtract the first column from each of the remaining columns.]

$$= \begin{vmatrix} \alpha_{22} & \alpha_{23} & \alpha_{24} \\ \alpha_{32} & \alpha_{33} & \alpha_{34} \\ \alpha_{42} & \alpha_{43} & \alpha_{44} \end{vmatrix} - \alpha_{21}\begin{vmatrix} 1 & 1 & 1 \\ \alpha_{32} & \alpha_{33} & \alpha_{34} \\ \alpha_{42} & \alpha_{43} & \alpha_{44} \end{vmatrix}$$

$$- \alpha_{31}\begin{vmatrix} \alpha_{22} & \alpha_{23} & \alpha_{24} \\ 1 & 1 & 1 \\ \alpha_{42} & \alpha_{43} & \alpha_{44} \end{vmatrix} - \alpha_{41}\begin{vmatrix} \alpha_{22} & \alpha_{23} & \alpha_{24} \\ \alpha_{32} & \alpha_{33} & \alpha_{34} \\ 1 & 1 & 1 \end{vmatrix}$$

$$= S_{11} - \alpha_{21}B_{21} - \alpha_{31}B_{31} - \alpha_{41}B_{41}, \text{ say.}$$

Now the first diagonal element of S^{-1} is $S_{11}/|S|$. Evidently this element is greater than one if and only if $(\alpha_{21}B_{21} + \alpha_{31}B_{31} + \alpha_{41}B_{41})$ is positive. Adding the first two terms, we obtain

$$\alpha_{21}B_{21} + \alpha_{31}B_{31} = (\alpha_{31}\alpha_{22} - \alpha_{21}\alpha_{32} + \alpha_{21}\alpha_{34} - \alpha_{31}\alpha_{24})(\alpha_{44} - \alpha_{43})$$
$$+ (\alpha_{21}\alpha_{33} - \alpha_{31}\alpha_{23} - \alpha_{21}\alpha_{34} + \alpha_{31}\alpha_{24})(\alpha_{44} - \alpha_{42})$$

$$(1A.21)$$

The first of the four bracketed expressions may be written

$$\xi \equiv \alpha_{31}\alpha_{22}(1 - \mu_2) - \alpha_{21}\alpha_{32}(1 - \mu_3)$$

where $\mu_2 \equiv \alpha_{24}/\alpha_{22}$ and $\mu_3 \equiv \alpha_{34}/\alpha_{32}$. Now the inequalities (1A.10) imply that the diagonal element is the largest element in each row (see the proof of Theorem 1A.3); hence $\mu_2 < 1$. Moreover, it follows from (1A.10) that $\mu_2 < \mu_3$. Evidently ξ is positive if $\mu_3 \geq 1$; but from (1A.10) and the fact that $(1 - \mu_3) < (1 - \mu_2)$, it is positive also if $\mu_3 < 1$. The third bracketed component of (1A.21) has a structure similar to that of the first; hence it too is positive. The second and fourth bracketed expressions are already known to be positive. Hence $(\alpha_{21}B_{21} + \alpha_{31}B_{31})$ is positive. By similar reasoning, $(\alpha_{31}B_{31} + \alpha_{41}B_{41})$ and $(\alpha_{21}B_{21} + \alpha_{41}B_{41})$ are positive. It follows by addition that $(\alpha_{21}B_{21} + \alpha_{31}B_{31} + \alpha_{41}B_{41})$ is positive.   Q.E.D.

Proof of (c): It suffices to show that, if the $(1, 2)$th element of S^{-1} is positive, the $(1, 3)$th and the $(1, 4)$th elements must be negative. In view of (a) above, this amounts to showing that, if A_{21} is positive, both A_{31} and A_{41} must be negative, where A_{ij} is the cofactor of the (i, j)th element of S. We first prove the following lemma.

Lemma: $\alpha_{ij} > \alpha_{is}\dfrac{\alpha_{rj}}{\alpha_{rs}}$ *implies* $A_{ji} < 0$ $\quad i \neq j \neq r \neq s$.

Proof: Without loss of generality, we may concentrate on the case $i = 1$, $j = 2$. Suppose first that $\alpha_{12} > \alpha_{13}\alpha_{42}/\alpha_{43}$. We seek to show that A_{21} is negative. Dividing each column of A_{21} by its first element, the second row by α_{34}/α_{14}, and the third row by α_{43}/α_{13}, we obtain

$$
A_{21} = -\beta \begin{vmatrix} 1 & 1 & 1 \\ \dfrac{\alpha_{32}\alpha_{14}}{\alpha_{12}\alpha_{34}} & \dfrac{\alpha_{33}\alpha_{14}}{\alpha_{13}\alpha_{34}} & 1 \\ \dfrac{\alpha_{42}\alpha_{13}}{\alpha_{12}\alpha_{43}} & 1 & \dfrac{\alpha_{44}\alpha_{13}}{\alpha_{14}\alpha_{43}} \end{vmatrix}
$$

where $\beta \equiv \alpha_{12}\alpha_{34}\alpha_{43} > 0$. From the inequalities (1A.10), $\alpha_{44}\alpha_{13}/\alpha_{14}\alpha_{43}$ is greater than one and $(\alpha_{33}\alpha_{12} - \alpha_{32}\alpha_{13})$ positive. Hence

$$
A_{21} < -\beta \begin{vmatrix} 1 & 1 & 1 \\ \dfrac{\alpha_{32}\alpha_{14}}{\alpha_{12}\alpha_{34}} & \dfrac{\alpha_{33}\alpha_{14}}{\alpha_{13}\alpha_{34}} & 1 \\ \dfrac{\alpha_{42}\alpha_{13}}{\alpha_{12}\alpha_{43}} & 1 & 1 \end{vmatrix}
$$

$$
= -\beta A'_{21}, \quad \text{say.}
$$

Suppose that $\alpha_{42}\alpha_{13} < \alpha_{12}\alpha_{43}$. Then, since $\alpha_{33}\alpha_{14}/\alpha_{13}\alpha_{34} > 1$ [from (1A.10)],

$$A'_{21} > \begin{vmatrix} 1 & 1 & 1 \\ * & * & * \\ 1 & 1 & 1 \end{vmatrix} = 0$$

Hence

$$A_{21} < 0 \quad \text{if} \quad \alpha_{42}\alpha_{13} < \alpha_{12}\alpha_{43} \tag{1A.22a}$$

Applying the same argument to the transpose of A_{21} we find that

$$A_{21} < 0 \quad \text{if} \quad \alpha_{12}\alpha_{34} > \alpha_{14}\alpha_{32} \tag{1A.22b}$$

That establishes the Lemma.

We return to the proof of (c). Suppose $A_{21} > 0$. Then, in view of the Lemma,

$$\alpha_{13} > \alpha_{12}\alpha_{43}/\alpha_{42} \quad \text{and} \quad \alpha_{14} > \alpha_{12}\alpha_{34}/\alpha_{32}$$

Applying the Lemma to these inequalities, we conclude that A_{31} and A_{41} must be negative.   Q.E.D.

Proof of (d): In view of the above numerical example, it suffices to show that the sum of a diagonal and an off-diagonal element in the same row of S^{-1} must be positive. In particular, it suffices to show that

$$A_{11} + A_{21} = \begin{vmatrix} \alpha_{22} & \alpha_{23} & \alpha_{24} \\ \alpha_{32} & \alpha_{33} & \alpha_{34} \\ \alpha_{42} & \alpha_{43} & \alpha_{44} \end{vmatrix} - \begin{vmatrix} \alpha_{12} & \alpha_{13} & \alpha_{14} \\ \alpha_{32} & \alpha_{33} & \alpha_{34} \\ \alpha_{42} & \alpha_{43} & \alpha_{44} \end{vmatrix}$$

$$= \begin{vmatrix} \alpha_{22} - \alpha_{12} & \alpha_{23} - \alpha_{13} & \alpha_{24} - \alpha_{14} \\ \alpha_{32} & \alpha_{33} & \alpha_{34} \\ \alpha_{42} & \alpha_{43} & \alpha_{44} \end{vmatrix}$$

is positive. Dividing the second row by α_{32}, the third row by α_{42}, the second column by α_{43}/α_{42}, and the third column by α_{34}/α_{32}, we obtain

$$A_{11} + A_{21} = \alpha_{43}\alpha_{34} \begin{vmatrix} \alpha_{22} - \alpha_{12} & (\alpha_{23} - \alpha_{13})\dfrac{\alpha_{42}}{\alpha_{43}} & (\alpha_{24} - \alpha_{14})\dfrac{\alpha_{32}}{\alpha_{34}} \\ 1 & \dfrac{\alpha_{33}}{\alpha_{32}}\dfrac{\alpha_{42}}{\alpha_{43}} & 1 \\ 1 & 1 & \dfrac{\alpha_{44}}{\alpha_{42}}\cdot\dfrac{\alpha_{32}}{\alpha_{34}} \end{vmatrix} \tag{1A.23}$$

The diagonal elements in (1A.23) are all positive and, from the inequalities (1A.10), the last two diagonal elements are greater than one. If $\alpha_{24} \leq \alpha_{14}$ the cofactor of the (2, 2)th element in (1A.23) is clearly positive. If, alternatively, $\alpha_{24} > \alpha_{14}$, the same is true; for, from (1A.19) and (1A.10),

$$\frac{\alpha_{22}}{\alpha_{24}} > \frac{\alpha_{12}}{\alpha_{14}} \quad \text{implies} \quad \frac{\alpha_{22} - \alpha_{12}}{\alpha_{24} - \alpha_{14}} > \frac{\alpha_{22}}{\alpha_{24}} > \frac{\alpha_{32}}{\alpha_{34}}$$

It follows that

$$A_{11} + A_{21} > \alpha_{43}\alpha_{34} \begin{vmatrix} \alpha_{22} - \alpha_{12} & (\alpha_{23} - \alpha_{13})\dfrac{\alpha_{42}}{\alpha_{43}} & (\alpha_{24} - \alpha_{14})\dfrac{\alpha_{32}}{\alpha_{34}} \\ 1 & 1 & 1 \\ 1 & 1 & \dfrac{\alpha_{44}}{\alpha_{42}} \cdot \dfrac{\alpha_{32}}{\alpha_{34}} \end{vmatrix} \quad (1A.24)$$

If $\alpha_{23} \leq \alpha_{13}$, the coefficient of the (3, 3)th element in (1A.24) is clearly positive. If, alternatively, $\alpha_{23} > \alpha_{13}$, the same is true; for from (1A.19) and (1A.10)

$$\frac{\alpha_{22}}{\alpha_{23}} > \frac{\alpha_{12}}{\alpha_{13}} \quad \text{implies} \quad \frac{\alpha_{22} - \alpha_{12}}{\alpha_{23} - \alpha_{13}} > \frac{\alpha_{22}}{\alpha_{23}} > \frac{\alpha_{42}}{\alpha_{43}}$$

It follows finally that

$$A_{11} + A_{21} > \alpha_{43}\alpha_{34} \begin{vmatrix} * & * & * \\ 1 & 1 & 1 \\ 1 & 1 & 1 \end{vmatrix} = 0 \quad \text{Q.E.D.}$$

Perhaps the most interesting feature of the original (two-by-two) Stolper–Samuelson Theorem is the element of *conflict* it establishes between the real factor rewards of the two factors: Given the conditions (1A.5) relating to relative factor intensities, *any* change in relative commodity prices works against one and in favor of the other. From Theorems 1A.4 and 1A.5(d) we now see that, if a generalized version of (1A.5) is satisfied, the element of conflict is preserved when $n \leq 4$. When $n = 4$ not all factor rewards need unambiguously increase or decrease; we can be sure, however, that at least one will increase and at least two decrease.

The Dual Samuelson–Rybczynski Theorem

Already, in Eq. (1.24) of the text, we have noted the duality of the factor reward-commodity price relationship and the commodity output-factor endowment relationship. It follows from Eq. (1.24) that Theorems (1A.1)–(1A.5), which are overtly concerned with the factor reward-commodity price relationship $\partial w_j / \partial p_i$, apply equally to the commodity output-factor endowment relationship $\partial X_i / \partial V_j$.

The establishment of Eq. (1.24) is a simple matter. In the notation of this appendix we may write the equilibrium full-employment and price-cost relations as

$$V' = AX' \tag{1A.25a}$$

and

$$p = wA \tag{1A.25b}$$

respectively. (A prime indicates the transpose.) From Eq. (1A.25a), if prices (and therefore factor rewards and the input-output coefficients a_{ij}) are held constant, $dV' = A(dX')$, so that $dX' = A^{-1}(dV')$. In particular, if only the jth factor endowment changes

$$dX_i = \beta_{ij}(dV_j) \tag{1A.26a}$$

where β_{ij} is the (i, j)th component of A^{-1}. From Eq. (1A.25b), on the other hand, $dp = (dw)A + w(dA)$. From Eq. (1A.1), however, $w(dA) = 0$; hence $dw = A^{-1}(dp)$. In particular, if only the ith price changes

$$dw_j = \beta_{ij}(dp_i) \tag{1A.26b}$$

Equation (1.24) follows from Eqs. (1A.26a) and (1A.26b).

Partial Correspondence of Factors and Products

We end this section on a destructive note. Suppose that only members of a proper subset of industries J have an associated factor. Is it then true that $\partial\theta_i/\partial\pi_i > 1$, $\partial\theta_i/\partial\pi_j < 0$ $(j \neq i)$ for $i, j \in J$?

We should not expect this to be so when J contains more than three elements. Unfortunately it is not even true when J contains two elements. This may be established by considering the simplest three-by-three case, with the inequalities (1A.10) holding for $i = 1, 2$.

One's hopes are raised by the fact that the algebraic cofactors of α_{ii} $(i = 1, 2, 3)$ are necessarily positive and the algebraic cofactors of α_{3i} and α_{i3} $(i = 1, 2, 3)$ are necessarily negative. If it could be shown that the determinant of S is necessarily positive, one could fill in the signs of all components of S^{-1} except those of the $(2, 3)$th and $(2, 1)$th components. One would know moreover that the $(3, 3)$th term is greater than one. However, the determinant of S can be negative, as the following example shows:

$$S = \begin{pmatrix} \frac{5}{13} & \frac{2}{13} & \frac{6}{13} \\ \frac{5}{15} & \frac{3}{15} & \frac{7}{15} \\ \frac{4}{11} & \frac{2}{11} & \frac{5}{11} \end{pmatrix}, \qquad |S| = \frac{-1}{11 \times 13 \times 15}$$

A3. UNEQUAL NUMBERS OF FACTORS AND PRODUCTS

In Sec. A2 we have examined the possibility of extending the Stolper–Samuelson and Samuelson–Rybczynski Theorems to cover situations with arbitrary but equal numbers of factors and products. We now consider the implications of relaxing the requirement that factors and products be equal in number.

More Products than Factors

We consider first a world of just three products and two factors. This is the simplest context in which the problems to be discussed can be adequately formulated. It must be supposed that, initially, commodity prices and factor rewards are consistent with the production of all three goods; otherwise we are back to the two-by-two case, or worse. Of course, it is not necessary that all three commodities be produced in positive amounts; in the case under consideration there is an inevitable and unavoidable element of indeterminacy in production.[21] But it *is* necessary that, within limits to be described presently, it be a matter of indifference to producers whether they produce all three goods, or just two, or (a singular possibility) just one.

In the world we have just described it is obviously impossible to associate one factor with each product. The most we can contrive is to restrict the matrix S so that each factor is associated with a product. Thus, after a suitable renumbering of products, the inequalities (1A.10) must be specialized to

$$\frac{\alpha_{ii}}{\alpha_{ji}} > \frac{\alpha_{is}}{\alpha_{js}} \qquad \begin{array}{l} i, j = 1, 2 \qquad i \neq j \\ s = 1, 2, 3 \qquad s \neq i \end{array} \qquad (1A.27)$$

Figure 1A.1 illustrates an initial equilibrium. The three one-dollar iso-revenue curves possess a common tangent line the slope of which represents the equilibrium ratio of factor rewards. The ray OP_i indicates the profit-maximizing ratio of factors in the ith industry and will be referred to as the ith "factor ray." The relative slopes of the three factor rays in Fig. 1A.1 are implied by (1A.27). Provided the ratio of factor endowments can be represented by a ray (the "endowment ray") of gentler slope than that of OP_2 and steeper slope than that of OP_1, something of all three commodities can be produced, though the actual production mix will be indeterminate. If the endowment ray lies between the first and third factor rays, something of all three commodities may be produced, or something of just the first and second, or something of just the first and third. If the endowment ray lies between the second and third factor rays, something of all three goods may

---

[21] This indeterminacy corresponds to the fact that through each point on the production possibility surface it is possible to draw a straight line each point of which is on the surface. Cf. [12], pp. 7n, 19; also Chap. 6, Sec. 1 below.

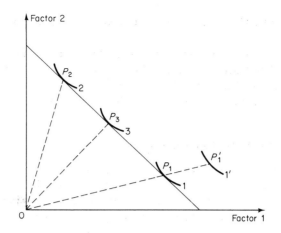

FIGURE 1A.1

be produced, or something of just the first and second, or something of just the second and third. If, finally, the endowment ray coincides with the third factor ray, something of all three commodities may be produced, or something of just the first and second, or something of just the third.

Suppose that the initial equilibrium is disturbed by a small decline in the price of the first commodity. The first isorevenue curve moves out from the origin in proportion to the price cut and assumes the position shown by the dotted curve of Fig. 1A.1. It is now impossible to find a pair of factor rewards such that all three goods could be produced. If the endowment ray lies between the first and third factor rays, only the first and third commodities will be produced; if it lies between the second and third factor rays, only the second and third goods will be produced; and if it coincides with the third factor ray only the third good will be produced. In the second and third of these three cases—when the endowment ray lies in or on the "cone" P_2OP_3—relative factor rewards remain at their initial levels, and both factors gain by virtue of their improved purchasing power over the first commodity. In the first case, however, we are back on familiar ground. Both in the first and in the third industry the ratio of the first to the second factor rises. It follows that in terms of the first and third goods (and, since the price of the third good in terms of the second is unchanged, in terms of the second also) the real reward of the first factor declines while the real reward of the second factor increases. If, on the other hand, the price of the first good *increases* slightly, something of both the first and second goods must be produced, whatever the endowment ratio. The ratio of the first to the second factor falls in both industries, hence the real reward of the first factor rises unambiguously and the real reward of the second factor falls.[22]

---

[22] Notice that when the endowment ray lies in or on the cone P_2OP_3 the real reward of the first factor increases whatever the direction of the price change.

Suppose next that the price of the third product changes. (It is unnecessary to separately consider a change in the second price. It is clear from Fig. 1A.1 that the implications of such a change are symmetrical with those of a change in the first price, and they may in fact be obtained from the preceding paragraph by simply interchanging "first" and "second.") If the price falls, production of the third commodity ceases, relative factor rewards remain unchanged and both factors benefit in terms of their increased purchasing power over the third commodity. This is so, whatever the endowment ratio. If, however, the price rises, the range of possible outcomes is wider. Thus if the endowment ray lies in the interior of the cone P_1OP_3, or in the interior of the cone P_2OP_3, the real reward of one factor must rise and that of the other factor fall. But if the endowment ray coincides with the common edge OP_3 of the two cones, the first and second industries both prove to be unprofitable in the new equilibrium, relative factor rewards remain unchanged, and the real rewards of both factors increase in terms of the first and second commodities.

We dwell briefly on a second special case before attempting to generalize. Suppose that at initial prices and factor rewards four commodities could be produced and that each industry requires positive amounts of each of three factors of production. The appropriate specialization of the inequalities

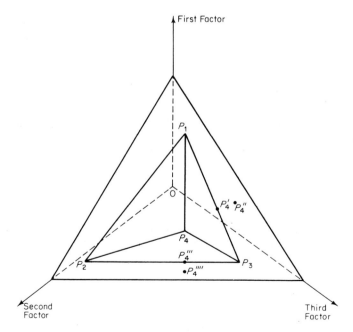

FIGURE 1A.2

(1A.10) is now

$$\frac{\alpha_{ii}}{\alpha_{ji}} > \frac{\alpha_{is}}{\alpha_{js}} \qquad \begin{array}{l} i, j = 1, 2, 3 \\ s = 1, 2, 3, 4 \end{array} \qquad \begin{array}{l} i \neq j \\ s \neq i \end{array} \tag{1A.28}$$

In an initial equilibrium each of four one-dollar isorevenue surfaces is tangential to a plane the partial slopes of which indicate ratios of factor rewards. In Fig. 1A.2, which depicts a special case, the four points of tangency are marked by $P_1, \ldots, P_4$. ($P_4', \ldots, P_4''''$ mark alternative positions for the fourth tangency.) In accordance with the assumption that positive amounts of every commodity can be produced, the factor endowment ray must be supposed to lie in the interior of the finite cone generated by the four factor rays $OP_1, \ldots, OP_4$. In accordance with conditions (1A.28) each of the first three factor rays is an edge of that cone;[23] the fourth factor ray may or may not be an edge.

Suppose that the equilibrium is disturbed by a slight fall in the price of the first commodity, so that the one-dollar isorevenue surface of that commodity shifts out from the origin. What happens to outputs and factor rewards depends on the precise orientation of the endowment ray. If P_2, P_3, and P_4 are not colinear and if the endowment ray lies in the cone formed by the second, third, and fourth factor rays, the first industry must prove to be unprofitable in the new equilibrium. Relative factor rewards will remain

---

[23] The general theorem underlying the construction of Figs. 1A.1 and 1A.2 is as follows. Each column of S corresponds to a factor ray. Suppose that commodities have been numbered so that

$$\frac{\alpha_{ii}}{\alpha_{ji}} > \frac{\alpha_{is}}{\alpha_{js}} \qquad \begin{array}{l} i = 1, \ldots, r \\ s, j = 1, \ldots, n \quad s \neq i, \; j \neq i \\ n \geq r \end{array} \tag{1A.29}$$

Then the vector $\alpha_i \equiv (\alpha_{1i}, \alpha_{2i}, \ldots, \alpha_{ri})$, $i = 1, \ldots, r$, must be an extreme vector (edge) of the cone generated by the n initial factor rays.

Proof: Suppose it were possible to write α_i as a non-negative combination of the other vectors, so that

$$\alpha_i = \sum_{\substack{v=1 \\ v \neq i}}^{n} \lambda_v \alpha_v$$

possesses a solution with non-negative λ_v, not all zero. Suppose without loss that $i \neq 1$ and deduct α_{1i} times the ith equation from α_{ii} times the first equation. The resulting equation,

$$0 = \sum_{\substack{v=1 \\ v \neq i}}^{n} \lambda_v (\alpha_{ii}\alpha_{1v} - \alpha_{1i}\alpha_{iv}),$$

must have a semi-positive solution. But this is impossible since, from (1A.29), all coefficients of the λ_v are positive.

unchanged and all factors will benefit in terms of their command over the first commodity. If, on the other hand, the endowment ray lies outside that cone (as it must if P_2, P_3, and P_4 are colinear), the first commodity must be produced in the new equilibrium. Either it continues to be possible to produce all four commodities (as when P_2, P_3, and P_4 are colinear), or one of the other three commodities proves to be unprofitable, or two of the other three prove to be unprofitable (as when the endowment ray cuts the line P_1P_4 in Fig. 1A.2). If it remains possible to produce three (or even four) goods, we again find ourselves governed by the results of Sec. A2; in particular, it follows from (1A.28) and Theorem 1A.3 that if the fourth industry proves unprofitable the first factor will suffer and the others benefit from the price change. Otherwise, we are in a situation with more factors than products. Suppose, alternatively, that the price of the first commodity *rises* slightly. Then the first isorevenue surface shifts towards the origin and, whatever the position of the endowment ray, something of the first good must be produced in the new equilibrium. Either it continues to be possible to produce all four goods (as when P_2, P_3, and P_4 are colinear), or one of the other three goods proves to be unprofitable, or two of the other three prove to be unprofitable (as when OP_4'''' is the fourth factor ray and the endowment ray cuts the line P_1P_4'''' south of the line P_2P_3). In any but the last of these cases we find ourselves effectively in a three-by-three world and subject to the conclusions of Sec. A2.[24]

The implications of a change in the price either of the second or of the third product are symmetrical with those of a change in the first product and may be obtained from the preceding paragraph by interchanging "first" and "second" or "third." Nor, if the fourth factor ray is an edge of the cone generated by the four factor rays, does a change in the fourth price furnish any new possibilities. A change in the fourth price is worthy of special attention only if the fourth factor ray lies in or on the cone generated by the first *three* factor rays alone (as in Fig. 1A.2). Suppose that this is the case and that the price of the fourth product declines. Then the fourth isorevenue surface shifts out from the origin, the fourth industry proves to be unprofitable in the new equilibrium, relative factor rewards remain unchanged, and all real rewards increase in terms of the fourth commodity. If, however, the price rises, the possibilities are more numerous. The fourth isorevenue surface shifts towards the origin, the fourth commodity is necessarily producible in the new equilibrium, and at least one of the first three industries must reveal itself to be unprofitable. In fact two of the three may turn out to be unprofitable (as when P_4 is in the interior of the triangle $P_1P_2P_3$ and the endowment ray cuts one of the lines P_1P_4, P_2P_4, P_3P_4), or even all three (as when the endowment ray passes through P_4).

---

[24] If the endowment ray lies in or on the cone generated by the second third and fourth factor rays, it is possible for the real reward of the first factor to increase, whatever the direction of change of p_1. Cf. footnote 22.

There are elements of asymmetry in the above conclusions. There is, however, a common thread running through them. Moreover, the same common features can be discerned in the general case of n products and r factors ($n > r$). *If the factor endowment is such that r commodities (including the ith) must be produced in positive amounts to ensure full employment, any change in the ith price will render unprofitable not more than $n - r$ industries* (exactly $n - r$ if no r initial production points lie in an ($r - 1$)-hyperplane) *and excluding the ith. To any r of those commodities* (including the ith) *which remain producible after the price change, the results of Sec. A2 remain applicable. Otherwise, either all real rewards rise together, or the results of Sec.* A2 *apply, or fewer goods are produced in the new equilibrium than there are factors,* depending on the orientations of the n factor rays and of the endowment ray. (Figures 1A.1 and 1A.2 provide illustrations.) The ith product must be produced if and only if the ith factor ray provides an edge both for every r-edged cone containing the endowment ray and for the cone generated by the n initial factor rays. The inequalities (1A.10), or an appropriate primed specialization of them, ensures that the ith factor ray is an edge of the cone generated by the n initial factor rays.[25]

All of the preceding discussion has rested on the supposition that price changes are autonomous *and arbitrary*. It is possible, however, to take a broader point of view and to treat the country under consideration as a small number of a trading community. From this point of view one can say a little more about the distributional implications of changes in commodity prices, for then the vector of price changes must be treated as endogenous and its elements as related. Thus suppose for the time being that the endowment rays of the several countries coincide and that the countries have a common technology. Then if all commodities are produced it will in each country be not unprofitable to produce all of them. (It is immaterial if in fact a country produces less than the entire range.) Moreover, unless world demand functions are quite odd, small price changes must be consistent with the continued world production of positive amounts of all goods. But if price changes are so restricted[26] we are back in a simple and familiar world to which Theorems 1A.4 and 1A.5 apply. Figure 1A.3 illustrates for the three-by-two case.

To achieve such simplicity it is not necessary to assume that the two endowment rays are identical. It is enough that any cone formed by r initial factor rays which contains one country's endowment ray also contains the other countries' endowment rays. If this condition is not met a much wider range of price changes is consistent with positive world production of all

[25] See footnote 23.
[26] The price change must be such that, before and after the change, the price plane and the production possibility surface must be tangential in a straight line. Cf. footnote 21.

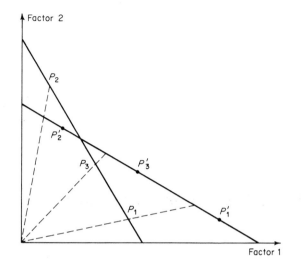

FIGURE 1A.3

commodities, for it is no longer necessary that each country should find it possible to produce all goods.

More Factors than Products

If there are three factors and two products (the Classical case[27]) one cannot determine factor rewards from the marginal conditions alone. To complete the system one must add equations requiring that all factors be fully employed. Unfortunately these additional conditions contribute complicated (factor) substitution terms to our derived relations between product prices and factor rewards. To obtain clear-cut results it becomes necessary to impose restrictions on the matrix of substitution terms, a possibility we do not explore here.

[27] The allusion is to the classical discussion of the distributional implications of the relaxation of the Corn Laws. Three factors were recognized (labor, land, and capital) and two groups of products (agricultural products, represented by corn, and manufactured goods).

chapter 2

A Simple Open Economy

We seek now to extend our analysis to open economies. It is convenient, however, to make the transition in stages. Thus in the present chapter we consider a trading country which is very small, in the sense that its purchases and sales bear insignificantly on world prices. It follows that p, to be interpreted now as the *world* price of the second commodity in terms of the first, that is, as the terms of international trade, is given.

Such an economy is described by Eqs. (1.9)–(1.15) which, given the p_i, forms a closed system. We have already addressed several comparative statical questions to that system. Thus in Chap. 1 we explored some of the implications of a change in the factor endowment and of a change in the price ratio. We now investigate a series of closely related questions: What is the effect of a technological change on outputs, on real factor rewards, and on the distribution of income? What are the consequences of a tariff or excise tax for the same list of variables? Thus it will be clear that, formally at least, the present chapter is simply a lengthy extension of its predecessor.

Occasionally we shall be interested in the responses of imports and exports. It is convenient therefore to write down explicitly the community's budget restraint:

$$p_1 d_1 + p_2 d_2 = p_1 y_1 + p_2 y_2 \qquad (2.1)$$

Denoting by $z_i \equiv d_i - y_i$ the community's excess (or import) demand for the ith commodity, the restraint may be expressed alternatively as

$$p_1 z_1 + p_2 z_2 = 0 \qquad (2.1')$$

Except where the contrary is indicated, it will be assumed that neither industry is completely idle.

1. THE IMPLICATIONS OF TECHNICAL IMPROVEMENTS

We consider first the implications of technical improvements—for outputs, factor proportions, and real factor rewards. Mill and Edgeworth were the pioneers in this field[1] and in many respects their analyses have hardly been improved on. The Mill–Edgeworth manner of posing and solving the problems associated with technical improvements is, however, subject to an important limitation. Improvements are assumed to play no favorites; they are assumed to be neither "labor-saving" nor "capital-saving," but "neutral." This assumption, implicit rather than explicit, was a natural one in the light of the continuing influence, even in Edgeworth's time, of the labor theory of value. But, like a horse's blinkers, it had the effect of obscuring a whole range of interesting problems: What will be the impact on the terms of trade of a labor-saving improvement in the export industry? Of a capital-saving improvement in the import-competing industry? And what is the relation between technical improvements, on one hand, and real factor rewards and the distribution of national income, on the other?

Technical improvements are frequently embodied in new types of equipment, or call for the learning of new manipulative skills. And usually they make possible the production of what is, strictly speaking, a brand new commodity. To stay within our "two-by-two" economy, however, we suppose that the improvement involves simply a new way of combining existing factors in the production of one or both of the two existing products.

In search of precision, let us rewrite the production relationship for the first industry as

$$X_1 = F_1(\lambda K_1, \lambda' L_1)$$

that is, as

$$y_1 = \lambda' l_1 f_1\left(\frac{\lambda}{\lambda'} k_1\right)$$

where λ and λ' are shift parameters each of which is initially equal to unity. Then a capital-saving improvement will be indicated by an increase in λ: The preimprovement output can be produced with less capital $[1/(1 + d\lambda)$ times the old amount] and the old amount of labor. In similar fashion, a

[1] See Mill [11] and Edgeworth [2] and [3].

labor-saving improvement will be indicated by an increase in λ': The pre-improvement output can be produced with $1/(1 + d\lambda')$ of the old amount of labor in combination with the old amount of capital. And a neutral improvement will be indicated by equal increases in both λ and λ': The preimprovement output can be produced with $1/(1 + d\lambda) = 1/(1 + d\lambda')$ of each of the old inputs. But evidently an improvement might involve *unequal* changes in λ and λ'; nor need λ and λ' change in the same direction. We are led, therefore, to offer the following more general definitions of "factor biased" improvements: An improvement is capital-saving, labor-saving or neutral according as λ/λ' increases, decreases or does not change. Evidently a neutral improvement involves only a renumbering of the isoquants. In the case of factor-biased improvements, however, there is involved some "tilting" of the isoquants. The precise nature of the tilting will be made clear shortly.[2]

There are six "pure" cases that might be considered; for improvements may be biased towards either of the two industries and towards either of the two factors, or they may be neutral as to industry or factor or both. And one can imagine, of course, an indefinite number of "mixed" cases.[3] It will be

[2] The classification of improvements offered here is not exhaustive. It only discriminates between improvements which preserve the linear homogeneity of the production function, leave the list of required factors unchanged, and for which a given proportionate increase in the "saved" input would be a perfect substitute *at all levels of output.* All other improvements remain unclassified.

The classification is related to but not equivalent to that of Hicks ([7], pp. 121–22), which is based on the behavior, *at constant inputs,* of the marginal rate of factor substitution. A labor-saving improvement in our sense for example, is labor-saving in Hicks' sense if and only if the elasticity of factor substitution is less than one. For detail, see Jones [9].

Finally it is worth noting an implication of the special "multiplicative" character of our definitions: In a Cobb–Douglas production function neutral and biased innovations are quite indistinguishable. Thus

$$\lambda K^\alpha L^{1-\alpha} = (\lambda^{1/\alpha}K)^\alpha L^{1-\alpha} = K^\alpha(\lambda^{1/1-\alpha}L)^{1-\alpha} = K^\alpha(\lambda'L)^{1-\alpha}$$

The difficulty flows, of course, from the similar multiplicative form of the Cobb–Douglas functions. One possible escape is to define improvements in, say, additive form:

$$X = (K + \lambda)^\alpha(L + \lambda')^{1-\alpha}$$

with λ and λ' initially zero. On the other hand, an additive classification of improvements would break down if the production function were also assumed to be additive:

$$\alpha(K + \lambda) + (1 - \alpha)L = \alpha K + (1 - \alpha)\left(L + \frac{\alpha}{1 - \alpha}\lambda\right)$$
$$= \alpha K + (1 - \alpha)(L + \lambda')$$

In general, whenever specific algebraic forms of the production function are adopted, one must be careful to choose a "nonconformable" classification of improvements.

[3] Attention is drawn to one such case, that in which an improvement is equally saving of a particular factor in each industry. Clearly an improvement of this kind is precisely equivalent to an increase, in appropriate degree, of the supply of the factor saved. The argument of Chap. 2, Sec. 2 covers the case nicely.

sufficient for our present purposes, however, to consider just three pure cases:[4] A capital-saving improvement of the simple kind which can be represented by an increase in λ, with λ' constant; a labor-saving improvement, analogously defined with $d\lambda = 0$ and $d\lambda' > 0$; and a neutral improvement, with $d\lambda = d\lambda' > 0$; all improvements are assumed to have incidence in the first industry.

For the study of these three cases, some revisions of our formal model are required. Thus the production relations (1.9), must now be written as

$$y_1 = \lambda' l_1 f_1\left(\frac{\lambda}{\lambda'} k_1\right)$$

$$y_2 = l_2 f_2(k_2) \tag{2.3}$$

and the marginal conditions (1.11) become

$$r = p_1 \lambda f'_1 = p_2 f'_2$$

$$w = p_1(\lambda' f_1 - \lambda k_1 f'_1) = p_2(f_2 - k_2 f'_2) \tag{2.4}$$

The full employment conditions (1.10) are retained, so that our revised system consists of Eqs. (2.3), (2.4) and (1.10).

Imagine, then, that a capital-saving improvement has taken place in the first industry. From Eqs. (2.4), bearing in mind that $\lambda = \lambda' = 1$,

$$\frac{dk_1}{d\lambda} = -\left[k_1 + \frac{k_2 f'_1}{f''_1(k_2 - k_1)}\right]$$

$$\frac{dk_2}{d\lambda} = -\frac{k_1 f'_2}{p f''_2(k_2 - k_1)} \tag{2.5}$$

Thus if the first industry happens to be relatively capital-intensive ($k_2 < k_1$), both expressions are negative; that is, labor is substituted for capital in both industries. This result does not perhaps appeal immediately to one's intuition. But recall that in the new equilibrium the old commodity price and cost ratios must be reestablished. Since the first industry has benefited from the improvement it follows that the factor price ratio must redress the balance by moving in favor of the second capital-intensive industry; in relation to wage rates rents must fall. For this reason alone, k_2 must fall; for this reason, *and* because the effect of a capital-saving improvement is to raise the marginal product of the existing labor input, k_1 must fall. If, on the other hand, the first industry happens to be relatively capital-intensive ($k_1 > k_2$), the balance of costs can be restored only by an increase in the wage:rent ratio. It follows that k_2 must increase. But in the case of k_1 there are two conflicting tensions, easily identifiable with the two terms in the square brackets of Eqs. (2.5):

[4] The examination of other cases is required in Prob. 2.1.

On the one hand, the marginal physical productivity of capital has fallen as a direct result of the improvement; on the other hand, the relative reward of capital has fallen. The outcome for k_1 is indeterminate.

We have already hinted at the direction in which, in each of the two cases, real factor rewards must change. Precise expressions are easily obtained. The real rental of capital, in terms of the first commodity, is $\lambda f_1'$; in terms of the second commodity, it is f_2'. Availing ourselves of Eqs. (2.5), and recalling that $\lambda = 1$,

$$\frac{dr_1}{d\lambda} = \frac{d(\lambda f_1')}{d\lambda} = p\frac{df_2'}{d\lambda} = -\left(\frac{k_1 f_1'}{k_2 - k_1}\right) \tag{2.6a}$$

The real reward of labor, on the other hand, is $w_1 = (f - \lambda k_1 f_1')$ in terms of the first commodity and $w_2 = (f_2 - k_2 f_2')$ in terms of the second. Again making use of Eqs. (2.5),

$$\frac{dw_1}{d\lambda} = \frac{d(f_1 - \lambda k_1 f_1')}{d\lambda} = p\frac{d(f_2 - k_2 f_2')}{d\lambda} = \frac{k_1 k_2 f_1'}{k_2 - k_1} \tag{2.6b}$$

Thus, the change in each factor's real reward, however the reward is measured, depends on the sign of $(k_2 - k_1)$, that is, on the relative factor-intensities of the two industries. If the first or progressive industry is relatively capital-intensive, the real reward of capital increases and that of labor decreases. If, on the other hand, the first industry is relatively labor-intensive, capitalists suffer and laborers benefit from the improvement.

Let us suppose now that the improvement is labor-saving. It would be unnecessarily tedious to plod through a detailed analysis of essentially the same kind as that just completed. Analogy suggests that, in this case, when $k_2 > k_1$, both k_1 and k_2 will increase, and the real reward of capital will fall; that of labor will rise. When, however, $k_1 > k_2$, k_2 will fall, the behavior of k_1 will be indeterminate, and the real reward of labor will fall; that of capital will rise. The results of the derivations are merely listed:

$$\frac{dk_1}{d\lambda'} = k_1 - \frac{f_1 - k_1 f_1'}{f_1''(k_2 - k_1)}$$

$$\frac{dk_2}{d\lambda'} = -\frac{f_2 - k_2 f_2'}{pf_2''(k_2 - k_1)} \tag{2.7}$$

and

$$\frac{dr_1}{d\lambda'} = \frac{df_1'}{d\lambda'} = p\frac{df_2'}{d\lambda'} = -\frac{f_1 - k_1 f_1'}{k_2 - k_1}$$

$$\frac{dw_1}{d\lambda'} = \frac{d}{d\lambda'}(\lambda' f_1 - k_1 f_1') = p\frac{d}{d\lambda'}(f_2 - k_2 f_2') = k_2\frac{(f_1 - k_1 f_1')}{(k_2 - k_1)} \tag{2.8}$$

Let us suppose, finally, that the improvement is factor-*neutral*. This, it will be recalled, is the case that was considered by Mill and Edgeworth. Initially, at unchanged factor prices, costs in the first industry fall relatively to those of the second industry. If $k_2 > k_1$, the balance of costs will be redressed by an increase in the ratio of wage rates to rents. It follows that in both industries the labor:capital ratio will fall. If, on the other hand, $k_1 > k_2$, wage rates must suffer a relative decline and, in both industries, the labor:capital ratio will rise. These conclusions may be confirmed by differentiating Eqs. (2.4) with respect to λ, with $d\lambda' = d\lambda$, or, more easily, by simply adding Eqs. (2.5) to Eqs. (2.7) and Eqs. (2.6) to Eqs. (2.8):

$$\left.\frac{dk_1}{d\lambda}\right|_{\lambda=\lambda'} = -\frac{pf_2}{f''_1(k_2 - k_1)}$$

$$\left.\frac{dk_2}{d\lambda}\right|_{\lambda=\lambda'} = -\frac{f_1}{p^2 f''_2(k_2 - k_1)} \tag{2.9}$$

and

$$\left.\frac{dw_1}{d\lambda}\right|_{\lambda=\lambda'} = p\left.\frac{dw_2}{d\lambda}\right|_{\lambda=\lambda'} = -\frac{f_1}{k_2 - k_1}$$

$$\left.\frac{dw_1}{d\lambda}\right|_{\lambda=\lambda'} = p\left.\frac{dw_2}{d\lambda}\right|_{\lambda=\lambda'} = \frac{k_2 f_1}{k_2 - k_1} \tag{2.10}$$

A simple diagram may assist in the understanding of the foregoing argument.[5] Select quantities of the two commodities which, given p, cost the same amount. Corresponding to the two quantities are two isoquants, one for each commodity. (See Fig. 2.1). It is assumed that, both before and after the improvement, the isoquants intersect once only. It follows that they possess a single common tangent, the isocost line CC. The slope of the isocost line is, of course, proportional to the ratio of factor rewards. The values of k_1 and k_2 are represented by the slopes of OP_1 and OP_2, respectively. It will suffice to consider a labor-saving improvement, which involves an equiproportionate *leftward* displacement of the isoquant labelled "1." Similar diagrams can be drawn to illustrate the effects of a capital-saving improvement, which involves an equiproportionate *downward* displacement of the same curve; or of a neutral improvement which involves a *scale contraction* of the curve.

Imagine first that $k_1 < k_2$ [Fig. 2.1(a)]. It is clear, then, that at given factor rewards k_1 must rise. But factor rewards cannot be considered as given: We know already that the wage:rent ratio will rise. The isocost line

---

[5] A similar diagram may be found in Findlay and Grubert [4]. The reader is warned, however, that I have not followed Findlay and Grubert in their definition of a factor-saving improvement.

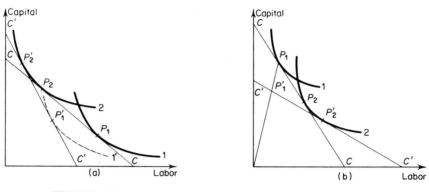

FIGURE 2.1

becomes steeper and the new tangencies occur at P_1' and P_2'. Both k_1 and k_2 are larger than before the improvement. Figure 2.1(b), on the other hand, has been drawn on the assumption that $k_1 > k_2$. The isoquant for the first commodity is again displaced leftwards. But this time k_2 decreases and the change in k_1 is indeterminate. (The figure illustrates the hairline possibility that k_1 does not change at all.)

We have not yet considered the effects of an improvement on the two *outputs*. Before doing so, however, let us collect the results obtained to date In Table 2.1 an arrow pointing up indicates that the variable indicated at the top of the column has increased as the result of the improvement. A downward-pointing arrow indicates that the variable has decreased in value. And

TABLE 2.1: Implications of Improvement in First Industry

	k_1 (i)	k_2 (ii)	Real Wage (iii)	Real Rent (iv)	y_1 (v)	y_2 (vi)
			$k_1 > k_2$			
Labor-saving	?	↘	↘	↗	?	?
Capital-saving	↘	↘	↘	↗	↗	↘
Neutral	↘	↘	↘	↗	↗	↘

	k_1 (vii)	k_2 (viii)	Real Wage (ix)	Real Rent (x)	y_1 (xi)	y_2 (xii)
			$k_2 > k_1$			
Labor-saving	↗	↗	↗	↘	↗	↘
Capital-saving	?	↗	↗	↘	?	?
Neutral	↗	↗	↗	↘	↗	↘

a question mark indicates that our assumptions are not strong enough to restrict the direction of change. The results obtained so far are summarized in columns (i)–(iv) and (vii)–(x).

Study of Table 2.1 suggests the following generalizations. If the improvement is saving of the factor used intensively in the progressive industry, or if the improvement is neutral, the rate of real reward of the factor used intensively in the progressive industry will rise and the intensity of its use will fall in both industries; the rate of real reward of the other factor will fall, and the intensity of its use will rise in both industries. If, however, the improvement is saving of the factor used intensively in the other, static industry, the real rate of reward of that factor will fall and the intensity of its use in the other industry will rise; the intensity of its use in the progressive industry may change in either direction, or not at all; and the real rate of reward of the other factor will rise.

It remains only to consider the effects of an improvement on outputs. Fortunately this problem can be disposed of quickly. We already know the effects of the improvement on the factor ratios k_1 and k_2. From that information we in most cases can infer the effects on outputs. Consider a labor-saving improvement with incidence in the first industry. Suppose that $k_1 < k_2$. We know that, in this case, both k_1 and k_2 rise. Hence, to preserve the full employment of both factors, l_1 must increase and l_2 fall. But if l_2 falls and k_2 rises then the output of the second commodity must fall [because $y_2 = l_2 f_2(k_2)$ and $f_2' > 0$]; the output of the first commodity will, of course, increase. The box diagram affords an easy geometric illustration. Consider Fig. 2.2. Production is initially at P, with k_1 represented by the slope of O_1P and k_2 represented by the slope of O_2P. The post-improvement production point is P', with higher k_1 and k_2. Evidently the production of the first commodity has increased, that of the second decreased. The outcomes in

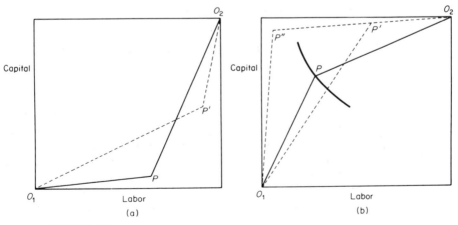

FIGURE 2.2

TABLE 2.2: Implications of Improvement in Second Industry

$$k_1 > k_2$$

	k_1 (i)	k_2 (ii)	Real Wage (iii)	Real Rent (iv)	y_1 (v)	y_2 (vi)
Labor-saving	↗	↗	↗	↘	↘	↗
Capital-saving	↗	?	↗	↘	?	?
Neutral	↗	↗	↗	↘	↘	↗

$$k_2 > k_1$$

	k_1 (vii)	k_2 (viii)	Real Wage (ix)	Real Rent (x)	y_1 (xi)	y_2 (xii)
Labor-saving	↘	?	↘	↗	?	?
Capital-saving	↘	↘	↘	↗	↘	↗
Neutral	↘	↘	↘	↗	↘	↗

other cases can be settled in similar fashion and are interred in columns (v), (vi), (xi), and (xii) of Table 2.1. Note that whenever the change in *either* k_1 or k_2 is indeterminate so are the changes in both outputs. Thus, if $k_1 > k_2$, the effect on k_1 of a labor-saving improvement in the first industry is indeterminate. In terms of Fig. 2.2(b), production may move to P', the production of both commodities increasing; or to P'', the output of the second commodity increasing and that of the first either increasing or decreasing, depending on whether the renumbering of the isoquants for the first commodity outweighs or is outweighed by the movement towards O_1.

Table 2.2 is added for completeness. The entries may be obtained by analogy from the preceding analysis. The problems associated with technical improvements will be studied further in Chap. 4.

2. THE IMPLICATIONS OF A CHANGE IN THE TERMS OF TRADE

The implications of a change in a country's terms of trade are, for the most part, comparatively straightforward. Indeed, many of them follow immediately from the analysis of Chap. 1. Suppose, for example, that the terms of trade improve slightly. We may infer from the convexity of the production frontier [Fig. 1.6(a)], that the export industry will expand, and the import-competing industry contract.[6] Suppose, further, that the export industry is relatively labor-intensive. Then we can infer, from the price change alone *without knowing the response of outputs*, that the capital:labor

[6] See also Prob. 1.2.

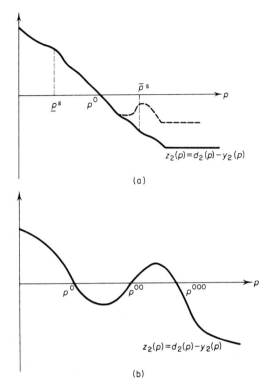

(a)

$z_2(p) = d_2(p) - y_2(p)$

(b)

$z_2(p) = d_2(p) - y_2(p)$

FIGURE 2.3

ratio will rise in each industry and that, therefore, real wages will rise, real rents fall. If, on the other hand, the export industry is relatively capital-intensive, the capital:labor ratio will fall in each industry, real wages will fall, and real rents rise.[7]

When we turn to the relationship between the terms of trade and the volume of imports and exports, our conclusions are much less certain. From Fig. 1.3 we can derive a curve of excess or import demand per capita for the second commodity, $z_2(p)$, as in Fig. 2.3(a). The excess demand for the first commodity, $z_1(1/p)$, appears in Fig. 2.3(a) as an *area* equal to (minus) the product

[7] Our discussion has been conducted under the assumption of incomplete specialization. If that assumption is abandoned, so must be our conclusions. If the country is initially completely specialized, outputs will not respond to an improvement in the terms of trade. Nor, therefore, will *relative* factor rewards: With incomes constant in terms of the exported commodity, each factor will benefit from access to cheaper imports. If, on the other hand, specialization initially is incomplete but becomes complete in the course of the tariff reduction, the outcome is a little more difficult to pin down. Up to the point of complete specialization, the argument of the text holds; beyond it, the present argument takes over. The factor which up to the point of complete specialization suffered a declining income experiences, after that point, a change of fortune. Whether the earlier losses are recouped depends, of course, on how far the terms of trade improve.

of p and z_2 [cf. Eq. (2.1′)]. Figure 1.3 yields a monotonic z_2-curve. However, our assumptions do not rule out nonmonotonic shapes like that of the dotted curve in Fig. 2.3(a). We know that an increase in the relative price of the second commodity will stimulate activity in the second industry. The demand response, however, is ambiguous. It can be split into a pure substitution effect, which is necessarily negative, and an income effect, which may be of either sign. If the second commodity is inferior in consumption, the income effect will be positive and, in extreme cases, may outweigh both the substitution effect and the production or supply effect. We can say with certainty only that a sufficient condition for the excess demand for the second commodity to decrease is that it be not inferior in consumption, and that a necessary condition for excess demand to increase is that the second commodity be inferior.

The assumption that the community behaves like a single individual does not suffice to rule out upward sloping stretches of the excess demand curve. It does suffice, however, to rule out multiple autarkic equilibria. To see this, let us provisionally suppose the contrary. Then, as Fig. 2.3(b) illustrates, steady increases in p (beginning at $p = 0$) take the economy first through a phase in which the second commodity is imported, then through an exporting phase, then through a second importing phase, and so on. Now consider Fig. 2.4. TT is the country's production possibility curve. At the terms of trade p', the country is in the second phase, with the second commodity exported. At the improved terms of trade p'', the country is in the third phase, with the second commodity imported. But evidently the relevant community indifference curves, i' and i'', intersect, indicating that the succession of phases indicated by Fig. 2.3(b) are inconsistent with the assumption that the community behaves like an individual.

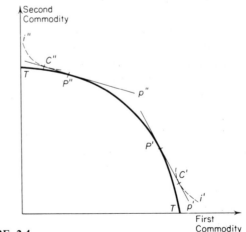

FIGURE 2.4

The Offer Curve

The information contained in Fig. 2.3(a) may be alternatively summarized by the heavy curve *GOG* of Fig. 2.5; and the information contained in Fig. 2.3(b) may be displayed also in the complicated curve *GOG* of Fig. 2.5. The slope of the p^0-line indicates the autarkic terms of trade. If the world price ratio moves in favor of the second commodity, to a level indicated by the

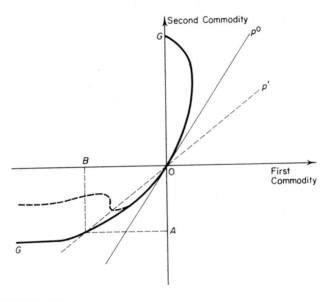

FIGURE 2.5

p'-line, the country will offer to export *OA* of the second commodity in exchange for *OB* of the first, both quantities being expressed per capita. If, alternatively, the price ratio moves in favor of the first commodity, the country will offer to import the second commodity. Consider all possible terms of trade, and the country's import and export responses to each. The locus of potential trading points generated in this way is the country's "offer" or "reciprocal demand" curve *GOG*. The dotted curve of Fig. 2:5 corresponds to the dotted curve of Fig. 2.3(a).

While the excess demand curve z_2 and the offer curve *GOG* display the same information, it will not always be a matter of indifference which is used in later discussion. Where a symmetrical treatment of the two commodities is desirable, for example, it will usually be more convenient to adopt the offer curve as the basic tool. Where possible generalizations of the analysis beyond the two-goods case are to be emphasized, it will always be more convenient to work with excess demand curves.

3. THE IMPLICATIONS OF A TARIFF

The imposition of an import duty, or the extension of an existing duty, has the effect of raising the domestic relative price of the imported commodity. It is hardly surprising, therefore, that in many details the implications of a tariff are similar to those of a deterioration of the terms of trade. Thus the import-competing industry expands, and the export industry contracts; the real reward of whichever factor is employed relatively intensively in the import-competing industry rises, and the real reward of the other factor contracts.[8]

That much is straightforward. The more difficult questions concern the impact of the tariff on the demand for imports. To simplify, we will assume that the community behaves like a single consumer. Intuitively, one would expect the imposition or extension of a tariff to curtail the demand for imports (at given terms of trade). But suppose that the tariff revenue is turned back to the public.[9] This addition to income will tend to *stimulate* the demand for imports. Is it possible that the stimulus from this source might dominate all other influences bearing on the demand for imports? Evidently we must now distinguish the domestic price ratio, which we continue to represent by the symbol p, from the external or world price ratio, which we will denote by p^*, a constant. Thus, if τ stands for the *ad valorem* rate of import duty, and if the second commodity is exported, so that p^* is the country's *terms of trade*, then

$$p(1 + \tau) = p^* \tag{2.11}$$

and

$$\frac{dp}{d\tau} = -\frac{p^*}{(1 + \tau)^2} = -\frac{p}{1 + \tau} \tag{2.12}$$

The per capita tariff proceeds, which are turned back to the public, are, in terms of the first commodity, $\tau z_1/(1 + \tau)$.[10] (z_i, it will be recalled, is the per capita import demand for the ith commodity.) Hence per capita real income, in terms of the first commodity, is

$$q_1 = y_1 + py_2 + \frac{\tau z_1}{1 + \tau} \tag{2.13}$$

---

[8] This is the form in which the Stolper–Samuelson theorem was first formulated. See Stolper and Samuelson [25]; also Chap. 1, Sec. 2, above.

[9] For a problem involving an alternative assumption, see Prob. 2.8.

[10] The tariff proceeds, in terms of the second commodity, are $(z_1/p) - (z_1/p^*) = \tau z_1/p^*$. In terms of the first commodity, therefore, they are $\tau z_1/(1 + \tau)$.

From Eq. (2.13), and making use of the relation[11]

$$\frac{dy_1}{d\tau} + p\frac{dy_2}{d\tau} = 0$$

we obtain the key relationship between real income and the rate of duty:

$$\frac{dq_1}{d\tau} = -\frac{p}{1+\tau}y_2 + \frac{z_1}{(1+\tau)^2} + \frac{\tau}{1+\tau}\cdot\frac{dz_1}{d\tau} \qquad (2.14)$$

In international equilibrium, the value of imports equals the value of exports, that is $z_1 + p^*z_2 = 0$; hence Eq. (2.14) reduces to

$$\frac{dq_1}{d\tau} = -\frac{p}{1+\tau}d_2 + \frac{\tau}{1+\tau}\cdot\frac{dz_1}{d\tau} \qquad (2.15)$$

With these results at our disposal, we return to our question. The per capita local demand for the imported commodity may be written as $d_1(p, q_1)$. Hence

$$\frac{dd_1}{d\tau} = \frac{\partial d_1}{\partial p}\cdot\frac{dp}{d\tau} + \frac{\partial d_1}{\partial q_1}\cdot\frac{dq_1}{d\tau} \qquad (2.16)$$

Substituting into Eq. (2.16) from Eq. (2.12) and Eq. (2.15), and making use of the Slutzky breakdown of $\partial d_1/\partial p$, we obtain

$$\frac{dd_1}{d\tau} = \frac{-p}{1+\tau}\cdot\frac{\partial d_1}{\partial p}\bigg| + \frac{\tau}{1+\tau}\cdot m_1\cdot\frac{dz_1}{d\tau} \qquad (2.17)$$

where $(\partial d_1/\partial p)|$ is the pure substitution effect of the price change. Finally, $z_1 = d_1 - y_1$; hence, making use of Eq. (2.17),

$$\frac{dz_1}{d\tau} = \frac{p\left(\dfrac{dy_1}{dp} - \dfrac{\partial d_1}{\partial p}\bigg|\right)}{1 + \tau(1 - m_1)} \qquad (2.18)$$

Now dy_1/dp is known to be negative, and $(\partial d_1/\partial p)|$ is necessarily positive. Hence the numerator is negative and the sign of (2.18) will be opposite to that of the denominator. If the initial situation is one of free trade, so that $\tau = 0$, the denominator must be positive and the response of import demand to the raising of the tariff must be negative.[12] This finding is illustrated by

---

[11] See Prob. 2.7.
[12] This statement needs qualification if the government spends part of the tariff proceeds. See Kemp [22] for details.

Fig. 2.6(a). In that figure the offer curve corresponding to the initial rate of duty is unbroken, and the offer curve associated with the new and higher rate of duty is broken; the initial trading equilibrium is at P, the new equilibrium is at P'.

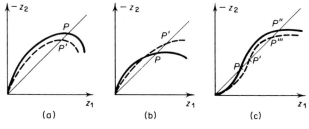

FIGURE 2.6

Suppose, however, that the initial situation is not one of free trade, so that $\tau > 0$, and that

$$m_1 > 1 + \frac{1}{\tau}, \quad \text{that is,} \quad m_2 < -\frac{1}{\tau} \tag{2.19}$$

implying that the exported commodity is inferior. Then the response of import demand to an increase in the rate of duty will be positive.[13] One is tempted to illustrate the outcome with Fig. 2.6(b). The latter, however, is based on the possibility that at some terms of trade the same nonzero offer will be forthcoming at different rates of duty. Under less restrictive demand assumptions than ours this possibility must be accepted. It must also be accepted when the assumption of fixed factor supplies is abandoned[14] or when the government spends part of the tariff proceeds in accordance with preferences which differ from those of the public.[15] As Fig. 2.7 shows, however, the possibility must be ruled out as inconsistent with the assumptions adopted here.[16] We are driven to the conclusion, then, that only Fig. 2.6(c) suitably illustrates the odd outcome. Notice, however, that Fig.

[13] In his "Memorandum on Fiscal Policy" [24] Marshall noted that the "Giffen Paradox" might operate in respect of imports of wheat into England and that, if it did, a tariff on wheat might turn the terms of trade against England. (See also Kemp [22].)

In his later *Money Credit and Commerce* [18], Marshall makes no mention of this possibility, the figure on p. 356 being thoroughly conventional. In his early *Pure Theory of Foreign Trade* [17], however, Marshall included an enigmatic diagram (Fig. 13) which might be interpreted as illustrating the Giffen effect; but this is pure speculation.

Finally, it may be noted that, in his editorial commentary in the 1949 edition of *Pure Theory*, Mr. Dorrance states that Fig. 13 has been reproduced on p. 356 of *Money Credit and Commerce*. This is not so: In the "reproduction" the curves labelled E and E' have been interchanged.

[14] See Chap. 5.

[15] See Lerner [23] and Prob. 2.8.

[16] This statement needs qualification in the limiting and exceptional case in which both the production possibility curve and the relevant indifference curve are right-angled.

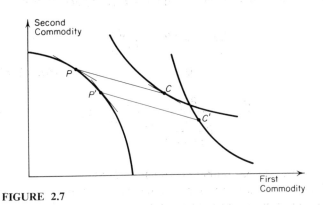

FIGURE 2.7

2.6(c) illustrates a situation in which, for each level of duty, multiple equilibria exist. In such a situation, by careful choice of the initial and new equilibria it is always possible to arrange that an increase in the rate of duty "results in" a curtailment of import demand—compare P'' with P' (or P''').

4. SOME IMPLICATIONS OF AN EXCISE TAX

Finally, we consider some of the implications of the imposition of an excise tax. This section is, therefore, companion to Sec. 4 of Chap. 1. We continue to assume that the community behaves like a single consumer.

It is assumed that an excise tax, at *ad valorem* rate $100t$ per cent, is imposed on the first or imported commodity. If we continue to denote consumers' prices by p_1 and p_2, the price received by producers of the taxed commodity must be $p_2/(1+t)$. [This reverses the conventions of Chap. 1, Sec. 4.] Since consumers' prices are determined on world markets and are assumed to be uninfluenced by the behavior of the country under consideration, the effect of the tax must be to reduce the price received by producers of the first commodity and thus discourage production and encourage imports. This may be easily confirmed. Thus

$$\frac{dz_1}{dt} = \frac{dd_1}{dt} - \frac{dy_1}{dt}$$

$$= \frac{\partial d_1}{\partial q} \cdot \frac{dq}{dt} - \frac{\partial y_1}{\partial \dfrac{p_1}{(1+t)}} \cdot \frac{d \dfrac{p_1}{(1+t)}}{dt}$$

Per capita income, however, is still equal to $p_1 q_1 + p_2 q_2$. Hence

$$\frac{dq}{dt} = p_1 \frac{dq_1}{dt} + p_2 \frac{dq_2}{dt}$$

$$= 0 \qquad\qquad \text{(from Prob. 1.2)}$$

and

$$\frac{dz_1}{dt} = \frac{\partial y_1}{\partial \dfrac{p_1}{(1+t)}} \cdot \frac{p_1}{(1+t)^2} > 0, \qquad\qquad (2.20)$$

a result which should be compared with Eq. (2.18).

Similarly, an excise tax imposed on the second or export good reduces the net price received by its producers, curtails output, and reduces exports. Indeed, a sufficiently high tax will result in a change of export commodity.

PROBLEMS

Technical Improvements

2.1 Derive expressions for $dk_i/d\lambda$, $dw_i/d\lambda$ and $dy_i/d\lambda$ ($i = 1, 2$) on the assumption that $d\lambda' = \rho d\lambda$.

2.2 Rewrite the production functions as $X_i/L_i = \lambda' f_i[(\lambda/\lambda')k_i]$. Plot X_i/L_i against k_i and show how the locus responds to change in λ and λ'.

2.3 Suppose that both production functions are of the Cobb–Douglas form (see Prob. 1.8). Derive expressions for $dw_1/d\lambda$, $dw_1/d\lambda'$, $(dw_1/d\lambda)|_{\lambda=\lambda'}$, $dr_1/d\lambda$, $dr_1/d\lambda'$, $(dr_1/d\lambda)|_{\lambda=\lambda'}$ and confirm the suspicions expressed in footnote 2 concerning the power of Cobb–Douglas functions to discriminate between neutral and biased improvements.

The Offer Curve

2.4 " . . . the course of agricultural technology in the early decades of the nineteenth century may well have accentuated the disparity between the terms on which labor was available to industry in the U.S.A. and England. In America improvements in agriculture took the form primarily of increasing output per head and the increase initially was probably more rapid than in industry; in England on the other hand, agricultural improvement was devoted primarily to increasing yields per acre and, even where there was an increase in output per head, the abundance of labor made it difficult for the laborer to enjoy the increase. In America agricultural improvements raised, and in England prevented, a rise in the terms on which labor was available to industry." (Habakkuk [5], p. 14.) Does the last sentence follow from its predecessors?

2.5 Generalize Eqs. (2.12) and (2.14) to cover the possibility that $\tau > 0$. Consider the cases $m_1 > 1 + 1/\tau$ and $1 < m_1 < 1 + 1/\tau$.

2.6 Trace the offer curve of a country which consumes the two goods in fixed proportions.

The Offer Curve and Tariffs

2.7 Derive expressions for $dy_i/d\tau$ $(i = 1, 2)$. Show that $p_1(dy_1/d\tau) + p_2(dy_2/d\tau) = 0$.

2.8 Suppose that the government spends the tariff revenue instead of handing it over to the public. Derive an expression for $dz_1/d\tau$. Is it possible for this expression to be positive?

2.9 Derive an expression for $dz_1/d\tau$ on the assumption that the *domestic* price is constant. Can you say anything about its sign?

REFERENCES

On Technical Change

[1] Amano, Akihiro, "Neoclassical Biased Technical Progress and a Neoclassical Theory of Economic Growth," *Quarterly Journal of Economics*, LXXVIII, No. 310 (February 1964), 129–38.

†[2] Edgeworth, F. Y., "The Theory of International Values," *Economic Journal*, IV, No. 13 (March 1894), 35–50.

†[3] Edgeworth, F. Y., "On a Point in the Pure Theory of International Trade," *Economic Journal*, IX, No. 1 (March 1899), 35–50.

[4] Findlay, Ronald and Harry Grubert, "Factor Intensities, Technological Progress, and the Terms of Trade," *Oxford Economic Papers*, XI, No. 1 (February 1959), 111–21.

[5] Habakkuk, H. J., *American and British Technology in the Nineteenth Century*. Cambridge: Cambridge University Press, 1962.

[6] Harrod, R. F., *Towards a Dynamic Economics*. London: Macmillan & Company Ltd., 1948.

[7] Hicks, J. R. *The Theory of Wages*. London: Macmillan & Company Ltd., 1932.

[8] Jones, Ronald W., "'Neutral' Technological Change and the Isoquant Map," *American Economic Review*, LV, No. 4 (September 1965), 848–55.

[9] Jones, Ronald W., "Comments on Technical Progress," *The Philippine Economic Journal*, V, No. 2 (Second Semester 1966), 313–32.

[10] Kemp, Murray C., "Some Difficulties in the Concept of Economic Input," in National Bureau of Economic Research, *Output, Input, and Productivity Measurement*, pp. 340–44. Princeton: Princeton University Press, 1961.

†[11] Mill, J. S., *Principles of Political Economy*, ed. Sir W. J. Ashley, Book III, Chap. XVIII, Sec. 5. London: Longmans, Green & Company, 1909.

[12] Solow, Robert, M., "Technical Change and the Aggregate Production Function," *Review of Economics and Statistics*, XXXIX, No. 3 (August 1957), 312–20.

[13] Solow, Robert M., "Investment and Technical Progress," in *Mathematical Methods in the Social Sciences*, eds. Kenneth J. Arrow, Samuel Karlin and Patrick Suppes, pp. 89–104. Stanford: Stanford University Press, 1959.

[14] Uzawa, H., "Neutral Inventions and the Stability of Growth Equilibrium," *Review of Economic Studies*, XXVIII (2), No. 76 (February 1961), 117–24.

On The Offer Curve

[15] Edgeworth, F. Y., *Papers Relating to Political Economy*, II, 31–40. London: Macmillan & Company Ltd., 1925.

[16] Johnson, Harry G., "International Trade, Income Distribution, and the Offer Curve," *Manchester School of Economic and Social Studies*, XXVII, No. 3 (September 1959), 241–60.

†[17] Marshall, Alfred, *The Pure Theory of Foreign Trade*. London: London School of Economics and Political Science, 1930, 1935, and 1949.

[18] Marshall, Alfred, *Money, Credit and Commerce*, Appendix J. London: Macmillan & Company Ltd., 1923.

On Tariffs

[19] Bhagwati, Jagdish, "The Gains from Trade Once Again," *Oxford Economic Papers*, New Series, XX, No. 2 (July 1968), 137–48.

†[20] Heckscher, Eli, "The Effect of Foreign Trade on the Distribution of Income," *Ekonomisk Tidskrift*, XXI (1919), 497–512 (in Swedish). Reprinted, in translation by Svend and Nita Laursen, in *Readings in the Theory of International Trade*, eds. Howard S. Ellis and Lloyd A. Metzler, 272–300. Philadelphia: The Blakiston Company, 1949.

[21] Kemp, Murray C., "Some Issues in the Analysis of Trade Gains," *Oxford Economic Papers*, New Series, XX, No. 2 (July 1968), 149–61.

[22] Kemp, Murray C., "Note on a Marshallian Conjecture," *Quarterly Journal of Economics*, LXXX, No. 320 (August 1966), 481–84.

†[23] Lerner, Abba P., "The Symmetry between Import and Export Taxes," *Economica*, New Series, III, No. 3 (August 1936), 306–13.

[24] Marshall, Alfred, "Memorandum on Fiscal Policy," in *Official Papers by Alfred Marshall*, 382–83. London: Macmillan & Company Ltd., for The Royal Economic Society, 1926.

†[25] Stolper, Wolfgang F., and Paul A. Samuelson, "Protection and Real Wages," *Review of Economic Studies*, IX, No. 1 (November 1941), 58–73. Reprinted in *Readings in the Theory of International Trade*, eds. Howard S. Ellis and Lloyd A. Metzler, 333–57. Philadelphia: The Blakiston Company, 1949.

chapter 3

A Trading World

In Chap. 2 it was assumed that the country under consideration produced and consumed on such a small scale that the effect of its purchases and sales on world markets could be ignored. The international terms of trade, p^*, were determined independently of that country's behavior; hence in examining the country's response to disturbances of various kinds—tariffs and technical improvements, for example—one could treat p^* as a constant.

1. A MODEL OF A TRADING WORLD

If that special case is abandoned, we must introduce an additional restriction to pin down p^*. An obvious candidate is the requirement that the world demand for one or other of the two commodities, say the second, be equal to the world supply. Now, as we have seen in Chap. 1, each country's aggregate demand for the second commodity depends on the price of that commodity in terms of the first commodity (the *numéraire*). The aggregate supply by each country also depends on the price ratio. Hence for each country net import demand, defined as the difference between aggregate local demand and aggregate local supply, depends on the local price ratio. However, under conditions of free trade, with no costs of transport, the same price ratio prevails everywhere. It follows that the required restriction can be written as[1]

$$Lz_2(p) + L^*z_2^*(p^*) = 0$$

$$p = p^*$$

(3.1)

where z_2^* is the rest of the world's net import demand for the second commodity per capita and L^* is the rest of the world's labor endowment. The determination of the equilibrium terms of trade p' is depicted in Fig. 3.1. In

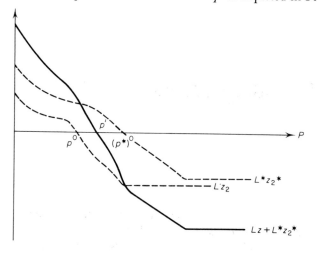

FIGURE 3.1

[1] Alternatively, one could make use of the condition of equilibrium in the first commodity market:

$$Lz_1(p) + L^*z_1^*(p^*) = 0$$

$$p = p^*$$

(3.1')

Note that Eqs. (3.1') are not independent of Eqs. (3.1); one can be obtained from the other with the aid of the two national budget constraints:

$$d_1 + p^*d_2 = y_1 + p^*y_2$$

$$d_1^* + p^*d_2^* = y_1^* + p^*y_2^*$$

that is,

$$z_1 + p^*z_2 = 0$$

$$z_1^* + p^*z_2^* = 0$$

Thus it follows from the constraints that, if $Lz_2 + L^*z_2^* = 0$, then

$$Lz_1 + L^*z_1^* = 0$$

and

$$Lz_1 - p^*L^*z_2^* = 0$$

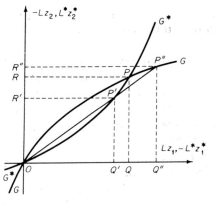

FIGURE 3.2

the case illustrated, the equilibrium is unique, with the home country exporting the second commodity and importing the first. The possibility of multiple equilibria is considered in Secs. 2 and 3.

Sometimes it is convenient to write Eq. (3.1) in the equivalent form[2]

$$Lz_1\left(\frac{1}{p}\right) - p^*L^*z_2^*(p^*) = 0$$
$$p = p^* \tag{3.2}$$

with the familiar geometric representation of Fig. 3.2. In that figure, the terms of trade are represented by the slope of a radius vector, and the quantities demanded and supplied at those terms of trade are indicated by the intersection of the radius vector with the home and foreign "offer curves," GOG and G^*OG^*, respectively. At the terms of trade indicated by the slope of $OP'P''$, for example, the rest of the world offers OQ' of the first commodity in exchange for OR' of the second commodity, while the home country offers OR'' of the second commodity in exchange for OQ'' of the first. Evidently at those terms of exchange world trade is in disequilibrium: The world excess demand for the second commodity is $R'R''$. In the case illustrated, the equilibrium terms of trade are indicated by the slope of OP. At those terms of trade, world demand is equal to world supply in each market.

That completes the construction of our static model of world trade. The model, or simple variations of it, will be the starting point for the comparative statical calculations of Chap. 4. The balance of the present chapter is devoted to certain properties of the world equilibrium. Thus in Sec. 2 we consider the so-called Heckscher–Ohlin Theorem; Sec. 3 is devoted to the fashionable question of "factor price equalization"; and in Sec. 4 we discuss conditions for the dynamic stability of the model.

[2] See footnote 1.

2. PROPERTIES OF TRADING EQUILIBRIA—THE HECKSCHER–OHLIN THEOREM

Consider two countries in autarkic equilibrium. Trade is suddenly freed. Is it possible to predict the direction trade will take, knowing only the observable characteristics of the autarkic equilibria? An answer to this question is contained in the so-called Heckscher–Ohlin Theorem: *If conditions of production are the same in both countries, each country will export the commodity which in the autarkic state is relatively intensive in its use of the country's relatively abundant factor.*

Before we can judge the truth or falsity of this proposition, it is necessary to agree on the sense in which we shall speak of a factor's relative scarcity or abundance. There are two obvious possibilities. The first is to say that capital is relatively scarce or abundant at home if the capital:labor endowment ratio is, respectively, lower or higher at home than abroad. It is not difficult to see, however, that on this definition the Heckscher–Ohlin proposition is untrue: To find a counter example one has only to imagine that each country has a strong preference for the commodity produced with relatively large quantities of its abundant factor.

An alternative definition runs in terms of the two autarkic wage-rental ratios. On this definition, a country is said to be relatively well endowed with a factor if in the autarkic equilibrium the relative reward of that factor is lower than abroad. Even on this definition, however, the Heckscher–Ohlin Theorem is untrue unless restrictions are placed on preferences and on the form of the production functions. In the balance of this section we shall endeavor to establish these propositions.

As a first step, let us consider again Fig. 3.1, which is drawn on the implicit assumption that both the autarkic and free-trade equilibria are unique. Under free trade the home country exports the second commodity, that is, the commodity which in the autarkic state is priced less favorably at home than abroad. Suppose now that the second commodity is relatively labor-intensive at all wage:rental ratios. The p^s-curve is then positively sloped, as in Fig. 1.2(a), and the autarkic ω^* exceeds the autarkic ω; that is, the home country exports the commodity which uses relatively large quantities of its abundant factor. Suppose, alternatively, that the second commodity is relatively capital-intensive at all wage:rental ratios. The p^s-curve is then negatively sloped, as in Fig. 1.2(b), and the autarkic ω exceeds the autarkic ω^*; again the home country exports the commodity which is relatively intensive in its use of the abundant factor. For these two cases, therefore, the Heckscher–Ohlin proposition appears to be verified. Suppose, however, that the relative factor-intensities of the two commodities vary with the wage:rental ratio: The case of "factor intensity reversal," illustrated by Fig. 1.2(c). Then a counter example to the Heckscher–Ohlin proposition may be constructed. Figure 3.3 contains such an example.

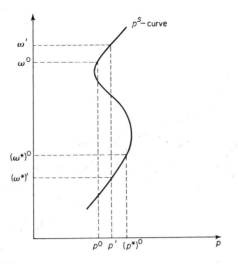

FIGURE 3.3

It is tempting to conclude from the above discussion that the Heckscher–Ohlin proposition is valid if "factor intensity reversal" is ruled out. However, that discussion was based on the assumption that the two autarkic equilibria are unique. Before accepting the qualified version of the Heckscher–Ohlin Theorem, therefore, it is desirable that we explore the implications of multiplicity of autarkic equilibria. A special case may be disposed of immediately. Thus suppose that the range defined by the highest and lowest equilibrium autarkic price ratios for one country contains no point of overlap with the corresponding range for the other country. In this case, as Fig. 3.4

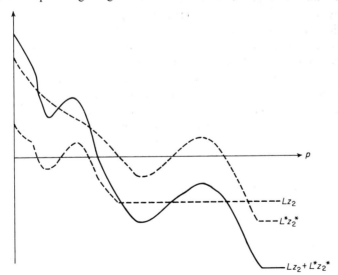

FIGURE 3.4

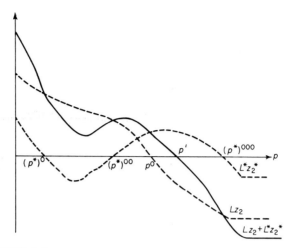

FIGURE 3.5

illustrates, the Heckscher-Ohlin proposition remains valid.[3] The interesting cases, therefore, are those in which the two ranges overlap, as in Fig. 3.5. That figure displays three alternative foreign autarkic equilibria (two stable equilibria, at $(p^*)^0$ and $(p^*)^{000}$, bracketing a single unstable equilibrium, at $(p^*)^{00}$), a unique home autarkic equilibrium (at p^0), and a unique free-trade equilibrium (at p') with the home country exporting the second commodity. If the autarkic price $(p^*)^{000}$ prevails abroad, only that part of Fig. 3.4 to the right of p^0 is relevant and we are, in effect, back to the situation depicted by Fig. 3.1. That the Heckscher–Ohlin proposition is valid follows from our earlier discussion. If, however, either $(p^*)^0$ or $(p^*)^{00}$ prevails before trade, the proposition is invalid. Thus imagine that $(p^*)^0$ prevails, and suppose that the second or home export industry is relatively labor-intensive. Then from the inequality $(p^*)^0 < p^0$ we infer that $(\omega^*)^0 < \omega^0$, implying that the home country exports the commodity which uses relatively large quantities of the relatively *scarce* factor labor. A similar conclusion emerges if the second commodity is relatively capital-intensive. Moreover, the whole argument remains valid if the foreign autarkic equilibrium falls at $(p^*)^{00}$ rather than at $(p^*)^0$. It is worth emphasizing, however, that in constructing a counter example to the Heckscher–Ohlin proposition it has not been necessary to assume that one of the autarkic equilibria is unstable.

It is clear therefore that the Heckscher–Ohlin Theorem is invalid, at least in the unqualified form in which we have stated it. However, it is possible to

---

[3] Notice that a multiplicity of autarkic equilibria does not imply a multiplicity of free-trade equilibria. Nor does a multiplicity of free-trade equilibria imply a multiplicity of autarkic equilibria.

rephrase the theorem so that it is proof against multiple autarkic equilibria: *If conditions of production are the same in both countries and if factor-intensities do not reverse themselves there exists a pair of autarkic equilibria such that when trade is opened each country will export the commodity which in the autarkic state is relatively intensive in its use of the country's relatively abundant factor.*

3. PROPERTIES OF TRADING EQUILIBRIA—THE EQUALIZATION OF FACTOR REWARDS

If trade were completely free, unhampered by transport costs or artificial obstacles like tariffs, the same product prices would prevail in all countries. If each country had the same list of primary factors of production, would the same be true of factor rewards? Common sense and common observation suggest that equalization of rewards is unlikely. But equalization is not impossible and considerable interest has been shown in a set of sufficient conditions for equalization developed by Abba Lerner and Paul Samuelson. That the conditions never will be satisfied in practice is very likely. Nevertheless the "factor price equalization theorem" is interesting if only because it focuses attention on the obstacles to equalization.

The Theorem

Suppose that each of two countries competitively produces (or could produce) something of (the same) two products with (the same) two factors, that returns to scale are constant and returns to proportions diminishing, and that the same production functions prevail in each country. Suppose, furthermore, that, for a given equilibrium p, the solution of Eqs. (1.2), for k_i and ω, is unique, and that trade between the two countries is free, subject to no impediment whatever. Then the same real and relative factor rewards must prevail in each country.

For under free trade the same product price ratio must prevail in each country. The solution of Eqs. (1.2) is unique, hence each commodity must be produced with the same factor proportions in each country. It follows that the marginal product (and real reward) of each factor, in whatever industry, must be the same in each country.

That, in a nutshell, is the "factor price equalization theorem" for the two factors/two products case. But, in pursuit of brevity, we have glided over two important questions. In the first place, we have assumed that under free trade each country produces something of each commodity; in other words, that each country is incompletely specialized in the production of its export commodity. But is incomplete specialization by both countries *possible*? In the second place, we have assumed that Eqs. (1.2) possess a unique solution. We now go over the same ground rather more carefully.

Consider any equilibrium world price ratio and choose units of the two commodities which, at those prices, are of equal value. In Fig. 3.6 the unit isoquants are labelled I_1I_1 and I_2I_2. If something is produced of each commodity (a) it must be possible to find a factor reward ratio such that the two isoquants are tangential to the same isocost line. Provided neither isoquant lies uniformly above the other, this will always be so; and, given the restrictions imposed on the production functions in Chap. 1, the isocost line will be negatively sloped. To ensure that both factors are fully employed,

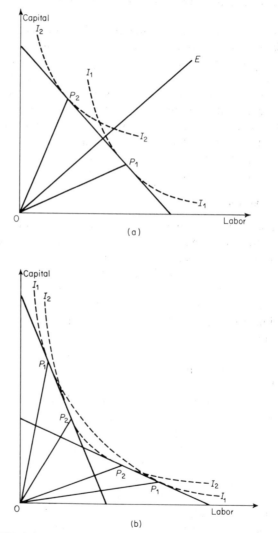

FIGURE 3.6

it is necessary also that (b) the factor endowment ray OE, the slope of which indicates the ratio of the two factor endowments, should lie in or on an edge of the cone P_1OP_2. Following Chipman, we shall call P_1OP_2 the "cone of diversification."[4] If (b) is not satisfied, complete specialization is inevitable. If both (a) and (b) are satisfied, incomplete specialization, actual or incipient, is inevitable.

Suppose that (a) and (b) are satisfied. What of uniqueness? Let us consider first the possibility that the two unit isoquants intersect once, as in Fig. 3.6(a). In view of the homogeneity of the production functions, we may infer that one commodity [in Fig. 3.6(a), the first] is uniformly, at all factor reward ratios, more labor-intensive than the other. In this case, there is quite clearly only one isocost line which can produce the required double tangency. The equilibrium ratio of factor rewards is uniquely determined and must be the same in each country. From the homogeneity of the production functions we may infer that real rewards also must be the same in each country. If, on the other hand, the isoquants intersect more than once, as in Fig. 3.6(b), there will be more than one common tangent; there will also be more than one cone of diversification, with no points in common (save in the degenerate case in which a double intersection is in fact a tangency). If in this case the two factor endowment rays lie in different cones of diversification, the equalization of factor rewards is impossible. If, however, the two endowment rays lie in the same cone equalization is inevitable. *Whatever the number of intersections*, therefore, *factor rewards are equalized if and only if the two endowment rays lie in the same cone of diversification*.

Once this is understood the question of uniqueness, which has been a dominant theme in the discussion of "factor price equalization," ceases to be of interest. In fact the uniqueness of the solution of Eqs. (1.2) is neither necessary nor sufficient for the equalization of rewards. When Eqs. (1.2) possess a unique solution, the equalization of rewards may fail because one endowment ray (or both) lies outside the (uniquely defined) cone of diversification. When the equations possess multiple solutions, so that there are many cones of diversification, the endowment ray (equivalently, the full employment conditions) of each country will "select" just one; and rewards will be equalized if and only if the two rays select the same solution.

The above discussion has run in terms of a single equilibrium world price ratio. If the price ratio changes the unit isoquants will shift and with them, the cones of diversification. The equalization of factor rewards may be inevitable with one price ratio, impossible with another.

The whole argument can be reviewed in terms of Fig. 1.2. Consider first Figs. 1.2(a) and 1.2(b), in both of which the reversal of factor intensities is ruled out. The range of commodity prices consistent with incomplete

[4] See Chipman [9], p. 21, n.3.

specialization at home is $(p^s - \bar{p}^s)$; the corresponding range for the foreign country is $[(p^s)^* - (\bar{p}^s)^*]$, not shown. It can be seen that if and only *if the two price ranges overlap and the equilibrium free-trade price ratio falls in the overlap, will factor rewards be equalized.* Notice that each part of the condition is necessary: Even when the two price ranges overlap, the equilibrium price ratio may fall outside the overlap—evidently much depends on demand conditions. When we turn to Fig. 1.2(c), which illustrates the possibility of factor intensity reversal, matters are not so simple; then, clearly, the italicized condition is not sufficient for factor price equalization (though it remains necessary). In that case it is necessary and sufficient for factor price equalization that the italicized condition be satisfied and that the factor endowment ratios *k and k* fall between the same adjacent intersections of the R_1- and R_2- curves* so that the autarkic equilibria (p^0, ω^0) and $[(p^*)^0, (\omega^*)^0]$ lie on the same monotonic section of the p^s-curve. If the two factor endowment ratios fall on opposite sides of a point of intersection of the R_1- and R_2-curves, then the two factor reward ranges $(\underline{\omega} - \bar{\omega})$ and $(\underline{\omega}^* - \bar{\omega}^*)$ have no point in common, at least one country must specialize completely, and the possibility of factor reward equalization can be ruled out.

Suppose that the above condition for the equalization of factor rewards is not satisfied. We know that free trade will not effect an international equality of factor rentals. What then *will* be the effect of trade on factor rentals? The answer depends on the number of times the R_1- and R_2-curves intersect and on the multiplicity of the two autarkic equilibria.

Let us suppose first that the R_i-curves do not intersect (Fig. 3.7(a)). If in each country the autarkic equilibrium is unique, the equilibrium free-trade price ratio must lie between the two pretrade price ratios, and the two free-trade factor reward ratios must lie closer together (or, more accurately, not further apart) than before the opening of trade. If, however, the autarkic equilibrium is not unique, this conclusion cannot be established. Thus suppose that the two excess demand curves are as displayed in Fig. 3.5. Then, as we have seen, the equilibrium free-trade price ratio need not lie between the two autarkic price ratios. It follows that the gap between the home and foreign wage:rental ratios may widen rather than narrow: $|(\omega^*)^0 - \omega^0| < |(\omega^*)' - \omega'|$. Figure 3.7(a), drawn on the assumption that the first industry is relatively capital-intensive, illustrates the possibility. It should be noted that for this outcome it is necessary that under free trade at least one country be completely specialized; thus, in the case illustrated by Fig. 3.7(a), the home country is completely specialized in producing the second commodity.

Let us suppose next that the overall factor endowment ratios, k and k^*, are separated by a single intersection of the R_i-curves, as in Fig. 3.7(b). And let us imagine for the time being that the two autarkic equilibria are unique. We know nothing about the relative values of the pretrade commodity price ratios. We do know, however, that after the opening of trade *either* each

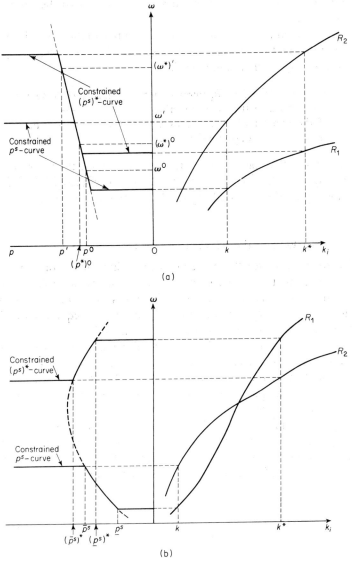

FIGURE 3.7

country will export the commodity which at the respective initial wage:rental ratios is labor-intensive *or* each country will export its capital-intensive commodity. It follows that *either* the wage:rental ratio will rise in both countries *or* it will fall in both countries. The gap between the two ratios may either widen or narrow. If either or both of the autarkic equilibria are not unique it no longer is true that the two wage:rental ratios must move in the same direction. However, our principal conclusion, that the gap may widen or narrow, stands.

The same kind of reasoning can be applied to situations in which k and k^* are separated by two, three, . . . intersections of the R_i-curves. In general, if the autarkic equilibria are unique then:

(a)   if the number of R_1–R_2 intersections is odd, the two wage:rental ratios must move in the same direction,

(b)   if the number of intersections is even (and positive), the two ratios must move in opposite directions.

In both cases, the opening of trade may either push the wage:rental ratios closer together or pry them further apart. The recognition of multiple autarkic equilibria does nothing to change this unsatisfactory general conclusion.

The Equalization of Factor Prices

The so-called factor "price" equalization theorem is concerned not with factor *prices*, that is, with the prices of more or less durable *capital assets*, but with factor *rentals*, that is, with the prices of factor *services*. To avoid begging the quite separate question of factor *price* equalization the entire discussion so far has been conducted in terms of factor rentals.

In fact the equalization of rentals is neither a necessary nor a sufficient condition of factor price equalization. For the relation between a factor's rental and its price is determined by (among other things) the rate of interest; and it is only in special circumstances that the same rate of interest will prevail in both countries.

To pose the problem of valuation in its simplest context let us imagine that capital is both immortal (nondepreciable) and nonaugmentable. A unit of capital will be expected to generate a series of uniform yields through time, the yield per unit of time being equal to its marginal product. In terms of the first commodity, the present value of the series is

$$\text{P.V.} = \left[\frac{1}{(1+i)} + \frac{1}{(1+i)^2} + \frac{1}{(1+i)^3} + \cdots\right] f_1'$$
$$= \frac{f_1'}{i}$$

where i is the rate of interest per annum (and $1/i$ is the "number of years' purchase"). The market value of a unit of capital, in terms of the *numéraire*, the first commodity, will in equilibrium equal the present value of the expected yields. If the market price were to exceed the present value, excess supply would appear (normally) and the price would fall; if the present value were to exceed the market price, excess demand would appear (normally) and the price would rise.

Now there is nothing in our present assumptions to ensure that a common rate of interest will prevail in the two countries. It follows that the price of capital will in general differ from one country to another. And this is so even though the conditions of factor *rental* equalization are satisfied. It is entirely possible for capital to earn the same real rentals everywhere yet to exchange internally at substantially different market prices.

This conclusion, however, depends essentially on the assumption that the capital asset is not itself produced. If capital were produced in both countries, with the same technology, the paradox would vanish. For from factor rental equalization it follows that the cost of producing capital, and hence the market price of capital *and the rate of interest* must be the same in both countries. *This result does not require that capital itself be internationally traded.* It requires only that at least two other traded commodities be produced in both countries. And it requires that *both* countries produce capital. Suppose, by way of contrast, that one country produces capital while the other does not. In view of the equalization of factor rentals, the failure of one country to produce capital must be the result of a demand price (for the first unit of output) lower than that prevailing in the other country. But this inequality implies that the marginal rate of time preference and the implicit rate of interest are higher than in the other country.

4. PROPERTIES OF TRADING EQUILIBRIA—STABILITY

In Chap. 4 we shall explore some of the comparative static properties of a world trading equilibrium. In particular, we shall examine the implications of small, once-over changes in preferences, in resource endowments, in technical conditions and in taxes for the several variables of the system—the volume of imports and exports, the terms of trade, factor rewards and factor proportions. Such exercises are most useful if the initial equilibrum is stable, so that when the system is disturbed it moves towards a new and neighboring equilibrium. In the present section, therefore, we consider the conditions of local stability for each of two alternative dynamic generalizations of the static model described in Sec. 1.

(i) We consider first a model in which the dynamic element is provided by a "*tâtonnement*" process of price adjustment. Suppose that the international terms of trade are slightly displaced from an equilibrium value defined by Eq. (3.2) and that, as a result, the world demand for the first commodity exceeds the supply, while (therefore) the world supply of the second commodity exceeds the demand. Suppose, further, that, under pressure of excess demand, the world price of the second commodity rises. More specifically, suppose that the rate of price increase is itself an increasing function of the excess demand. Then we may write the differential equation

$$\frac{dp}{dt} = g\left[L^*z_2^*(p) - \frac{L}{p} z_1\left(\frac{1}{p}\right) \right] \qquad g(0) = 0, \quad g' > 0 \qquad (3.3)$$

Eq. (3.3) may be viewed as a dynamical generalization of Eq. (3.2).

For the displaced terms of trade to return to the initial equilibrium value it is necessary and sufficient that $dg/dp < 0$, that is, since $g' > 0$, that $d[L^*z_2^*(p) - Lz_1(1/p)/p]/dp < 0$. Carrying out the differentiation, and equating $pL^*z_2^*$ to Lz_1, we obtain

where

$$\Delta \equiv 1 + \xi + \xi^* < 0 \qquad (3.4)$$

$$\xi \equiv \frac{1}{pz_1} \cdot \frac{dz_1}{d\frac{1}{p}}$$

and

$$\xi^* \equiv \frac{p}{z_2^*} \cdot \frac{dz_2^*}{dp}$$

are, respectively, the total price elasticities of home and foreign import demand, evaluated at the equilibrium terms of trade.[5]

(ii) This is not the only way in which dynamic elements may be injected into the static system (3.2). In the dynamic extension just considered it was assumed that for each commodity demand and supply adjust immediately and completely to the prevailing price ratio, but that, during any prescribed interval of time, the response of price to the market forces of demand and supply is only partial. We now turn these assumptions about and assume that the quantity offered by each country adjusts sluggishly to the prevailing price ratio while the price ratio always adjusts instantaneously to clear markets. In particular we imagine that in each country outputs move at specified rates per unit of time in the profit-maximizing direction.

In a complete analysis one would have to admit the possibility that, out of equilibrium, a country's production might be inefficient, with the production point falling inside the production possibilities curve, so that, within limits, the two outputs might move independently of each other. For such an analysis four adjustment equations would be needed, one for each output in each country. Evidently the calculations would be exceedingly complicated.[6]

[5] Condition (3.4) sometimes is referred to as the "Marshall–Lerner condition." Never were adjectives so incongruously applied. Marshall developed a quite different stability condition (see Marshall [34] and [35], and Samuelson [36], pp. 266–67); and Lerner was concerned neither with a barter nor with a dynamical economy (see Lerner [33]).

[6] Perhaps for this reason, no analysis admitting inefficient production has yet been attempted.

To avoid these and other complications, it will be assumed that disequilibrium outputs always lie on the two production possibility curves. Then in each country changes in one output imply changes in the other output, with both described by the same adjustment equation. Equally important, it is possible to ignore the effect of output changes on income. To see this, recall that in the discussion of local stability only a small neighborhood of an equilibrium point is involved. Thus all output changes take place along the production possibilities curve close to the equilibrium point. It follows that, whatever the commodity employed as *numéraire*, to a sufficiently close approximation output changes leave income unchanged. But if output changes do not affect income they do not affect home demand and are reflected without magnification and without diminution in the country's offer. It follows that, as in our discussion of the process of price adjustment, we can confine our analysis to Edgeworth's clock hands (the offer curves) without bothering about the detailed micromechanism behind the clock face.

Under competitive conditions, with constant returns and no taxes, the "profit-maximizing direction" is always towards the equilibrium output. Hence, if barred z's indicated the per capita amounts actually offered and unbarred z's the ideal or long-run offers, our dynamic adjustment equations take the form[7]

$$-\frac{d\bar{z}_2}{dt} = g[\bar{z}_2 - z_2(p)] \qquad g(0) = 0 \quad g' > 0$$

$$-\frac{d\bar{z}_1^*}{dt} = g^*\left(\bar{z}_1^* - z_1^*\left(\frac{1}{p}\right)\right) \qquad g^*(0) = 0 \quad g^{*\prime} > 0 \qquad (3.5)$$

$$L^*\bar{z}_1^* = Lp\bar{z}_2$$

Substituting for p in the first two members of Eqs. (3.5), expanding g and g^* around the equilibrium value of p, say p^0, abandoning nonlinear terms, and choosing units of quantity so that $g'(0) = g^{*\prime}(0) = 1$, Eqs. (3.5) reduce to

$$-\frac{d\bar{z}_2}{dt} = (1 + \epsilon)[\bar{z}_2 - z_2(p^0)] - \frac{L^*}{L}\frac{\epsilon}{p^0}\left(\bar{z}_1^* - z_1^*\left(\frac{1}{p^0}\right)\right)$$

$$-\frac{d\bar{z}_1^*}{dt} = -\frac{L}{L^*}p^0\epsilon^*[\bar{z}_2 - z_2(p^0)] + (1 + \epsilon^*)\left(\bar{z}_1^* - z_1^*\left(\frac{1}{p^0}\right)\right)$$

$$(3.6)$$

where

$$\epsilon \equiv \frac{p}{z_2} \cdot \frac{dz_2}{dp}$$

[7] Remember that z_2 and z_1^* have been defined as excess *demands* and are, therefore, negative in equilibrium.

and

$$\epsilon^* \equiv \frac{1}{pz_1^*} \cdot \frac{dz_1^*}{d\left(\frac{1}{p}\right)}$$

are, respectively, the home and foreign elasticities of export supply. The system (3.6) is locally stable if and only if

$$1 + \epsilon + \epsilon^* > 0$$

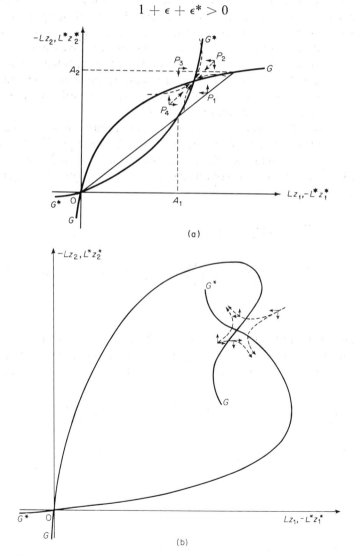

FIGURE 3.8

that is,[8]

$$\Delta \equiv 1 + \xi + \xi^* < 0 \qquad (3.7)$$

This condition is also sufficient for the local stability of system (3.5). Since the characteristic roots of the coefficient matrix

$$\begin{pmatrix} 1 + \epsilon & -\dfrac{L^*}{L}\dfrac{\epsilon}{p^0} \\[2ex] -\dfrac{L}{L^*}p^0\epsilon^* & 1 + \epsilon^* \end{pmatrix} \qquad (3.8)$$

are neither purely imaginary nor zero and since there are no multiple roots, condition (3.7) is also necessary.

Thus the stability conditions for our present quantity-adjusting model are the same as for our earlier price-adjusting model. The offer curves of Fig. 3.8(a) satisfy condition (3.7), those of Fig. 3.8(b) do not. (In the latter case the curves intersect in a saddlepoint.) The heavy arrows indicate the forces operating on the quantities actually traded. Thus at point P_1 in Fig. 3.8(a) the terms of trade p are represented by the slope of OP_1. At those terms of trade the ideal offer of the first commodity is OA_1, and the ideal offer of the second commodity is OA_2. Accordingly, the offer of the first commodity contracts and the offer of the second expands, as indicated by the heavy arrows issuing from P_1. The arrows issuing from P_2, P_3, and P_4 bear similar interpretations. Notice that, in the stable case, the approach to equilibrium is direct, not oscillatory. If trade is initially at P_1 or P_3 the path to equilibrium can at most cross one offer curve; if the initial trade point is P_2 or P_4 the path cannot cross an offer curve even once. This is the diagrammatic counterpart to the fact that the characteristic roots of (3.8) are real.

PROBLEMS

A Trading World

3.1 Suppose that the home country has a higher capital:labor ratio than the foreign country: $k > k^*$. If neither country is completely specialized, is the overall capital:output ratio higher at home than abroad? That is, is

$$K/(X_1 + pX_2) > K^*/(X_1^* + pX_2^*)?$$

Is the answer different if each country is completely specialized?

[8] See the Appendix on Elasticities for the relationship which exists between import demand elasticities and export supply elasticities.

The Equalization of Factor Rentals

3.2 Suppose that the production functions of two countries differ only by a "scale factor"; that is, that for given factor inputs, the output of one country is λ times that of another, with the same λ for each industry. Can you formulate a theorem on *relative* factor rental equalization?

3.3 Suppose that the simple "two-by-two" world considered in Sec. 3 is complicated by the introduction of nontraded (and possibly different) commodities in each country. Is it possible to formulate a theorem on the equalization of factor rewards *in terms of the traded commodities*?

3.4 Suppose that for both industries the elasticity of substitution is constant. How many times at most can the R_i-curves intersect? [Cf. Prob. (1.7).]

3.5 Suppose that in both industries the production functions are of the Cobb–Douglas type. How many times may the R_i-curves cross? [Cf. Prob. (1.8).]

3.6 Consider a production function of the form

$$[\alpha L^{-\beta} + (1 - \alpha)K^{-\beta}]^{-1/\beta} \qquad 0 < \alpha < 1, \beta > -1$$

Prove that:

(a) Returns to scale are constant;

(b) Both marginal products are positive and decreasing;

(c) The isoquants are convex to the origin;

(d) The elasticity of substitution [defined in Prob. (1.7)] is equal to $1/(1 + \beta)$ and ranges from zero to infinity;

(e) The function approaches the Cobb–Douglas form as β approaches zero. Hint: use L'Hospital's Rule. (Functions of the above type have been introduced, and thoroughly dissected, by Arrow *et al.* [5].)

3.7

(a) Write down Eqs. (1.2) for functions of the form considered in Prob. (3.6).

(b) Prove that the R_i-curves may intersect once at most. At what value of (w/r) will the R_i-curves cross?

(c) Find an expression for $d \log \omega / d \log p$. What value does $E_{p.(w/r)}$ assume when $\beta_1 = \beta_2$ (that is, when $\sigma_1 = \sigma_2$)?

3.8 Suppose that the R_i-curves touch at a single point. What will be the shape of the p^s-curve?

Leontief's "Paradox"

3.9 Leontief found that, for the United States, exports were more labor-intensive than import-competing goods. He inferred that the overall labor:capital endowment ratio was higher in the U.S. than in those countries with which the U.S. trades, and reconciled this conclusion with common sense by equating one U.S. laborer to three foreign laborers (on the grounds that U.S. labor works

harder, is more amenable to shift work, and so on). Is Leontief's inference a necessary one? (Leontief's findings are summarized in two articles, [15] and [16]. For
a summing up of the controversy inspired by Leontief's work, see Brown [8].)

3.10 Rewrite Eqs. (3.6) as a system of difference equations in $\bar{z}_1^*$ and $\bar{z}_2$,
solve them, and write down the local stability conditions.

3.11 As early as 1877 Marshall ([34], Chap. II) developed a dynamic
generalization of Eq. (3.2) on the assumption that each country's offer moves at
a determinable rate per unit of time in the direction of the amount which would be
offered in exchange for the current volume of imports if unlimited time were available
for the adjustment. Denoting by $G^*(-L\bar{z}_2)$ and $G(-L^*\bar{z}_1^*)$ the offer curves of the
foreign and home countries, respectively, the formal Marshallian model is

$$
\left.
\begin{aligned}
-\frac{d}{dt}(L^*\bar{z}_1^*) &= h_1[G^*(-L\bar{z}_2) + L^*\bar{z}_1^*] \\
-\frac{d}{dt}(L\bar{z}_2) &= h_2[G(-L^*\bar{z}_1^*) + L\bar{z}_2]
\end{aligned}
\right\}
\qquad
\begin{aligned}
h_i' &> 0, \quad h_i(0) = 0 \\
i &= 1, 2
\end{aligned}
$$

(a) Show that if the h_i are expanded linearly around the equilibrium
values of $L\bar{z}_2$ and $L^*\bar{z}_1^*$, and if the units of quantity are chosen so
that $h_1'(0) = h_2'(0) = 1$, the model reduces to

$$
-\frac{d}{dt}(L^*\bar{z}_1^*) = L^*[\bar{z}_1^* - z_1^*(1/p^0)] - p^0 e^* L[\bar{z}_2 - z_2(p^0)]
$$

$$
-\frac{d}{dt}(L\bar{z}_2) = -\frac{e}{p^0} L^*[\bar{z}_1^* - z_1^*(1/p^0)] + L[\bar{z}_2 - z_2(p^0)]
$$

where

$$
e^* \equiv \frac{\bar{z}_2}{G^*} \cdot \frac{dG^*}{d\bar{z}_2}
$$

and

$$
e \equiv \frac{\bar{z}_1}{G} \cdot \frac{dG}{d\bar{z}_1^*}
$$

are the elasticities of the foreign and home offer curves, respectively.

(b) Show that stability requires either that e and e^* are of opposite sign
or, if e and e^* are of the same sign, that $ee^* < 1$, that is,

$$
\frac{1+\xi}{\xi} \cdot \frac{1+\xi^*}{\xi^*} < 1
$$

Show further that, if ξ and ξ^* are of like sign, this latter inequality
reduces to

$$
\Delta \equiv 1 + \xi + \xi^* < 0
$$

and that, if ξ and ξ^* are of opposite sign, it reduces to

$$\Delta \equiv 1 + \xi + \xi^* > 0$$

In addition to the Marshallian reference [34], the reader may consult Marshall [35], Samuelson[36], pp. 266–67, and Kemp [32], pp. 66–69.

REFERENCES

A Trading World

†[1] Edgeworth, F. Y., *Papers Relating to Political Economy*, Vol. II, 31–40. London: Macmillan and Company Ltd., 1925.

†[2] Marshall, Alfred, *The Pure Theory of Foreign Trade*. London: The London School of Economics and Political Science, 1930, 1935, and 1949.

[3] Marshall, Alfred, *Money Credit and Commerce*, Appendix J. London: Macmillan and Company Ltd., 1923.

The Heckscher–Ohlin Theorem

†[4] Inada, Ken-ichi, "A Note on the Heckscher–Ohlin Theorem," *Economic Record*, XLIII, No. 101 (March 1967), 88–96.

[5] Johnson, Harry G., *International Trade and Economic Growth*, Chap. I. London: George Allen and Unwin Ltd., 1958.

†[6] Jones, Ronald W., "Factor Proportions and the Heckscher–Ohlin Theorem," *Review of Economic Studies*, XXIV(1), No. 63 (1956–57), 1–10.

The Equalization of Factor Rewards

[7] Arrow, K. J., H. B. Chenery, B. S. Minhas, and R. M. Solow, "Capital–Labor Substitution and Economic Efficiency," *Review of Economics and Statistics*, XLIII, No. 3 (August 1961), 225–50.

[8] Brown, A. J., "Professor Leontief and the Pattern of World Trade," *Yorkshire Bulletin of Economic and Social Research*, IX, No. 2 (November 1957), 63–75.

[9] Chipman, John S., "A Survey of the Theory of International Trade: Part 3, The Modern Theory," *Econometrica*, XXXIV, No. 1 (January 1966), 18–75.

†[10] Gale, David and Hukukane Nikaidô, "The Jacobian Matrix and Global Univalence of Mappings," *Mathematischen Annalen*, 159 (1965), 81–93.

†[11] Heckscher, Eli F., "Utrikshandelns verkan påinkomstfördelningen," *Ekonomisk Tidskrift*, XXI (1919), Del 2, 1–32. Reprinted, in English translation by Svend and Nita Laursen, as "The Effect of Foreign Trade on the Distribution of

National Income," *Readings in the Theory of International Trade*, eds. Howard S. Ellis and Lloyd A. Metzler, pp. 272–300. Philadelphia: The Blakiston Company, 1949.

†[12] Inada, Ken-ichi, "Factor Intensity and the Stolper–Samuelson Condition," *Econometrica*, to be published.

[13] Inada, Ken-ichi, "Free Trade, Capital Accumulation and Factor Price Equalization," *Economic Record*, XLIV, No. 107 (September 1968), 322–41.

[14] Kemp, Murray C. and Leon L. F. Wegge, "On the Relation between Commodity Prices and Factor Rewards," *International Economic Review*, to be published.

[15] Leontief, Wassily, "Domestic Production and Foreign Trade: the American Capital Position Re-examined," *Proceedings of the American Philosophical Society*, XCVII (September 1953), 332–49.

[16] Leontief, Wassily, "Factor Proportions and the Structure of American Trade: Further Theoretical and Empirical Analysis," *Review of Economics and Statistics*, XXXVIII, No. 4 (November 1956), 386–407.

†[17] Lerner, Abba P., "Factor Prices and International Trade," *Economica*, New Series, XIX, No. 1 (February 1952), 1–16. Reprinted in Abba P. Lerner, *Essays in Economic Analysis*. London: Macmillan and Company Ltd., 1953.

†[18] McKenzie, Lionel W., "Equality of Factor Prices in World Trade," *Econometrica*, XXIII, No. 2 (July 1955), 239–57.

[19] McKenzie, Lionel W., "The Inversion of Cost Functions: A Counter-Example," *International Economic Review*, VIII, No. 3 (October 1967), 271–78.

[20] McKenzie, Lionel W., "Theorem and Counter-Example," *International Economic Review*, VIII, No. 3 (October 1967), 279–85.

[21] Minhas, Bagicha S., "The Homohypallagic Production Function, Factor-Intensity Reversals, and the Heckscher–Ohlin Theorem," *Journal of Political Economy*, LXX, No. 2 (April 1962), 138–57.

[22] Pearce, I. F., "More About Factor Price Equalization," *International Economic Review*, VIII, No. 3 (October 1967), 255–70.

[23] Reiter, Stanley, "Efficient International Trade and Equalization of Factor Prices," *International Economic Review*, II, No. 1 (January 1961), 29–64.

[24] Samuelson, Paul A., "International Trade and the Equalization of Factor Prices," *Economic Journal*, LVIII, No. 2 (June 1948), 163–84.

†[25] Samuelson, Paul A., "International Factor Price Equalization Once Again," *Economic Journal*, LIX, No. 2 (June 1949), 181–97.

†[26] Samuelson, Paul A., "Prices of Factors and Goods in General Equilibrium," *Review of Economic Studies*, XXI(1), No. 54 (1953)–54), 1–20.

†[27] Samuelson, Paul A., "Equalization by Trade of the Interest Rate along with the Real Wage," in Robert E. Baldwin *et al.*, eds., *Trade, Growth and the Balance of Payments*, pp. 35–52. Chicago: Rand McNally & Co., 1965.

[28] Samuelson, Paul A., "Summary on Factor Price Equalization," *International Economic Review*, VIII, No. 3 (October 1967), 286–95.

†[29] Uekawa, Yasuo, "On the Generalization of the Stolper–Samuelson Theorem," *Econometrica*, to be published.

[30] Uzawa, Hirofumi, "Prices of the Factors of Production in International Trade," *Econometrica*, XXVII, No. 2 (July 1959), 448–68.

Stability

†[31] Amano, Akihiro, "Stability Conditions in the Pure Theory of International Trade: A Rehabilitation of the Marshallian Approach," *Quarterly Journal of Economics*, LXXXII, No. 2 (May 1968), 326–39.

[32] Kemp, Murray C., *The Pure Theory of International Trade*. Englewood Cliffs, N. J.,: Prentice–Hall, Inc., 1964.

[33] Lerner, Abba P., *The Economics of Control*. New York: The Macmillan Company, 1946.

†[34] Marshall, Alfred, *The Pure Theory of Foreign Trade*, Chap. II. London: The London School of Economics and Political Science, 1930, 1935, and 1949.

[35] Marshall, Alfred, *Money Credit and Commerce*, Appendix J. London: Macmillan and Company Ltd., 1923.

[36] Samuelson, Paul, *Foundations of Economic Analysis*. Cambridge, Mass.: Harvard University Press, 1947.

APPENDIX*

The International Equalization of Factor Rewards in the General Case of n Goods and r Factors

The discussion of "factor price equalization" was confined for the most part to the simple two factors-two products case. We now seek to extend that discussion to cover situations in which both factors and products are arbitrary in number.

Suppose then that we are given a vector of equilibrium world commodity prices and told that there are no impediments to trade and that something of each of n commodities is produced, though not necessarily in each country. Under what conditions can we infer that each of r primary factors of production receives the same reward in each country?

Given the price vector, we can choose equal-valued commodity units and then define the corresponding unit isoproduct surfaces, n in number. Either these surfaces do or do not possess a common negatively sloped tangent

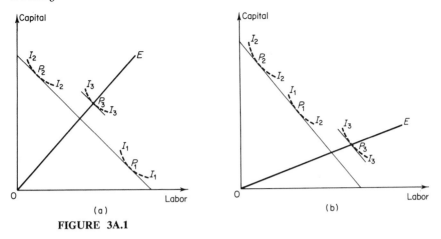

FIGURE 3A.1

plane. If they do not possess a common tangent plane, the international equalization of factor rewards is impossible, at least at the given equilibrium prices. Figure 3A.1 provides an illustration with $n = 3, r = 2$. Suppose that one country's endowment ray passes through P_3 and that the endowment ray of a second country lies in the interior of the cone of diversification P_1OP_2. It might be imagined that an international equilibrium is possible with the first country producing only the third commodity and the second country producing the first and second commodities, and with the same relative factor rewards prevailing in both countries. In the first country, however, there would be a profit incentive to abandon production of the third commodity and take up the production of either of the remaining commodities. An equilibrium of the type described is therefore impossible. In any true equilibrium each country must produce two commodities, a different pair in each country; and this implies the international *inequality* of factor rewards.

For the international equalization of factor rewards, the existence of a common tangent plane is necessary but not sufficient. Suppose that such a plane exists and is unique. Then it is still possible that the relative factor rewards implied by the plane are inconsistent with the full employment of all factors. To ensure full employment it is necessary that the endowment ray of each country should lie inside the cone of diversification defined by the n points of tangency. Suppose, alternatively, that such a plane exists but is not unique. (If $n < r$ and if such a plane exists, it cannot possibly be unique.) Each plane defines a different cone of diversification; moreover, the several cones have no points in common. It is possible therefore for the endowment rays of two countries to lie in different cones; again, full employment can be maintained in each country only if factor rewards differ from country to country. Figure 3A.2 provides an illustration, with $n = 2, r = 3$. Suppose that there exists a plane which has negative slopes and is tangent to the first and second isoproduct surfaces (not shown) at P_1 and P_2, respectively. Only

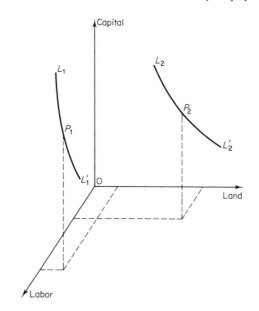

FIGURE   3A.2

one plane can be tangent at P_1 and P_2. P_1OP_2 is the corresponding (degenerate) cone of diversification. Evidently an indefinite number of additional planes and cones can be generated by rolling the initial tangent plane round the two isoproduct surfaces. The two loci of tangencies are labelled L_1L_1' and L_2L_2'. Between points of L_1L_1' and L_2L_2' there exists a one-to-one relationship, with points between P_1 and L_1 associated with points between P_2 and L_2. It follows that no two cones have points in common.

For the international equalization of factor rewards it is necessary therefore that the endowment rays of each country compared should lie in the same cone of diversification. The satisfaction of this condition also suffices.

Notice that in the above exposition it has not been necessary to treat separately each of the three cases: $n > r$, $n = r$, $n < r$. The same general rule applies in all cases.[9]

Notice finally that for the international equalization of factor rewards it is not necessary that all n commodities be produced in each country compared. If $n > r$ there is an inevitable element of indeterminacy in the relative composition of outputs; in particular, some outputs may be zero. It *is* necessary, however, that the production of all commodities be possible without loss.

The subject of this appendix is reconsidered in Chap. 5, Sec. 2 and in Chaps. 8 and 9.

---

[9] Chipman and others have claimed that when $n < m$, international "factor price equalization" will not take place unless additional restrictions are imposed on the production functions. This view is, I think, a mistaken one. See [9], pp. 31–32.

chapter 4

A Trading World—
Comparative Statics

We are now in a position to examine the comparative statical properties of the two-countries, two-commodities, two-factors trading world which was constructed in Chap. 3. To explore the implications of all possible parametric variations would be tedious. It suffices to consider the effects, on the terms of trade, outputs, and the distribution of income, of changes in the level of import duties, of changes in demand, of international transfers, and of economic expansion.

1. TARIFF CHANGES

We know from Chap. 1 that if we can determine the response of p to a change in the rate of duty we can immediately infer the response of outputs, real factor rewards, and the distribution of earned income. Under the assumption that the community behaves like a single individual, we examined in Chap. 2 the conditions under which a tariff gives rise to an increase in the demand for imports at given terms of trade. If those conditions are satisfied, the terms of trade deteriorate and *a fortiori* the internal price ratio, $p = p^*/(1 + \tau)$, falls. However, the conditions are extremely rigorous, and we would normally expect a tariff to turn the terms of trade in favor of the country imposing it. But then the domestic price ratio is subject to conflicting pulls: On the one hand, the terms of trade improve; on the other hand, the tariff spread between the terms of trade and the domestic price ratio is widened. Can we say anything more?

In international equilibrium the home country's demand for imports, Lz_1, must equal the foreign country's demand for imports (expressed in terms of the first commodity), $p^*L^*z_2^*$. Hence the condition of equilibrium takes the form

$$Lz_1 = L\left[d_1\left(q_2, \frac{1}{p}\right) - y_1\right] = p(1 + \tau)L^*z_2^*[p(1 + \tau)] \qquad (4.1)$$

We seek $dp/d\tau$. Differentiating Eq. (4.1) totally with respect to τ, we obtain

$$-\frac{Lz_1}{p}(1 + \xi + \xi^*)\frac{dp}{d\tau} + Lpm_1\frac{\partial q_2}{\partial \tau} = pL^*z_2^*(1 + \xi^*) \qquad (4.2)$$

Now

$$q_2 = \frac{y_1}{p} + y_2 + \frac{\tau}{1 + \tau}\left(\frac{z_1}{p}\right)$$

Hence

$$\frac{\partial q_2}{\partial \tau} = \frac{z_1}{p(1 + \tau)^2\Omega}$$

where $\Omega \equiv (1 + \tau m_2)/(1 + \tau)$. Substituting for $\partial q_2/\partial \tau$ in Eq. (4.2), and solving for $dp/d\tau$, we obtain

$$\frac{dp}{d\tau} = -\frac{p}{\Delta(1 + \tau)}\left(\xi^* + \frac{m_2}{\Omega}\right) \qquad (4.3)$$

Clearly the price change may be of either sign or zero. The ambiguity stems from the fact that p is subject to the two conflicting pulls already referred to. In particular, if the stability condition $\Delta < 0$ is satisfied[1]

$$\frac{dp}{d\tau} \gtreqless 0 \quad \text{as} \quad \xi^* + \frac{m_2}{\Omega} \gtreqless 0 \qquad (4.4)$$

Of special interest is the case in which $\xi^* + (m_2/\Omega) = 0$, for then both real factor rewards and the distribution of *earned* income remain unchanged. If trade is initially free, $\Omega = 1$ and the condition takes the simple form $-\xi^* = m_2$;[2] that is, the marginal propensity to buy the exported commodity must

---

[1] See Prob. 4.1.

[2] The reader should compare this condition with that implied by Eq. (1.27). At this point, also, he might consider Prob. 4.2. The condition $-\xi^* = m_2$ was first obtained by Lerner [2], p. 130.

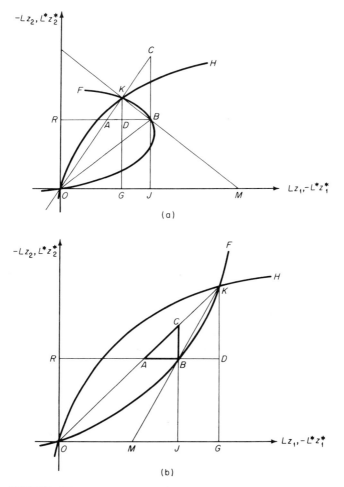

FIGURE 4.1

equal minus the elasticity of import demand. Note that if neither commodity is inferior, the paradox can appear only when the demand for imports is inelastic. If, however, the first or imported commodity is inferior the paradox can appear even when the demand for imports is elastic. The two cases are illustrated by Figs. 4.1(a) and 4.1(b) respectively. OH is the pre-tariff offer curve of the home or tariff-imposing country; OF is the offer curve of the rest of the world. The initial terms of trade, and the post-tariff domestic price ratio in the tariff-imposing country, are represented by the slope of OK; the post-tariff terms of trade are represented by the slope of OB. The *ad valorem* rate of duty is given by $CB/BJ = BA/RA$. K is the initial, pre-tariff trading point; B is the post-tariff trading point. (K also indicates the volume of imports which would be demanded *by private citizens* if the government retained the tariff proceeds, either in the form of the first commodity, or of the second, or in some mixed form.) The tariff revenue, in terms of the second commodity, is BC; converting at the *internal* price ratio, the revenue is, in terms of the first commodity, AB. Clearly, then, the marginal propensity to consume the first commodity, m_1, is DB/AB; and the marginal propensity to consume the second, m_2, is AD/AB. For small τ the chord through B and K can be considered to coincide with the tangent at K. Hence the elasticity of the foreign demand for imports, evaluated at K, is given by

$$-\xi^* = \frac{OG}{OM} = \frac{AD}{AB} = m_2$$

2. DEMAND SHIFTS

Let us suppose that, trade between the two countries E and G having been in equilibrium, there is a considerable increase in E's demand for G's goods, unaccompanied by any corresponding increase of demand on the part of G. The first result will be an increase in the amount of E's goods which her importing merchants will be able to obtain in return for each bale of G's goods. The second will be that merchants will be able and compelled to offer more of E's goods in G's markets for each G bale: their mutual competition will force them to do so. That is to say, the terms of international trade will be altered in G's favor. But how far will the movement go?[3]

This problem was posed and answered by Marshall nearly fifty years ago. His solution became the subject of a lengthy controversy, which only recently has been laid to rest.[4] Much of the disagreement was the product of failure to define with sufficient care the concept "increase in demand." As will become clear in a moment, both the behavior of the terms of trade and the bearing of the two demand elasticities on the outcome depend upon the type of demand shift postulated.

Let us suppose that there is an increase in the demand by the rest of the world for the export of the home country. Three types of demand shift will be recognized, though of course the possibilities are unlimited. First, one might imagine an increase, in uniform proportion, of the amount of the first commodity offered in exchange *for a given amount of the second*. It is this kind of demand shift that Marshall himself had in mind. If we write the import demand function of the rest of the world as $L^*z_2^*(p/\mu_1)$, where μ_1 is a

[3] Marshall [8], p. 177.
[4] A resolution of the problem and a bibliography may be found in Kemp [7]. Problems (4.8)–(4.11) were suggested by statements made by participants in the controversy.

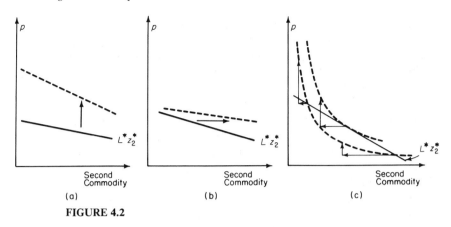

FIGURE 4.2

parameter initially equal to one, a demand shift of this kind may be represented by an increase in μ_1. Diagrammatically, it is represented by a vertical shift upwards of the demand curve [Fig. 4.2(a)], or by a horizontal shift of the offer curve [Fig. 4.3(a)]. It will be evident that the elasticity of import demand, ξ^*, evaluated at a constant z_2^* is invariant under demand shifts of this kind.

As a second possibility, we might imagine an increase, in uniform proportion, of the amount of the first commodity offered *at given terms of trade.* It is this kind of shift which is implicit in Graham's contribution to the controversy.[5] If we rewrite the import demand function of the rest of the world as $\mu_2 L^* z_2^*(p)$, where μ_2 is a second parameter, also initially equal to one, a

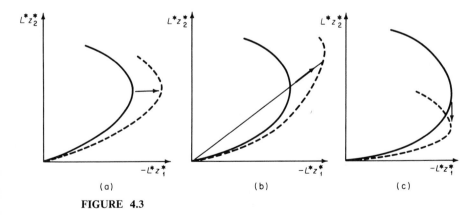

FIGURE 4.3

[5] For references see Kemp [7].

It is noteworthy that in the *Principles* Marshall recognized as increases in demand only shifts which, in the sense of the text, are Grahamesque: "When we say that a person's demand for anything increases, we mean that he will buy more of it than he would before at the same price." See Marshall [9], p. 97.

demand shift of the present kind may be represented by an increase in μ_2. Diagrammatically it is represented by a horizontal shift of the demand curve [Fig. 4.2(b)], or by a radial projection of the offer curve [Fig. 4.3(b)]. If evaluated at constant p, the elasticity of import demand is invariant under demand shifts of this kind.

Finally, we might imagine a decrease, in uniform proportion, of the amount of the second commodity demanded in return for a given amount of the first. If we write the import demand function in yet another guise, $(1/\mu_3)L^*z_2^*(p/\mu_3)$, where μ_3 is a third parameter of demand, initially equal to one, a demand shift of this kind might be represented by an increase in μ_3. Diagrammatically, the rest of the world's offer curve shifts down in uniform proportion [Fig. 4.3(c)]; in terms of demand curves, the representation is a trifle more complicated: Each point on the old demand curve must be imagined to move to the left in uniform proportion and then vertically until contact is made with the curve of unitary elasticity which passes through the initial point [Fig. 4.2(c)]. If evaluated at constant z_1, the elasticity of demand is invariant under shifts of this kind.

The implications of each of the three types of demand shift will be considered in turn.

Marshallian Demand Shifts

It is a necessary condition of international equilibrium that the value of the home country's imports, Lz_1, should equal the value of its exports, $pL^*z_2^*$; in notation convenient to a discussion of Marshallian shifts,

$$Lz_1\left(\frac{1}{p}\right) = pL^*z_2^*\left(\frac{p}{\mu_1}\right) \tag{4.5}$$

Differentiating with respect to μ_1, and solving,

$$\frac{dp}{d\mu_1} = \frac{p\xi^*}{\Delta} \tag{4.6}$$

where, of course,

$$\Delta = 1 + \xi + \xi^*$$

Hence

$$\frac{dz_1}{d\mu_1} = -\frac{z_1\xi\xi^*}{\Delta} \tag{4.7}$$

and

$$\frac{dz_2^*}{d\mu_1} = -\frac{z_2^*\xi^*(1+\xi)}{\Delta} = \frac{z_2^*\xi^*\epsilon}{\Delta} \tag{4.8}$$

It follows that, provided $\Delta < 0$ and both demand curves are downward sloping,[6] the terms of trade will move in favor of the country for the export of which there has been an increase in demand; the volume of that country's imports will also increase. If, in addition, that country's import demand is elastic ($\xi < -1$, that is, $\epsilon > 0$), the volume of its exports will increase too. If the market is unstable ($\Delta > 0$), these conclusions stand in need of fairly obvious revision.[7]

Grahamesque Demand Shifts

In the notation convenient to a discussion of demand shifts of the second kind, the condition of international equilibrium is

$$Lz_1\left(\frac{1}{p}\right) = p\mu_2 L^* z_2^*(p)$$

Differentiation yields

$$\frac{dp}{d\mu_2} = -\frac{p}{\Delta} = \frac{-1}{\xi^*} \cdot \frac{dp}{d\mu_1} \tag{4.9}$$

$$\frac{dz_1}{d\mu_2} = \frac{z_1\xi}{\Delta} = \frac{-1}{\xi^*} \cdot \frac{dz_1}{d\mu_1} \tag{4.10}$$

$$\frac{d\mu_2 z_2^*}{d\mu_2} = \frac{z_2^*(1 + \xi)}{\Delta} = -\frac{z_2^*\epsilon}{\Delta} = \frac{-1}{\xi^*} \cdot \frac{dz_2^*}{d\mu_1} \tag{4.11}$$

Thus if we ignore the factor $-1/\xi^*$, the effects of Marshallian and Grahamesque shifts are identical.[8] The factor $-1/\xi^*$ simply translates a horizontal Grahamesque shift into a vertical Marshallian shift:

$$\frac{\partial}{\partial\mu_2}[\mu_2 z_2^*(p)] = z_2^* = \frac{-1}{\xi^*} \cdot \frac{\partial}{\partial\mu_1}\left[E_2^*\left(\frac{p}{\mu_1}\right)\right]$$

Demand Shifts of the Third Kind

In the notation appropriate to a discussion of demand shifts of the third kind, the condition of international equilibrium is

$$Lz_1\left(\frac{1}{p}\right) = \frac{pL^* z_2^*(p/\mu_3)}{\mu_3}$$

[6] Under most of the more familiar dynamic generalizations of Eq. (4.5), $\Delta < 0$ is the condition of stability. See Chap. 3, Sec. 4.

[7] See Prob. 4.10.

[8] See Prob. 4.11.

It follows that

$$\frac{dp}{d\mu_3} = \frac{p(1 + \xi^*)}{\Delta} = -\frac{p\epsilon^*}{\Delta} \tag{4.12}$$

$$\frac{dz_1}{d\mu_3} = \frac{-z_1\xi(1 + \xi^*)}{\Delta} = \frac{z_1\xi\epsilon^*}{\Delta} \tag{4.13}$$

$$\frac{d(z_2^*/\mu_3)}{d\mu_3} = \frac{-z_2^*(1 + \xi)(1 + \xi^*)}{\Delta} = \frac{-z_2^*\epsilon\epsilon^*}{\Delta} \tag{4.14}$$

Thus if we ignore the multiplicative factor $-(1 + \xi^*)$, the effects are identical with those of a Grahamesque shift. The factor simply translates one kind of shift into the other:

$$\frac{\partial}{\partial\mu_3}\left[\frac{1}{\mu_3} z_2^*\left(\frac{p}{\mu_3}\right)\right] = -z_2^*(1 + \xi^*) = -(1 + \xi^*)\frac{\partial}{\partial\mu_2}[\mu_2 z_2^*(p)]$$

The results contain one surprise: A demand shift of the third type gives rise to a favorable movement of the rest of the world's terms of trade if the import demand of the rest of the world is inelastic.

Generalized Demand Shifts

We have explored the implications of just three among the infinity of types of demand shift that we might have recognized. By writing the foreign demand function as

$$\mu_4 z_2^*(\mu_5 p)$$

and adding

$$\frac{d\mu_5}{d\mu_4} = \lambda \qquad \lambda \geq 0$$

we might consider a general class of demand shifts, into which the three considered fit as special cases. This possibility is further considered in Prob. 4.9.

3. INTERNATIONAL TRANSFERS

Imagine that one country is called upon to make a net payment to another country. The payment can be effected, of course, only by exporting goods and services. The deprivation of those goods and services constitutes the primary burden of the payment. The question which has long interested economists is whether the paying country must suffer, in addition, a secondary burden in the form of a deterioration of its terms of trade.[9] The nature of the payment is, from this point of view, of no consequence: It may be a war indemnity payable by the government of a defeated country; or it may be a loan, or repayment of a loan, or interest on a loan, either between two governments or between individuals or between individuals and a government; or it may be a gift, or a subscription. In the vast literature concerning the "transfer problem" it has usually been assumed that the payment is unilateral or unrequited, that is, not in discharge of a debt incurred by the importation (in the period under study) of goods and services. But clearly payments in discharge of ordinary commercial debts raise exactly the same range of problems as do other kinds of payments; the origin of the debt is immaterial.

Imagine that the governments of the rest of the world must pay T units of the first commodity, their export, to the government of the home country. We wish to know the effect of the payment on the terms of trade, p, and, in particular, we wish to know the conditions under which the payment will have *no* effect on the terms of trade. Now every payment poses a pair of budgetary problems: How does the paying government obtain the means of payment? How does the receiving government dispose of the proceeds? And the effect of a payment on the terms of trade depends on the manner in which the budgetary problems are resolved. It follows that analysis can proceed only after specific assumptions have been made concerning the fiscal arrangements of the countries involved in the payment. The possible assumptions are legion: It could be assumed that the paying government levies an income tax with a yield equal to the payment and that the receiving government hands over the amount transferred to the public, or we might suppose both budgetary problems to be solved by expansion or cutback in the rate of government spending; or the level of a sales tax might be the variable which adjusts to accommodate the payment, or the rate of import duty; or some mixture of the foregoing alternatives might be adopted. Clearly not all possibilities can be explored. It will be assumed here that each country varies the average rate of personal income tax to absorb the shock of the payment.[10]

Before the payment is made, the home or receiving country imports $Lz_1(1/p)$ of the first commodity; after the payment its imports rise to $Lz_1(1/p) + m_1T$. The imports of the rest of the world fall from $L^*z_2^*(p)$ to $[L^*z_2^*(p) - (m_2^*T/p)]$. The condition of international equilibrium is that the receiving country's imports should exceed the value of the rest of the world's imports by T:

$$Lz_1\left(\frac{1}{p}\right) + m_1T = pL^*z_2^*(p) - m_2^*T + T$$

[9] See, for example, Mill [12], p. 43.
[10] See also Probs. 4.15 and 4.16.

Differentiating with respect to T, and setting $T = 0$, we obtain

$$\frac{dp}{dT} = \frac{m_2^* - m_2}{L^* z_2^* \Delta} = \frac{m_1 - m_1^*}{L^* z_2^* \Delta} = \frac{m_1 + m_2^* - 1}{L^* z_2^* \Delta} \qquad (4.15)$$

Thus the terms of trade will be unaffected by the payment if

$$m_1 + m_2^* = 1 \qquad (4.16)$$

that is, if the sum of the two marginal propensities to import is unity: The receiving country's imports rise by $m_1 T$; those of the rest of the world fall by $m_2^* T$ (in terms of the first commodity); hence, without any change in the terms of trade, the result of income effects alone, there emerges an export surplus of just the required magnitude:

$$(m_1 + m_2^*)T = T$$

(Note that this result is quite independent of the initial value of T.) If, on the other hand,

$$m_1 + m_2^* < 1$$

the surplus generated by income effects alone is inadequate and must be augmented by an adjustment of the terms of trade. How far the terms of trade must move is determined by the value of Δ, a fact which should not surprise us at this stage. If, finally,

$$m_1 + m_2^* > 1$$

the income-generated surplus will be more than enough to effect the payment. Provided $\Delta < 0$, the terms of trade will require revision in favor of the *paying* country.[11]

4. ECONOMIC EXPANSION

In this section I shall explore the implications of economic expansion for production, the terms of trade, and real income.[12] Eventually it will be

---

[11] One is led to ask whether the transfer might give rise to an improvement in the welfare of the paying country, a deterioration in the welfare of the receiving country. It can be shown that this outcome is impossible, at least in the context of the present model and provided that $\Delta < 0$. See Prob. 4.17.

[12] This section builds on the discussion of technological improvements and changes in factor endowment contained in Chaps. 1 and 2.

necessary to distinguish carefully between the two kinds of expansionary agents—technical improvements and growth of factor supplies. For the time being, however, we need not bother with distinctions; we suppose merely that an expansion occurs, in the sense that the community's production frontier shifts out from the origin, so that at the prevailing prices it will be profitable to expand the production of at least one of the two commodities. If we represent the expansionary agent by θ we may then write

$$X_1 = X_1(\theta, p)$$

$$X_2 = X_2(\theta, p)$$

Evaluated at the prevailing prices, the impacts on the outputs X_1 and X_2 of a change in θ are $\partial X_1/\partial\theta$ and $p(\partial X_2/\partial\theta)$, respectively. For the present, $\partial X_1/\partial\theta$ and $p(\partial X_2/\partial\theta)$ are simply taken as given; later we shall have to evaluate them for various types of expansionary agents: Technological improvements of one kind or another, expansions in the supply of one or other of the two factors. The remaining partial derivatives, $\partial X_1/\partial p$ and $\partial X_2/\partial p$, we have already encountered and evaluated.[13]

Writing $Z_i \equiv Lz_i$, the condition of international equilibrium is

$$Z_1\left(\frac{1}{p}, \theta\right) = pZ_2^*(p)$$

Hence, differentiating with respect to θ,

$$\left(Z_2^* + p\frac{dZ_2^*}{dp} + \frac{1}{p^2} \cdot \frac{\partial Z_1}{\partial 1/p}\right)\frac{dp}{d\theta} = \frac{\partial Z_1}{\partial\theta}$$

whence

$$\frac{dp}{d\theta} = \frac{\partial Z_1}{\partial\theta}\bigg/ Z_2^*\Delta$$

The outcome for the terms of trade, then, depends on the value of $\partial Z_1/\partial\theta$. Now if $D_i \equiv Ld_i$ and if $Q_i \equiv Lq_i$ are, respectively, aggregate demand for the ith commodity and aggregate income in terms of the ith commodity, we may write

$$Z_1 = D_1(p, Q_1) - X_1(p, \theta)$$

[13] See Prob. 1.2.

so that[14]

$$\frac{\partial Z_1}{\partial \theta} = m_1 \frac{\partial Q_1}{\partial \theta} - \frac{\partial X_1}{\partial \theta}$$

$$= \frac{\partial Q_1}{\partial \theta}(m_1 - \beta)$$

where

$$\beta = \frac{\dfrac{\partial X_1}{\partial \theta}}{\dfrac{\partial Q_1}{\partial \theta}}$$

measures the degree of participation by the first industry in the general expansion of output. It follows, finally, that

$$\frac{dp}{d\theta} = \frac{(m_1 - \beta)\dfrac{\partial Q_1}{\partial \theta}}{Z_2^* \Delta} = -\frac{(m_1 - \beta)\dfrac{\partial Q_1}{\partial \theta}}{Z_2 \Delta} \qquad (4.17)$$

Evidently the condition for no change in the terms of trade is that

$$\beta = m_1: \qquad (4.18)$$

at constant prices the first industry shares in the general expansion of output in the same degree that it shares in the general expansion of consumption. If $\beta < m_1$, the output of the first industry expands by less than demand, and the demand for imports rises; the terms of trade move against the expanding country. If, on the other hand, $\beta > m_1$, the output of the first industry expands by more than demand, and the demand for imports falls; the terms of trade move in favor of the expanding country. The three possibilities are illustrated by Fig. 4.4. In each branch of the figure the initial and post-expansion production points are represented by P_0 and P_1, respectively, and the initial and postexpansion consumption points are represented by C_0 and C_1, respectively. β and m_1 are represented by P_0B/P_0D and C_0E/C_0F, respectively; but their *relative* magnitudes may be more easily ascertained by comparing the slopes (referred to the vertical axis) of C_0C_1 and P_0P_1, respectively.

---

[14] The value of m_1 may depend on the source of the expansion. In particular it will probably be very different in the case of an expansion of the labor force than in the case of either an accumulation of capital or of a technical improvement.

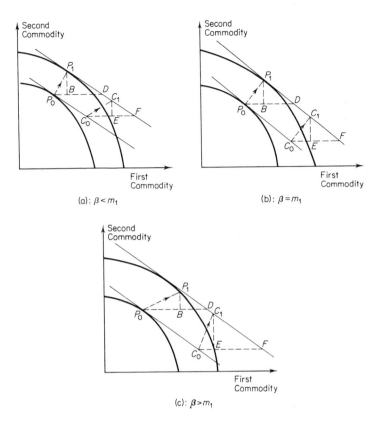

FIGURE 4.4

The case in which the expanding country's terms of trade deteriorate, the rest of the world benefiting from the expansion, is of special interest. For it suggests the possibility, first noted by Edgeworth,[15] that the expanding country might be worse off after the expansion than before. Now this is not the place for a detailed exploration of the welfare effects of an expansion; nor, since we have not yet specialized our discussion by differentiating expansion based on technological acquisitions from expansion based on enlargement of the factor endowment, are we equipped to do so. We may, however, ask the following important questions. Is it possible that the terms of trade may move so far against the expanding country that it cannot keep up its old pattern of aggregate consumption? If so, what are the conditions under which that outcome may be expected?

---

[15] Edgeworth [19], pp. 40–42. For a brief sketch of the history of thought on this topic, see Kemp [22], pp. 467–68.

The rate of change of real income, Q_1, is

$$\frac{dQ_1}{d\theta} = \frac{\partial Q_1}{\partial \theta} + \frac{\partial Q_1}{\partial p} \cdot \frac{dp}{d\theta}$$

$$= \frac{\partial Q_1}{\partial \theta} + X_2 \frac{dp}{d\theta} \qquad \text{(from Prob. 1.2)}$$

The rate of increase in the cost of the initial consumption basket, on the other hand, is $D_2(dp/d\theta)$. It follows that the country is better or worse off in the above-defined sense, as

$$\frac{\partial Q_1}{\partial \theta} + X_2 \frac{dp}{d\theta} > \quad \text{or} \quad < D_2 \frac{dp}{d\theta}$$

that is, as

$$\frac{\partial Q_1}{\partial \theta} - Z_2 \frac{dp}{d\theta} \gtrless 0$$

or, substituting from Eq. (4.17), as

$$1 + \frac{m_1 - \beta}{\Delta} \gtrless 0 \qquad (4.19)$$

And the country's net gain, possibly negative, may be defined as[16]

$$\frac{\partial Q_1}{\partial \theta}\left(1 + \frac{m_1 - \beta}{\Delta}\right)$$

Thus the condition of the expanding country's *damnification*, to adopt Edgeworth's picturesque expression, is

$$\begin{aligned}
\Delta + m_1 - \beta > 0 \quad \text{if} \quad \Delta < 0 \\
\Delta + m_1 - \beta < 0 \quad \text{if} \quad \Delta > 0
\end{aligned} \qquad (4.20)$$

That the possibility of loss exists is remarkable. The flavor of paradox may be removed, perhaps, by observing that an expanding country could not possibly be damnified if it were to follow a suitable policy of trade restriction. That this is so follows from the fact that, while the country's production frontier has expanded, its trading possibilities, summarized by the offer

---

[16] For completeness, the net gain of the rest of the world is

$$-\left(\frac{m_1 - \beta}{\Delta}\right) \cdot \frac{\partial Q_1}{\partial \theta}$$

and the net gain of the world as a whole is simply $\partial Q_1/\partial \theta$. These measures of gain are not to be taken too seriously. Not only do they fail to measure gain *per caput*; they do not even measure the compensating variation, that is, the amount of which, after the innovation, the community could be deprived without *net* ill or beneficial effect.

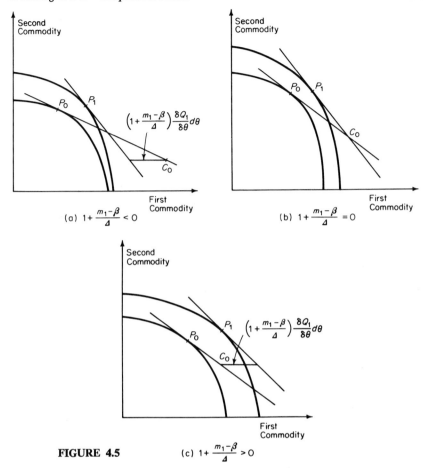

FIGURE 4.5

(a) $1 + \dfrac{m_1 - \beta}{\Delta} < 0$

(b) $1 + \dfrac{m_1 - \beta}{\Delta} = 0$

(c) $1 + \dfrac{m_1 - \beta}{\Delta} > 0$

curve of the rest of the world, have not contracted, but remained as they were; its consumption possibilities therefore must have expanded. Figure 4.5 illustrates three possibilities.

To complete our discussion we must indicate how to assign specific form to β (or, what amounts to the same thing, to $\partial Q_1/\partial\theta$ and $\partial X_1/\partial\theta$) for each of the several factor-saving improvements identified in Chap. 2 and for changes in the nation's endowment of each of the two productive factors.

Changes in Factor Endowment

Suppose that the supply of labor increases. We know that

$$\frac{\partial X_1}{\partial L} = \frac{k_2 f_1}{k_2 - k_1}$$

$$\frac{\partial X_2}{\partial L} = -\frac{k_1 f_2}{k_2 - k_1}$$

(1.20b)

and that[17]

[17] See Prob. 1.9.

$$\frac{\partial Q_1}{\partial L} = \frac{\partial X_1}{\partial L} + p\,\frac{\partial X_2}{\partial L} = f_1 - k_1 f_1'$$

Hence
$$\beta = \frac{\partial X_1}{\partial L} \bigg/ \frac{\partial Q_1}{\partial L} = \frac{k_2}{k_2 - k_1} \cdot \frac{f_1}{f_1 - k_1 f_1'}$$

Thus if $k_2 > k_1$, that is, if the import-competing industry is labor-intensive, β must exceed unity, $(m_1 - \beta)$ must be negative (if we rule out the possibility that the second commodity is inferior in consumption), and the terms of trade of the expanding country must improve (assuming that $\Delta < 0$); damnification is impossible.[18] But if $k_1 > k_2$, that is, if the import-competing industry is capital-intensive, β is negative; $(m_1 - \beta)$ is positive (if we rule out the possibility that the first commodity is inferior in consumption); and the terms of trade must move against the expanding country (if $\Delta < 0$); damnification is possible but, of course, not inevitable.

If, on the other hand, the supply of *capital* increases,[19]

$$\frac{\partial X_1}{\partial K} = \frac{-f_1}{k_2 - k_1}$$

$$\frac{\partial X_2}{\partial K} = \frac{f_2}{k_2 - k_1} \tag{1.20a}$$

and
$$\frac{\partial Q_1}{\partial K} = \frac{\partial X_1}{\partial K} + p\,\frac{\partial X_2}{\partial K}$$
$$= f_1'$$

Hence
$$\beta = \frac{k_1}{k_1 - k_2} \cdot \frac{f_1}{k_1 f_1'}$$

Thus if $k_1 > k_2$, that is, if the import-competing industry is capital-intensive, β must exceed unity, $(m_1 - \beta)$ must be negative (if, again, we rule out the possibility that the second commodity is inferior), and the terms of trade must move in favor of the expanding country (if $\Delta < 0$); damnification is possible, but not inevitable. The reader will note the symmetry between these results and those set out in the preceding paragraph.

If, finally, the supplies of both factors increase, in the same proportion,

$$\frac{\partial X_1}{\partial K}\bigg|_{k \text{ constant}} = \frac{\partial X_1}{\partial K} + \frac{1}{k}\frac{\partial X_1}{\partial L} \qquad k = \frac{K}{L}$$

$$= \frac{(k_2 - k)f_1}{k(k_2 - k_1)} = \frac{L_1}{K} f_1$$

[18] Damnification would not be impossible if the increase in the labor supply were so large that the expanding country found it profitable to begin exporting the first commodity and importing the second. Throughout this section we confine our attention to very small changes in factor supplies and to very minor innovations. It cannot be assumed that all our results carry over to the case of large changes either in factor supplies or in costs.

[19] See Prob. 1.9.

$$= \frac{X_1}{K}$$

and

$$\left.\frac{\partial X_2}{\partial K}\right|_{k \text{ constant}} = \frac{\partial X_2}{\partial K} + \frac{1}{k}\frac{\partial X_2}{\partial L}$$

$$= \frac{(k - k_1)f_2}{k(k_2 - k_1)} = \frac{L_2}{K}f_2$$

$$= \frac{X_2}{K}$$

Hence

$$\left.\frac{\partial Q_1}{\partial K}\right|_{k \text{ constant}} = \frac{Lf_1}{K} + p\frac{L_2 f_2}{K} = \frac{Q_1}{K}$$

and

$$\beta = \frac{X_1}{Q_1} \qquad (4.21)$$

In the present case β must be a positive fraction: Damnification is possible, no matter which industry is labor-intensive, but it is not inevitable. Note that the general case, in which the supplies of both factors change, but not necessarily in the same proportion or direction, can be handled by replacing k in the above formulae by any constant, positive or negative.[20]

TABLE 4.1: Effect on Real Income of Increase in Factor Supply

Source of Expansion	$k_2 > k_1$	$k_1 > k_2$
Increase in Labor Supply	Damnification Impossible	Damnification Possible
Increase in Capital Supply	Damnification Possible	Damnification Impossible
Equiproportionate Increases in Both Factors	Damnification Possible	Damnification Possible

Technological Improvements

In assessing the implications of technological improvements we will find the results of Chap. 2 highly serviceable. In Tables 2.1 and 2.2, for example, are set out the directions in which each output changes in response to each type of improvement. From those tables, and assuming only that neither commodity is inferior in consumption and that markets are stable ($\Delta < 0$), we can rule out certain cases as incompatible with damnification of the expanding country. For, whenever at constant prices the output of the export commodity declines under the impact of an improvement, the terms of trade must move in favor of the growing country, whence damnification is impossible. In any case it is a very easy matter to deploy the methods of

[20] See Prob. 4.18.

Chap. 2 to derive the change in the terms of trade corresponding to each type of improvement. For these reasons we confine our attention here to a single type, factor-neutral improvements.

Suppose that a factor-neutral improvement occurs in the first or import-competing industry. Then, by straightforward calculations,

$$\frac{\partial Q_1}{\partial \lambda} = X_1$$

Moreover, since $d\lambda$ is the proportional reduction in the cost of producing the first commodity, we have

$$\frac{\partial X_1}{\partial \lambda} = \frac{1}{p} \cdot \frac{\partial X_1}{\partial \left(\frac{1}{p}\right)}$$

It follows that

$$\beta = \frac{\dfrac{\partial X_1}{\partial \lambda}}{\dfrac{\partial Q_1}{\partial \lambda}} = \frac{1}{pX_1} \cdot \frac{\partial X_1}{\partial (1/p)} \equiv e_1,$$

the "general equilibrium" or *mutatis mutandis* elasticity of supply of the first commodity along the curve of production possibilities. Since as a result of the improvement the first industry attracts resources initially employed in the second industry, β must be greater than one. Hence, if we rule out the possibility of inferior goods and unstable markets, the terms of trade must move in favor of the expanding country; damnification is impossible.

If, on the other hand, the incidence of the improvement is in the second or export industry it is easy to see that

$$\beta = 1 - e_2 < 0$$

where $e_2 \equiv (p/X_2)(\partial X_2/\partial p)$ is the "general equilibrium" elasticity of supply of the second commodity. The terms of trade move against the expanding country, and damnification is possible, regardless of factor intensities.

If, finally, the improvement is equally cost-saving in each industry

$$\beta = \frac{X_1}{Q_1}$$

Hence β is a positive fraction and the direction of change of the terms of trade depends on the relative magnitudes of m_1 and β; damnification is possible, no matter which industry is labor-intensive, but it is not inevitable.

In the special case in which the Engel curves are straight lines through the origin, so that the marginal propensity to consume the imported commodity, m_1, is equal to the average propensity, D_1/Q_1, it is evident that m_1 must exceed β, for

$$\frac{D_1}{Q_1} > \frac{X_1}{Q_1}$$

and the terms of trade must turn against the expanding country.[21]

The analysis of the preceding paragraph can be easily extended to cover the possibility of factor-neutral improvements which strike both industries but with unequal severity.[22]

Edgeworth, in his pioneering discussion of technological improvements,[23] had confined his attention to improvements with incidence in the export industries. We see now that damnification is possible even when the improvement plays no favorites. Note, however, that neutral improvements confined to the import industries cannot possibly result in loss to the expanding country. We can envisage factor-neutral improvements which, while not confined exclusively to the import-competing industry, are nevertheless biased towards it in varying degree. And presumably there is some critical degree of bias beyond which damnification may be ruled out as impossible.[24]

TABLE 4.2: Effect on Real Income of Neutral Improvements

Incidence of Improvements	$k_2 > k_1$	$k_1 > k_2$
Import-competing Industry	Damnification Impossible	Damnification Impossible
Export Industry	Damnification Possible	Damnification Possible
Both	Damnification Possible	Damnification Possible

PROBLEMS

On Tariffs

4.1 Introduce into the system composed of Eqs. (2.13) and (4.1) separate demand functions for laborers and landlords. Derive a generalization of condition (4.4).

[21] That we reached the same conclusion in the case of an equiproportionate increase in the supplies of both factors should occasion no surprise.
[22] See Prob. 4.19.
[23] Edgeworth [19] and [20]. Mill made the same assumption (Mill [23]).
[24] See Prob. 4.19.

4.2 Compare conditions (1.14) and (4.4). We have seen that, under our customary assumptions concerning demand, (1.14) can be ruled out. Can (4.4) be ruled out on the same or similar grounds? If not, why not?

4.3 Consider a three-commodities world—one export, one import, and one nontraded domestic good for each country. One country imposes an import duty and distributes the proceeds to the public. Is it inevitable that the terms of trade will move in its favor?

4.4 Derive a condition, analogous to Eq. (4.4) for $dp/d\tau = 0$, on the assumption that the government spends the tariff revenue instead of passing it on to the public. (Compare this problem with Prob. 1.5.)

4.5 Suppose, as in Prob. 4.4, that the government spends the tariff revenue instead of passing it on to the public. Under what conditions will the terms of trade move against the tariff-imposing country? (Compare this problem with Prob. 2.7.)

4.6 Show that to every duty on the imported commodity there corresponds a duty on the exported commodity which assigns the same values to all "real" variables. Show that if the import duty is applied to the foreign price and the export duty to the domestic price the corresponding rates of duty are equal. (See Marshall [3], pp. 180–81; Lerner [2].)

4.7 Suppose that the home country disturbs a free-trade equilibrium by imposing a small import duty, and that the foreign country retaliates. How large, in relation to the home duty, must be the foreign duty if the terms of trade are to return to their initial free-trade level?

On Demand Shifts

4.8 Provide an algebraic representation of the demand shifts discussed in this chapter in terms of the rest of the world's *supply* function, $-Z_1^*(1/p)$.

4.9 Rewrite Eqs. (4.6)–(4.14) in terms of the supply elasticities, ϵ and ϵ^*.

4.10 In discussing the effect of demand shifts on the volume and terms of trade, Marshall confined himself to stable situations with elastic demands and offer curves convex to the "export" axes: hence to situations in which $\Delta < 0$. He concluded that

> . . . in every possible combination of a large, medium or small elasticity on the part of [the demand by the rest of the world], with a large, medium, or small elasticity on the part of [the demand of the home country], one general rule holds. The more elastic the demand of either country, the elasticity of the other country being given, the larger will be the volumes both of [the rest of the world's] exports and of her imports; but the more also will her exports be enlarged relatively to her imports; or, in other words, the less favorable to her will be the terms of trade. Thus both sides of the trade will be very greatly enlarged, if both elasticities are great. But if both are small [the home country's] exports will be increased only a little; while [the rest of the world's] will be increased by the original [increase in demand] and a *very* little more in addition. (Marshall [8], p. 178.)

Is Marshall's solution correct?

Marshall also discusses ([8], pp. 180 ff., 344–46) the case of a horizontal shift to the *left* of the offer curve, a shift which he associates with the imposition by the rest of the world of a uniform and general import or export tax the proceeds of which are spent by the governments concerned on their export commodities. His solution ([8], p. 185) is consistent with that offered for the case of rightward shifts.

4.11 Graham contested Marshall's conclusions (see Problem 4.10):

> While valid for [the home country], they will certainly not hold for [the rest of the world]. The more elastic the demand of [the rest of the world], the demand of [the home country] being given, the *smaller* will be the volume of [the rest of the world's] imports and exports, and the *less* will her exports be enlarged relatively to her imports. [The rest of the world's] demand having increased (shift of the demand schedule to the right), and the terms of trade having consequently moved against [the rest of the world, the latter] will, on Marshall's very definition of elasticity take a quantity of imports which will vary in *inverse* relationship with the elasticity of her demand schedule. [The rest of the world's] exports, as well as her imports, will be smaller in volume when her demand schedule (for imports) shows an elastic trend than they would be if it were inelastic, both because, her imports being smaller in volume, few imports will, on this account, be required in payment, and also because the terms of trade will not be so adverse as they would be were her demand inelastic. The terms of trade will, of course, have moved against [the rest of the world], but they will certainly not carry as far in that direction if her demand for [the home country's] goods is elastic as they would were it inelastic. (Graham [6], pp. 601–2.)

Graham was not explicit about his assumptions. It appears reasonable to assume, however, that he had in mind the same conditions as those postulated by Marshall: Stability, elastic demands, and convex offer curves. On the basis of those assumptions, and using the implicit Grahamesque definition, are Graham's statements correct?

4.12 Imagine that there is an increase in the import demand of the home country. For each of the three types of increase, what is the effect on the terms of trade?

4.13 Suppose that the foreign demand function can be given the representation

$$\mu_4 Z_2^*(\mu_5 p) \qquad \mu_4, \mu_5 = 1$$

Obtain expressions for $dp/d\mu_4$, $dZ_1/d\mu_4$, and $dZ_2^*/d\mu_4$ on the assumption that $d\mu_5/d\mu_4 = \lambda$.

What values must λ assume to ensure that $dp/d\mu_4 = 0$? That $dZ_1/d\mu_4 = 0$? That $dZ_2^*/d\mu_4 = 0$?

On the Transfer Problem

4.14 Suppose that the home country has imposed an import duty at an *ad valorem* rate of 100τ per cent, and that the rest of the world has imposed a duty at a rate of $100\tau^*$ per cent. Under what conditions will a transfer payment to the home country have no effect on the terms of trade? (Assume that in each country the tariff receipts are handed over to the public and that the transfer is added to or subtracted from the tariff receipts.)

4.15 Derive a condition, analogous to Eq. (4.16), for the case in which all countries allow the rate of import duty, rather than the rate of personal income tax, to adjust to accommodate a transfer payment. *Hint:* Mathematically, the "setup" of the problem is very similar to that of Prob. 4.14. But the two tariff proceeds must now be treated as constants, τ and τ^* as variables.

4.16 Derive a condition, analogous to Eq. (4.16), for the case in which the accommodating fiscal device is (a) a general and uniform sales tax, (b) a general and uniform excise tax, (c) government expenditure on public works.

4.17 Is it possible for a unilateral transfer to turn the terms of trade so far in favor of the paying country that the latter is better off after the transfer than before and the receiving country worse off?

On Economic Expansion

4.18 Derive an expression for β, analogous to Eq. (4.21), for the case in which $dL/L = \rho(dK/K)$, where ρ is any constant, positive or negative. Is there some critical value of ρ beyond which damnification is impossible? If so, does the critical value depend on which industry is labor-intensive?

4.19 Derive an expression for β, analogous to Eq. (4.22), for the case in which, at constant factor prices, the proportionate reduction of costs in the import-competing industry is ρ times the proportionate reduction of costs in the export industry. Is there some critical value of ρ beyond which damnification is impossible? If so, does the critical value depend on which industry is labor-intensive?

REFERENCES

On Tariffs

[1] Kemp, Murray C., "Note on a Marshallian Conjecture," *Quarterly Journal of Economics*, LXXX, No. 320 (August 1966), 481–84.

†[2] Lerner, Abba P., "The Symmetry Between Import and Export Taxes," *Economica*, New Series, III, No. 3 (August 1936), 306–13. Reprinted in Abba P. Lerner, *Essays in Economic Analysis*, 123–33. London: Macmillan and Company Ltd., 1953. References are to the *Essays*.

†[3] Marshall, Alfred, *Money Credit and Commerce*, pp. 180, 346 ff. London: Macmillan and Company Ltd., 1923.

†[4] Metzler, Lloyd A., "Tariffs, the Terms of Trade, and the Distribution of National Income," *Journal of Political Economy*, LVII, No. 1 (February 1949), 1–29.

[5] Metzler, Lloyd A., "Tariffs, International Demand, and Domestic Prices," *Journal of Political Economy*, LVII, No. 4 (August 1949), 345–51.

On Demand Shifts

†[6] Graham, Frank D., "The Theory of International Values," *Quarterly Journal of Economics*, XLVI, No. 3 (August 1932), 581–616.

[7] Kemp, Murray C., "The Relation Between Changes in International Demand and the Terms of Trade," *Econometrica*, XXIV, No. 1 (January 1956), 41–46.

†[8] Marshall, Alfred, *Money Credit and Commerce*, pp. 177 ff., 342 ff. London: Macmillan and Company Ltd., 1923.

[9] Marshall, Alfred, *Principles of Economics*, 8th ed. London: Macmillan and Company Ltd., 1920.

On the Transfer Problem

[10] Bastable, C. F., "On Some Applications of the Theory of International Trade," *Quarterly Journal of Economics*, IV, No. 1 (October 1889), 1–17.

[11] Johnson, Harry G., *International Trade and Economic Growth*, Chap. VII. London: George Allen & Unwin, 1958.

†[12] Mill, J. S., *Essays on Some Unsettled Questions of Political Economy*. London: The London School of Economics and Political Science, 1948.

[13] Mill, J. S., *Principles of Political Economy*, ed. Sir W. J. Ashley, Part III, Chap. XXI, Sec. 4. London: Longmans, Green and Company, 1909.

†[14] Samuelson, Paul A., "The Transfer Problem and Transfer Costs," *Economic Journal*, LXII, No. 2 (June 1952), 278–304, and LXIV, No. 2 (June 1954), 264–89.

[15] Wicksell, Knut, "International Freights and Prices," *Quarterly Journal of Economics*, XXXII, No. 3 (February 1918), 404–10.

On Economic Expansion

[16] Amano, Akihiro, "International Factor Movements and the Terms of Trade," *Canadian Journal of Economics and Political Science*, XXXII, No. 4, (November 1966), 511–19.

[17] Bastable, C. F., *The Theory of International Trade*, 4th ed., App. C, Sec. 2. London: Macmillan & Company Ltd., 1903.

[18] Bhagwati, Jagdish, "International Trade and Economic Expansion," *American Economic Review*, XLVIII, No. 5 (December 1958), 941–53.

†[19] Edgeworth, F. Y., "The Theory of International Values. I," *Economic Journal*, IV, No. 1 (March 1894), 35–50.

†[20] Edgeworth, F. Y., "On a Point in the Pure Theory of International Trade," *Economic Journal*, IX, No. 1 (March 1899), 125–28.

[21] Johnson, Harry G., *International Trade and Economic Growth*, Chap. III. London: George Allen and Unwin Ltd., 1958.

[22] Kemp, Murray C., "Technological Change, the Terms of Trade and Welfare," *Economic Journal*, LXV, No. 3 (September 1955), 457–74.

†[23] Mill, J. S., *Principles of Political Economy*, ed. Sir W. J. Ashley, Book III, Chap. XVIII, Sec. 5. London: Longmans, Green & Company, 1909.

General Reference

[24] Mundell, R. A., "The Pure Theory of International Trade," *American Economic Review*, L, No. 1 (March 1960), 67–110.

chapter 5

Variable Factor Supply
and the Theory of International Trade*

To this point factor supplies have been assumed to be completely inelastic with respect to variations in real factor rewards. The assumption is an obviously convenient one. But evidently it cannot be justified by analytical convenience alone. Its defense must rest either on (a) a plea of "sufficient" realism or on (b) a demonstration that the answers to the usual comparative statical questions are insensitive, at least regarding sign, to modifications of the assumption. But any demarcation of "sufficient" realism presupposes information concerning sensitivity. In the final analysis, therefore, the defense must rest on (b).

The present chapter contains an analysis of several familiar problems under the assumption of variable factor supplies. Particular attention is paid to the effects on factor rewards and outputs of an import duty; but it is shown that the method of analysis may be adapted to other problems, notably the problem of determining the shape of a country's offer curve. The reader must brace himself for a veritable Wonderland of possibilities. It will emerge, for example, that with variable factor supplies an increase in the price of a commodity (the upshot, let us say, of an import duty) may give rise to a *reduction* in its output; that this curious possibility is not inconsistent with the usual static assumptions concerning household

119

behavior or with the postulate of market stability; and that, with variable factor supplies, a country's offer curve may bend back on itself, a deterioration of the terms of foreign trade giving rise to an increased demand for imports.

1. THE FORMAL MODEL—REVISED VERSION

Let us begin by formally revising the fundamental model of Chap. 1, Sec. 1. The model consists of Eqs. (1.1), (1.2), and (1.7), and has been given a geometrical interpretation in Fig 1.2. It has been the starting point of all our intervening expeditions. But it is based on the assumption of completely inelastic factor supplies, an assumption which we now wish to abandon.

In view of the homogeneity properties of our model, it suffices to consider the possibility that the supply of *one* of the two factors responds to price and income changes. Throughout the present chapter, therefore, it will be assumed that capital remains in absolutely fixed supply but that the supply of labor, or, more conveniently, the demand for leisure, depends on the price of leisure (the money wage rate), on the money prices of the two commodities, and on the imputed money value of the total stock of leisure, $\bar{H}$. In the absence of money illusion, the demand for leisure is a homogeneous function and any price can be chosen as deflator. Let us choose the price of the first commodity for this task. This allows us to write the supply of labor as

$$L = \bar{H} - H(p, w_1; w_1\bar{H})$$

where

$$w_1 \equiv \frac{w}{p_1} = f_1 - k_1 f_1'$$

is the real wage in terms of the first commodity. The system can now be rounded out by adding the production equations

$$X_i = L_i f_i(k_i) \qquad i = 1, 2 \tag{1.1}$$

the marginal conditions

$$r_1 = f_1' = p f_2'$$
$$w_1 = f_1 - k_1 f_1' = p(f_2 - k_2 f_2') \tag{1.2}$$

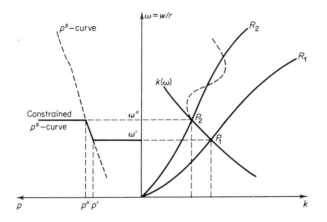

FIGURE 5.1

and the requirement that each factor be fully employed,

$$L_1 + L_2 = \bar{H} - H(p, w_1; w_1\bar{H})$$

$$k_1L_1 + k_2L_2 = K$$

$$(5.1)$$

If we treat p as a parameter, Eqs. (5.1), (1.1), and (1.2) form a system of eight equations in X_i, k_i, L_i, w_1, and r_1 ($i = 1, 2$). For convenience it is assumed that the first commodity is relatively capital-intensive; but none of our conclusions depends on that assumption.

Figure 1.2(a) is easily revised to accommodate our new assumptions. The supply of labor (and, since the supply of capital is fixed, the overall capital: labor ratio) depends on the real wage, w_1, and on the commodity price ratio, p. But p and (in view of the homogeneity properties of our system) w_1 are related uniquely to the ratio of factor rewards, $\omega = w/r$. We therefore may inscribe in the right-hand half of Fig. 1.2 a curve $k(w/r)$ which relates the overall endowment ratio to the ratio of factor rewards. The intersections of this curve with the two R_i-curves determine the limits within which the ratio of factor rewards may lie. In Fig 5.1, for example, the k-curve intersects the R_1- and R_2-curves at P_1 and P_2, respectively, the intersections marking off a range of feasible factor reward ratios, ω' to ω'', and a corresponding range of commodity price ratios, p' to p'', which are consistent with incomplete specialization. Note however that nothing in our assumptions prevents the *k*-curve from bending back (as does the dotted curve of Fig 5.1) and marking off a *second* range of feasible factor reward ratios, and a second range of commodity price ratios, consistent with incomplete specialization.

2. THE RELATIONSHIP BETWEEN COMMODITY PRICES, FACTOR PRICES, AND OUTPUTS

We turn now to the central issues to be treated in this chapter. As a first step, we seek expressions for dX_1/dp and dX_2/dp. That poses a purely technical problem, and not a particularly difficult one. Of greater difficulty is the problem of casting the two expressions in forms which lend themselves to further analysis. In particular, we shall want to enquire whether perverse signs $[(dX_1/dp) > 0, (dX_2/dp) < 0]$ are consistent with the assumptions of the traditional analysis of consumer behavior and with the assumption of market stability. With this ultimate objective in mind, three definitions are introduced at the outset. First, the partial elasticity of demand for labor by the *i*th industry is defined as

$$\eta_{L_i} = \frac{w_1}{L_i} \cdot \frac{\partial L_i}{\partial w_1} \qquad i = 1, 2$$

$$= w_1/k_1^2 f_1'' \qquad \text{[from Eqs. (1.2)]} \qquad (5.2)$$

The second definition also has an air of familiarity. It is, indeed, closely related to the elasticity of the price locus, discussed at length in Chap. 1, Sec. 2. Suppose w_1 is treated as a parameter of our new system, Eqs. (5.1), (1.1), and (1.2). Then the elasticity of price with respect to wages, E_{pw_1}, is defined as the percentage change in the price of the second or labor-intensive good that must accompany a one per cent change in the wage rate. It is obtained by differentiating the system totally with respect to w_1 and solving for dp/dw_1:

$$E_{pw_1} = \frac{w_1}{p} \cdot \frac{dp}{dw_1}$$

$$= \frac{k_1 - k_2}{k_1} \cdot \frac{f_2 - k_2 f_2'}{f_2} \qquad (5.3)$$

Both terms are positive fractions, hence[1]

$$0 < E_{pw_1} < 1$$

[1] The reader may compare this inequality with inequality (1.23).

Finally, let us define the partial elasticities of labor supply with respect to the commodity price ratio,

$$e_{Lp} = \frac{p}{L} \cdot \frac{\partial L}{\partial p} = -\frac{p}{L} \cdot \frac{\partial H}{\partial p} \tag{5.4}$$

and with respect to the real wage rate,

$$e_{Lw_1} = \frac{w_1}{L} \cdot \frac{\partial L}{\partial w_1} = -\frac{w_1}{L} \cdot \frac{\partial H}{\partial w_1} - \frac{\bar{H}}{L} m_H, \tag{5.5}$$

where $m_H = w_1(\partial H/\partial w_1 H)$ is the marginal propensity to consume leisure.

Pushing on now to the derivation of dX_1/dp and dX_2/dp, we have, from Eqs. (1.1),

$$\frac{dX_1}{dp} = f_1 \frac{dL_1}{dp} + L_1 f_1' \frac{dk_1}{dp} \tag{5.6}$$

From the full employment relations (5.1),

$$L_1 = \frac{k_2(\bar{H} - H) - K}{k_2 - k_1}$$

Hence

$$\frac{dL_1}{dp} = \left\{ \left[L\frac{dk_2}{dp} - k_2\left(\frac{\partial H}{\partial p} + \frac{\partial H}{\partial w_1}\frac{dw_1}{dp}\right) \right][k_2 - k_1] \right.$$
$$\left. - L(k_2 - k_1)\left(\frac{dk_2}{dp} - \frac{dk_1}{dp}\right) \right\} \div (k_2 - k_1)^2 \tag{5.7}$$

Now

$$\frac{dk_1}{dp} = \frac{dk_1}{dw_1}\frac{dw_1}{dp}$$

$$= -\frac{1}{k_1 f_1''}\frac{dw_1}{dp} \qquad \text{[from Eqs. (1.2)]}$$

$$= -\frac{k_1}{w_1}\eta_{L_1}\frac{dw_1}{dp} \qquad \text{[from Eqs. (5.2)]}$$

$$= -\frac{k_1}{pE_{pw_1}}\eta_{L_1} \qquad \text{[from Eq. (5.3)]} \tag{5.8a}$$

Similarly,

$$\frac{dk_2}{dp} = -\frac{k_2}{pE_{pw_1}}\eta_{L_2} \tag{5.8b}$$

Substituting from Eqs. (5.8) into Eq. (5.7), and noting that $k \equiv k_1(L_1/L) + k_2(L_2/L)$,

$$\frac{dL_1}{dp} = - \frac{L}{pE_{pw_1}} \cdot \frac{k_2}{k_2 - k_1} \left\{ \frac{L_1}{L} \frac{k_1}{k_2} \eta_{L_1} + \frac{L_2}{L} \eta_{L_2} - (E_{pw_1} e_{Lp} + e_{Lw_1}) \right\}$$

Hence, substituting in Eq. (5.6),

$$\frac{dX_1}{dp} = - \frac{Lf_1}{pE_{pw_1}} \frac{k_2}{k_2 - k_1} \left\{ \frac{L_1}{L} \frac{k_1}{k_2} \left[\frac{f_1 + (k_2 - k_1)f_1'}{f_1} \right] \eta_{L_1} \right.$$

$$\left. + \frac{L_2}{L} \eta_{L_2} - (E_{pw_1} e_{Lp} + e_{Lw_1}) \right\} \tag{5.9}$$

From Eqs. (1.2), however,

$$\frac{f_1 + (k_2 - k_1)f_1'}{f_1} = \frac{f_2}{f_2 + (k_1 - k_2)f_2'}$$

and, from Eq. (5.3),

$$1 - E_{pw_1} = \frac{k_2}{k_1} \cdot \frac{f_2 + (k_1 - k_2)f_2'}{f_2}$$

Hence Eq. (5.9) reduces to

$$\frac{dX_1}{dp} = - \frac{Lf_1}{pE_{pw_1}} \cdot \frac{k_2}{k_2 - k_1} \left\{ \frac{L_1}{L} (1 - E_{pw_1})^{-1} \eta_{L_1} + \frac{L_2}{L} \eta_{L_2} \right.$$

$$\left. - (E_{pw_1} e_{Lp} + e_{Lw_1}) \right\} \tag{5.10a}$$

and we may conclude that

$$\frac{dX_1}{dp} > 0 \quad \textit{if and only if}$$

$$E_{pw_1} e_{Lp} + e_{Lw_1} < \frac{L_1}{L} (1 - E_{pw_1})^{-1} \eta_{L_1} + \frac{L_2}{L} \eta_{L_2} \tag{5.11a}$$

Following a line of reasoning similar to that of the preceding paragraph, we find that

$$\frac{dX_2}{dp} = \frac{Lf_2}{pE_{pw_1}} \cdot \frac{k_1}{k_2 - k_1} \left\{ \frac{L_1}{L} \eta_{L_1} + (1 - E_{pw_1}) \frac{L_2}{L} \eta_{L_2} - (E_{pw_1} e_{Lp} + e_{Lw_1}) \right\}$$

$$\tag{5.10b}$$

and that therefore

$$\frac{dX_2}{dp} < 0 \quad \text{if and only if}$$

$$E_{pw_1}e_{Lp} + e_{Lw_1} < \frac{L_1}{L}\eta_{L_1} + (1 - E_{pw_1})\frac{L_2}{L}\eta_{L_2} \qquad (5.11b)$$

The left-hand side of the inequalities (5.11) happens to be equal to the percentage change in the quantity of labor employed in response to a one per cent change in the real wage rate, assuming that prices adjust to the new wage rate. It will be referred to as the "elasticity of employment."

The right-hand sides of the inequalities (5.11) are negative and, since E_{pw_1} is a positive fraction, stand in the relationship

$$\frac{L_1}{L}\eta_{L_1} + (1 - E_{pw_1})\frac{L_2}{L}\eta_{L_2} > \frac{L_1}{L}(1 - E_{pw_1})^{-1}\eta_{L_1} + \frac{L_2}{L}\eta_{L_2}$$

Suppose that both inequalities (5.11) are satisfied. Now let the left-hand term $(E_{pw_1}e_{Lp} + e_{Lw_1})$ increase. In this way we pass through successive phases which, reading down, correspond to the rows of Table 5.1. Note that the combination $(+, +)$ is impossible.[2]

TABLE 5.1

dX_1/dp	dX_2/dp
+	−
−	−
−	+

Are the perverse outcomes at all likely? In particular, are they consistent with conventional utility theory and with the postulate of stability in the labor market? These questions must now be explored.

The static theory of the household does contain some restrictions on the left-hand side of the inequalities (5.11), but the restrictions are not sufficiently severe to rule out the possibility of perversity. Thus if e_{Lp} and e_{Lw_1} are split into pure substitution elasticities (indicated by a bar) and income terms, the left-hand side of (5.11) becomes

$$(\bar{e}_{Lw_1} + E_{pw_1}\bar{e}_{Lp}) - (1 - \alpha_2 E_{pw_1})m_H \qquad (5.12)$$

where α_2 is the fraction of earned income $(w_1 L)$ that is spent by laborers on

---

[2] This would not be so if the first commodity were labor-intensive. In that case the combination $(-, -)$ would be ruled out.

the consumption of the second commodity. Now if neither commodity is inferior, the income term is necessarily greater than minus one. And the substitution terms, $(\bar{e}_{Lw_1} + E_{pw_1}\bar{e}_{Lp})$, can be negative only if the first commodity and leisure are complementary in consumption (implying $\bar{e}_{Lp} < 0$). It follows that the left-hand side of (5.11) can be less than minus one only if the first (or capital-intensive) commodity and leisure are complementary goods. One obvious corollary of this is that labor's total share (w_1L, expressed in units of the first commodity) must increase as p rises, as long as the first commodity and leisure are substitutes.[3, 4] It is clear, however, that even the ruling out of complementarity does not suffice to rule out the inequalities (5.11).

Further bounds on the response of the labor supply to a wage change can be derived by requiring stability of the labor market. Since p, the domestic commodity-price ratio, is treated as a parameter, given by the terms of trade and the rate of import duty, we enquire into the stability of the labor market when commodity prices are constant but the wage rate is disturbed from its equilibrium position. Furthermore we may assume that, in this short-run disequilibrium state, capital is occupationally immobile: K_1 and K_2 may be considered constant. The condition for (Hicksian) stability is that at a wage rate higher than equilibrium (but in the neighborhood of equilibrium) the quantity of labor supplied should exceed the quantity of labor demanded. Alternatively stated, the labor market is stable if and only if the elasticity of the labor supply curve exceeds the elasticity of the demand curve for labor.

With the wage rate changing and commodity prices constant, the elasticity of labor supply is merely the term e_{Lw_1} examined earlier. In computing the elasticity of demand for labor, it is necessary to realize that, with capital immobile between occupations, one of Eqs. (1.2), equating the rent of capital in the two occupations, is no longer binding.[5] It is easy to show that the elasticity of the demand for labor is the weighted sum of each industry's η_{L_i}, the weights being the fractions of the total labor supply employed in each industry. That is, stability in the labor market requires

$$e_{Lw_1} > \frac{L_1}{L}\eta_{L_1} + \frac{L_2}{L}\eta_{L_2} \qquad (5.13)$$

[3] The same statement holds true if labor's share is measured in units of the second commodity, for it can be easily shown that $(1 - E_{pw_1})^{-1}$ times expression (5.12) must be less than minus one if labor's total share is to fall. If leisure and the first commodity are substitutes, this possibility is ruled out because $(1 - E_{pw_1})^{-1}(1 - \alpha_2 E_{pw_1})$ is a positive fraction.

[4] It is an easy matter to show that not only the real wage bill but also labor's relative share of real national income (however measured) may fall. Thus when labor supply is variable a tariff may turn the distribution of income against the factor used intensively in the import-competing industry *even when the effect of the tariff is to raise the domestic price of the import-competing good.* (Cf. Chap. 4, Sec. 1.)

[5] It follows that in the disequilibrium state the solution does not lie along the production-efficiency locus.

A comparison of this stability condition[6] with inequalities (5.11) reveals that it is not strong enough to rule out the perverse outcomes: $dX_1/dp > 0$ and $dX_2/dp < 0$. Again, much depends upon the "cross" term, e_{Lp}.

Thus the bounds imposed upon our various elasticities by the theory of household behavior and by the postulate of stability in the labor market have failed to rule out the possibility of perverse responses of output to price changes. Even if it is assumed that the elasticity of labor supply with respect to the wage rate (e_{Lw_1}) is zero, the "cross" effect of commodity price increases on labor supply, represented by the term e_{Lp}, conceivably may permit such a reduction in employment that outputs respond inversely to price movements. This case is most likely to occur if leisure and the capital-intensive commodity are complementary.

3. THE OFFER CURVE

It is clear, then, that the response of outputs to price changes may be perverse if labor supply is variable. This perhaps suggests that the country's offer curve might also exhibit some peculiar features in this case. Harry Johnson[7] has recently suggested that if the demand behavior of wage-earners differs from that of capitalists, the offer curve can bend back on itself: A higher price for imports might increase, rather than reduce, the quantity of imports demanded. In large part this possibility rests upon the underlying redistribution of income accompanying the change in the relative price of imports and the assumption that marginal propensities to import differ among income groups.

In this section the previous analysis is extended to demonstrate two propositions concerning the effect of variable labor supply on the offer curve. But, to isolate the effect of variable labor supply, we reject the assumption that a pure transfer of income between capitalists and wage-earners affects the composition of aggregate demand.

The two propositions can be stated at the outset. First, it is possible for the offer curve to bend back on itself, so that a greater quantity of imports is demanded at a higher price. For this to happen it is necessary that a reduced quantity of labor be forthcoming at a higher wage, and that the reduction be even greater than that required to reduce the production of importables at the higher price. Second, the absolute value of the elasticity of the offer curve is reduced as a consequence of labor being in variable supply if and only if the elasticity of employment is negative. Neither of these propositions is obvious. For an increase in the labor supply increases the quantity of

---

[6] It is worth mentioning, perhaps, that condition (5.13) is also necessary for Samuelsonian dynamic stability. If in a state of disequilibrium dw/dt is proportional to the excess demand for labor, $w(t)$ fails to converge if condition (5.13) is not satisfied.

[7] See Johnson [6] and [7].

importables demanded through an income effect, but since importables are assumed to be labor-intensive, it also increases the quantity of importables produced. It is necessary to determine which effect is dominant.

Suppose that the *second* commodity is imported. The demand for imports, Z_2, is the demand for the imported commodity, D_2, less the domestic production of the second commodity. Since we are ignoring distributional considerations, we may write the total demand for the imported commodity as a function of the price ratio, p, and of aggregate real income in terms of the exported commodity, $X_1 + pX_2$. Noting further that the quantities produced depend on the domestic price ratio and on factor supplies, we may write

$$Z_2 = D_2[p, X_1(p, L) + pX_2(p, L)] - X_2(p, L)$$

Differentiating totally with respect to p, defining the marginal propensity to consume X_2 as $m_2 \equiv p \dfrac{\partial D_2}{\partial(X_1 + pX_2)}$, and noting that[8]

$$\frac{\partial X_1}{\partial p} + p \frac{\partial X_2}{\partial p} = 0$$

and that[9]

$$\frac{\partial X_1}{\partial L} + p \frac{\partial X_2}{\partial L} = f_1 - k_1 f_1' = p(f_2 - k_2 f_2')$$

we obtain

$$\frac{dZ_2}{dp} = \frac{\partial D_2}{\partial p} + \frac{m_2}{p}\left[X_2 + (f_1 - k_1 f_1')\frac{dL}{dp}\right] - \left(\frac{\partial X_2}{\partial p} + \frac{\partial X_2}{\partial L}\cdot\frac{dL}{dp}\right) \qquad (5.14)$$

Noting further that, from Eqs. (1.20b) and (5.3),

$$\frac{\partial X_2}{\partial L} = \frac{(f_2 - k_2 f_2')}{E_{pw_1}}$$

Eq. (5.14) reduces to

$$\frac{dZ_2}{dp} = \left(\frac{\partial D_2}{\partial p} + \frac{m_2}{p}\cdot X_2 - \frac{\partial X_2}{\partial p}\right) - (f_2 - k_2 f_2')\left(\frac{1}{E_{pw_1}} - m_2\right)\frac{dL}{dp} \qquad (5.15)$$

---

[8] That is, the slope of the production possibility curve, $(\partial X_1/\partial p)/(\partial X_2/\partial p)$, is, under perfect competition, equal to minus the price ratio. (Cf. Prob. 1.2.)

[9] The first of the two equalities states that the addition to total output (valued in terms of the first commodity) that results from the efficient employment of an increment of labor is equal to the marginal product of labor in the first industry. This is perhaps sufficiently obvious without elaborate proof. The second of the two equalities simply reproduces part of Eq. (1.2).

The two propositions we wish to establish follow readily from Eqs. (5.14) and (5.15). If employment is constant: $dL/dp = 0$ and the elasticity of the offer curve is simply p/Z_2 times the first bracketed expression in Eq. (5.15); the latter is assumed to be negative. Since both E_{pw_1} and m_2 are positive fractions, the second bracketed expression is positive. It follows that for perverse results we need $dL/dp < 0$. It follows also that the absolute value of the elasticity varies directly with dL/dp. Finally, for the production of X_2 to decrease as its price rises it is necessary that

$$\frac{\partial X_2}{\partial p} + \frac{\partial X_2}{\partial L} \cdot \frac{dL}{dp}$$

be negative. But, from Eq. (5.14), this does not ensure $(dZ_2/dp) > 0$.[10]

4. GEOMETRIC ILLUSTRATIONS

The argument of Sec. 2 and 3 has been concise and, at some points, difficult. Fortunately, much of it can be clothed in simple geometry.

Figure 5.2 depicts a three-dimensional production surface.[11] Suppose point Q is the initial point of equilibrium, OX_1^0 of the first commodity and OX_2^0 of the second commodity being produced by the fixed capital resource in conjunction with $(\bar{H} - H^0)$ units of labor. OH^0 represents the consumption of leisure. In the commodity space, resources K and L $(= \bar{H} - H^0)$ support the transformation schedule AA, the slope of which at Q is (minus) p^0, the initial relative price of the second commodity. The intersection of the surface and a plane through Q perpendicular to the X_2-axis is the $\bar{X}_2\bar{X}_2$-locus showing the relationship between leisure (and therefore labor inputs) and the production of the first commodity. The curvature of $\bar{X}_2\bar{X}_2$ reflects the diminishing marginal product of labor in producing the first commodity. Similarly, the locus $\bar{X}_1\bar{X}_1$, along which the production of the first commodity is constant, reflects the relationship between leisure (and labor) and the output of the second commodity.

[10] These conclusions do not depend on our selection of the second or imported commodity as relatively labor-intensive. Differentiating Eqs. (1.1), (1.2), and (5.1) with respect to p, solving for dL/dp, and substituting in Eq. (5.15), we obtain

$$\frac{dZ_2}{dp} = \left(\frac{\partial D_2}{\partial p} + \frac{m_2}{p} X_2 - \frac{\partial X_2}{\partial p}\right) + \frac{L}{p^2} \cdot \frac{1}{E_{pw_1}} \cdot \left(\frac{1}{E_{pw_1}} - m_2\right)(e_{Lw_1} + E_{pw_1}e_{Lp})$$

If X_2 were relatively capital-intensive, E_{pw_1} would be negative; but $\dfrac{1}{E_{pw_1}}\left(\dfrac{1}{E_{pw_1}} - m_2\right)$ would be positive as before.

[11] Cf. Walsh [13].

One other locus is sketched: The dashed curve p^0p^0. This traces out on the surface the collection of points for which the slope of curves such as AA have the same value, p^0, as at the initial point Q. As the locus is traversed from M in the X_1X_2-plane to N in the X_1Z-plane it cuts both higher and higher $\bar{X}_1\bar{X}_1$-curves and lower and lower $\bar{X}_2\bar{X}_2$-curves. This is the graphical counterpart of the familiar theorem of Samuelson and Rybczynski, according to which a reduction in the labor endowment (from M to N) with constant p must result in a decrease in the production of the second or labor-intensive commodity and an increase in the first or capital-intensive commodity. (Cf. Chap. 1, Sec. 2.)

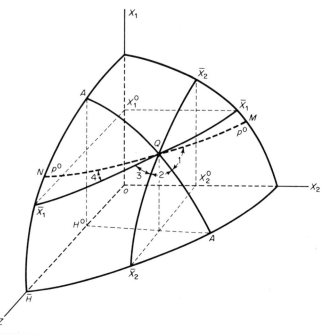

FIGURE 5.2

Suppose p increases from the initial value p^0 at Q. The economy responds by moving from Q to some point south of line MN. The increase in the relative price of the labor-intensive good will, of course, drive up the wage rate. If the quantity of employment is unchanged, production of the second commodity will increase, and that of the first decrease, along the transformation curve AA. If the increase in p (and in the wage rate) should call forth an increased quantity of labor, the movement from Q will be towards Region 1; in this case the "normal" production changes will be accentuated. If, on the other hand, a higher p and wage rate should elicit a smaller supply of labor, three possibilities are suggested. For a small decline in employment (Region 2), the production of the second commodity will increase, and that of the first decrease, as before. If employment falls far enough, however, production of both commodities will be *reduced* (Region 3). But most paradoxical of all is the possibility that employment may fall so sharply that not only is production of the second or labor-intensive commodity reduced, but output of the first or capital-intensive commodity is *increased*.

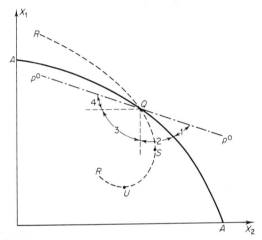

FIGURE 5.3

A locus of possible equilibrium positions, each consistent with the supply function of labor, could be drawn on the production surface. Since our interest lies in the changes in output, however, we concentrate on the "shadow" thrown by such a locus on the $X_1 X_2$-commodity space. In Fig 5.3, the projection of the AA-transformation schedule through the initial point Q is shown by the solid curve.

The dashed $p^0 p^0$-line through Q is the projection of the $p^0 p^0$-line of Fig. 5.2 onto the $X_1 X_2$-plane. As can easily be checked by referring to Eq. (1.20b), the slope of the projection is $-k_2 f_1 / k_1 f_2$. Since p^0 is held constant, k_1 and k_2, are constant and this curve is, indeed, a straight line. Now $-k_2 f_1 / k_1 f_2$ equals $(1 - E_{p w_1})$ times $(f_1 - k_1 f_1')/(f_2 - k_2 f_2')$,[12] or a positive fraction times the price ratio, p. Thus the $p^0 p^0$-line must be flatter than the transformation schedule at Q.[13]

The locus $RQSUR$ represents a "production-possibilities" curve when labor supply is variable. Its shape throughout reflects a negative elasticity of employment. From the initial point at Q the curve must pass south of line

[12] This may be checked by substituting for $E_{p w_1}$ from Eq. (5.3).
[13] Note that $p^0 p^0$ itself becomes the locus of possible outputs if the elasticity of labor supply is infinite.

p^0p^0 with a higher relative price, $p > p_0$ (and, therefore, a higher wage). The four regions marked in Fig. 5.3 correspond to those in Fig. 5.2. As drawn, higher relative prices for the second commodity lead initially to greater production of that commodity and cutbacks in the production of the first commodity until point S is reached. From S to U, the production of the second commodity falls as the elasticity of employment falls below the critical mark of Eq. (5.6b). Finally, from U to R the production of the first commodity actually rises as its relative price falls.[14]

Two points should be made in comparing the locus RR with the AA-transformation schedule. First, in our model the slope of RR at Q *cannot* be equal to the price ratio (or AA-slope) there unless the elasticity of employment is zero. What this reflects is the asymmetrical effect of price changes on the various factors of production, a point already well established by the Samuelson–Stolper tariff discussion. (Cf. Chap. 1, Sec. 2).

Secondly, the section SUR does not reflect inferior production possibilities, for leisure is a good, as well as X_1 and X_2. More leisure is consumed at U than at S.

PROBLEMS

5.1 In what respects, if any, does our earlier analysis of the transfer problem and of economic expansion (Chap. 4, Secs. 3 and 4) require modification in the light of variable labor supply?

5.2 Would you expect the opening up of trade to make the overall factor endowment ratios more unequal? Cf. Heckscher [5], p. 293, and Ohlin [9], pp. 118–19.

5.3 Suppose that for each of two trading countries the k-curve is positively sloped. Is the range of possible variation in the ratio of factor rewards greater than in the case of fixed factor supplies, or is it less? Is the international equalization of factor rentals more likely, or less likely? Would your answers be different if the k-curves had been assumed to be negatively sloped?

5.4 Given relative commodity prices and a possibly backward sloping supply curve of labor, what is the effect of a small increase in the capital endowment on the value of output?

5.5 "For any given production function, with stability conditions met, the larger the absolute value of [the elasticity of labor supply], the smaller will be the change in output as the ... [capital endowment] ... changes." (Krueger [9], 328. Bracketed expressions added.) Is this true for a two-commodity world?

5.6 It was assumed in Sec. 1, "for convenience," that the first commodity is relatively capital-intensive. Show that "none of our conclusions depends on that assumption."

[14] However, UR cannot rise more steeply than the p-line passing through U (not shown), the slope of which is $-k_2f_1/k_1f_2$.

REFERENCES

[1] Caves, Richard E., *Trade and Economic Structure, Models and Methods*. Chap. IV. Cambridge, Mass.: Harvard University Press, 1960.

[2] Haberler, Gottfried, *The Theory of International Trade with its Applications to Commercial Policy*, trans. Alfred Stonier and Frederic Benham. Chap. XII. London: William Hodge and Company, Limited, 1936.

[3] Haberler, Gottfried, "Some Problems in the Pure Theory of International Trade," *Economic Journal*, LX, No. 2 (June 1950), 223–40.

[4] Haberler, Gottfried, "Real Cost, Money Cost and Comparative Advantage," *International Social Science Bulletin*, III (Spring 1950), 48–52.

[5] Heckscher, Eli, "The Effect of Foreign Trade on the Distribution of Income," *Economisk Tidskrift*, XXI (1919), 479–512 (in Swedish). Reprinted, in translation by Svend and Nita Laursen, in *Readings in the Theory of International Trade*, eds. Howard S. Ellis and Lloyd A. Metzler, 272–300. Philadelphia: The Blakiston Company, 1949.

[6] Johnson, Harry G., "International Trade, Income Distribution, and the Offer Curve," *Manchester School*, XXVII, No. 2 (September 1959), 241–60.

[7] Johnson, Harry G., "Income Distribution, the Offer Curve, and the Effects of Tariffs," *Manchester School*, XXVIII, No. 2 (September 1960), 215–42.

[8] Kemp, Murray C. and Ronald W. Jones, "Variable Labour Supply and the Theory of International Trade," *Journal of Political Economy*, LXX, No. 1 (February 1962), 30–36.

[9] Krueger, Anne O., "The Implications of a Backward Bending Labor Supply Curve," *Review of Economic Studies*, XXIV(4), No. 81 (October 1962), 327–28.

[10] Ohlin, Bertil, *Interregional and International Trade*. Cambridge, Mass.: Harvard University Press, 1933.

[11] Vanek, Jaroslav, "An Afterthought on the "Real Cost–Opportunity Cost" Dispute and Some Aspects of General Equilibrium Under Conditions of Variable Factor Supplies," *Review of Economic Studies*, XXVI, No. 3 (June 1959), 198–208.

[12] Viner, Jacob, *Studies in the Theory of International Trade*, pp. 516–26. London: George Allen & Unwin Ltd., n.d.

[13] Walsh, V. C., "Leisure and International Trade," *Economica*, New Series, XXIII, No. 3 (August 1956), 253–60.

chapter 6

Nontraded Commodities*

Every country, even Kuwait, produces commodities which are neither imported nor exported. High costs of transport, prohibitive tariffs, export or import embargoes based on considerations of defense, international disparities in preferences or in levels of income per capita—all and any of these can account for the existence of commodities which, at least within a wide range of factor rewards and costs of production, have no export market. In most moderately to heavily industrialized countries the production of domestic or nontraded goods represents more than one-half of total output. It is desirable therefore that we work some of the exercises of Chap. 4 on the revised assumption that at least one commodity is not traded. That is the purpose of the present chapter.

The existence of purely domestic industries, it will be seen, again presents many of the possibilities first encountered in Chap. 5, where factor supplies were allowed to respond to price changes. These similarities are not surprising, perhaps, when it is observed that purely domestic industries serve as a kind of reservoir which may release factors to the international sector, or absorb factors from that sector, in response to variations in prices.

It is now necessary to distinguish at least three commodities. In what follows, commodity 0 is assumed to be purely domestic, commodity 1 is assumed to be imported, and commodity 2 is assumed to be exported. We continue to assume that there are just two factors of production, capital and labor. Retaining the first commodity as *numéraire*, we must cope with two price ratios, denoted by π_0 and π_2. The first of these is the relative price of the domestic good, the second is the relative home price of the exported commodity. As usual, asterisks relate variables to the foreign country. The home country's terms of trade, for example, are denoted by π_2^*.

1. BASIC RELATIONSHIPS

On the production side, our new model has several special features. It bears emphasizing, however, that the novelties flow from the fact that there are now three products and only two factors, *not* from the fact that one of the commodities is purely domestic. Throughout the present section, indeed, the *zero*th good may be viewed indifferently as tradeable or domestic.

First we note that if all commodities are produced in positive amounts, π_2 and π_0 cannot vary independently of each other. Thus suppose that π_2 is assigned the value π_2^0. Putting aside the possibility of reversal of relative factor intensities, we can infer the corresponding unique equilibrium ratio of factor rewards $(w/r)^0$ and, hence, the uniquely determined π_0^0 at which it is just profitable to produce the *zero*th commodity. Thus we may write $\pi_0 = \pi_0(\pi_2)$.

The precise form of the functional relationship may be explored with the aid of some of our earlier results. Thus from Eq. (1.6)

$$\frac{\omega}{\pi_2} \cdot \frac{d\pi_2}{d\omega} = -\frac{\omega}{k_1 + \omega} + \frac{\omega}{k_2 + \omega}$$

and

$$\frac{\omega}{\pi_0} \cdot \frac{d\pi_0}{d\omega} = -\frac{\omega}{k_1 + \omega} + \frac{\omega}{k_0 + \omega}$$

Hence, dividing one equation by the other,

$$\frac{\pi_2}{\pi_0} \cdot \frac{d\pi_0}{d\pi_2} = \frac{k_1 - k_0}{k_1 - k_2} \cdot \frac{k_2 + \omega}{k_0 + \omega} \tag{6.1}$$

It follows that $d\pi_0/d\pi_2$ is positive if the *zero*th and second commodities are either both more capital-intensive or both less capital-intensive than the *numéraire;* if the *numéraire* is less capital-intensive than one commodity and more capital-intensive than the other, $d\pi_0/d\pi_2$ is negative. Unfortunately, nothing can be said about the magnitude of the elasticity (6.1).

Figure 6.1 illustrates the conclusions summarized in Eq. (6.1). Three unit isoquants are shown, tangent to the same constant cost line, at P_0, P_1 and P_2, respectively, and therefore reflecting the equality of π_0 and π_2. In the case shown, $k_1 < k_2 < k_0$. We should therefore expect an increase in π_2

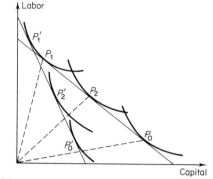

FIGURE 6.1

to be associated with an increase in π_0. Suppose that π_2 increases, so that in the new equilibrium less of the second commodity is exchanged against the old amount of the first. For this to happen it is necessary that the factor used more intensively in the second than in the first industry, namely capital, should become relatively more expensive, so that all constant cost lines are tilted towards the vertical. P_1' and P_2' are the new equilibrium points. The *zero*th industry is even more capital-intensive than the second industry; hence its relative price also must rise. This increase in price is indicated by the fact that P_0' lies on an isoquant representing less than the initial output.

Next we turn our attention to the three-dimensional production possibility surface. Our chief purpose will be to show that the surface is composed of straight lines, that is, that it is a ruled surface; and to draw out some of the implications of this fact. The dimensions of the accompanying box (Fig. 6.2) are determined by the given factor endowments K and L. The south-west and north-east corners are the origins for systems of isoquants for the first and second industries, respectively. Suppose that $\pi_2 = \pi_2^0$ and $\omega = \omega^0$. Suppose further that the first industry's output is arbitrarily fixed at X_1^0. On the corresponding isoquant is marked that point O_0 at which the marginal rate of factor substitution is equal to $-\omega^0$. O_0 forms the south-west corner of a smaller box containing the isoquants of the *zero*th and second industries. Since by assumption something is produced of each commodity, one can find on the contract locus O_0O_2 a point P at which the common marginal rate of substitution is equal to $-\omega^0$. Points O_0 and P therefore correspond to a point on the production possibility surface at which the surface is touched by the price plane defined by π_2^0. The three capital:labor ratios are indicated by the slopes of O_1O_0, O_0P, and O_2P. Consider now a higher output of the first commodity, say X_1'. If π_2, and therefore ω, is unchanged, so are the three capital:labor ratios. Hence a second production mixture indicated by points O_0' and P' also is consistent with the set of commodity prices and factor

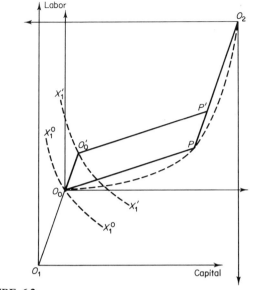

FIGURE 6.2

rewards. Indeed by sliding O_0P from left to right one may generate any number of alternative output mixtures, all of them consistent with the same commodity prices and all lying on a straight line imbedded in the production surface. The production surface is therefore ruled, as in Chap. 5.

It follows that, if prices are consistent with incomplete specialization, prices alone do not suffice to pin down a country's output. If the *zero*th commodity is a purely domestic good it suffices to know in addition the demand for that commodity. However, if all three commodities are tradeable and if in equilibrium both countries are incompletely specialized (in the sense that no industry is unprofitable) there exists an essential indeterminacy in the allocation of (determinate) world output between the two trading partners and, therefore, in the pattern of world trade. More specifically, it is possible to dispense with trade in one good without impairing the efficiency of world production and without reducing the gains from trade for either country. Moreover, in the face of small disturbances of whatever kind, the identity of the commodity in which trade is dispensable does not change. For small disturbances, therefore, that commodity has the properties of a domestic good. In the case of incomplete specialization, indeed, our stipulation that the *zero*th good be genuinely domestic merely removes the indeterminacy of national outputs and the pattern of world trade. It has no bearing on equilibrium world prices or on factor rewards in either country. In Secs. 2–5 it will be assumed that each country is incompletely specialized. Those of our results which relate to commodity prices and factor rewards therefore have a field of application wider than the context will indicate.

2. The Offer Curve

It was one of the most striking conclusions of Chap. 5 that when factor supplies are variable the offer curve might bend back on itself, so that the demand for imports falls when the terms of trade improve. We shall now see that the existence of a nontraded commodity throws up the same possibility.

We seek an expression for

$$\frac{dZ_1}{d\pi_2} = \frac{dD_1}{d\pi_2} - \frac{dX_1}{d\pi_2} \tag{6.2}$$

the rate of change of home import demand per unit change in the terms of trade, it being understood that all other variables, including π_0, adjust *mutatis mutandis*. The calculation is a tedious one, chiefly because, as we have just seen, $dX_1/d\pi_2$ cannot be inferred from knowledge of production possibilities only. In the absence of information about demand, $dX_1/d\pi_2$ is indeterminate. Our procedure, therefore, is first to calculate the effect of a change in π_2 on X_0, the output of the domestic commodity, and on k_0, the capital:labor ratio in the domestic industry. Armed with this information we can infer the extent to which factors are released to the foreign sector. We then calculate the effect of the change in π_2 on k_1 and k_2, the capital:labor ratios in the foreign sector, and hence the changes in outputs necesary to maintain full employment of both factors.

Equilibrium in the market for the domestic commodity requires that

$$L_0 f_0(k_0) \equiv X_0 = D_0 \tag{6.3}$$

The release of labor from the domestic industry is therefore

$$\frac{dL_0}{d\pi_2} = -\frac{1}{f_0}\left(\frac{dD_0}{d\pi_2} - L_0 f_0' \frac{dk_0}{d\pi_2}\right) \tag{6.4}$$

The additional labor absorbed by the first or import-competing industry is then calculated from the revised full employment conditions

$$L_0 + L_1 + L_2 = L$$
$$L_0 k_0 + L_1 k_1 + L_2 k_2 = K \tag{6.5}$$

Thus

$$\frac{dL_1}{d\pi_2} = -\frac{k_2 - k_0}{k_2 - k_1} \cdot \frac{dL_0}{d\pi_2} + \frac{1}{k_2 - k_1} \Sigma L_i \frac{dk_i}{d\pi_2} \tag{6.6}$$

The changes in the capital:labor ratios, on the other hand, can be calculated from the marginal conditions

$$\pi_0 f'_0 = f'_1 = \pi_2 f'_2$$

$$\pi_0(f_0 - k_0 f'_0) = f_1 - k_1 f'_1 = \pi_2(f_2 - k_2 f'_2)$$

(6.7)

They are

$$\frac{dk_0}{d\pi_2} = \frac{f_0}{(\pi_0)^2 f''_0(k_0 - k_1)} \cdot \frac{d\pi_0}{d\pi_2}$$

$$\frac{dk_1}{d\pi_2} = \frac{f_2}{f''_1(k_2 - k_1)} = \frac{f_0}{f''_1(k_0 - k_1)} \cdot \frac{d\pi_0}{d\pi_2}$$

(6.8)

$$\frac{dk_2}{d\pi_2} = \frac{f_1}{(\pi_2)^2 f''_2(k_2 - k_1)}$$

We can now calculate

$$\frac{dX_1}{d\pi_2} = \frac{d}{d\pi_2} L_1 f_1(k_1) = f_1 \frac{dL_1}{d\pi_2} + L_1 f'_1 \frac{dk_1}{d\pi_2}$$

(6.9)

In view of Eqs. (6.4), (6.6) and (6.8), Eq. (6.9) reduces to

$$\frac{dX_1}{d\pi_2} = -\frac{f_1}{f_0} \cdot \frac{k_2 - k_0}{k_2 - k_1} \cdot \frac{dD_0}{d\pi_2} + Q_1$$

(6.10)

where

$$Q_1 \equiv \frac{\pi_2 L_0 f_1(f_2)^2}{(\pi_0)^3 f_0 f''_0(k_2 - k_1)^2} + \frac{\pi_2 L_1(f_2)^2}{f''_1(k_2 - k_1)^2} + \frac{L_2(f_1)^2}{(\pi_2)^2 f''_2(k_2 - k_1)^2}$$

(6.11)

is necessarily negative. From Eq. (6.8) we derive an alternative expression for $d\pi_0/d\pi_2$:

$$\frac{d\pi_0}{d\pi_2} = \frac{f_2}{f_0} \cdot \frac{k_0 - k_1}{k_2 - k_1}$$

(6.12)

It follows that Eq. (6.10) can be written as

$$\frac{dX_1}{d\pi_2} = \frac{f_1}{f_0} \cdot \frac{k_2 - k_0}{k_1 - k_0} \cdot \frac{d\pi_0}{d\pi_2} \cdot \frac{dD_0}{d\pi_2} + Q_1$$

$$= \alpha \frac{d\pi_0}{d\pi_2} \frac{dD_0}{d\pi_2} + Q_1$$

(6.13)

where

$$\alpha \equiv \frac{f_1}{f_0} \cdot \frac{k_2 - k_0}{k_1 - k_0}$$

From Eqs. (6.2) and (6.13)

$$\frac{dZ_1}{d\pi_2} = \frac{dD_1}{d\pi_2} - \alpha \frac{d\pi_0}{d\pi_2} \cdot \frac{dD_0}{d\pi_2} - Q_1 \qquad (6.14)$$

But

$$D_i = Ld_i(\pi_0, \pi_2, q_1) \qquad i = 0, 1$$

where

$$q_1 = \pi_0 y_0 + y_1 + \pi_2 y_2 \qquad (6.15)$$

with

$$\frac{\partial q_1}{\partial \pi_0} = y_0, \quad \frac{\partial q_1}{\partial \pi_2} = y_2 \qquad (6.16)$$

Hence

$$\frac{\partial D_i}{\partial \pi_2} = L\left\{\left(\frac{\partial d_i}{\partial \pi_0} + \frac{m_i}{\pi_i} y_0\right)\frac{d\pi_0}{d\pi_2} + \left(\frac{\partial d_i}{\partial \pi_2} + \frac{m_i}{\pi_i} y_2\right)\right\} \qquad i = 0, 1 \quad (6.17)$$

where $m_i \equiv \pi_i(\partial d_i/\partial q_1)$ is the marginal propensity to consume the ith commodity ($\pi_1 = 1$). Introducing the Slutzky decompositions of $\partial d_i/\partial \pi_0$ and $\partial d_i/\partial \pi_2$, and converting to elasticities, Eqs. (6.17) become

$$\frac{\partial D_i}{\partial \pi_2} = L\left\{\frac{d_i}{\pi_0}\bar{\eta}_{i0}\frac{\partial \pi_0}{\partial \pi_2} + \frac{d_i}{\pi_2}(\bar{\eta}_{i2} + \theta_i m_i)\right\} \qquad i = 0, 1 \qquad (6.18)$$

where

$$\bar{\eta}_{ij} \equiv \frac{\pi_j}{d_i} \cdot \frac{\partial d_i}{\partial \pi_j}\bigg| \qquad\qquad i = 0, 1; j = 0, 2 \quad (6.19)$$

is the compensated elasticity of demand for the ith commodity with respect to the relative price of the jth commodity and

$$\theta_i \equiv -\frac{\pi_2 z_2}{\pi_i d_i} \qquad i = 0, 1 \qquad (6.20)$$

is the (positive) ratio of export earnings to total expenditure on the ith commodity. Substituting from Eq. (6.18) into Eq. (6.14), we find that

$$\frac{dZ_1}{d\pi_2} = \frac{D_1}{\pi_0} \bar{\eta}_{10} \frac{d\pi_0}{d\pi_2} + \frac{D_1}{\pi_2} (\bar{\eta}_{12}\theta_1 m_1)$$

$$- \alpha \frac{d\pi_0}{d\pi_2} \left[\frac{D_0}{\pi_0} \bar{\eta}_{00} \frac{d\pi_0}{d\pi_2} + \frac{D_0}{\pi_2} (\bar{\eta}_{02} + \theta_0 m_0) \right] - Q_1 \quad (6.21)$$

Suppose that the capital:labor ratio of the domestic industry falls between those of the export and import-competing industries, so that $d\pi_0/d\pi_2$ and $-\alpha$ are positive. Suppose, moreover, that $\bar{\eta}_{10}$, $\bar{\eta}_{12}$, and $\bar{\eta}_{02}$ are negative. Then clearly $dZ_1/d\pi_2$ may be negative, so that the home offer curve bends back on itself.

3. THE TERMS OF TRADE, THE BALANCE OF PAYMENTS AND UNILATERAL TRANSFERS

The home country's balance of payments, in terms of the first commodity, is

$$B_1 = \pi_2^* Z_2^* - Z_1 \quad (6.22)$$

For stability it is necessary that

$$\frac{dB_1}{d\pi_2^*} \equiv Z_2^* + \pi_2^* \frac{dZ_2^*}{d\pi_2^*} - \frac{dZ_1}{d\pi_2^*} \quad (6.23)$$

be negative. We already have an expression for $dZ_1/d\pi_2^*$. It remains to evaluate $dZ_2^*/d\pi_2^*$. By an argument similar to that which culminated in Eq. (6.21), we find that

$$\frac{dZ_2}{d\pi_2} = \frac{D_2}{\pi_0} \bar{\eta}_{20} \frac{d\pi_0}{d\pi_2} + \frac{D_2}{\pi_2} (\bar{\eta}_{22} + \theta_2 m_2)$$

$$+ \frac{d\pi_0}{d\pi_2} \left[\frac{D_0}{\pi_0} \bar{\eta}_{00} \frac{d\pi_0}{d\pi_2} + \frac{D_0}{\pi_2} (\bar{\eta}_{02} + \theta_0 m_0) \right] - Q_2 \quad (6.24)$$

where

$$Q_2 \equiv \frac{L_0 f_1(f_2)^2}{\pi_0 f_0 f_0''(k_2 - k_1)^2} - \frac{L_1(f_2)^2}{f_1''(k_2 - k_1)^2} - \frac{L_2(f_1)^2}{(\pi_2)^3 f_2''(k_2 - k_1)^2} \quad (6.25)$$

and is necessarily positive. Star all variables in Eq. (6.24) and we have $dZ_2^*/d\pi_2^*$.

It is a short step, left to the reader, to the relationship between a unilateral transfer and the terms of trade.[1]

4. TARIFF CHANGES

We next consider the implications, for the terms of trade π_2^*, and the domestic price ratio π_2, of the imposition of a small import duty. It will be assumed that the proceeds of the duty are handed over to and spent by the general public.

As a first step we calculate the tariff-induced change in home import demand, with the world terms of trade supposed to be unchanged. It will be apparent that this exercise is very similar to that which engaged us in Sec. 2. The chief difference is that income now includes the tariff proceeds $\tau z_1/(1 + \tau)$:

$$q_1 = \pi_0 y_0 + y_1 + \pi_2 y_2 + \frac{\tau}{1 + \tau} z_1 \qquad (6.26)$$

Since $\tau = 0$ initially,

$$\frac{\partial q_1}{\partial \tau} = z_1 \qquad (6.27)$$

Instead of Eq. (6.2) we have

$$\frac{dZ_1}{d\tau} \equiv \frac{dD_1}{d\tau} - \frac{dX_1}{d\tau}$$

$$= \left(\frac{dD_1}{d\pi_2} \cdot \frac{d\pi_2}{d\tau} + \frac{\partial D_1}{\partial \tau} \right) - \frac{dX_1}{d\tau} \qquad (6.28)$$

and, instead of Eq. (6.13),

$$\frac{dX_1}{d\tau} = \alpha \frac{d\pi_0}{d\pi_2} \left(\frac{dD_0}{d\pi_2} \cdot \frac{d\pi_2}{d\tau} + \frac{\partial D_0}{\partial \tau} \right) + Q_1 \frac{d\pi_2}{d\tau} \qquad (6.29)$$

Substituting in Eq. (6.28) for $dX_1/d\tau$, and recalling Eq. (6.14) and the fact that $d\pi_2/d\tau = -\pi_2$,

$$\frac{1}{Z_1} \frac{dZ_1}{d\tau} = \frac{1}{Z_1} \cdot \frac{dZ_1}{d\pi_2} \cdot \frac{d\pi_2}{d\tau} + \frac{1}{Z_1} \left(\frac{\partial D_1}{\partial \tau} - \alpha \frac{d\pi_0}{d\pi_2} \frac{\partial D_0}{\partial \tau} \right)$$

$$= -\frac{\pi_2}{Z_1} \frac{dZ_1}{d\pi_2} + \left(m_1 - m_0 \frac{\alpha}{\pi_0} \frac{d\pi_0}{d\pi_2} \right) \qquad (6.30)$$

[1] See Prob. 6.4.

In view of our findings in Sec. 2, this expression may be of either sign. If world commodity markets are stable, the terms of trade of the home country will improve when $(1/Z_1)(dZ_1/d\tau)$ is negative, deteriorate when it is positive. This conclusion stands in sharp contrast to that reached in Chap. 4 where purely domestic goods were ignored and where it was shown that for the terms of trade to turn against the tariff-imposing country it is necessary that the government spend part of the tariff proceeds.

It remains to determine whether the Lerner–Metzler possibility, that an import duty may depress the internal price of imports in terms of exports, emerges under the revised assumptions of the present chapter. We first seek the conditions under which the internal price ratio π_2 will be undisturbed by the imposition of a tariff. Now international equilibrium is defined by

$$Z_1 = \pi_2^* Z_2^* \tag{6.31}$$

so that

$$\frac{dZ_1}{d\tau} = \left(Z_2^* + \pi_2^* \frac{dZ_2^*}{d\pi_2^*} \right) \frac{d\pi_2^*}{d\tau}$$

$$= Z_2^*(1 + \xi^*) \frac{d\pi_2^*}{d\tau} \tag{6.32}$$

where $\xi^* \equiv (\pi_2^*/Z_2^*)(dZ_2^*/d\pi_2^*)$ is the total price elasticity of foreign import demand. Since π_2 is assumed to be constant, however,

$$d\pi_2^*/d\tau = d[\pi_2(1 + \tau)]/d\tau = \pi_2$$

Hence

$$\frac{dZ_1}{d\tau} = \pi_2^* Z_2^*(1 + \xi^*) \tag{6.33}$$

Our main task, therefore, is to evaluate $dZ_1/d\tau$. Now constant π_2 implies constant π_0. On the other hand, home income increases by the amount of the tariff proceeds, $Z_1 d\tau$. This gives rise to an increase in the demand for imports

$$dD_1 = m_1 Z_1 d\tau \tag{6.34}$$

It also boosts the demand for the domestic good, by $m_0 Z_1 d\tau/\pi_0$. To meet this increase in demand, resources are drawn from the foreign sector, resulting in a change in the home output of the imported commodity. Thus the imposition of the tariff results in the absorption by the domestic industry of $dX_0/f_0 = m_0 Z_1 d\tau/\pi_0 f_0$ additional units of labor and $k_0 dX_0/f_0 = k_0 m_0 Z_1 d\tau/\pi_0 f_0$ additional units of capital. From Prob. 1.10, therefore, the output of the first industry changes by

$$dX_1 = -\frac{f_1}{f_0} \cdot \frac{k_2 - k_0}{k_0(k_2 - k_1)} \cdot \frac{m_0}{\pi_0} \cdot Z_1 \, d\tau \tag{6.35}$$

Combining Eqs. (6.34) and (6.35), we have

$$\frac{dZ_1}{d\tau} \equiv \frac{dD_1}{d\tau} - \frac{dX_1}{d\tau}$$

$$= \left[m_1 + \frac{m_0}{\pi_0} \cdot \frac{f_1}{f_0} \cdot \frac{k_2 - k_0}{k_0(k_2 - k_1)} \right] Z_1 \qquad (6.36)$$

Finally, from Eqs. (6.31), (6.33), and (6.36), we infer our required condition

$$1 + \xi^* = m_1 + \frac{m_0}{\pi_0} \cdot \frac{f_1}{f_0} \cdot \frac{k_2 - k_0}{k_0(k_2 - k_1)} \qquad (6.37)$$

which, when $m_0 = 0$, coincides with the expression obtained in Chap. 4. As Eq. (6.37) makes clear, the injection of a domestic commodity may either weaken or strengthen the condition, depending on the sign of $(k_2 - k_0)/(k_2 - k_1)$. If the marginal propensity to buy the imported commodity falls short of the critical value defined by Eq. (6.37), the terms of trade will move so far in favor of the home country that even the internal price ratio π_2 will increase. If m_1 exceeds that value, π_2 will fall.

Suppose that π_2 does increase. It is tempting to say then that the tariff has failed to protect the import-competing industry and, perversely, has protected the export industry. That would indeed be a reasonable interpretation if the purely domestic good could be ignored. We know, however, that $d\pi_0/d\pi_2$ may be of either sign. Thus the tariff may force up both price ratios, or it may force them to move in opposite directions. In the first case, clearly, the import-competing industry is discouraged; whether both of the other industries are stimulated, or just one, remains uncertain. In the second case, the export industry is stimulated, and the domestic industry discouraged; the net effect on the import-competing industry is uncertain.

5. CHANGES IN FACTOR ENDOWMENTS

It was shown in Chap. 1, Sec. 2, that with fixed product prices an increase in a country's capital endowment would give rise to a more than proportionate increase in the output of the commodity in which capital is used relatively intensively and to a decline in the output of the other commodity. Putting aside the possibility of inferiority in consumption, therefore, an increase in the capital endowment would result in a decline in import demand if the imported commodity were relatively capital-intensive and to an increase in import demand if it were relatively labor-intensive.

When a nontraded commodity is introduced, matters become much more complicated. An increase in the capital endowment raises income, and part of the additional income is spent on the domestic commodity. The expansion of the domestic industry draws both factors from the foreign sector, in the ratio k_0. Depending on the relative values of the three k's, it is possible that import demand may increase even though *in relation to the export industry* the import-competing industry is capital-intensive ($k_1 > k_2$). That this is so will perhaps come as no surprise after the discussion of Sec. 4. The formal demonstration can be brief.

If we could ignore the domestic industry, the effect of the increase in the capital endowment would be to change the output of the first industry by[2]

$$-\frac{f_1}{k_2 - k_1} dK \qquad (6.38)$$

In the present context we must think of this as merely the direct effect of the change in endowment, to which must be added the indirect effect operating through the change in scale of the domestic industry. The calculation of the indirect effect will be our main task in this section.

The increase in the capital endowment raises total income by $w_1 dK$. The increase in income inflates the demand for (and therefore the output of) the domestic commodity by

$$\frac{m_0}{\pi_0} w_1 \, dK$$

The additional output requires an additional capital intake of

$$dK_0 = \frac{k_0}{f_0} \left(\frac{m_0}{\pi_0} w_1 \, dK \right)$$

and an additional labor intake of

$$dL_0 = \frac{1}{k_0} dK_0$$

From Prob. 1.10, this flow of factors changes the output of the first industry by

$$-\frac{f_1}{k_0} \cdot \frac{k_2 - k_0}{k_2 - k_1} \cdot dK_0 = -\frac{f_1}{f_0} \cdot \frac{k_2 - k_0}{k_2 - k_1} \cdot \frac{m_0}{\pi_0} w_1 \, dK \qquad (6.39)$$

Adding expressions (6.38) and (6.39), we obtain the net effect on the output of the first industry of the change in capital endowment

$$dX_1 = -\frac{f_1}{k_2 - k_1} \left[1 + (k_2 - k_0) \frac{m_0}{\pi_0 f_0} w_1 \right] dK \qquad (6.40)$$

[2] See Chap. 1, Sec. 2.

On the other hand, the income-induced change in demand for the first commodity is

$$dD_1 = m_1 w_1 dK \qquad (6.41)$$

Hence the required change in import demand is

$$dZ_1 \equiv dD_1 - dX_1$$

$$= \left\{ m_1 w_1 + \frac{f_1}{k_2 - k_1} \left[1 + (k_2 - k_0) \frac{m_0}{\pi_0 f_0} w_1 \right] \right\} dK \qquad (6.42)$$

If k_2 is less than k_0 and k_1, this expression could be positive, a conclusion which contrasts sharply with that reached in Chap. 4.

6. FINAL COMMENTS

It would be possible to recalculate the implications of technical improvements of several kinds. This would be tedious. Moreover, the student will learn more by performing these calculations himself. They are therefore left as Prob. 6.3.[3]

PROBLEMS

6.1 Suppose that the home country imposes a small import duty and that the government spends the proceeds in proportions α_0, α_1, α_2 on the three commodities ($\Sigma \alpha_i = 1$). Find counterparts to Eqs. (6.30) and (6.37) on the alternative assumptions (a) that the government pays duty on its purchases and (b) that the government does not pay duty.

6.2 Suppose that the community's labor endowment increases slightly. Derive expressions for the consequential changes in (a) outputs, (b) factor rewards, and (c) import demand.

6.3 Suppose that factor-neutral technical improvements take place in (a) the domestic industry, (b) the export industry, (c) the import-competing industry of a small country. What will be the implications for internal prices, factor rewards and outputs?

6.4 Derive a counterpart to Eq. (5.15), employing the assumptions of the present chapter.

[3] See also Komiya [1].

REFERENCES

†[1] Komiya, Ryutaro, "Non-Traded Goods and the Pure Theory of International Trade," *International Economic Review*, VIII, No. 2 (June 1967), 132–52.

[2] McDougall, I. A., "Non-Traded Goods and the Transfer Problem," *Review of Economic Studies*, XXXII (1), No. 89 (January 1965), 67–84.

[3] McDougall, I. A., "Tariffs and Relative Prices," *Economic Record*, XLII, No. 98 (June 1966), 219–43.

†[4] Melvin, James R., "Production and Trade with Two Factors and Three Goods," *American Economic Review*, LVIII, No. 5, Part 1 (December 1968), 1249–68.

[5] Pearce, I. F., "The Problem of the Balance of Payments," *International Economic Review*, II, No. 1 (January 1961), 1–28.

[6] Samuelson, Paul A., "Price of Factors and Goods in General Equilibrium," *Review of Economic Studies*, XXI, No. 1 (October 1953), 1–20.

[7] Samuelson, Paul A., "Equalization by Trade of the Interest Rate along with the Real Wage," in R. E. Baldwin, *et al.* (eds.), *Trade, Growth, and the Balance of Payments. Essays in Honor of Gottfried Haberler*, 35–52. Chicago: Rand McNally & Company, 1955.

chapter 7

Intermediate Goods*

It has been pretended so far that final goods are produced with primary, nonproducible factors of production, with no mention of intermediate goods. This is indeed the usual practice in the theory of international trade. Yet the bulk of international trade is precisely in intermediate goods—produced commodities which serve as inputs in the production of other commodities.[1]

The principal purpose of the present chapter is to show how the standard Heckscher–Ohlin model of trade can be extended to accommodate intermediate goods and to confirm that the principal theorems proved in earlier chapters carry over with only trivial changes. In other words, the purpose of this chapter is to defend the neglect of intermediate goods in earlier (and later) chapters.

Intermediate goods may be more or less durable in use and economists have long worked with a rough and ready distinction between circulating capital, which is used up or transformed within a single arbitrarily defined period, and fixed capital, which retains its form (though its quantity may shrink) over at least two periods. Fixed capital plays an especially important role in the analysis of economic change. Since two separate chapters are devoted to that subject, we concentrate here on circulating capital.

We continue to recognize two primary factors of production, labor and capital, and two finished products. We suppose, however,

[1] See [15], pp. 159–99.

that the product of each industry serves also as an input for the other industry. The basic production relationships are then

$$X_1 = F_1(K_1, L_1, X_{21}) - X_{12}$$
$$X_2 = F_2(K_2, L_2, X_{12}) - X_{21}$$

(7.1)

where F_j and X_j are, respectively, the gross and net outputs of the jth industry, X_{ij} is the amount of the ith product used in the jth industry, and the F_j are subject to restrictions similar to those imposed in Chap. 1, Sec. 2. Alternatively, drawing on the homogeneity of F_j, we may rewrite Eqs. (7.1) as

$$F_1\left(\frac{K_1}{X_1 + X_{12}}, \frac{L_1}{X_1 + X_{12}}, \frac{X_{21}}{X_1 + X_{12}}\right) = F_1(a_{K1}, a_{L1}, a_{21}) = 1$$
$$F_2\left(\frac{K_2}{X_2 + X_{21}}, \frac{L_2}{X_2 + X_{21}}, \frac{X_{12}}{X_2 + X_{21}}\right) = F_2(a_{K2}, a_{L2}, a_{12}) = 1$$

(7.1')

where a_{ij} stands as usual for the amount of the ith factor used in the production of one unit of the jth commodity, with $i = K, L, 1, 2$ and $j = 1, 2$, and where by convention $a_{ii} \equiv 0$.

The production relations must be supplemented by formal statements of the full employment conditions, the implications of perfect competition and the marginal conditions of profit maximization. The requirement that both factors be fully employed can be expressed as

$$a_{L1}X_1 + a_{L2}X_2 = L$$
$$a_{K1}X_1 + a_{K2}X_2 = K$$

(7.2)

From the assumptions of perfect competition, free entry and incomplete specialization it follows that in each industry price equals average cost:

$$a_{L1}w + a_{K1}r + a_{21}p_2 = p_1$$
$$a_{L2}w + a_{K2}r + a_{12}p_1 = p_2$$

(7.3)

To help give expression to the assumption of profit maximization, we introduce the definitions

$$\chi_1 \equiv \{a_{K1}, a_{L1}, a_{21} \mid 1 = F_1(a_{K1}, a_{L1}, a_{21})\}$$
$$\chi_2 \equiv \{a_{K2}, a_{L2}, a_{12} \mid 1 = F_2(a_{K2}, a_{L2}, a_{12})\}$$

The problem facing the individual firm is that of minimizing its unit costs of production:

$$\min_{(a_{L1}, a_{K1}, a_{21}) \in \chi_1} (wa_{L1} + ra_{K1} + p_2 a_{21})$$

$$\min_{(a_{L2}, a_{K2}, a_{12}) \in \chi_2} (wa_{L2} + ra_{K2} + p_1 a_{12})$$

As necessary conditions of cost minimization we have

$$wda_{L1} + rda_{K1} + p_2 da_{21} = 0$$
$$wda_{L2} + rda_{K2} + p_1 da_{12} = 0 \qquad (7.4)$$

where it is understood that the input increments are consistent with Eqs. (7.1′).

That completes our specification of the economy. It will prove convenient, however, to have the key equations (7.2)–(7.4) on a common footing. With this goal in mind we differentiate Eqs. (7.2) and, after some slight rearrangement, obtain

$$\lambda_{L1} \hat{X}_1 + \lambda_{L2} \hat{X}_2 = \hat{L} - (\lambda_{L1} \hat{a}_{L1} + \lambda_{L2} \hat{a}_{L2})$$
$$\lambda_{K1} \hat{X}_1 + \lambda_{K2} \hat{X}_2 = \hat{K} - (\lambda_{K1} \hat{a}_{K1} + \lambda_{K2} \hat{a}_{K2}) \qquad (7.5)$$

where λ_{ij} is the proportion of the community's endowment of the ith primary factor employed by the jth industry (so that $\lambda_{i1} + \lambda_{i2} = 1$) and $\hat{X}_i \equiv dX_i/X_i$, etc. In similar fashion we obtain from Eqs. (7.3)

$$\theta_{L1} \hat{w} + \theta_{K1} \hat{r} = \hat{p}_1 - \theta_{21} \hat{p}_2 - (\theta_{L1} \hat{a}_{L1} + \theta_{K1} \hat{a}_{K1} + \theta_{21} \hat{a}_{21})$$
$$\theta_{L2} \hat{w} + \theta_{K2} \hat{r} = \hat{p}_2 - \theta_{12} \hat{p}_1 - (\theta_{L2} \hat{a}_{L2} + \theta_{K2} \hat{a}_{K2} + \theta_{12} \hat{a}_{12})$$

where θ_{ij} is the share of the ith factor in the costs of the jth industry (so that $\theta_{L1} + \theta_{K1} + \theta_{21} = 1 = \theta_{L2} + \theta_{K2} + \theta_{12}$). From Eqs. (7.4), however, the bracketed expressions vanish, so that

$$\theta_{L1} \hat{w} + \theta_{K1} \hat{r} = \hat{p}_1 - \theta_{21} \hat{p}_2$$
$$\theta_{L2} \hat{w} + \theta_{K2} \hat{r} = \hat{p}_2 - \theta_{12} \hat{p}_1 \qquad (7.6)$$

Our next step is to eliminate the $\hat{a}_{ij}$ from Eqs. (7.5). To this end, we introduce σ_{ij}^k, the partial elasticity of substitution between factors i and j in the kth industry.[2] It can be shown[3] that

$$\hat{a}_{L1} = \theta_{L1}\sigma^1_{LL}\hat{w} + \theta_{K1}\sigma^1_{KL}\hat{r} + \theta_{21}\sigma^1_{2L}\hat{p}_2$$

$$\hat{a}_{K1} = \theta_{L1}\sigma^1_{KL}\hat{w} + \theta_{K1}\sigma^1_{KK}\hat{r} + \theta_{21}\sigma^1_{2K}\hat{p}_2$$

$$\hat{a}_{21} = \theta_{L1}\sigma^1_{2L}\hat{w} + \theta_{K1}\sigma^1_{K2}\hat{r} + \theta_{21}\sigma^1_{22}\hat{p}_2$$

and that

$$\hat{a}_{L2} = \theta_{L2}\sigma^2_{LL}\hat{w} + \theta_{K2}\sigma^2_{KL}\hat{r} + \theta_{12}\sigma^2_{L1}\hat{p}_1$$

$$\hat{a}_{K2} = \theta_{L2}\sigma^2_{KL}\hat{w} + \theta_{K2}\sigma^2_{KK}\hat{r} + \theta_{12}\sigma^2_{K1}\hat{p}_1$$

$$\hat{a}_{12} = \theta_{L2}\sigma^2_{1L}\hat{w} + \theta_{K2}\sigma^2_{K2}\hat{r} + \theta_{12}\sigma^2_{11}\hat{p}_1$$

Substituting, Eqs. (7.5) become

$$\lambda_{L1}\hat{X}_1 + \lambda_{L2}\hat{X}_2 + (\lambda_{L1}\theta_{L1}\sigma^1_{LL} + \lambda_{L2}\theta_{L2}\sigma^2_{LL})\hat{w}$$
$$+ (\lambda_{L1}\theta_{K1}\sigma^1_{KL} + \lambda_{L2}\theta_{K2}\sigma^2_{KL})\hat{r}$$
$$= \hat{L} - \lambda_{L2}\theta_{12}\sigma^2_{L1}\hat{p}_1 - \lambda_{L1}\theta_{21}\sigma^1_{2L}\hat{p}_2$$

$$\lambda_{K1}\hat{X}_1 + \lambda_{K2}\hat{X}_2 + (\lambda_{K1}\theta_{L1}\sigma^1_{KL} + \lambda_{K2}\theta_{L2}\sigma^2_{KL})\hat{w}$$
$$+ (\lambda_{K1}\theta_{K1}\sigma^1_{KK} + \lambda_{K2}\theta_{K2}\sigma^2_{KK})\hat{r}$$
$$= \hat{K} - \lambda_{K2}\theta_{12}\sigma^2_{K1}\hat{p}_1 - \lambda_{K1}\theta_{21}\sigma^1_{2K}\hat{p}_2$$

(7.7)

Eqs. (7.6) and (7.7) form the basis of all further manipulations.

The apparatus set up, we now use it to determine whether the Stolper–Samuelson theorem carries over to a world with intermediate goods. Specifically, we wish to know whether an increase in the price of the ith good results in an unambiguous increase in the real reward of whichever primary factor is used relatively intensively in the ith industry and in an unambiguous decline in the real reward of the other factor.

From Eqs. (7.6)

$$\begin{pmatrix} \hat{w} \\ \hat{r} \end{pmatrix} = \frac{1}{|\theta|} \begin{pmatrix} \theta_{K2} + \theta_{K1}\theta_{12} & -(\theta_{K2}\theta_{21} + \theta_{K1}) \\ -(\theta_{L2} + \theta_{L1}\theta_{12}) & \theta_{L2}\theta_{21} + \theta_{L1} \end{pmatrix} \begin{pmatrix} \hat{p}_1 \\ \hat{p}_2 \end{pmatrix}$$

(7.8)

where

$$|\theta| \equiv \begin{vmatrix} \theta_{L1} & \theta_{K1} \\ \theta_{L2} & \theta_{K2} \end{vmatrix}$$

---

[2] For a definition see [1], p. 504. Notice that we are flouting convention by allowing $i = j$.
[3] See [1], p. 508.

is positive if the first industry is relatively labor-intensive and negative if it is relatively capital-intensive. Now

$$\theta_{K2}(1 - \theta_{L1}) + \theta_{K1}(\theta_{12} + \theta_{L2}) > 0$$

hence

$$\theta_{K2} + \theta_{K1}\theta_{12} > \theta_{K2}\theta_{L1} - \theta_{K1}\theta_{L2} \equiv |\theta| \qquad (7.9a)$$

Similarly,

$$\theta_{L2}\theta_{21} + \theta_{L1} > |\theta| \qquad (7.9b)$$

$$-(\theta_{L2} + \theta_{L1}\theta_{12}) < |\theta| \qquad (7.9c)$$

$$-(\theta_{K2}\theta_{21} + \theta_{K1}) < |\theta| \qquad (7.9d)$$

It follows that if $|\theta|$ is positive the diagonal elements of the coefficient matrix of Eqs. (7.8) are greater than one and the off-diagonal elements negative; and that if $|\theta|$ is negative the off-diagonal elements are greater than one and the diagonal elements negative. The Stolper–Samuelson Theorem follows immediately.

We switch our attention now to the Samuelson–Rybczynski Theorem. Setting $\hat{p}_1 = \hat{p}_2 = \hat{w} = \hat{r} = 0$ in Eqs. (7.7), we obtain

$$\begin{pmatrix} \lambda_{L1} & \lambda_{L2} \\ \lambda_{K1} & \lambda_{K2} \end{pmatrix} \begin{pmatrix} \hat{X}_1 \\ \hat{X}_2 \end{pmatrix} = \begin{pmatrix} \hat{L} \\ \hat{K} \end{pmatrix}$$

as in the absence of intermediate goods.

Thus both the Stolper–Samuelson Theorem and the Samuelson–Rybczynski Theorem emerge unscathed by the recognition of intermediate goods. If this is found surprising, the reader may take comfort in the following rough-and-ready logic. The true capital intensity of an industry after allowing for the capital intensity of produced inputs, is some weighted average of the apparent capital intensities of the two industries. The weights depend on the θ_{ij}. Now if the economy is viable $\theta_{ij} < 1$, hence in calculating an industry's true capital intensity one must attach a greater weight to its own apparent capital intensity than to that of the other industry. If therefore an industry is apparently the more capital-intensive, it must be truly the more capital-intensive.

PROBLEMS

7.1 Suppose that there is just one primary factor of production but that in each industry the list of inputs includes the product of the other industry. Deduce the shape of the net production possibilities curve.

REFERENCES

[1] Allen, R. G. D., *Mathematical Analysis for Economists*. London: Macmillan and Co. Ltd., 1938.

[2] Amano, Akihiro, "Intermediate Goods and the Theory of Comparative Advantage: a Two-Country, Three-Commodity Case," *Weltwirtschaftliches Archiv*, XCVI, No. 2 (1966), 340–45.

[3] Jones, Ronald W., "Comparative Advantage and the Theory of Tariffs: a Multi-Country Multi-Commodity Model," *Review of Economic Studies*, XXVIII (3), No. 77 (June 1961), 161–75.

[4] Melvin, James R., "Intermediate Goods in Production Theory: the Differentiable Case," *Review of Economic Studies*, XXXVI(1), No. 105 (January 1968), 124–131.

[5] Melvin, James R., "Intermediate Goods, the Production Possibility Curve, and the Gains from Trade," *Quarterly Journal of Economics*, to be published.

[6] Melvin, James R., "Production and Trade with Intermediate Inputs," unpublished.

[7] McKenzie, Lionel W., "Specialization and Efficiency in World Production," *Review of Economic Studies*, XXI (3), No. 56 (June 1954), 165–80.

[8] McKenzie, Lionel W., "Specialization in Production and the Production Possibility Locus," *Review of Economic Studies*, XXIII (1), No. 60 (October 1955), 56–64.

[9] McKinnon, Ronald I., "Intermediate Products and Differential Tariffs: A Generalization of Lerner's Symmetry Theorem," *Quarterly Journal of Economics*, LXXX, No. 4 (November 1966), 584–615.

[10] Reiter, Stanley, "Trade Barriers in Activity Analysis," *Review of Economic Studies*, XX (3), No. 53 (June 1953), 174–180.

[11] Samuelson, Paul A., "Prices of Factors and Goods in General Equilibrium," *Review of Economic Studies*, XXL (1), No. 54 (1953–54), 1–20.

[12] Samuelson, Paul A., "Equalization by Trade of the Interest Rate Along with the Real Wage," in Robert E. Baldwin, *et al*, eds., *Trade, Growth, and the Balance of Payments. Essays in Honor of Gottfried Haberler*. Chicago: Rand McNally & Co., 1955.

[13] Travis, William Penfield, *The Theory of Trade and Protection*. Cambridge, Mass.: Harvard University Press, 1964.

[14] Vanek, Jaroslav, "Variable Factor Proportions and Inter-Industry Flows in the Theory of International Trade," *Quarterly Journal of Economics*, LXXVII, No. 1 (February 1963), 129–42.

[15] Yates, P. Lamartine, *Forty Years of Foreign Trade*. London: George Allen and Unwin Ltd., 1959.

chapter 8

*Variable Returns to Scale**

The assumption of constant returns to scale has been maintained throughout the seven preceding chapters. It has been a very convenient assumption since it has enabled us to focus attention on factor *proportions* and output *ratios* without much bothering about the size of a country's resource endowment or the scale of its productive and trading operations. It is conceivable, however, that Nature is blind to the comforts of academic economists. Accordingly, in the present chapter there are sketched some of the implications of variable returns to scale. We shall be especially interested in the extent to which the basic theorems of constant returns technology, *viz.* the Stolper–Samuelson, Samuelson–Rybczynski, and Factor Price Equalization Theorems, carry over to more general contexts. We shall also examine the implications of variable returns for the stability of equilibrium.

Economies and diseconomies of scale may be internal to the firm, or external to it. If economies of scale are internal to the firm, the upshot, in a static world, is at most a single producer in each country; and if in equilibrium the economy-generating industry is much smaller than the other industry, or if the country which specializes in the product of that industry is much larger than its trading partner, it seems probable that world production will be in the hands of a single producer. In any case, perfectly competitive marginal cost pricing cannot possibly prevail in that industry.[1]

Economies that are external to the firm, however, are quite consistent with constant or rising marginal costs for individual firms and, hence, with perfectly competitive conditions. On the other hand, marginal private cost now exceeds marginal social cost, and this may give rise to certain analytical complications: For one thing, the production point may lie inside the community's production possibilities curve; and, even if that complication is avoided, one cannot be sure that in equilibrium the price ratio (which measures the marginal rate of substitution in consumption) will be equal to the slope of the production possibilities curve (which measures the marginal rate of substitution in production).

These complications are, however, not inseparable from external economies of scale. By restricting our attention to specific kinds of external economies, it will be possible to avoid the complications without evading the issues posed by variable returns. It will turn out, indeed, that only when economies are of a very special type can many of the problems listed in our opening paragraph be properly posed. Thus consider the Stolper–Samuelson, Samuelson–Rybczynski, and Factor Price Equalization Theorems. These have been proved under the assumption that each production function is homogeneous of degree one. To avoid irrelevant complications associated with inter-industrial differences in the degree of homogeneity, it seems necessary, therefore, that we should now assume

(a) that the homogeneity of the industry production functions is of degree greater or less than one, but the same in each industry.[2]

It seems appropriate that we assume also

(b) that for the individual firm returns to scale are constant, that is, that equiproportionate changes in the firm's inputs, *the output of the industry being constant*, give rise to changes in the firm's output in the same proportion.

---

[1] It should not be inferred from this that the recognition of internal economies requires the complete recasting of our earlier analysis. If entry to each industry were perfectly free, the "monopolist" would be in effective competition with an indefinite number of potential producers and would be driven to equate price and average cost. Moreover, if to our standard assumptions (inelastic factor supplies, absence of joint products, absence of intermediate goods) we add the further assumption that the degree of monopoly is the same in each industry, average cost pricing would achieve the same allocation of resources as marginal cost pricing. The extent of the revisions required by internal economies therefore should not be exaggerated.

For trade models with internal economies incorporated, see Negishi [9] and [10].

[2] See, however, Probs. 8.1–8.3.

Note that this assumption removes any possibility of conflict between variable returns and marginal productivity factor pricing. The "adding-up problem" still has a solution since each factor is paid not the value of its marginal product to the *industry* but the value of its marginal product as seen by the individual *firm*—and the firm's production function is homogeneous of first degree in the firm's inputs. Finally, we assume

> (c) that all economies external to the firm are (i) internal to the industry of which the firm is a member, (ii) "output-" rather than "factor-generated,"[3] and (iii) "neutral," in the sense that at a given ratio of factor rentals the optimal factor ratio is independent of the industry's output.

The most general form of the individual firm's production function which possesses the above properties is

$$x = g(X) \cdot F(v_1, v_2) \qquad g(X) > 0 \quad \text{for} \quad X > 0$$

where x is the firm's output, X is the industry's output, v_1 and v_2 are the firm's inputs of capital and labor, respectively, and F is homogeneous of degree one in v_1 and v_2 ($dg/dX > 0$ for external economies, $dg/dX < 0$ for diseconomies). The industry's production may be written as

$$X = g(X)F(K, L) \tag{8.1}$$

This reduces to the special form of Eqs. (1.1) when $g \equiv 1$, that is, when external effects are absent. Differentiating Eq. (8.1) logarithmically we obtain

$$(1 - \omega)\hat{X} = \epsilon_K \hat{K} + \epsilon_L \hat{L} \tag{8.2}$$

where $\omega \equiv X(dg/dX)/g$ is the partial elasticity of the individual firm's output with respect to the industry's output,[4] ϵ_i is the partial elasticity of the firm's output with respect to the ith input, and the "hat" is an operator which tells us that the relative change of the variable is to be considered ($\hat{X} = dX/X$, etc.) From the homogeneity of F we infer that $\epsilon_K + \epsilon_L = 1$ and, therefore, that when $\hat{K} = \hat{L}$ Eq. (8.2) reduces to

$$\hat{X} = \frac{\hat{K}}{1 - \omega} = \frac{\hat{L}}{1 - \omega} \tag{8.3}$$

---

[3] The economies are output-generated if the output or inputs of one firm are dependent on the output of a second firm. The economies are factor-generated if the output or inputs of one firm are dependent on one or more inputs of a second firm. In the special case in which all factors generate economies with equal severity and incidence the distinction collapses. For more details, see Kemp [15].

[4] The symbol ω has been used in earlier chapters to denote the ratio of factor rewards.

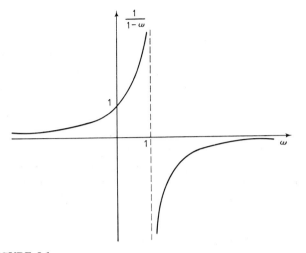

FIGURE 8.1

$1/(1 - \omega)$ is therefore a measure of the type of scale returns prevailing in the industry: If $\omega < 0$ the industry displays decreasing returns to scale, if $0 < \omega < 1$ the industry exhibits increasing returns, and in the uninteresting case in which $\omega \geq 1$ we are in the land of Cockaigne.

It follows from assumptions (a)–(c) that the community will operate on the production frontier and that in equilibrium the ratio of the two marginal private costs will be equal to the ratio of the two marginal social costs; private self-interest will therefore ensure that, as long as something of each commodity is produced, the marginal social rate of substitution will be the same in production as in consumption. In partial equilibrium terms, equilibrium may be illustrated by Fig. 8.2. $D_i D_i$ is the demand curve for the ith commodity; $C_i C_i$ is the firm's marginal (and average) cost curve, drawn on the assumption that the industry's output is constant at the equilibrium level

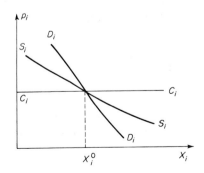

FIGURE 8.2

X_i^0; and S_iS_i is the industry's "supply curve," that is, the locus of minimum unit costs (for the firm and for the industry) for given outputs. In a static world it is reasonable to suppose that each firm has perfect knowledge, in particular that it is aware of the presence and magnitude of the external economies. It may be wondered, then, why a single firm does not expand, "internalize" the economies and ensure decreasing marginal and average costs, and drive out all competitors. The answer is that a single firm may indeed do this. However, the "public good" nature of the externalities implies that any potential newcomer, whatever the projected scale of output, could produce at the same unit costs as the sole producer. Freedom of entry therefore ensures that even a single producer behaves competitively, equating price with marginal (and average) cost. The number of firms and the scale of output of individual firms is indeterminate; but it is also irrelevant.

1. THEORETICAL BACKGROUND

We shall in due course review most of the propositions established in earlier chapters. First, however, we must set out the basic equations appropriate to an economy with variable returns to scale. These have their analogues in Chap. 1 and give expression to the assumptions of full employment, perfect competition, and profit maximization. Until further notice it is assumed that specialization is incomplete.

Let a_{ij} again stand for the amount of the ith factor used in the production of a unit of the jth commodity, where $i = K, L$ and $j = 1, 2$. Then the requirement that both factors be fully employed may be expressed as

$$\begin{pmatrix} a_{K1} & a_{K2} \\ a_{L1} & a_{L2} \end{pmatrix} \begin{pmatrix} X_1 \\ X_2 \end{pmatrix} = \begin{pmatrix} K \\ L \end{pmatrix} \tag{8.4}$$

From the assumptions of perfect competition, free entry, and incomplete specialization it follows that in each industry price equals average cost

$$\begin{pmatrix} a_{K1} & a_{L1} \\ a_{K2} & a_{L2} \end{pmatrix} \begin{pmatrix} r \\ w \end{pmatrix} = \begin{pmatrix} p_1 \\ p_2 \end{pmatrix} \tag{8.5}$$

It remains to give expression to the assumption of profit maximization. The production function of a typical producer in the ith industry may be written, with obvious adaptations of notation, as

$$x_i = g^i(X_i) \cdot F^i(v_{1i}, v_{2i})$$

or, drawing on the first degree homogeneity of F^i, as

$$1 = g^i(X_i) \cdot F^i(a_{Ki}, a_{Li}) \qquad i = 1, 2 \qquad (8.6)$$

Let $\chi^i(X_i)$ be the set $\{a_{Ki}, a_{Li}\}$ each member of which satisfies Eq. (8.6):

$$\chi^i(X_i) \equiv \{a_{Ki}, a_{Li} \mid g^i(X_i) \cdot F^i(a_{Ki}, a_{Li}) = 1\}$$

Then the problem facing the individual firm is that of minimizing its unit costs:

$$\min_{(a_{Ki}, a_{Li}) \in \chi^i(X_i)} (ra_{Ki} + wa_{Li})$$

As a necessary condition of cost minimization we have

$$rda_{Ki} + wda_{Li} = 0 \qquad i = 1, 2 \qquad (8.7)$$

where it is understood that the two increments are consistent with Eq. (8.6).

That completes our specification of the economy. It will prove convenient, however, to place the key equations on a common footing by rewriting Eqs. (8.4) and (8.5) in terms of relative changes of the variables. Differentiating Eqs. (8.4) and rearranging slightly, we obtain

$$\begin{pmatrix} \lambda_{K1} & \lambda_{K2} \\ \lambda_{L1} & \lambda_{L2} \end{pmatrix} \begin{pmatrix} \hat{X}_1 \\ \hat{X}_2 \end{pmatrix} = \begin{pmatrix} \hat{K} \\ \hat{L} \end{pmatrix} - \begin{pmatrix} \lambda_{K1}\hat{a}_{K1} + \lambda_{K2}\hat{a}_{K2} \\ \lambda_{L1}\hat{a}_{L1} + \lambda_{L2}\hat{a}_{L2} \end{pmatrix} \qquad (8.8)$$

where λ_{ij} is again the proportion of the community's endowment of the ith factor employed by the jth industry (so that $\lambda_{i1} + \lambda_{i2} = 1$). In similar fashion we obtain from Eqs. (8.5)

$$\begin{pmatrix} \theta_{K1} & \theta_{L1} \\ \theta_{K2} & \theta_{L2} \end{pmatrix} \begin{pmatrix} \hat{r} \\ \hat{w} \end{pmatrix} = \begin{pmatrix} \hat{p}_1 \\ \hat{p}_2 \end{pmatrix} - \begin{pmatrix} \theta_{K1}\hat{a}_{K1} + \theta_{L1}\hat{a}_{L1} \\ \theta_{K2}\hat{a}_{K2} + \theta_{L2}\hat{a}_{L2} \end{pmatrix} \qquad (8.9)$$

where θ_{ij} is again the share of the ith factor in the costs of jth industry (so that $\theta_{Kj} + \theta_{Lj} = 1$). It is easily verified that

$$\det(\lambda_{ij}) \equiv |\lambda| = \lambda_{K1} - \lambda_{L1}$$
$$\det(\theta_{ij}) \equiv |\theta| = \theta_{K1} - \theta_{K2} \qquad (8.10)$$

and that $|\lambda|$ and $|\theta|$ are both positive or both negative according as production of the first or second commodity is relatively capital-intensive.

Our next step is to eliminate the $\hat{a}_{ij}$ from Eqs. (8.8) and (8.9) with the aid of Eqs. (8.7). To convert Eqs. (8.7) into the required "hatted" form is a trivial matter. We must remember, however, that the relative changes in the variables are constrained to satisfy Eqs. (8.6), with constant industrial outputs X_i. They are therefore based on *partial* differentials and will be distinguished by a double "hat":

$$\theta_{K1}\hat{\hat{a}}_{K1} + \theta_{L1}\hat{\hat{a}}_{L1} = 0$$
$$\theta_{K2}\hat{\hat{a}}_{K2} + \theta_{L2}\hat{\hat{a}}_{L2} = 0 \tag{8.11}$$

We next introduce, as a convenient short-hand, the elasticity of substitution σ_i for the ith production function. The two elasticities are defined by

$$\hat{\hat{a}}_{K1} - \hat{\hat{a}}_{L1} = -\sigma_1(\hat{r} - \hat{w})$$
$$\hat{\hat{a}}_{K2} - \hat{\hat{a}}_{L2} = -\sigma_2(\hat{r} - \hat{w}) \tag{8.12}$$

and are assumed to be positive. Again the double "hat" is appropriate since the two elasticities are defined in relation to movements around given industrial isoquants. Solving Eqs. (8.11) and (8.12) for the $\hat{\hat{a}}_{ij}$'s we obtain

$$\hat{\hat{a}}_{K1} = -\theta_{L1}\sigma_1(\hat{r} - \hat{w})$$
$$\hat{\hat{a}}_{L1} = \theta_{K1}\sigma_1(\hat{r} - \hat{w})$$
$$\hat{\hat{a}}_{K2} = -\theta_{L2}\sigma_2(\hat{r} - \hat{w})$$
$$\hat{\hat{a}}_{L2} = \theta_{K2}\sigma_2(\hat{r} - \hat{w}) \tag{8.13}$$

Finally, we convert the $\hat{\hat{a}}_{ij}$'s into $\hat{a}_{ij}$'s by relaxing the assumption that the X_i's are constant and adding to Eqs. (8.13) terms which allow for the additional effects of changing X_i. From Eq. (8.3) we infer that $-\omega$ is the elasticity of a_{ij} with respect to changes in X_j. Hence our revised equations are

$$\hat{a}_{K1} = \hat{\hat{a}}_{K1} - \omega\hat{X}_1 = -\theta_{L1}\sigma_1(\hat{r} - \hat{w}) - \omega\hat{X}_1$$
$$\hat{a}_{L1} = \hat{\hat{a}}_{L1} - \omega\hat{X}_1 = \theta_{K1}\sigma_1(\hat{r} - \hat{w}) - \omega\hat{X}_1$$
$$\hat{a}_{K2} = \hat{\hat{a}}_{K2} - \omega\hat{X}_2 = -\theta_{L2}\sigma_2(\hat{r} - \hat{w}) - \omega\hat{X}_2$$
$$\hat{a}_{L2} = \hat{\hat{a}}_{L2} - \omega\hat{X}_2 = \theta_{K2}\sigma_2(\hat{r} - \hat{w}) - \omega\hat{X}_2 \tag{8.14}$$

Substituting from Eqs. (8.14) into Eqs. (8.8) and (8.9), we obtain

$$(1 - \omega)\lambda\begin{pmatrix}\hat{X}_1 \\ \hat{X}_2\end{pmatrix} = \begin{pmatrix}\hat{K} \\ \hat{L}\end{pmatrix} + (\hat{r} - \hat{w})\begin{pmatrix}\delta_K \\ -\delta_L\end{pmatrix} \tag{8.15}$$

and

$$\theta \begin{pmatrix} \hat{r} \\ \hat{w} \end{pmatrix} = \begin{pmatrix} \hat{p}_1 \\ \hat{p}_2 \end{pmatrix} + \omega \begin{pmatrix} \hat{X}_1 \\ \hat{X}_2 \end{pmatrix} \tag{8.16}$$

where $\delta_K \equiv \lambda_{K1}\theta_{L1}\sigma_1 + \lambda_{K2}\theta_{L2}\sigma_2$, $\delta_L \equiv \lambda_{L1}\theta_{K1}\sigma_1 + \lambda_{L2}\theta_{K2}\sigma_2$, $\lambda \equiv (\lambda_{ij})$, and $\theta \equiv (\theta_{ij})$.

Equations (8.15) and (8.16) will form the basis of all further manipulations. The four equations contain eight variables. The best we can hope for, therefore, is that we can solve for four variables in terms of the remaining four. This will suffice however to allow us to examine the sensitivity to changes in assumptions of two of the theorems established in earlier chapters—the Stolper–Samuelson Theorem and the Samuelson–Rybczynski Theorem.

2. THE STOLPER–SAMUELSON THEOREM

The Stolper–Samuelson Theorem, it will be recalled, tells us that under conditions of constant returns to scale a small increase in the price of any commodity gives rise to an increase in the real reward of whichever factor is used relatively intensively in the production of that commodity, and to a decrease in the real reward of the other factor. Is the conclusion still valid under conditions of variable returns?

The remarkable thing about the Stolper–Samuelson Theorem is the total absence of any reference to factor endowments and commodity outputs. The theorem is valid whatever the behavior of endowments and outputs, provided only that the country remains incompletely specialized in production. When the assumption of constant returns is abandoned, however, all this changes; it becomes vital that the background behavior of endowments and outputs be spelled out in detail. In what follows we shall distinguish two ideal cases: (a) that in which outputs are held constant, with endowments left free to assume equilibrating values; and (b) that in which endowments are controlled, with outputs free to vary.

Case (a): outputs constant. In this case scale effects are suppressed and hence can play no part in the relationship between commodity prices and factor rewards. One would expect, therefore, that the Stolper–Samuelson Theorem would carry over without change. That this is indeed the case can be checked by substituting $\hat{X}_1 = \hat{X}_2 = 0$ in Eqs. (8.16). Then

$$\theta \begin{pmatrix} \hat{r} \\ \hat{w} \end{pmatrix} = \begin{pmatrix} \hat{p}_1 \\ \hat{p}_2 \end{pmatrix} \tag{8.17}$$

as in the case of constant returns.

Case (b): endowments constant. In this case outputs vary in response to the price change, hence scale effects must be allowed for. Solving Eqs. (8.15) for $\hat{X}_1$ and $\hat{X}_2$, and substituting into Eqs. (8.16), we obtain

$$\theta' \begin{pmatrix} \hat{r} \\ \hat{w} \end{pmatrix} = \begin{pmatrix} \hat{p}_1 \\ \hat{p}_2 \end{pmatrix} \tag{8.18}$$

where

$$\theta' \equiv \theta + \frac{\omega}{1-\omega} \cdot \frac{1}{|\lambda|} \begin{pmatrix} -(\lambda_{L2}\delta_K + \lambda_{K2}\delta_L) & \lambda_{L2}\delta_K + \lambda_{K2}\delta_L \\ \lambda_{L1}\delta_K + \lambda_{K1}\delta_L & -(\lambda_{L1}\delta_K + \lambda_{K1}\delta_L) \end{pmatrix}$$

Suppose that the first commodity is relatively capital-intensive, so that $|\theta|$ and $|\lambda|$ are positive. Then the Stolper–Samuelson conclusions carry over if and only if

$$\theta' > 0 \quad \text{and} \quad |\theta'| > 0 \tag{8.19a}$$

$$or$$

$$\theta' < 0 \quad \text{and} \quad |\theta'| < 0 \tag{8.19b}$$

Inspection of θ', however, reveals that it is impossible for all elements of θ' to be negative; at most two elements can be negative. It follows that the Stolper–Samuelson conclusions carry over if and only if conditions (8.19a) are satisfied. Suppose next that the first commodity is relatively *labor-intensive*, so that $|\theta|$ and $|\lambda|$ are negative. Then by reasoning similar to that just used it can be shown that the Stolper–Samuelson conclusions carry over if and only if

$$\theta' > 0 \quad \text{and} \quad |\theta'| < 0$$

Consolidating these conclusions, we may say that *the Stolper–Samuelson conclusions carry over if and only if*

$$\theta' > 0 \quad and \quad |\theta|, |\theta'| \quad are\ of\ similar\ sign \tag{8.20}$$

If

$$\theta' > 0 \quad and \quad |\theta|, |\theta'| \quad are\ of\ opposite\ sign \tag{8.21}$$

the obverse of the Stolper–Samuelson conclusions is true: An increase in the price of any commodity results in a decline in the real reward of the factor used relatively intensively in the production of that commodity and in an increase in the real reward of the other factor.

Suppose that θ' is positive. Then the additional requirement that $|\theta|$ and $|\theta'|$ be of similar sign can be clarified slightly by noting that

$$|\theta'| = \alpha |\theta| \tag{8.22}$$

where

$$\alpha \equiv 1 - \frac{\omega}{1 - \omega} \cdot \frac{\delta_K + \delta_L}{|\theta| \cdot |\lambda|} \tag{8.23}$$

It follows that $|\theta|$ and $|\theta'|$ are of similar sign if and only if α is positive, that is, if and only if

$$\omega < \frac{|\theta| \cdot |\lambda|}{|\theta| \cdot |\lambda| + \delta_K + \delta_L} \tag{8.24}$$

If we add the assumption that the elasticity of substitution is the same in both industries, so that $\sigma_1 = \sigma_2 = \sigma$, this condition reduces to

$$\omega < \frac{|\theta| \cdot |\lambda|}{|\theta| \cdot |\lambda| + \sigma(1 - |\theta| \cdot |\lambda|)} \tag{8.24a}$$

In the special Cobb–Douglas case, when $\sigma = 1$, the condition is simply

$$\omega < |\theta| \cdot |\lambda| > 0 \tag{8.24b}$$

Figures 8.3(a) and 8.3(b) illustrate cases in which conditions (8.20) and (8.21), respectively, are satisfied, that is, cases in which the Stolper–Samuelson and obverse Stolper–Samuelson conclusions are valid. The initial unit isoquants of the two industries are labelled I_1 and I_2, with the second commodity assumed to be relatively capital-intensive. Units of quantity are chosen so that initially the two commodity prices are equal. The initial equilibrium is represented by points P_1 and P_2, at which the respective

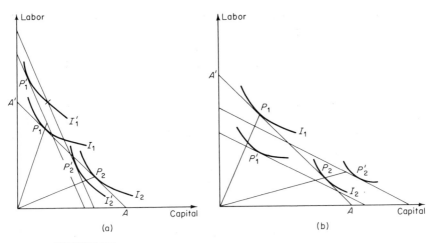

(a)　　　　　　　　(b)

FIGURE 8.3

isoquants are tangential to the common isocost line AA'. This equilibrium is disturbed by an increase in the price of the second commodity. If condition (8.20) is satisfied, as in Figure 8.3(a), the change in price gives rise to an increase in the rental:wage rate ratio and, therefore, to an increase in the labor:capital ratio in both industries. To maintain the full employment of both factors it is therefore necessary for the second industry to expand and for the first to contract. As a result of these output changes the two unit isoquants shift, the first out from the origin, the second towards the origin. The new equilibrium is indicated by P_1' and P_2'. In the obverse Stolper–Samuelson case, on the other hand, with condition (8.21) satisfied, the rental:wage rate ratio falls, the labor:capital ratio falls in both industries, the first industry expands while the second contracts, the first unit isoquant shifts in and the second moves out. The new equilibrium is indicated by P_1' and P_2' in Figure 8.3(b).

3. THE SAMUELSON–RYBCZYNSKI THEOREM

The Samuelson–Rybczynski Theorem, proved in Chap. 1, Sec. 2 under conditions of constant returns to scale, tells us that if product prices, and therefore factor rewards, are constant, an increase in the community's endowment of any factor will give rise to an increase in the output of whichever industry uses the augmented factor relatively intensively and to a decline in the output of the other industry. The theorem was recognized to be dual to the Stolper–Samuelson Theorem. Is the conclusion still valid under conditions of variable returns?

When we abandon the assumption of constant returns we find ourselves in a dilemma. For it is no longer possible simultaneously to vary the community's factor endowment and to hold steady both the ratio of product prices and the ratio of factor rewards; at least one ratio must be set free. As in our discussion of the Stolper–Samuelson Theorem, therefore, we shall distinguish two cases, depending on whether product prices or factor rewards are controlled.˙

Case (a): factor rewards constant. If the ratio of factor rewards is controlled, and the ratio of product prices allowed to find its equilibrium level, the effect on outputs of a change in the factor endowment can be inferred directly from Eqs. (8.15):

$$(1 - \omega)\lambda\left(\frac{\hat{X}_1}{\hat{X}_2}\right) = \left(\frac{\hat{K}}{\hat{L}}\right) \tag{8.25}$$

Except for the harmless multiplicative factor $(1 - \omega)$, these equations are precisely those which emerge under conditions of constant returns. It follows that the Samuelson–Rybczynski conclusions carry over without change.

Case (b): product prices constant. When product prices are controlled, with factor rewards free to vary, matters are not so simple. Solving Eqs. (8.16) for $(\hat{r} - \hat{w})$, substituting into Eqs. (8.15), and setting $\hat{p}_1 - \hat{p}_2 = 0$, we obtain

$$\lambda'\begin{pmatrix}\hat{X}_1 \\ \hat{X}_2\end{pmatrix} = \begin{pmatrix}\hat{K} \\ \hat{L}\end{pmatrix} \qquad (8.26)$$

where $\lambda' \equiv (1 - \omega)\lambda + \dfrac{\omega}{|\theta|}\begin{pmatrix}-\delta_K & \delta_K \\ \delta_L & -\delta_L\end{pmatrix}$ and

$$|\lambda'| = \alpha(1 - \omega)^2 |\lambda| \qquad (8.27)$$

It follows that the Samuelson–Rybczynski conclusions follow if and only if

$$\lambda' > 0 \quad \text{and} \quad |\lambda'|, |\lambda| \text{ are of similar sign} \qquad (8.28a)$$

or

$$\lambda' < 0 \quad \text{and} \quad |\lambda'|, |\lambda| \text{ are of opposite sign} \qquad (8.28b)$$

Inspection of λ' reveals however that $\lambda' < 0$ is impossible. Hence *the Samuelson–Rybczynski conclusions carry over if and only if condition* (8.28a) *is satisfied. If*

$$\lambda' > 0 \quad \textit{and} \quad |\lambda'|, |\lambda| \textit{ are of opposite sign} \qquad (8.29)$$

the obverse Samuelson–Rybczynski conclusions hold: An increase in the endowment of any factor results in a decline in the output of whichever industry uses that factor relatively intensively and in an increase in the output of the other industry.

Suppose that $\lambda' > 0$. Then the Samuelson–Rybczynski conclusions carry over if and only if α is positive. Recalling the conclusions of Sec. 2, we conclude that *if θ' and λ' are positive* either the Stolper–Samuelson and Samuelson–Rybczynski conclusions carry over or the obverse Stolper–Samuelson and Samuelson–Rybczynski conclusions hold, depending respectively on whether α is positive or negative. Under the italicized assumptions, therefore, the Stolper–Samuelson–Rybczynski duality persists. The assumptions, however, seem quite restrictive.

Figures 8.4(a) and 8.4(b) illustrate cases in which conditions (8.28a) and (8.29), respectively, are satisfied, that is, cases in which the Samuelson–Rybczynski and obverse Samuelson–Rybczynski conclusions are valid. The figures incorporate the same assumptions about relative factor intensities as Figs. 8.3. If condition (8.28a) is satisfied, as in Figure 8.4(a), an increase in the capital endowment gives rise to an increase in the output of the second (relatively capital-intensive) commodity, a decline in the output of the first

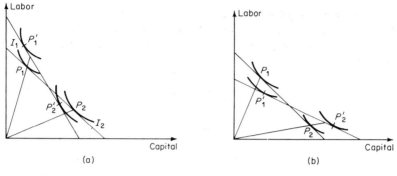

FIGURE 8.4

commodity, an increase in the rate of real rentals, and a decline in the rate of real wages. If condition (8.29) is satisfied, as in Fig. 8.4(b), all changes undergo a reversal of sign.

4. THE RELATION BETWEEN EQUILIBRIUM OUTPUTS AND COMMODITY PRICES

It is well known that, if returns to scale are constant and if market distortions are absent, the equilibrium output of a commodity responds positively (strictly, non-negatively) to an increase in its relative price. It is less well known that if each industry displays increasing returns, however mild, then, at least in a neighborhood of each axis, the response of equilibrium output must be perverse.[5]

To prove this, we solve Eqs. (8.16) for $(\hat{r} - \hat{w})$ and substitute in Eqs. (8.15); then set $\hat{K} = \hat{L} = 0$ and solve for $(\hat{X}_1 - \hat{X}_2)$:

$$\hat{X}_1 - \hat{X}_2 = \frac{\delta_K + \delta_L}{\alpha(1 - \omega)\,|\lambda| \cdot |\theta|}(\hat{p}_1 - \hat{p}_2) \qquad (8.30)$$

Thus output responds in the normal way to changes in price if and only if α is positive. From the definition (8.23), however, for ω positive α goes to

[5] In fact a much stronger proposition can be proved: If an industry displays increasing returns, however mild, then in a neighborhood of the other industry's axis the response of output to a change in commodity prices must be perverse *whatever the nature of returns in the other industry.* (For more details, see Prob. 8.3.)

Certain related (but not equivalent) propositions can be proved concerning the shape of the locus of production possibilities under conditions of increasing returns. It is widely believed that the locus becomes uniformly convex to the origin if returns to scale are sufficiently strongly increasing but remains uniformly concave if returns are only weakly increasing. In fact neither belief is generally valid. It can be shown, for example, that if an industry displays increasing returns, however mild, then in a neighborhood of the other industry's axis the locus must be convex *whatever the nature of returns in the other industry.* For proofs of this and other propositions, see Herberg [3] and Herberg and Kemp [4].

minus infinity as X_i goes to zero $(i = 1, 2)$; in fact

$$\lim_{X_i \to 0} \frac{d \ln (X_2/X_1)}{d \ln (p_2/p_1)} = -\frac{1}{\omega} \tag{8.31}$$

Finally, we note the intimate connection between the output-price relationship and the possibility of generalizing the Samuelson–Rybczynski Theorem. From the results established in the present section and in Section 3 it follows that, if when product prices are controlled the Samuelson-Rybczynski conclusions carry over, outputs must respond normally to small changes in product prices. The converse, however, is not true: It is quite possible for outputs to respond normally to price changes and the Samuelson–Rybczynski conclusions to be false.

5. THE OFFER CURVE

We turn now to the derivation of the offer curve of a country endowed with a variable-returns technology. In this section, therefore, we abandon our assumption that specialization is incomplete.

Given the simplifying assumptions (a)–(c) of the introduction, decreasing returns pose no new problems. We therefore concentrate on increasing returns, assumed for the balance of the chapter to be strong enough to reverse the convexity of the production frontier throughout its length.[6] Figure 8.5(a) depicts the production possibilities curve CC'. Any point on that curve represents a potential equilibrium of production. Thus if the

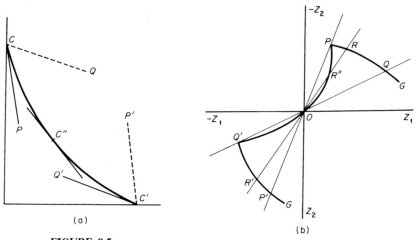

(a)

(b)

FIGURE 8.5

[6] But see Prob. 8.4.

international terms of trade could be represented by the tangent to CC' at C'', and if certain auxiliary conditions, to be explored presently, were satisfied, C'' would represent a production equilibrium.

Special interest attaches to the tangents to CC' at the end points, C and C'; and to the terms of trade corresponding to the slopes of those tangents. At the terms of trade CP, for example, production could well take place at C, implying that the second commodity is exported, the first imported; this possibility is represented also by point P in Fig. 8.5(b). But at those terms of trade, which are also depicted by the slope of $C'P'$, production could equally well take place at C', the opposite extreme of possibilities, implying that the first commodity is exported, the second imported; this possibility is represented also by point P' in Fig. 8.5(b). Thus at the terms of trade CP (or $C'P'$) there are two possible equilibrium offers; one for each commodity. The same is true of the terms of trade CQ (or $C'Q'$), as may be readily verified.

Suppose now that, beginning at CP (or $C'P'$), the terms of trade move in favor of the second commodity; suppose, in particular, that the new terms of trade can be represented by the tangent at C''. Evidently C and C' retain their eligibility as production equilibria; for at C the relative marginal cost of producing the second commodity is less than its relative price; and at C' the relative marginal cost of producing the *first* commodity is less than *its* relative price. But C'', also, represents a possible production equilibrium. And just as we have three possible production equilibria we have three possible trading equilibria or offers, represented by R, R', and R''. Two of the three equilibria involve complete specialization, and at least one lies in each of the first and third quadrants of Fig. 8.5(b).

Continuing in this way, we may trace out three segments of the offer curve GG: $P'Q'$, corresponding to complete specialization in the first commodity; PQ, corresponding to complete specialization in the second commodity; and $Q'OP$, corresponding to incomplete specialization. Note that along the segment $Q'OP$ any improvement of the terms of trade is associated with a *cut* in the equilibrium volume of exports (and in the equilibrium volume of production of the exported commodity).

There remain for consideration terms of trade lying outside the range defined by the slopes of CP and CQ. To each such terms of trade there will correspond a single offer and complete specialization. If the terms of trade become even more unfavorable to the first commodity than CQ, it will no longer pay to produce that commodity; if, on the other hand, the terms of trade become even more unfavorable to the second commodity than CP, it will no longer pay to produce *that* commodity. This is all sufficiently clear from Fig. 8.5.

In summary, then, at any given terms of trade there may be one, two, or three possible equilibria; if there are just one or two, they involve complete specialization; finally, in any equilibrium involving incomplete specialization, both output and offer respond perversely to small changes in the terms of trade.

6. INTERNATIONAL EQUILIBRIUM

If increasing returns prevail in the rest of the world also—and are of sufficient strength to ensure uniformly decreasing marginal social opportunity costs—the possible international equilibria will be defined by the intersection of two similarly-shaped offer curves. The intersections (other than at the origin) may be multiple or unique. Figures 8.6(a)–(c) illustrate the possibility of three, two, and one intersection, respectively. The pretrade terms of trade in each country may be identified as the slope of the appropriate offer curve at the origin. A little work with pencil and paper will reveal that, in contrast to the outcome under constant returns, the equilibrium terms of trade may well lie outside the limits defined by the two autarkic price ratios.

Consider the three trading possibilities displayed by Fig. 8.6(a): At point A_1 both countries are completely specialized; at A_2 neither country is completely specialized; and at A_3 one country is completely specialized, the other incompletely. These exhaust the cases that are likely to emerge; but for completeness we must examine the theoretically interesting case in which the pretrade price ratios are equal.[7] The offer curves in that case are tangential at the origin. Now if returns to scale had been constant, it would have been a valid inference from tangency that no trade would take place. That trade *can* take place when returns are increasing is clear from Fig. 8.6(b); indeed, in a dynamic world it is *inevitable* that trade will take place, for, as we shall see presently, the tangency equilibrium is dynamically unstable.

7. THE STABILITY OF INTERNATIONAL EQUILIBRIUM

So far we have directed our attention to the *possibility* of equilibrium and have carefully skirted all questions of stability. Yet the analysis of stability conditions involves some of the nicest problems associated with increasing returns.

What are reasonable dynamic postulates under conditions of increasing returns to scale? We know too much to expect a unique answer (see Chap. 3). Let us begin, therefore, with a sweeping assumption which will serve to radically narrow the possibilities: We shall suppose that whenever a country is in disequilibrium (that is, off its offer curve), it is because producers (not consumers) are in disequilibrium. Even then, one must be prepared to give at least two answers to the question, for what is reasonable depends on

---

[7] A sufficient, but by no means necessary, condition for the emergence of this case is that the trading countries have identical factor endowments and preferences.

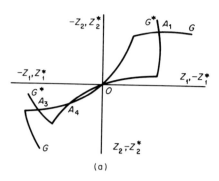

(a)

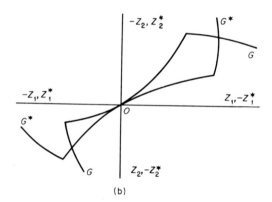

(b)

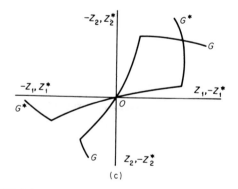

(c)

FIGURE 8.6

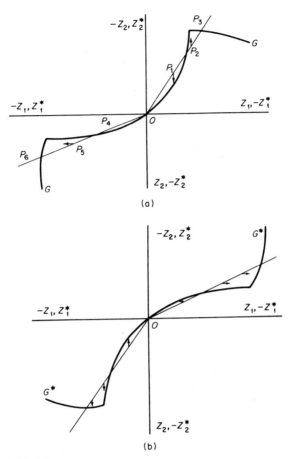

FIGURE 8.7

whether or not the country is completely specialized. Imagine that trade takes place at P_1, with the home country exporting the second commodity at terms of trade represented by the slope of OP_1 [Fig. 8.7(a)]. The home country is, of course, incompletely specialized. Since the country is producing and exporting less than the equilibrium quantities at those terms of trade, and since the country is producing under conditions of increasing returns to scale, the supply price of that volume of exports must exceed the terms of trade; hence the production and export of the second commodity must *contract*. If, on the other hand, the trading point were P_2, export would exceed the equilibrium quantity and the supply price would fall short of the terms of trade; hence the production and export of the second commodity would *expand*. The direction of the arrow emanating from P_5 is obtained by a similar line of reasoning.

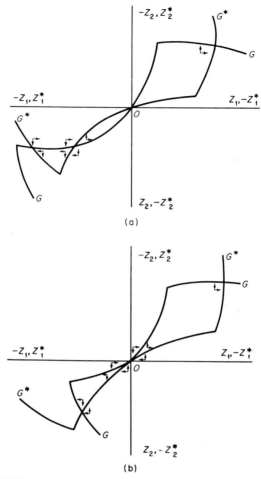

FIGURE 8.8

Trade could take place at P_3 and P_6 only if the public were temporarily consuming more of the export good than in the long run they would wish, a possibility which has been ruled out by assumption.

Figure 8.7(b) contains a similar arrow scheme for the rest of the world.

Applying the arrow schemes of Fig. 8.7(b) to Fig. 8.6(a), we obtain Fig. 8.8(a), from which it emerges that the three equilibria are alternatively stable and unstable. Both stable equilibria involve complete specialization by at least one country. Indeed it may be stated as a general rule that, given our dynamic assumptions, incomplete specialization by both countries is inconsistent with stability. The common sense of this rule is easy to uncover. Suppose that in an initial equilibrium both countries produce something of both commodities. Then any slight displacement of production from the equilibrium quantities will be cumulative. Whichever country gets a head start on the other will reap the cost advantages of greater production, and lower costs will encourage greater production with even lower costs, etc. Eventually the low cost country will either drive its competitor out of production or will itself become completely specialized.[8]

Similarly, by applying the arrow schemes of Fig. 8.7 to Fig. 8.6(b), we obtain Fig. 8.8(b), from which it emerges that the no-trade, freetrade equilibrium is unstable.

8. VARIABLE RETURNS AND THE EQUALIZATION OF RELATIVE FACTOR REWARDS

Chapter 3 contains a list of conditions which, in the simple two-commodities, two-factors, and two-countries case, are sufficient to ensure the international equalization of factor rewards. Prominent on that list is the condition of constant returns to scale. We now very briefly explore the possibility of factor reward equalization under conditions of variable returns. More specifically, we retain all the assumptions of earlier sections of the present chapter and add the additional assumption that production functions are the same in both countries.

It will be evident at once that under these assumptions the most that can be expected is *relative* factor reward equalization. For if absolute real factor rentals were the same in both countries not only would the capital:labor ratio for any particular industry be the same in each country,[9] but the scales of output would be the same also. Taken together, these two circumstances imply that the two countries possess identical factor endowments. In what follows we put aside this uninteresting special case and focus on the possibility of equalization of relative factor rewards.

It will prove convenient to reintroduce the curve relating the ratio of product prices to the ratio of factor rewards. The *price locus*, it will be recalled, was introduced in Chap. 1. It was shown there that its slope depends on the relative factor ratios in the two industries: The slope is positive if $k_1 > k_2$, negative if $k_1 < k_2$. As we have seen in Sec. 2, however, matters are very much more complicated when returns to scale are variable. If and only if condition (8.20) is satisfied does the old relationship carry over. In general the locus will not be monotonic but will look like the heavy curve of Fig. 8.9.

Under conditions of constant returns the position and shape of the price locus are independent of the community's factor endowment, at least in the

[8] The conclusions of this paragraph depend crucially on the assumption that both production frontiers are convex to the origin. If one country's production frontier (and therefore the associated offer curve) has normal shape, with $\omega \leq 0$, incomplete specialization by that country is quite compatible with international stability.

[9] This follows from the assumed neutrality of the external effects.

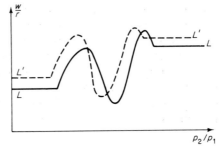

FIGURE 8.9

commodity price range consistent with incomplete specialization. Under conditions of variable returns this is no longer true; the locus must be redrawn for each specific relative factor endowment. (The only type of change in factor endowment which does not disturb the locus is one involving equiproportionate changes in both factors.) An increase in the capital endowment, for example, will require the replacement of LL by $L'L'$.

Consider two countries with price loci LL and $L'L'$. Relative factor reward equalization is *possible* if and only if the two loci intersect. To determine whether or not they intersect requires much more information than we have so far assumed. However it seems not worth exploring possible sufficiency conditions.[10] For even if an intersection is assured, relative factor reward equalization will be realized if and only if the prevailing world price ratio corresponds to a point of intersection. The probability that consumer preferences will dictate the establishment of one of the critical price ratios must be small indeed.

While even relative factor rental equalization must be considered a remote contingency, there remains the possibility that trade will promote more nearly equal relative factor rentals. That even this weaker possibility is uncertain is evident from Fig. 8.9. The reader will have no difficulty in constructing examples in which trade produces a *divergence* of relative rewards.

9. OTHER CASES BRIEFLY CONSIDERED

In the foregoing sections of this chapter our attention has been confined to external economies which preserve equality between the ratio of marginal private costs and the ratio of marginal social costs, and, furthermore, preserve the equality between the community's marginal rates of substitution, the first commodity for the second, in consumption and production. We now briefly consider other possibilities.

[10] In the first edition of this book I yielded to temptation, with unhappy results. See the first edition, pp. 122–27. The reader who wishes to pursue the matter further is referred also to Laing [13].

Economies with incidence external to the firm may be generated by a particular factor *input*, or by a particular *output;* their incidence may be external to the industry which generates them, or internal to it; and severity of the economies may vary from industry to industry and from factor to factor.[11] It would be a waste of time to attempt an analysis of all possibilities. Three will suffice: (a) Economies generated by the output of a single industry, say the first; (b) economies generated by a single input, with equal severity in each industry; and (c) economies generated by a single factor in a single industry, say the first. The incidence of the economies is, in each case, unimportant.[12] It is assumed, however, that the economies are sufficiently severe to render the production possibilities curve uniformly convex to the origin.

In case (*a*) the marginal rate of factor substitution is the same in both industries, so that the community must be operating on its production possibilities curve. But in the first industry marginal private cost exceeds marginal social cost. It follows that both the minimum p at which the country might completely specialize in the production of the second commodity, and the maximum p at which the country might completely specialize in the production of the first, will be *smaller* than the slopes of the production possibilities curve at its upper and lower extremities, respectively.[13] In

[11] For details, see Kemp [15].

[12] The justification of this assertion is distributed over the next three footnotes.

[13] These assertions are easily verified. If the output of the first commodity generates economies with incidence in the second industry the production functions may be written as

$$X_1(L_1, K_1)$$

$$X_2(L_2, K_2, X_1)$$

and the marginal conditions of efficient production as

$$\frac{\partial X_1}{\partial L_1} \bigg/ \frac{\partial X_1}{\partial K_1} = \left(\frac{\partial X_2}{\partial L_2} - \frac{\partial X_2}{\partial X_1} \cdot \frac{\partial X_2}{\partial L_2} \right) \bigg/ \left(\frac{\partial X_2}{\partial K_1} - \frac{\partial X_2}{\partial X_1} \cdot \frac{\partial X_1}{\partial K_1} \right)$$

Evidently the right-hand side is equal to the left-hand side if

$$\frac{\partial X_1}{\partial L_1} \bigg/ \frac{\partial X_1}{\partial K_1} = \frac{\partial X_2}{\partial L_2} \bigg/ \frac{\partial X_2}{\partial K_2}$$

This condition is satisfied under competition; hence, under competition the economy operates on the production possibilities curve.

But the slope of the production possibilities curve, which is equal to minus the ratio of marginal *social* costs, is

$$\left(-\frac{\partial X_2}{\partial L_2} + \frac{\partial X_2}{\partial X_1} \cdot \frac{\partial X_1}{\partial L_1} \right) \bigg/ \frac{\partial X_1}{\partial L_1} = -\frac{\partial X_2}{\partial L_2} \bigg/ \frac{\partial X_1}{\partial L_1} \cdot \frac{\partial X_2}{\partial X_1}$$

$$= -\frac{1}{p} + \frac{\partial X_2}{\partial X_1}$$

Evidently this is not equal to $(-1/p)$, the ratio of marginal *private* costs.

terms of Fig. 8.5(b), the limiting terms of trade lines are rotated anticlockwise from the positions they would occupy if marginal social cost were equal to marginal private cost. It also follows that, at any given terms of trade, the equilibrium point of imperfectly specialized production (if it exists) will be closer to C' than if marginal social and marginal private cost were equal; in terms of Fig. 8.10(a) the production point will be at P_0, not P_1. Hence the offer of the first commodity will be greater, or the demand for the first commodity less, than if the two marginal costs were equal. We may conclude,

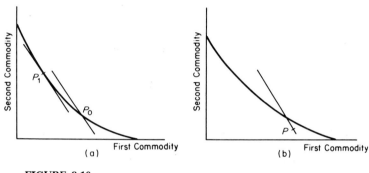

FIGURE 8.10

therefore, that in relation to its position when the marginal private and marginal social cost are equal, the offer curve will be rotated to the left. It may undergo some distortion in the process, but will retain the same general shape as that of GG in Fig. 8.5(b).

In case (b) not only is the marginal rate of factor substitution the same in each industry, ensuring that production is efficient, but the ratio of marginal social costs is equal to the ratio of marginal private costs.[14] The analysis of earlier sections applies immediately.

[14] In case (b), the production functions are

$$X_1(L_1, K_1, K_2)$$
$$X_2(L_2, K_2, K_1)$$

and the marginal conditions of efficient production may be written as

$$\left(\frac{\partial X_1}{\partial L_1} \Big/ \frac{\partial X_1}{\partial K_1}\right) - \left(\frac{\partial X_2}{\partial L_2} \Big/ \frac{\partial X_2}{\partial K_2}\right) = \left(\frac{\partial X_2}{\partial L_1} \Big/ \frac{\partial X_1}{\partial K_1}\right)\left[\left(\frac{\partial X_1}{\partial L_2} \Big/ \frac{\partial X_2}{\partial L_1}\right) - \left(\frac{\partial X_1}{\partial K_1} \Big/ \frac{\partial X_2}{\partial K_2}\right)\right]$$

From the assumption of competition we deduce that the left-hand side is zero; and, from the assumption that the economies fall with equal severity in each industry, the right-hand side is zero too.

In case (c), finally, not only is the ratio of marginal private cost not equal to the ratio of marginal social cost but production, if incompletely specialized, is inefficient.[15] In terms of Fig. 8.10(b), production may take place at P. But the general shape of the offer curve will be preserved.

Thus our conclusions concerning the shape of the offer curve under external economies and diseconomies of scale do not seem to depend on the type of externality which happens to prevail. Later, however, we shall have occasion to consider the welfare implications of the various types of external economy. Then we shall not get off so lightly (see Chap. 12).

The slope of the production possibilities curve is

$$-\left(\frac{\partial X_2}{\partial L_2} - \frac{\partial X_2}{\partial L_1}\right) \bigg/ \left(\frac{\partial X_1}{\partial L_1} - \frac{\partial X_1}{\partial L_2}\right)$$

But, under competition,

$$p\,\frac{\partial X_2}{\partial L_2} = \frac{\partial X_1}{\partial L_1}$$

and, from the assumption of equal severity of the economies,

$$p\,\frac{\partial X_2}{\partial L_1} = \frac{\partial X_1}{\partial L_2}$$

hence the slope of the production possibilities curve is equal to

$$-\frac{1}{p} = -\left(\frac{\partial X_2}{\partial L_2} \bigg/ \frac{\partial X_1}{\partial L_1}\right)$$

the ratio of marginal private costs.

[15] In case (c) the production functions are

$$X_1(L_1, K_1, L_2)$$
$$X_2(L_2, K_2)$$

and the marginal conditions of efficient production may be written as

$$\left(\frac{\partial X_1}{\partial L_1} \bigg/ \frac{\partial X_1}{\partial K_1}\right) - \left(\frac{\partial X_1}{\partial L_2} \bigg/ \frac{\partial X_1}{\partial K_1}\right) = \frac{\partial X_2}{\partial L_2} \bigg/ \frac{\partial X_2}{\partial K_2}$$

This condition will be satisfied under competition only if $(\partial X_1/\partial L_2) = 0$. But, by assumption, $(\partial X_1/\partial L_2) > 0$.

The slope of the production possibilities curve is

$$-\left(\frac{\partial X_1}{\partial L_1} \bigg/ \frac{\partial X_2}{\partial L_2}\right) + \left(\frac{\partial X_1}{\partial L_2} \bigg/ \frac{\partial X_2}{\partial L_2}\right)$$

This is equal to $-(1/p)$, the ratio of marginal private costs, only if $\partial X_1/\partial L_2 = 0$.

PROBLEMS

8.1 Suppose that in each industry the production function is homogeneous and of the form

$$X_i = L_i^{\theta_i} f_i(k_i)$$

Suppose that both factor endowments increase in the same proportion β. Show that

$$\hat{X}_i \equiv \frac{dX_i}{X_i} = \beta\theta_i$$

and that the proportionate increase in total output is β times a weighted average of the θ_i's:

$$\frac{dQ_1}{Q_1} = \beta\left(\frac{\theta_1 X_1 + p\theta_2 X_2}{X_1 + pX_2}\right) = \beta[\gamma\theta_1 + (1 - \gamma)\theta_2]$$

where $\gamma \equiv \dfrac{X_1}{(X_1 + pX_2)}$.

8.2 Suppose that returns are increasing at different rates in the two industries. Then we must distinguish ω_1 and ω_2, where $1/(1 - \omega_i)$ indicates the type of scale returns prevailing in the ith industry. Show that Eqs. (8.15) and (8.16) generalize to

$$\lambda\begin{pmatrix} (1 - \omega_1)\hat{X}_1 \\ (1 - \omega_2)\hat{X}_2 \end{pmatrix} = \begin{pmatrix} \hat{K} \\ \hat{L} \end{pmatrix} + (\hat{r} - \hat{w})\begin{pmatrix} \delta_K \\ -\delta_L \end{pmatrix}$$

and

$$\theta\begin{pmatrix} \hat{r} \\ \hat{w} \end{pmatrix} = \begin{pmatrix} \hat{p}_1 \\ \hat{p}_2 \end{pmatrix} + \begin{pmatrix} \omega_1\hat{X}_1 \\ \omega_2\hat{X}_2 \end{pmatrix}$$

respectively.

8.3 Building on the answer to Prob. 8.2, show that Eq. (8.30) generalizes to

$$\hat{X}_1 - \hat{X}_2 = \frac{\Gamma_1 + \alpha'\Gamma_2}{\omega_1(\Gamma_1 + \alpha'\Gamma_2) - \alpha'(1 - \omega_1)|\lambda| \cdot |\theta|}(\hat{p}_1 - \hat{p}_2)$$

where $\Gamma_1 \equiv \lambda_{L1}\delta_K + \lambda_{K1}\delta_L$, $\Gamma_2 \equiv \lambda_{L2}\delta_K + \lambda_{K2}\delta_L$ and

$$\alpha' \equiv [(\omega_1 - \omega_2)\Gamma_1 + (1 - \omega_2)|\lambda| \cdot |\theta|]/[(\omega_2 - \omega_1)\Gamma_2 + (1 - \omega_1)|\lambda| \cdot |\theta|].$$

Then prove the proposition stated in the first paragraph of footnote 5.

8.4 Throughout the discussion of offer curves in Sec. 5 it was assumed that the production frontier is uniformly convex to the origin. Suppose now that returns are only mildly increasing in each industry, so that the production frontier has a concave section separated by two convex sections. Deduce the shape of the offer curve.

8.5 Write down the formal dynamic system underlying Fig. 8.8.

8.6 Suppose that the home country's offer curve is of the shape illustrated by Fig. 8.5(b) and that the foreign offer curve is of the conventional shape associated with constant returns. Examine the multiplicity and stability of possible solutions.

8.7 What will be the effect of an import duty on the shape of the offer curve of Fig. 8.5(b)?

8.8 Does our earlier conclusion, that a tariff normally will give rise to an improvement of a country's terms of trade, hold when returns to scale are increasing?

8.9 Draw import demand and export supply curves for the case of strongly increasing returns.

8.10 Prove the proposition stated in footnote 8.

REFERENCES

The Stolper–Samuelson and Samuelson–Rybczynski Theorems

†[1] Jones, Ronald W., "Variable Returns to Scale in General Equilibrium Theory," *International Economic Review*, X (October 1968), 261–72.

[2] Minabe, Nobuo, "The Stolper–Samuelson Theorem under Conditions of Variable Returns to Scale," *Oxford Economic Papers*, XVIII, No. 2 (July 1966) 204–12.

The Production Possibilities Curve

†[3] Herberg, Horst, "On the Curvature of the Transformation Curve in Case of Homogeneous Production Functions," *Zeitschrift für die gesamte Staatswissenschaft*, to appear.

[4] Herberg, Horst and Murray C. Kemp, "Some Implications of Variable Returns to Scale," *Canadian Journal of Economics*, II, No. 3 (August 1969).

The Offer Curve and International Equilibrium

[5] Lerner, Abba P., "The Diagrammatic Representation of Cost Conditions in International Trade," *Economica*, XXXIV, No. 3 (August 1932), 346–56.

[6] Lerner, Abba P., "The Diagrammatic Representation of Demand Conditions in International Trade," *Economica*, New Series, I, No. 4 (August 1934), 306–13.

†[7] Matthews, R. C. O., "Reciprocal Demand and Increasing Returns," *Review of Economic Studies*, XVII, No. 2 (February 1950), 149–58.

[8] Meade, J. E., *A Geometry of International Trade*, Chap. V. London: George Allen & Unwin Ltd., 1952.

[9] Negishi, Takashi, "International Trade between Similar Countries with Factor Mobility," unpublished.

[10] Negishi Takashi, "Increasing Returns, Factor Market Distortions and Trade," unpublished.

[11] Tinbergen, J., *International Economic Cooperation*, Appendix 1, Amsterdam: Elsevier, 1945.

[12] Tinbergen, J., *International Economic Integration*, Appendix II. Amsterdam: Elsevier, 1954.

The Equalization of Relative Factor Rewards

[13] Laing, N. F., "Factor Price Equalization in International Trade and Returns to Scale," *Economic Record*, XXXVII, No. 3 (September 1961), 339–51.

Technical Equipment

[14] Adams, Robert W. and John T. Wheeler, "External Economies and the Supply Curve," *Review of Economic Studies*, XX, No. 1 (November 1951), 24–39.

[15] Kemp, Murray C., "The Efficiency of Competition as an Allocation of Resources: I. External Economies of Production," *Canadian Journal of Economics and Political Science*, XXI, No. 1 (February 1955), 30–42.

[16] Meade, J. E., "External Economies and Diseconomies in a Competitive Situation," *Economic Journal*, LXII, No. 1 (March 1951), 54–67.

chapter 9

The International Migration
of Factors of Production

Throughout the preceding chapters we have adhered to the assumption, inherited from the Classical economists, that primary factors of production are internationally immobile—or, more accurately, that they do not move in response to purely *economic* incentives. This has been a most convenient assumption, for it has made it possible to study the response of each country separately to a change in world prices. When the assumption is abandoned, it is necessary to recognize that changes in commodity prices entail changes in factor rewards in all countries and therefore give rise to equilibrating movements of factors between countries. The extent of the movements will depend on conditions of demand and supply in all trading countries. Hence it is impossible to calculate the implications of a price change for one country without considering the implications for all countries.

In the present chapter we explore some of the implications of allowing factors to migrate in response to international differences in rewards. The international migration of labor and of capital raise similar problems. To avoid repetition, therefore, attention will for the most part be focused on the implications of capital mobility, with labor assumed completely immobile. In the concluding sections, however, some of the special problems raised by the international migration of labor will be noted and briefly analyzed.

181

Throughout the present chapter it will be assumed that the world factor endowment is given; capital accumulation and decay, and population change, are ruled out. This is a drastic simplification, but it does permit us to concentrate on a few basic relationships which can be expected to prevail in any economy, whether stationary or evolving. The role of these relationships in a growing world will be discussed in Chap. 11.

Given this overriding assumption, our chief task will be to pin down the international allocation of capital by suitably extending our earlier models of the international economy. We shall also rework under the more general assumptions some of our familiar comparative statical exercises. In particular, because the results will be needed in later chapters, we shall explore the implications of changes in import duties and in taxes on foreign earnings.

The remaining assumptions of earlier chapters—two countries, perfect competition, absence of risk—are taken over without change. It will be assumed also that, if it is a net creditor, the home country either exports the second commodity or exports nothing; and that, if it is a net debtor, the home country exports the second commodity or exports both commodities. The second commodity is, in this sense, the "natural" export of the home country.

1. FORMAL EXTENSIONS OF THE MODEL AND SOME PRELIMINARY RESULTS

We must now, for the first time,[1] work with models incorporating more than two traded goods. The conditions of market equilibrium appropriate to such models are considerably more complicated than those examined in earlier chapters. We therefore begin by setting out the equilibrium conditions in detail. While our later calculations will be based on a model with just three traded goods (two produced goods and the services of capital), we may with little additional effort set out the conditions in full generality.

Free Trade

Suppose that n countries trade freely in m commodities, that each country absorbs some of each commodity, and that prices are quoted in terms of a common international currency. Let p_i^r be the price of the ith commodity in country r. Then, in market equilibrium,

$$p_i^r = p_i^s \qquad r, s = 1, 2, \ldots, n; \, i = 1, 2, \ldots, m \qquad (9.1)$$

That is, for each commodity the same price prevails everywhere.

[1] In the appendices to Chaps. 1 and 3 we have already tackled some special problems associated with trade in many goods.

Tariff-Ridden Trade

If the assumption of free trade is relaxed, the conditions of equilibrium assume a more complicated form. Suppose then that the rth country is free to tax both its imports and its exports of each commodity but must refrain from discriminating between countries; that its imports of the ith commodity are taxed at an *ad valorem* rate of $100\tau_i^r$ per cent; and that its exports of the same commodity are taxed at a rate of $100\tau_i^{r*}$ per cent, with the import duty applied to the foreign price and the export duty applied to the domestic price. No restrictions are placed on the signs of τ_i^r and τ_i^{r*}; however, we do rule out subsidies of 100 per cent and above. Now in market equilibrium and in the absence of direct import controls the domestic price in the rth country cannot exceed the foreign price corrected for the import duty:

$$p_i^r \leq p_i^s(1 + \tau_i^r) \qquad s = 1, 2, \ldots, n; i = 1, 2, \ldots, m \qquad (9.2\text{a})$$

(If the inequality were not satisfied, traders would have an incentive to expand the rth country's imports.) Of course the weak inequality becomes an equality if the rth country's gross imports from the sth country are positive. Similarly, in market equilibrium without direct controls over exports the foreign price cannot exceed the rth country's domestic price corrected for the export duty:

$$p_i^s(1 + \tau_i^{r*}) \geq p_i^s \qquad s = 1, 2, \ldots, n; \quad i = 1, 2, \ldots, m \qquad (9.2\text{b})$$

(If the inequality were not satisfied, traders would have an incentive to expand the rth country's exports.) Of course the weak inequality becomes an equality if the rth country's gross exports to the sth country are positive.

In stating the conditions of equilibrium in this way we free ourselves of the necessity of pretending that we know in advance whether the rth country is a net importer from or exporter to the sth country. The importer-exporter status of the rth country in relation to the sth country is determined by the market and we, economist-observers interested only in writing down equilibrium conditions general enough to cover all possible outcomes, do not need to know what the market decides.

Combining inequalities (9.2a) and (9.2b) we find that, in market equilibrium and in the absence of direct controls over trade, the import and export duties imposed on any particular commodity must satisfy the further inequality

$$(1 + \tau_i^r)(1 + \tau_i^{r*}) \geq 1 \qquad (9.3)$$

It follows that at most one rate of duty may be negative and that if either rate of duty is zero the other must be non-negative. If (9.3) is satisfied as a strict inequality, trade in the ith good between countries r and s must be in one direction only; that is, gross and net imports (exports) must be equal.

The equilibrium conditions (9.2a) and (9.2b) apply equally to trade in finished goods and to trade in factor services. Suppose that the rth country borrows from and/or lends capital to the sth country, with capital viewed as a homogeneous physical stock. Equivalently, we may view the rth country as importing and/or exporting from country s the services of capital. One then has only to identify capital services with the jth good to fit them into the preceding analysis.

It is of course more usual to tax the earnings of capital than to impose a duty on trade in capital services. But anything which can be achieved by a tax on earnings can be achieved by a duty on trade, and vice versa. If instead of an import duty and an export duty on trade in capital services one wishes to apply a tax (at a rate of $100t^r$ per cent) on the earnings of foreign capital invested in country r and a tax (at a rate of $100t^{r*}$ per cent) on the earnings of domestic capital invested abroad, one has only to apply a simple transformation. Instead of conditions (9.2a) and (9.2b), with $i = j$, we have

and

$$p_j^r(1 - t^r) \leq p_j^s \qquad r, s = 1, 2, \ldots, n \qquad (9.4a)$$

$$p_j^r \geq p_j^s(1 - t^{r*}) \qquad r, s = 1, 2, \ldots, n \qquad (9.4b)$$

respectively, with $t^r = \tau_j^r/(1 + \tau_j^r)$ and $t^{r*} = \tau_j^{r*}/(1 + \tau_j^{r*})$. If the rth country is a gross borrower, condition (9.4a) is satisfied as an equality; and if the rth country is a gross lender, condition (9.4b) is satisfied as an equality. Instead of inequality (9.3) we have

$$(1 - t^r)(1 - t^{r*}) \leq 1 \qquad (9.5)$$

from which it follows that at most one rate of tax can be negative and that if either rate of tax is zero the other must be non-negative. If (9.5) is satisfied as a strict inequality the gross and net debtor-creditor positions of the rth in relation to the sth country coincide.

To emphasize the complete parallelism between trade in final goods and trade in factor services we note further that, just as a suitable tax on the earnings of capital has the same effect as a given tariff on trade in capital services, so a suitable tax on the proceeds of trade in final goods has the same effect as a given tariff. Simple transformations are available, similar to those provided in the preceding paragraph.

Three Conventions

In later calculations it will be found convenient to "normalize" a country's tariff structure by supposing that imports are taxed only if net imports are positive and that exports are taxed only if net exports are positive. Given this convention, it follows from inequality (9.3) that in the absence of quantitative controls over trade all rates of duty are non-negative.

A second convention will be useful. Suppose that the rth country is either a net importer of the ith commodity from country s or a net exporter of the ith commodity to country s. Then at least one of the weak inequalities (9.2a) and (9.2b) must be satisfied as an equality. Given the normalizing convention just described, either

$$p_i^r = p_i^s(1 + \tau_i^r) \qquad \tau_i^r \geq 0, \quad \tau_i^{r*} = 0 \qquad (9.6a)$$

or

$$p_i^r(1 + \tau_i^{r*}) = p_i^s \qquad \tau_i^{r*} \geq 0, \quad \tau_i^r = 0 \qquad (9.6b)$$

Suppose however that we define the export duty as applicable not to the domestic price but to the foreign price. Then clearly it suffices to write the single equilibrium condition (9.6a), it being understood that τ_i^r is an import duty if net imports are positive and an export duty if net exports are positive, and that if τ_i^r is an export duty it is applied to the foreign price. Defined as applicable to the domestic price, the rate of export duty τ_i^{r*} may be calculated from the relation

$$(1 + \tau_i^{r*})(1 + \tau_i^r) = 1 \qquad (9.7)$$

whence

$$\tau_i^{r*} = - \frac{\tau_i^r}{1 + \tau_i^r} \qquad (9.8)$$

Suppose that the tariff structure of country r is normalized. Even so, any feasible pattern of trade can be attained by manipulating just $(m - 1)$ rates of duty. As a third convention, then, one tariff will be equated to zero.

Preliminary Results—Free Trade

In the balance of this chapter we shall be concerned with the special case in which $n = 2$ and $m = 3$. Reverting to familiar notation, the conditions of free-trade equilibrium (9.1) reduce in this case to

$$p_i = p_i^* \qquad i = 1, 2, 3$$

Alternatively, if we identify the third commodity with capital services and define r_i as the home rental per unit of capital, measured in terms of the ith commodity, we may write the conditions as

$$p_i = p_i^* \qquad i = 1, 2 \qquad (9.9a)$$

$$r_i = r_i^* \qquad i = 1, 2 \qquad (9.9b)$$

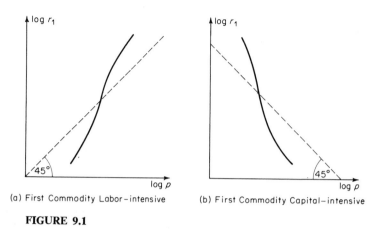

(a) First Commodity Labor-intensive   (b) First Commodity Capital-intensive

FIGURE 9.1

It is not difficult to see that if the available technology is everywhere the same, each country must in this case produce something of both commodities (or be on the verge of producing both). If technologies differ, however, this is not true. Consider Fig. 9.1 which, on the assumption of incomplete specialization, shows the relationship between the home commodity price ratio and the marginal product of capital in the first industry. In drawing Fig. 9.1(a) it has been assumed that the first commodity is uniformly labor-intensive; in drawing Fig. 9.1(b) it has been assumed that the first commodity is uniformly capital-intensive. Analogous curves can be drawn for the foreign country. If now we superimpose the home and foreign curves we obtain Fig. 9.2. Clearly the two curves may have no point of intersection, in which case a world equilibrium with incomplete specialization by both countries is ruled out on technological grounds. If the curves do have one or more points in

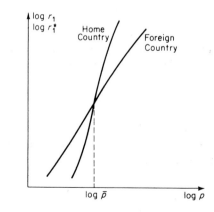

FIGURE 9.2

common such an equilibrium cannot be ruled out on purely technological grounds; nevertheless it does require that world demand and supply should establish a price ratio which corresponds to such a point. Thus in Fig. 9.2 there is a single point of intersection, with the associated price ratio $\bar{p}$; for incomplete specialization it is necessary that $\bar{p}$ should equate world demand and supply.

Preliminary Results—Tariff-ridden Trade

If we introduce import and export duties, and identify the home country with the rth, the conditions of equilibrium (9.2) reduce to

$$p_i \leq p_i^*(1 + \tau_i) \qquad i = 1, 2, 3$$

and

$$p_i(1 + \tau_i^*) \geq p_i^* \qquad i = 1, 2, 3$$

where τ_i is the duty imposed by the home country on its imports of the ith commodity and τ_i^* is the duty imposed by the home country on its exports of the ith commodity. Suppose now that we introduce the three conventions already described and, in particular, that trade in the second commodity is duty-free. The equilibrium conditions then reduce to[2]

$$p_1 = p_1^*(1 + \tau_1) \tag{9.10a}$$

$$p_2 = p_2^* \tag{9.10b}$$

$$p_3 = p_3^*(1 + \tau_3)$$

The third condition can be written equivalently as

$$p_i r_i(1 - t) = p_i^* r_i^* \qquad i = 1, 2 \tag{9.10c}$$

where, of course, r_i is the real rental of capital at home in terms of the ith commodity and t is the rate of tax applied to the foreigner's earnings in the home country. Finally, from Eqs. (9.10a) and (9.10b)

$$p(1 + \tau_1) = p^* \tag{9.11a}$$

and, applying Eqs. (9.10a) and (9.10b) to Eqs. (9.10c),

$$r_1(1 - t)(1 + \tau_1) = r_1^* \tag{9.11b}$$

and

$$r_2(1 - t) = r_2^* \tag{9.11c}$$

[2] The reader is reminded that, in the extreme case in which the home country is a net debtor and exports both commodities, the duty τ_1 must be an export duty (applied to the foreigner price).

We wish to know the implications of the import duty and the tax for the variety of possible patterns of international specialization. As a preliminary, we study the special case in which either τ_1 or t (but not both) is zero. For concreteness we suppose that $\tau_1 \neq 0$, $t = 0$; but nothing depends on that choice. It will be obvious that, if technology is everywhere the same, at least one country must specialize completely. If technology differs from country to country, this is not so; and Fig. 9.3 displays an equilibrium with both countries incompletely specialized. For such an equilibrium to emerge,

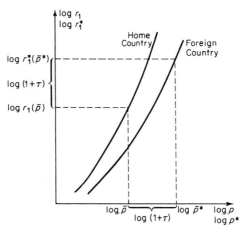

FIGURE 9.3

however, it is necessary, first, that there exist a p^*, say $\bar{p}^*$, which satisfies Eqs. (9.11), with $t = 0$, and, second, that the free play of world demand and supply throw up precisely that p^*. Whether the first condition is met depends on the two national technologies, which jointly determine the shapes of the two curves of Fig. 9.3, and on the two national factor endowments, from which we may deduce which p and p^* are consistent with incomplete specialization. Nothing more can be said without introducing much more specific assumptions than hitherto. Nor is it possible without additional assumptions to determine whether the second condition is satisfied. We may note however that when both countries are incompletely specialized the international allocation of capital is, at any given terms of trade, indeterminate: Any sufficiently small change in the allocation will leave marginal products (and therefore rates of return) unchanged in both countries; hence any one of an infinity of allocations would suit the owners of capital equally well. On the other hand, changes in the allocation of capital result in changes in the international distribution of income and, therefore, in the world excess demand for each commodity. Thus at each terms of trade, in particular at those which satisfy Eqs. (9.11), there is for each commodity a whole interval of values of excess

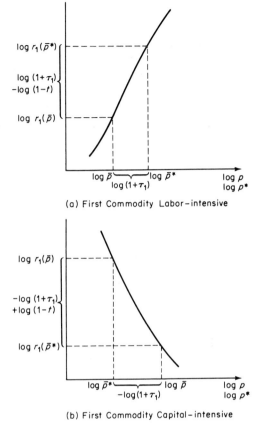

(a) First Commodity Labor-intensive

(b) First Commodity Capital-intensive

FIGURE 9.4

demand. If for one permissible allocation of capital excess demands do not vanish they yet may do so for another allocation. One hesitates then to describe the equilibrium depicted in Fig. 9.3 as singular or uninteresting.

Consider now the possibility that $\tau_1 \neq 0 \neq t$. We know that if technology is the same in both industries and if *either* the tax rate *or* the rate of duty differs from zero, at least one country must specialize completely. If, however, *both* the rate of duty *and* the rate of tax differ from zero *and bear just the right relationship to each other* (that is, lie on a particular plane curve determined by the shape of the curve in Fig. 9.1) both countries may be incompletely specialized. The possibility is illustrated by Fig. 9.4 with the home country a net creditor.

Suppose alternatively that technology differs from country to country. We know that in the absence of tariff and tax it is just possible for both countries to be incompletely specialized. We now add a related proposition: *If when trade is tariff-free and foreign earnings tax-free international price equilibrium is unique and involves the incomplete specialization of both countries, the same will be true after the imposition of a tariff and/or tax provided the tariff and tax are sufficiently small.* Suppose that the relative factor intensities of the two industries differ from one country to the other, and that in an initial tariff- and tax-free equilibrium both countries are incompletely specialized with the home country a net creditor.[3] Figure 9.5 illustrates. If this equilibrium is disturbed by the imposition of a sufficiently small tariff and/or a sufficiently small tax it is possible to find a terms of trade $p^* = \bar{p}^*$ such that Eqs. (9.11) are satisfied.

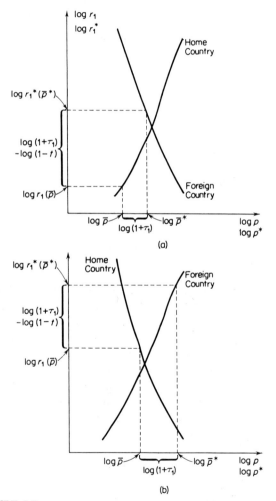

FIGURE 9.5

[3] It is easy to modify the proof to handle other cases. See Inada and Kemp [3].

It may be objected that world demand and supply may not be equated at $\bar{p}^*$. To overcome this objection it is necessary to examine in more detail the special properties of the model. It may be recalled first that when both countries are incompletely specialized the international allocation of capital is, at any given terms of trade, indeterminate: Any sufficiently small change in the allocation will leave marginal products (and therefore rates of return) unchanged in both countries, hence any one of an infinity of allocations would suit the owners of capital equally well. On the other hand, variations in the allocation of capital result in variations in the world excess demand for each commodity. Hence, provided the tariff and tax are sufficiently small, there will exist an allocation which will bring the commodity markets into equilibrium at the terms of trade $\bar{p}^*$. Suppose that this allocation is unique. If then we require that $p^* = \bar{p}^*$, the allocation of capital will be determinate. In this argument we have twice required that the rate of duty and the rate of tax be sufficiently small. It must be understood therefore that τ_1 and t lie in the intersection of the sets defined by these requirements.

The proof has relied on an interesting recursive property possessed by the model when both countries are incompletely specialized. Thus Eqs. (9.11), which reflect technological conditions only, determine the terms of trade p^*. Given the terms of trade, and that both countries are incompletely specialized, we may then obtain the international allocation of capital from the conditions of equilibrium in the commodity markets. This property does not appear if either country is completely specialized. The reason is that marginal factor productivities are in that case not independent of the balance of international indebtedness.

Elasticity of Import Demand

When international indebtedness is not zero, special care must be taken, in defining demand and supply elasticities, to make clear the relative scope of the *ceteris paribus* and *mutatis mutandis* clauses. Accordingly we round off this introductory section with some definitions. It will be assumed throughout that commodity and capital flows are unimpeded by taxes and tariffs.

In each country the demand for any commodity depends on the price ratio and on real income (in terms of the *numéraire*); the supply of the commodity depends on the price ratio and on the net international indebtedness J of the foreign country; hence the excess demand, being the difference between demand and supply, depends on all three variables. We therefore may write, for example,

$$Z_2^* = Z_2^*(p^*, Q_1^*, J) \qquad (9.12)$$

where

$$Q_1^* = X_1^* + p^* X_2^* - J r_1^* \qquad (9.13a)$$

(The term $J r_1^*$ indicates the net foreign earnings of the home country.) From the function Z_2^* we can derive the total price elasticity of foreign import demand, with foreign real income allowed to adjust to changes in p^* but with J held constant:

$$\xi_2^* = \frac{p^*}{Z_2^*}\left(\frac{\partial Z_2^*}{\partial p^*} + \frac{\partial Z_2^*}{\partial Q_1^*}\frac{\partial Q_1^*}{\partial p^*}\right) \tag{9.14}$$

Now from Eq. (9.13a)

$$\frac{\partial Q_1^*}{\partial p^*} = X_2^* - J\frac{\partial r_1^*}{\partial p^*}$$

$$= Z_2^*\left(\frac{X_2^*}{Z_2^*} - \mu^*\gamma^*\right)$$

where $\mu^* \equiv Jr_1^*/p^*Z_2^*$ stands for net foreign earnings as a proportion of home exports; and $\partial Z_2^*/\partial Q_1^* \equiv m_2^*/p^*$. Hence

$$\xi_2^* = \frac{p^*}{Z_2^*}\left[\frac{\partial Z_2^*}{\partial p^*} + \frac{m_2^*}{p^*}Z_2\left(\frac{X_2^*}{Z_2^*} - \mu^*\gamma^*\right)\right]$$

From this definition one can move to the more refined real-income-compensated elasticity $\bar{\xi}_2^*$ by introducing the Slutzky decomposition of the price slope:

$$\frac{\partial Z_2^*}{\partial p^*} = \frac{\partial Z_2^*}{\partial p^*}\bigg|_{\text{utility constant}} - \frac{m_2^* D_2^*}{p^*}$$

Thus

$$\xi_2^* = \bar{\xi}_2^* - m_2^*(1 + \mu^*\gamma^*) \tag{9.15}$$

where $\bar{\xi}_2^* \equiv (p^*/Z_2^*)(\partial Z^*/\partial p^*)\big|$. When $J = 0$, $\mu^* = 0$ and $\xi_2^* = \bar{\xi}_2^* - m_2^*$ as usual.

2. MARKET STABILITY

To describe the comparative statical properties of the model it will be useful to know the conditions under which the two commodity markets are stable. In particular, we should like to know the conditions under which an increase in p^*, considered as a parameter, results in a decline in the world excess demand for the second commodity, where the initial value of p^* is an equilibrium value. In the present section we set out necessary and sufficient conditions for stability in that sense.

Throughout the section it will be assumed that both tariff and tax are zero.

The task of generalizing the stability conditions to accommodate non-zero τ and t is left to the reader.[4]

It will be assumed also that at least one country is completely specialized. The reason for adopting this apparently restrictive assumption is that when both countries are incompletely specialized the comparative statical properties of the model can be determined from Eq. (9.9b) alone, without reference to excess demand functions. In any case, when both countries are incompletely specialized the question of stability as formulated above is meaningless. For it follows from Sec. 1 that when both countries are incompletely specialized and the terms of trade are treated as a parameter, the international allocation of capital is indeterminate. The response of J (and therefore of world excess demand) to a change in the parameter is, therefore, also indeterminate.

Algebraically, we seek the conditions under which $d(Z_2 + Z_2^*)/dp^* < 0$, where

$$Z_2 + Z_2^* \equiv Z_2(p, Q_1, J) + Z_2^*(p^*, Q_1^*, J) \qquad (9.16)$$

and

$$Q_1 = X_1 + pX_2 + Jr_1^* \qquad (9.13b)$$

$$Q_1^* = X_1^* + p^*X_2^* - Jr_1^* \qquad (9.13a)$$

The differentiation of expression (9.16) is to be performed subject to the requirement that equilibrium is maintained in the international capital market:

$$r_1 = r_1^* \qquad (9.9b)$$

Differentiating Eq. (9.16) totally with respect to p^*, and recalling that $p = p^*$, we obtain

$$
\frac{d}{dp^*}(Z_2 + Z_2^*) = \left(\frac{\partial Z_2}{\partial p} + \frac{\partial Z_2^*}{\partial p^*}\right) + \left(\frac{m_2}{p}\cdot\frac{\partial Q_1}{\partial p} + \frac{m_2^*}{p^*}\cdot\frac{\partial Q_1^*}{\partial p^*}\right)
$$
$$
+ \left(\frac{m_2}{p}\cdot\frac{\partial Q_1}{\partial J} + \frac{m_2^*}{p^*}\frac{\partial Q_1^*}{\partial J} + \frac{\partial Z_2}{\partial J} + \frac{\partial Z_2^*}{\partial J}\right)\frac{dJ}{dp^*} \qquad (9.17)
$$

where

$$m_2 \equiv p\,\frac{\partial Z_2}{\partial Q_1} \qquad (9.18a)$$

and

$$m_2^* \equiv p^*\,\frac{\partial Z_2^*}{\partial Q_1^*} \qquad (9.18b)$$

are, respectively, the home and foreign marginal propensities to consume the second commodity.

To evaluate the several partial derivatives in expression (9.17), we refer

[4] See Prob. 9.7.

back to Eqs. (9.13a) and (9.13b) and calculate that

$$\frac{\partial Q_1}{\partial p} = Z_2^* \left(\frac{X_2}{Z_2^*} + \mu^* \gamma^* \right) \tag{9.19a}$$

$$\frac{\partial Q_1}{dJ} = r_1^* \delta^* \tag{9.19b}$$

$$\frac{\partial Q_1^*}{\partial p^*} = Z_2^* \left(\frac{X_2^*}{Z_2^*} - \mu^* \gamma^* \right) \tag{9.19c}$$

$$\frac{\partial Q_1^*}{\partial J} = -r_1^* \delta^* \tag{9.19d}$$

where

$$\gamma \equiv \frac{p}{r_1} \cdot \frac{\partial r_1}{\partial p} \tag{9.20a}$$

$$\gamma^* \equiv \frac{p^*}{r_1^*} \cdot \frac{\partial r_1^*}{\partial p^*} \tag{9.20b}$$

and

$$\delta^* \equiv \frac{J}{r_1^*} \cdot \frac{\partial r_1^*}{\partial J} \tag{9.21a}$$

From the Stolper–Samuelson Theorem we know that, if something of each commodity is produced, γ and γ^* exceed one in absolute value; otherwise $\gamma = 1$ and $\gamma^* = 0$. If the foreign country is incompletely specialized, $\delta^* = 0$; otherwise, δ^* is negative. Finally, we break down the demand slopes $\partial Z_2 / \partial p$ and $\partial Z_2^* / \partial p^*$ into their Slutzky components and express them in elasticity form:

$$\frac{\partial Z_2}{\partial p} = \frac{Z_2}{p} \left(\xi_2 - m_2 \frac{D_2}{Z_2} \right) \tag{9.22a}$$

$$\frac{\partial Z_2^*}{\partial p^*} = \frac{Z_2^*}{p^*} \left(\xi_2^* - m_2^* \frac{D_2^*}{Z_2^*} \right) \tag{9.22b}$$

where $\xi_2 \equiv \dfrac{p}{Z_2} \cdot \left. \dfrac{\partial Z_2}{\partial p} \right|$ is the home real-income-compensated elasticity of excess demand for the second commodity and $\xi_2^* \equiv \dfrac{p^*}{Z_2^*} \cdot \left. \dfrac{\partial Z_2^*}{\partial p^*} \right|$ is the foreign compensated elasticity.

Substituting from Eqs. (9.19) and (9.22) into Eq. (9.17), noting that in equilibrium $Z_2 + Z_1^* = 0$, and recalling the duality relations (1.24), we obtain

$$\frac{d(Z_2 + Z_2^*)}{Z_2^*} = \{ -\xi_2 + \xi_2^* + (1 + \mu^* \gamma^*)(m_2 - m_2^*) \} \hat{p}^*$$

$$+ \mu^* \{ (m_2 - m_2^*) \delta^* + (\gamma - \gamma^*) \} \hat{J} \tag{9.23}$$

where the circumflex indicates relative changes ($\hat{p}^* = dp^*/p^*$, etc.). From

Eq. (9.9b), on the other hand,

$$(\delta + \delta^*)\hat{J} = (\gamma - \gamma^*)\hat{p}^* \qquad (9.24)$$

where

$$\delta \equiv -\frac{J}{r_1} \cdot \frac{\partial r_1}{\partial J} \qquad (9.21b)$$

Substituting from Eq. (9.24) into Eq. (9.23), we obtain our required stability condition:

$$d(Z_2 + Z_2^*) = Z_2^* \Delta \hat{p}^* < 0 \qquad (9.25)$$

where

$$\Delta \equiv -\xi_2 + \xi_2^* + (1 + \mu^* \gamma^*)(m_2 - m_2^*)$$

$$+ \mu^* \cdot \frac{\gamma - \gamma^*}{\delta + \delta^*} [(m_2 - m_2^*) \delta^* + (\gamma - \gamma^*)] \qquad (9.26)$$

The examination of certain special cases provides us with appropriate interpretations of the several components of Δ. Thus in the absence of international borrowing and lending $J = \mu^* = 0$ and $Z_2^* > 0$; hence the stability criterion reduces to

$$-\xi_2 + \xi_2^* + m_2 - m_2^* < 0 \qquad (9.27)$$

which is necessarily satisfied if $m_2^* \geq m_2$. If international indebtedness is frozen at some constant level, not necessarily zero, the criterion reduces to the slightly more complicated form:

$$Z_2^*[-\xi_2 + \xi_2^* + (1 + \mu^* \gamma^*)(m_2 - m_2^*)] < 0 \qquad (9.28)$$

Thus the influence of international indebtedness is registered by the term $Z_2^* \mu^* \gamma^*(m_2 - m_2^*)$. Put concisely but inelegantly, this term measures the effect on world demand for the second commodity of the international redistribution of income inherent in the price-induced change in the foreign return to capital. To see this, suppose first that the foreign country is incompletely specialized. If the second industry is relatively capital-intensive abroad, so that $\gamma^* > 1$, an increase in p^* results in an increase in r_1^*. This in turn shifts the international distribution of income in favor of the home country. The total amount redistributed is $J(\partial r_1^*/\partial p^*) \equiv Z_2^* \mu^* \gamma^*$. The net effect on world demand for the second commodity is therefore that sum times the difference in marginal propensities. If, on the other hand, the second industry is relatively labor-intensive abroad, an increase in p^* changes the distribution in the opposite direction. Suppose, alternatively, that the foreign country is completely specialized in the production of the first commodity, so that $\gamma^* = 0$ and the extra term vanishes. Then any change in the terms of trade leaves r_1^*, and therefore the international distribution of income, unchanged.

The residual term

$$Z_2^* \mu^* \frac{\gamma - \gamma^*}{\delta + \delta^*} [(m_2 - m_2^*) \delta^* + (\gamma - \gamma^*)] \qquad (9.29)$$

reflects the influence on world excess demand for the second commodity of the price-induced change in net international indebtedness. To check that this is so, suppose first that the foreign country is incompletely specialized and, therefore, the home country completely specialized. In this case $\delta^* = 0$, $\gamma = 1$ and the residual term (9.29) reduces to

$$\frac{Z_2^* \mu^*}{\delta} (1 - \gamma^*)^2 \qquad (9.30)$$

If $\gamma^* < -1$, so that $\gamma^* < \gamma$, the immediate effect of the price change is to open a gap between the return to capital at home and abroad: $r_1 > r_1^*$. Capital therefore moves to the home country and (again because $\gamma^* < \gamma$) world output of the second commodity increases. If, alternatively, $\gamma^* > 1$, so that $\gamma^* > \gamma$, the immediate effect of the price change is to make $r_1 < r_1^*$. Capital moves to the foreign country and (again because $\gamma^* > \gamma$) world output of the second commodity increases. Thus, whatever the sign of $(\gamma - \gamma^*)$, the reallocation of capital serves to stabilize commodity markets: Expression (9.30) is necessarily negative, the positivity of $(\gamma - \gamma^*)^2$ reflecting the dual role of $(\gamma - \gamma^*)$ in first directing the flow of capital and then ensuring a stabilizing output response. Suppose, alternatively, that the foreign country is completely specialized in the production of the first commodity. Then $\delta^* \neq 0$ and we must consider the additional term

$$Z_2^* \mu^* \frac{\gamma - \gamma^*}{\delta + \delta^*} (m_2 - m_2^*) \delta^* \qquad (9.31)$$

An interpretation is easy to find. When the foreign country is completely specialized, the price-induced reallocation of capital changes the foreign rate of capital rental r_1^* and therefore the rate of return on foreign investment. The implied redistribution of income between countries influences the world demand for the second commodity, in a direction determined by the difference between the two marginal propensities to buy the second commodity. Thus suppose that $\gamma > \gamma^*$, so that, immediately after the price change, $r_1 > r_1^*$. Capital leaves the foreign country. As a result, r_1^* rises and income is redistributed in favor of the home country. If $m_2 > m_2^*$, net demand for the second commodity rises; if $m_2 < m_2^*$, net demand falls. If, on the other hand, $\gamma < \gamma^*$, capital migrates to the foreign country; r_1^* falls, income is redistributed in favor of the foreign country, and net demand for the second commodity rises if $m_2 < m_2^*$, falls if $m_2 > m_2^*$. In summary, then, the additional distributional effect described by expression (9.31) may go either way. If (9.31) is negative, the redistribution reinforces the allocational effect described by (9.30); otherwise, the two effects pull against each other and the residual term (9.29) may even be of perverse sign.

3. TARIFF CHANGES

In this section we explore the implications of tariff changes for the terms of trade, the ratio of home prices, factor rewards, and the balance of international indebtedness. To minimize complications we assume throughout that the initial state is one of free trade with no taxes.

When both countries are incompletely specialized, most of the above comparative statical problems can be solved by manipulating Eq. (9.11b), without reference to other parts of the system. We begin therefore by considering the case in which both commodities are produced in each country. From Eq. (9.11b), with $\tau_1 = 0 = t$,

$$\gamma \hat{p} + d\tau_1 = \gamma^* \hat{p}^* \qquad (9.32)$$

From Eq. (9.11a), on the other hand,

$$\hat{p} + d\tau_1 = \hat{p}^* \qquad (9.33)$$

Hence

$$\hat{p}^* = -\frac{1 - \gamma}{\gamma - \gamma^*} d\tau_1 \qquad (9.34)$$

and

$$\hat{p} = -\frac{1 - \gamma^*}{\gamma - \gamma^*} d\tau_1 \qquad (9.35)$$

Thus the home country's terms of trade must improve if γ and γ^* are of opposite sign, that is, if each country's export commodity is relatively capital-intensive [as in Fig. 9.5(a)] or if each country's import commodity is relatively capital-intensive [as in Fig. 9.5(b)]. However the terms of trade cannot improve so markedly that the home country's internal price ratio moves in favor of the exported commodity—the tariff cannot fail to protect the imported commodity. In other cases, where γ and γ^* are of the same sign, both the external and the internal terms of trade may move in either direction, the outcome depending on the relative magnitudes of γ and γ^*.

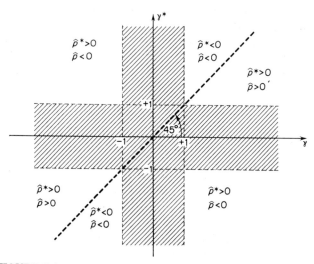

FIGURE 9.6

For these other cases, however, we have the following sweeping generalization: *The two price ratios must move in the same direction; in particular, any improvement in the external terms of trade must be so great that it carries the internal terms of trade with it, so that the tariff fails to protect the imported commodity.* Figure 9.6 summarizes the possible outcomes of a tariff when both countries are incompletely specialized.

When we recognize the possibility that at least one country is completely specialized in the production of its export commodity, matters become much more complicated. For then it is impossible to infer the comparative statical properties of the model from technological considerations alone. We need in addition the condition of market equilibrium[5]

$$Z_2(p, Q_1, J) + Z_2^*(p^*, Q_1^*, J) = 0 \qquad (9.36)$$

where home income is defined now as

$$Q_1 \equiv X_1 + pX_2 + \frac{Jr_1^*}{1 + \tau_1} + \frac{\tau_1}{1 + \tau_1}(p^*Z_2^* + Jr_1^*)$$

$$= X_1 + pX_2 + Jr_1^* + \frac{\tau_1}{1 + \tau_1} p^*Z_2^* \qquad (9.37)$$

This definition needs some explanation. The term $Jr_1^*/(1 + \tau_1)$ is the value at home, in terms of the first commodity, of net foreign earnings. To make

[5] If the capital market and the market for the second commodity are in equilibrium, so must be the market for the first commodity.

this clear, we define J', the amount of capital invested by the home country abroad, and J'', the amount of foreign capital invested in the home country. Evidently $J \equiv J' - J''$. Now the money value of the home country's gross foreign earnings is $p_1^* J' r_1^*$. Dividing by the home price of the first commodity, $p_1 = p_1^*(1 + \tau_1)$, this expression reduces to $J' r_1^*/(1 + \tau_1)$. On the other hand, the foreign country's earnings in the home country are $J'' r_1$. In view of Eq. (9.11b), therefore, the home country's *net* foreign earnings are

$$\frac{J' r_1^*}{1 + \tau_1} - J'' r_1 = \frac{J r_1^*}{1 + \tau_1}$$

The fourth term, $[\tau_1/(1 + \tau_1)][p^* Z_2^* + J r_1^*]$, represents the tariff revenue which, it is assumed, is handed over to the public. Thus the money value of the tariff revenue is $\tau_1 p_1^* Z_1$; expressed in terms of the first commodity the revenue amounts to $\tau_1 p_1^* Z_1/p_1 = [\tau_1/(1 + \tau_1)]Z_1$. From the condition for balance of payments equilibrium,

$$Z_1 - p^* Z_2^* - J' r_1^* + J'' r_1(1 + \tau_1) = 0 \tag{9.38}$$

and, from Eq. (9.11b), it becomes, finally, $[\tau_1/(1 + \tau_1)][p^* Z_2^* + J r_1^*]$.
From Eq. (9.11b), with $\tau_1 = 0 = t$,

$$d\tau_1 + \gamma \hat{p} - \gamma^* \hat{p}^* - (\delta + \delta^*)\hat{J} = 0 \tag{9.39}$$

From Eq. (9.36), on the other hand,

$$\left(\frac{\partial Z_2}{\partial p} + \frac{m_2}{p} \frac{\partial Q_1}{\partial p}\right)\frac{dp}{d\tau_1} + \left(\frac{m_2}{p} \frac{\partial Q_1}{\partial p^*} + \frac{\partial Z_2^*}{\partial p^*} + \frac{m_2^*}{p^*} \frac{\partial Q_1^*}{\partial p^*}\right)\frac{dp^*}{d\tau_1}$$

$$+ \left(\frac{m_2}{p} \frac{\partial Q_1}{\partial J} + \frac{\partial Z_2}{\partial J} + \frac{m_2^*}{p^*} \frac{\partial Q_1^*}{\partial J} + \frac{\partial Z_2^*}{\partial J}\right)\frac{dJ}{d\tau_1} + \frac{m_2}{p} \frac{\partial Q_1}{\partial \tau_1} = 0 \tag{9.40}$$

whence, substituting for the several partial derivatives,[6] introducing the Slutzky decomposition of the price slopes, and transferring to elasticities,

$$(-\xi_2 + m_2)\hat{p} + [\xi_2^* - m_2^* + (m_2 - m_2^*)\mu^* \gamma^*]\hat{p}^*$$
$$+ \mu^*[(\gamma - \gamma^*) + \delta^*(m_2 - m_2^*)]\hat{J} + m_2 d\tau_1 = 0 \tag{9.41}$$

---

[6] Most of these are familiar from Sec. 2. The partial derivative of home income with respect to the rate of duty is obtained from Eq. (9.37):

$$\partial Q_1/\partial \tau_1 = p^* Z_2^*$$

Substituting for $\hat{J}$ from Eq. (9.39), Eq. (9.41) reduces to

$$A\hat{p} + B\hat{p}* + Cd\tau_1 = 0 \tag{9.42}$$

where

$$A \equiv -\bar{\xi}_2 + m_2 + \frac{\mu^*\gamma}{\delta + \delta^*}\left[(\gamma - \gamma^*) + \delta^*(m_2 - m_2^*)\right]$$

$$B \equiv \bar{\xi}_2^* - m_2 + (m_2 - m_2^*)(1 + \mu^*\gamma^*) - \frac{\mu^*\gamma^*}{\delta + \delta^*}\left[(\gamma - \gamma^*) + \delta^*(m_2 - m_2^*)\right]$$

$$C \equiv \frac{\mu^*}{\delta + \delta^*}\left[(\gamma - \gamma^*) + \delta^*(m_2 - m_2^*)\right] + m_2$$

Eqs. (9.33) and (9.42) may be solved for $\hat{p}$ and $\hat{p}*$ in terms of $d\tau_1$:

$$\Delta\hat{p} + (B + C)\,d\tau_1 = 0 \tag{9.43a}$$
$$\Delta\hat{p}* + (C - A)\,d\tau_1 = 0 \tag{9.43b}$$

where

$$\Delta \equiv A + B.$$

We can now set out the conditions under which the terms of trade and the home price ratio will move in one direction or the other. In particular we can ascertain whether the paradoxical outcomes—that the terms of trade deteriorate ($\hat{p}* < 0$) and the home price of the protected commodity falls ($\hat{p} > 0$)—are possible. Suppose that commodity markets are stable, so that $Z_2^*\Delta < 0$. Then

$$\text{if} \quad Z_2^* > 0 \quad \begin{cases} \hat{p}* > 0 & \text{if and only if} \quad C - A > 0 \\ \hat{p} < 0 & \text{if and only if} \quad B + C < 0 \end{cases} \tag{9.44a}$$

and

$$\text{if} \quad Z_2^* < 0 \quad \begin{cases} \hat{p}* > 0 & \text{if and only if} \quad C - A < 0 \\ \hat{p} < 0 & \text{if and only if} \quad B + C > 0 \end{cases} \tag{9.44b}$$

If $Z_2^*\Delta > 0$ all right-hand inequalities are reversed.

Two special cases are of interest. If $J \equiv 0$, Z_2^* is necessarily positive and

$$A = -\bar{\xi}_2 + m_2$$
$$B = \bar{\xi}_2^* - m_2^*$$
$$C = m_2$$

Conditions (9.44) therefore reduce to

$$\hat{p}^* > 0 \quad \text{if and only if} \quad \bar{\xi}_2 > 0$$
$$\hat{p} < 0 \quad \text{if and only if} \quad \xi_2^* - m_2^* + m_2 < 0 \tag{9.45}$$

That is, the terms of trade turn in favor of the home or tariff-imposing country, and the internal price ratio moves in favor of the protected industry if and only if the uncompensated elasticity of foreign import demand ($\xi_2^* - m_2^*$) plus the home marginal propensity to buy the exported commodity is positive. These conclusions are identical with those reached in Chap. 4.

A second, less special case is that in which $J = \bar{J} \neq 0$, where $\bar{J}$ is a constant. Then

$$A = -\bar{\xi}_2 + m_2$$
$$B = \xi_2^* - m_2^* + (m_2 - m_2^*)\mu^*\gamma^*$$
$$C = m_2$$

Conditions (9.44a) reduce to:

$$\text{if } Z_2 > 0 \quad \begin{cases} \hat{p}^* > 0 \text{ if and only if } \bar{\xi}_2 > 0 \\ \hat{p} < 0 \text{ if and only if } \bar{\xi}_2 + (m_2 - m_2^*)(1 + \mu^*\gamma^*) < 0 \end{cases} \tag{9.46a}$$

and conditions (9.44b) to:

$$\text{if } Z_2^* < 0 \quad \begin{cases} \hat{p}^* > 0 \text{ if and only if } \bar{\xi}_2 < 0 \\ \hat{p} < 0 \text{ if and only if } \xi_2^* + (m_2 - m_2^*)(1 + \mu^*\gamma^*) > 0 \end{cases} \tag{9.46b}$$

Thus if the home country is an exporter, the terms of trade necessarily move in its favor. For an improvement in the terms of trade it is sufficient therefore that the home country be a net debtor. Conversely, if the home country imports both commodities (implying that it is a net creditor) its terms of trade necessarily deteriorate.[7] The reason is that market stability now requires $\Delta > 0$. Figures 9.7(a) and 9.7(b) illustrate the two cases. The figures are drawn on the assumption that the world terms of trade are given, at $(p^*)^0$, so that the foreign earnings of the home country, $\bar{J}r_1^*[(p^*)^0]$, also are constant. In Fig. 9.7 foreign earnings are represented by OA. The home country's trading opportunities are represented by a straight line through A (and A') with slope proportional to $(p^*)^0$. The initial pre-tariff equilibrium is,

[7] In this case trade, narrowly defined to embrace finished goods only, is all one way; hence p^* should perhaps not be called the "terms of trade."

say, at P where a trade indifference curve is tangent to the trading opportunities line. If now a tariff is imposed the home price ratio p declines; the new ratio is proportional, say, to the slope of BB' and indicates the terms on which trade takes place at home. As a result of the tariff, the home price of the first commodity rises and the home value of foreign earnings falls to $\bar{J}r_1^*[(p^*)^0]$, represented by OC. On the other hand the tariff proceeds,

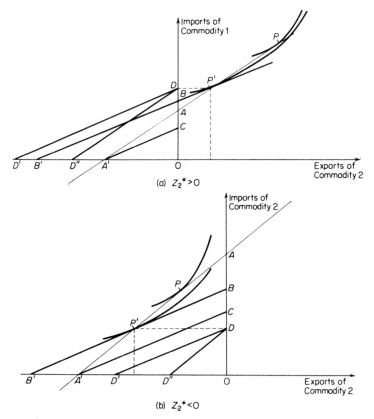

FIGURE 9.7

amounting to $A'B'$ in terms of the second commodity or BC in terms of the first, are passed on to the public so that the new trading opportunities, as viewed by the public, are indicated by BB' extended. The precise location of B on the vertical axis is determined by the requirement that the chosen trading point P', at which a new trade indifference curve is tangent to BB', must lie on AA' extended. Total imports of the first commodity are then OD. For this total an amount OD' is paid in terms of the second commodity. Of this amount, however, part is skimmed off at the customs house. Valued in terms of the second commodity this part is $D'D''$ $(= A'B')$; valued in terms of the first commodity this part is BC. It is clear from Fig. 9.7 that the imposition of a tariff necessarily curtails the home demand for imports of the first commodity and therefore, given market stability, turns the terms of trade in favor of the home country if $Z_2^* > 0$, against it if $Z_2^* < 0$.

From conditions (9.46) it is also clear that the effect of a tariff may be to turn home prices against the "protected" industry. For this outcome it is necessary and sufficient that

$$[\bar{\xi}_2^* - m_2^*(1 + \mu^*\gamma^*)] + m_2(1 + \mu^*\gamma^*) \gtrless \text{ as } Z_2^* \gtrless 0 \quad (9.47)$$

It will be recalled, however, that the square-bracketed expression is ξ_2^*, the uncompensated total price elasticity of foreign import demand when $J = \bar{J}$. Condition (9.47) can be recognized, therefore, as a simple extension of the Lerner–Metzler condition discussed in Chap. 4.

Returning to the general conditions (9.44a), we note that they can be written

$$\hat{p}^* > 0 \quad \text{if and only if} \quad C - A = \alpha(1 - \gamma) + \bar{\xi}_2 > 0$$

$$\hat{p} < 0 \quad \text{if and only if} \quad B + C = \alpha(1 - \gamma^*) + \bar{\xi}_2$$
$$+ (m_2 - m_2^*)(1 + \mu^*\gamma^*) < 0$$

where $\alpha \equiv \dfrac{\mu^*}{\delta + \delta^*}[(\gamma - \gamma^*) + (m_2 - m_2^*)\delta^*]$. Allowing for the tariff-induced reallocation of capital therefore introduces the new terms $\alpha(1 - \gamma)$ and $\alpha(1 - \gamma^*)$, respectively. In one case it is still possible to reach clearcut conclusions. Thus if the home country is completely specialized $\gamma = 1$, $\alpha(1 - \gamma) = 0$ and the terms of trade necessarily move in favor of the tariff-imposing country. In all other cases, however, both the terms of trade and the home price ratio move in either direction.

Given $\hat{p}$ and $\hat{p}^*$ it is a simple matter to calculate the change in real factor rewards. For example

$$\hat{r}_1 = \gamma\hat{p}$$
$$\hat{r}_1^* = \gamma^*\hat{p}^*$$

The change in the balance of international indebtedness, on the other hand, may be inferred from Eq. (9.39)—an inference which is left to the reader.

4. TAX CHANGES

In this section we follow a course parallel to that followed in Sec. 3 and consider the implication of a small tax t on the foreigner's earnings for the home country's terms of trade, for home prices, for factor rewards and for the international allocation of capital. As in Sec. 3, we assume that initially $\tau_1 = t = 0$.

We dispose first of the simple case in which both countries are incompletely specialized. In that case we need refer only to Eq. (9.11b), from which we calculate that, with $t = 0 = \tau_1$,

$$\hat{p} = \hat{p}^* = - \frac{dt}{\gamma - \gamma^*} \qquad (9.48)$$

Thus the two price ratios rise if $\gamma^* > \gamma$, fall if $\gamma > \gamma^*$. This is not difficult to understand. The ultimate effect of the tax must be to raise r_1^* above r_1. If $\gamma^* > \gamma$, this can be done only by raising p and p^*; if $\gamma^* < \gamma$, it can be accomplished only by a fall in the price ratio. Figure 9.8 illustrates for the case in which γ and γ^* are both positive.

When we recognize the possibility that at least one country is completely specialized in the production of its export commodity, we need also the condition of market equilibrium (9.36), with home income now defined by Eq. (9.13b) and foreign income by Eq. (9.13a).[8] From Eq. (9.11b), with $t = 0 = \tau_1$,

$$dt + (\gamma - \gamma^*)\hat{p} - (\delta + \delta^*)\hat{J} = 0 \qquad (9.49)$$

From Eq. (9.36), on the other hand,

$$\left(\frac{\partial Z_2}{\partial p} + \frac{\partial Z_2^*}{\partial p^*} + \frac{m_2}{p} \frac{\partial Q_1}{\partial p} + \frac{m_2^*}{p^*} \frac{\partial Q_1^*}{\partial p^*} \right) \frac{dp}{dt}$$

$$+ \left(\frac{m_2}{p} \frac{\partial Q_1}{\partial J} + \frac{\partial Z_2}{\partial J} + \frac{m_2^*}{p^*} \frac{\partial Q_1^*}{\partial J} + \frac{\partial Z_2^*}{\partial J} \right) \frac{dJ}{dt} = 0 \quad (9.50)$$

whence, substituting for the partial derivatives, decomposing the price slopes, and transferring to elasticities, in the usual way,

$$[-\bar{\xi}_2 + \bar{\xi}_2^* + (m_2 - m_2^*)(1 + \mu^* \gamma^*)]\hat{p}$$

$$+ \mu^*[(\gamma - \gamma^*) + \delta^*(m_2 - m_2^*)]\hat{J} = 0 \quad (9.51)$$

<hr/>

[8] Home income, in terms of the first commodity, is

$$Q_1 = X_1 + pX_2 + J'r_1^* - J''r_1$$
$$= X_1 + pX_2 + Jr_1^* - tJ''r_1^* \quad \text{[from Eq. (9.11b)]}$$
$$= X_1 + pX_2 + Jr_1^*$$

Similarly,

$$Q_1^* = X_1^* + p^*X_2^* - Jr_1^*$$

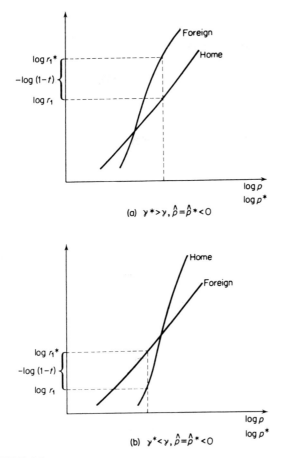

(a) $\gamma^* > \gamma, \hat{p} = \hat{p}^* < 0$

(b) $\gamma^* < \gamma, \hat{p} = \hat{p}^* < 0$

FIGURE 9.8

Substituting for $\hat{J}$ from Eq. (9.49), Eq. (9.51) becomes

$$Z_2^*\{\Delta\hat{p} + \frac{\mu^*}{\delta + \delta^*}[(\gamma - \gamma^*) + \delta^*(m_2 - m_2^*)]\}\, dt = 0 \quad (9.52)$$

Thus the home terms of trade improve if and only if $Z_2^*\Delta$ and

$$Z_2^* \frac{\mu^*}{\delta + \delta^*}[(\gamma - \gamma^*) + \delta^*(m_2 - m_2^*)] \quad (9.53)$$

are of opposite sign.

In seeking to interpret this conclusion it is useful to first consider the special case in which $J = \bar{J}$, a constant. Then, clearly, Eqs. (9.11b) and (9.49) must be abandoned; and Eq. (9.51) reduces to

$$[-\xi_2 + \xi_2^* + (m_2 - m_2^*)(1 + \mu^*\gamma^*)]\hat{p} = 0$$

Thus leaving aside the singular case in which the home export supply and foreign import demand curves coincide in a neighborhood of the initial equilibrium, so that the square-bracketed expression vanishes and $\hat{p}$ is indeterminate, we conclude that $\hat{p} = 0$. The imposition of a tax in this case has no real effects at all. Foreign earnings are taxed, but the proceeds of the tax are passed back to the very people taxed.

Thus any effects the tax may have on prices flow directly from the tax-induced reallocation of the world's capital. Expression (9.53) reflects the influence on net world demand for the second commodity of the capital flow induced by the tax change. The stability indicator, $Z_2^* \Delta$, then translates the change in demand into the required equilibrating price change. Thus suppose that the foreign country is incompletely specialized and, therefore, the home country completely specialized. In this case $\gamma = 1$, $\delta^* = 0$ and expression (9.53) reduces to

$$\frac{Z_2^* \mu^*}{\delta} (1 - \gamma^*)$$

A tax on foreign earnings has the effect of making home investment more profitable than foreign. Hence a reallocation of capital takes place in favor of the home country and r_1 is forced down to equality with $(1 - t)r_1^*$. The effect of the reallocation is to raise world output of the second commodity if $\gamma^* < -1$ and to lower it if $\gamma^* > 1$. If the commodity markets are stable $(Z_2^* \Delta < 0)$, these changes in output will be translated into price changes of opposite sign. If, on the other hand, the foreign country is completely specialized, $\delta^* \neq 0$ and (9.53) does not simplify to nearly the same degree. The tax-induced reallocation of capital forces up r_1^*, the rate of return on foreign investment, and thus brings about an international redistribution of income. How this redistribution affects world demand then depends on the relative values of m_2 and m_2^*, the marginal propensities to buy the second commodity.

Having solved for $\hat{p}$ it is a simple matter to obtain, from Eq. (9.49), an expression for $\hat{J}$. Then, given $\hat{p}$ and $\hat{J}$, one can solve for $\hat{r}_1$ and $\hat{r}_1^*$. There may be some ground for regarding the outcome $(\hat{J} < 0, \hat{r}_1 < 0, \hat{r}_1^* > 0)$ as "normal," but it is easy to construct examples in which some or all of the inequalities are reversed.

5. THE MIGRATION OF LABOR

That completes our analysis of international capital mobility. In the present section we briefly consider the implications of assuming that labor is internationally mobile, capital immobile.

As has already been indicated in the introductory paragraphs of this chapter, labor mobility and capital mobility involve almost symmetric modifications of the basic model of Chaps. 3 and 4. The chief asymmetry derives from the fact that the migration of labor does not necessarily entail the repatriation of earnings. Migrants may choose to remit part of their earnings, but the proportion may be quite small. Suppose that migrants from the home country choose to send home a constant fraction φ of their earnings. Then if V represents the net number of home emigrants and if w_1 is the home real wage in terms of the first commodity, our revised basic equations under conditions of free trade are:

$$w_1(p, V) = w_1^*(p, V) \qquad (9.54)$$

and

$$Z_2(p, Q_1, V) + Z_2^*(p, Q_1^*, V) = 0 \qquad (9.55)$$

where

$$Q_1 = X_1 + pX_2 + \varphi V w_1^* \qquad (9.56a)$$

and

$$Q_1^* = X_1^* + pX_2^* - \varphi V w_1^* \qquad (9.56b)$$

The revised condition for balance of payments equilibrium is

$$Z_1 + p^* Z_2 - \varphi V w_1^* = 0 \qquad (9.57)$$

At one extreme migrants send nothing home, $\varphi = 0$, and the symmetry of this model with the model of Sec. 2 is at a minimum. At the other, hardly feasible extreme, they send everything home, $\varphi = 1$, and the symmetry is very clear.

The symbol φ has been introduced as a constant. Alternatively, it could be treated as a variable, dependent on w_1^* and obtained as the solution of the following problem:

$$\max_{\varphi} U[(1 - \varphi)w_1^*, \varphi w_1^*]$$

where U is the migrants' utility function. For simplicity, however, φ will be treated as a constant.

If a tariff is imposed by the home country, the model becomes much more complicated. First we must rewrite home income as

$$Q_1 = X_1 + pX_2 + \frac{\varphi V w_1^*}{1 + \tau_1} + \frac{\tau_1}{1 + \tau_1}(p^* Z_2^* + \varphi V w_1^*)$$

$$= X_1 + pX_2 + \varphi V w_1^* + \frac{\tau_1}{1 + \tau_1} p^* Z_2^* \qquad (9.58)$$

The similarity of Eqs. (9.37) and (9.58) will be apparent. Second, the condition of labor market equilibrium becomes

$$w_1 = w_1^* \left(1 - \frac{\tau_1}{1 + \tau_1} \varphi\right) \tag{9.59}$$

The reason is the following. The purchasing power of the migrant's wage is the sum of two parts, the purchasing power of that portion of the wage which he retains and the purchasing power of the portion he remits:

$$(1 - \varphi)w_1^* + \varphi \frac{w_1^*}{1 + \tau_1} = w_1^* \left(1 - \frac{\tau_1}{1 + \tau_1} \varphi\right)$$

It would be tedious to rework Secs. 2 and 3 in full detail. On the other hand, the symmetry between the models of capital mobility and labor mobility is imperfect so that the analysis of labor mobility cannot be passed over with a mere wave of the hand. As a compromise we offer a brief analysis of stability and of the implications of a tariff—a skeleton consisting of the main equations, but little else.

First we derive the conditions of market stability appropriate to a world of labor mobility. Expression (9.17) carries over, with J replaced by V. From it we obtain, in place of Eq. (9.23),

$$\frac{d(Z_2 + Z_2^*)}{Z_2^*} = \{-\xi_2 + \xi_2^* + (m_2 - m_2^*)(1 + \varphi\lambda^*\epsilon^*)\}\hat{p}$$

$$+ \lambda^*\{(\epsilon - \epsilon^*) + (m_2 - m_2^*)(\varphi v^* + \varphi - 1)\}\hat{V} \tag{9.60}$$

where

$$\epsilon \equiv \frac{p}{w_1} \cdot \frac{\partial w_1}{\partial p} \tag{9.61a}$$

$$\epsilon^* \equiv \frac{p^*}{w_1^*} \cdot \frac{\partial w_1^*}{\partial p^*} \tag{9.61b}$$

$$v^* \equiv \frac{V}{w_1^*} \cdot \frac{\partial w_1^*}{\partial V} \tag{9.62a}$$

and

$$\lambda^* \equiv \frac{V w_1^*}{p Z_2^*} \tag{9.63}$$

From Eq. (9.54), on the other hand,

$$(\epsilon - \epsilon^*)\hat{p} - (v + v^*)\hat{V} = 0 \tag{9.64}$$

where

$$v \equiv -\frac{V}{w_1} \cdot \frac{\partial w_1}{\partial V} \tag{9.62b}$$

Substituting from Eq. (9.64) into Eq. (9.60), we obtain our new stability condition:

$$d(Z_2 + Z_2^*) = Z_2^* \Delta' < 0 \tag{9.65}$$

where

$$\Delta' = -\xi_2 + \xi_2^* + (m_2 - m_2^*)(1 + \varphi \lambda^* \epsilon^*)$$

$$+ \lambda^* \frac{\epsilon - \epsilon^*}{v + v^*} [(\epsilon - \epsilon^*) + (m_2 - m_2^*)(\varphi v^* + \varphi - 1)] \tag{9.66}$$

When $\varphi = 1$ the symmetry between Eqs. (9.65)–(9.66) and (9.25)–(9.26) is apparent. The special cases in which $V = 0$ and $V = \bar{V} \neq 0$ are left to the reader.

Next we consider the implications of imposing a tariff. Suppose first that both countries are incompletely specialized. Then, from Eq. (9.59),

$$\epsilon \hat{p} = \epsilon^* \hat{p}^* - \varphi \, d\tau_1 \tag{9.67}$$

which, in view of Eq. (9.33), reduces to

$$\hat{p} = -\frac{\varphi - \epsilon^*}{\epsilon - \epsilon^*} \, d\tau_1 \tag{9.68}$$

$$\hat{p}^* = -\frac{\varphi - \epsilon}{\epsilon - \epsilon^*} \, d\tau_1 \tag{9.69}$$

Equations (9.68) and (9.69) should be compared with Eqs. (9.35) and (9.34), respectively.

Suppose next that at least one country is completely specialized in the production of its export commodity. From Eq. (9.59) we calculate that

$$\epsilon \hat{p} - \epsilon^* \hat{p}^* - (v + v^*) \hat{V} + \varphi \, d\tau_1 = 0 \tag{9.70}$$

Substituting for $\hat{V}$ in Eq. (9.40), with J replaced by V, then substituting for the partial derivatives from Eqs. (9.56b) and (9.58), introducing the Slutzky decomposition of the price slopes, and switching to elasticities, we obtain

$$A' \hat{p} + B' \hat{p}^* + C' \, d\tau_1 = 0 \tag{9.71}$$

where

$$A' = -\xi_2 + m_2 + \frac{\lambda^* \epsilon}{v + v^*} [(\epsilon - \epsilon^*) + (m_2 - m_2^*)(\varphi v^* + \varphi - 1)]$$

$$B' = \xi_2^* - m_2 + (m_2 - m_2^*)(1 + \varphi \lambda^* \epsilon^*) - \frac{\lambda^* \epsilon^*}{v + v^*} [(\epsilon + \epsilon^*)$$
$$+ (m_2 - m_2^*)(\varphi v^* + \varphi - 1)]$$

$$C' = \frac{\varphi \lambda^*}{v + v^*} [(\epsilon + \epsilon^*) + (m_2 - m_2^*)(\varphi v^* + \varphi - 1)] + m_2$$

and

$$A' + B' = \Delta'$$

It follows, by reasoning familiar from Sec. 3, that if commodity markets are stable, so that $Z_2^* \Delta' < 0$, then

$$\text{if } Z_2^* > 0 \quad \begin{cases} \hat{p}^* > 0 & \text{if and only if} \quad C' - A' > 0 \\ \hat{p} < 0 & \text{if and only if} \quad B' + C' < 0 \end{cases} \tag{9.72a}$$

and

$$\text{if } Z_2^* < 0 \quad \begin{cases} \hat{p}^* > 0 & \text{if and only if} \quad C' - A' < 0 \\ \hat{p} < 0 & \text{if and only if} \quad B' + C' > 0 \end{cases} \tag{9.72b}$$

If commodity markets are unstable, so that $Z_2^* \Delta' > 0$, all righthand inequalities are reversed. The interpretation of conditions (9.72a) and (9.72b), and the consideration of special cases, is left to the reader.

6. FINAL REMARKS

We have explored the implications of assuming that *either* capital *or* labor is internationally mobile. It would be tedious to examine in detail the general case in which both factors are mobile. Some interesting features of that case will, however, be briefly noted.

Suppose that free trade prevails and that foreign income is free of tax. The first thing to notice is that if technology is the same everywhere both countries must be either incompletely specialized or on the verge of being incompletely specialized, with price equal to marginal cost in both industries. The second thing to notice is the element of indeterminacy in world factor allocation. Granted that both countries must be incompletely specialized, the same factor rewards and the same world outputs are consistent with quite different allocations of factors between countries.

The assumption that technology is the same everywhere is a very special one. Abandon the assumption and the rather paradoxical conclusions must be abandoned too. If technology is different from country to country, however, one must recognize a new paradox—that both factors may flee one country (the low productivity country) completely. This astonishing outcome is, however, the result of imagining that all factors are perfectly mobile. Introduce an immobile third factor, however insignificant, and the paradox evaporates.

PROBLEMS

9.1 Provide an algebraic proof of the proposition that labor may be worse off after the removal of barriers to migration than before.

9.2 Does an outflow of capital worsen the lot of the workers? This is a Classical problem, debated by McCulloch, Wakefield and Torrens. For references, see Thomas [12].

9.3 The migration of skilled workers from low income to high income countries has been regarded by some writers as "perverse." (Cf. Thomas [13].) Do you find such migration surprising?

9.4 Suppose that the home country exports both commodities and taxes *exports* of the first commodity. Revise conditions (9.44) and (9.72) accordingly.

9.5 Suppose that the home country is a net debtor and taxes the earnings of the foreign country. Revise condition (9.53) accordingly.

9.6 Suppose that one made a token allowance for the greater risk of foreign investment by re-writing Eq. (9.1) as

$$r_1 = \theta r_1^* \quad \begin{matrix} 0 < \theta < 1 & \text{if} \quad J > 0 \\ \theta > 1 & \text{if} \quad J < 0 \end{matrix}$$

Treating θ as a constant, revise the stability condition (9.25).

9.7 Show that, when $\tau \neq 0$, $t \neq 0$, the condition of market stability is

$$Z_2^* \Delta'' \hat{p}^* < 0$$

where

$$\Delta'' \equiv \frac{-\xi}{1 + \tau m_2} + \xi^* + (1 + \mu^* \gamma^*)\left(m_2 \frac{1 + \tau}{1 + \tau m_2} - m_2^*\right) + \mu^* \frac{\gamma - \gamma^*}{\delta + \delta^*}$$

$$\left[m_2 \frac{\tau(1 - \gamma) + (1 + \tau)\delta^*}{1 + \tau m_2} - m_2^* \delta^* + (\gamma - \gamma^*)\right]$$

Confirm that Δ'' reduces to Δ when $\tau = 0$.

REFERENCES

[1] Caves, Richard E., *Trade and Economic Structure. Models and Methods*, Chap. V. Cambridge, Mass.: Harvard University Press, 1960.

[2] Heckscher, Eli, "The Effect of Foreign Trade on the Distribution of Income," *Economisk Tidskrift*, XXI (1919), 497–512 (in Swedish). Reprinted, in translation by Svend and Nita Laursen, in *Readings in the Theory of International Trade*, eds., Howard S. Ellis and Lloyd A. Metzler, pp. 272–300. Philadelphia: The Blakison Company, 1949.

[3] Inada, Ken-ichi and Murray C. Kemp, "International Capital Movements and the Theory of International Trade," *Quarterly Journal of Economics*, LXXXIII, No. 2 (May 1969).

†[4] Jones, Ronald W., "International Capital Movements and the Theory of Tariffs and Trade," *Quarterly Journal of Economics*, LXXXI, No. 1 (February 1967), 1–38.

[5] Kemp, Murray C., "The Gain from International Trade and Investment: a Neo-Heckscher–Ohlin Approach," *American Economic Review*, LVI, No. 4 (September 1966), 788–809.

[6] Kemp, Murray C., "A Partial Theoretical Solution of the Problem of the Incidence of Import Duties," in J. N. Wolfe, ed., *Value, Capital, and Growth. Papers in honour of Sir John Hicks*, pp. 257–73. Edinburgh: Edinburgh University Press, 1968.

[7] Kindleberger, C. P., *International Economics*, new ed., Chap. 22. Homewood, Illinois: Richard D. Irwin, Inc., 1958.

[8] Meade, J. E., *The Theory of International Economic Policy. Volume Two. Trade and Welfare*, Chap. XXVII. New York: Oxford University Press, Inc., 1955.

[9] Mundell, R. A., "International Trade and Factor Mobility," *American Economic Review*, XLVII, No. 2 (June 1957), 321–37.

[10] Ohlin, Bertil, *Interregional and International Trade*. Cambridge, Mass.: Harvard University Press, 1933.

[11] Pigou, A. C., *Protective and Preferential Import Duties*, pp. 59–60. London: Macmillan & Company, Ltd., 1960.

[12] Thomas, Brinley, *Migration and Economic Growth. A Study of Great Britain and the Atlantic Economy*. Cambridge: Cambridge University Press, 1954.

[13] Thomas, Brinley, "International Factor Movements and Unequal Rates of Growth," *Manchester School*, XXIX, No. 1 (January 1961), 1–22.

part II

Trade and Investment in a Context of Growth

chapter 10

International Trade

and Economic Growth

Questions posed by economic growth have already been encountered in Chaps. 1, 2, and 4. In particular, we have explored the implications of technical improvements, of changes in a country's factor endowment, and of improvements in its terms of trade. However, the treatment of growth in those chapters was of the comparative statical kind: Once-over changes in data were imposed on the system "from outside" and the responses calculated.

In this Part we shall attempt to generalize the system so that at least some components of growth are generated "endogenously" by the system itself. The interesting questions then concern the *interaction* through time of growth, trade, and investment. Attention will be focused not so much on the matrix of trade and investment at any moment but on the pattern of its change, especially on the trends (if any) inherent in the system. And, where such trends are discernible, we shall compare them with the corresponding trends in a state of autarky.

In the present chapter we examine some of the interactions of trade and growth, sheltered by the assumption that international investment is zero. Now in a strictly barter world international investment can be effected only by the installation in one country of equipment owned by residents of the other country, that is, by

215

"direct investment." Thus our assumption implies that all equipment owned by residents of the home country is installed at home, and that all equipment owned by foreigners is installed abroad. The additional ingredient of international investment will be added in Chap. 11.

We shall work with simplifying assumptions as drastic as is consistent with the posing of the questions which interest us. Even so, the analysis will demand a considerable measure of concentration. To keep our discussion within the two-by-two framework familiar from earlier chapters we suppose that one of the two commodities produced is an investment good. This means that we must learn to distinguish between the *stock* of capital in existence at any point of time and the *flow* of newly produced investment goods. To be specific, we will suppose that the first commodity is a consumers' good, the second an investment good, so that p must be interpreted as the price of the investment good in terms of the consumers' good. Trade is completely free, so that $p = p^*$. Capital is assumed to be perfectly durable. Simple patterns of depreciation could be introduced without much complicating the analysis, but also without changing the general character of our conclusions. It is assumed that the labor forces of the home and foreign countries grow at the exponential rates $n \geq 0$ and $n^* \geq 0$, respectively. The average savings propensities, s and s^*, are assumed to be constant positive fractions, implying an income-elasticity of demand of one and an own price-elasticity of minus one in each country. The savings propensities themselves, however, may differ from country to country. Production functions also may differ from country to country. It will be assumed, however, that, at any given terms of trade compatible with incomplete specialization in both countries, the relatively capital-intensive industry is the same in each country; that is $k_1[\omega(p)] \gtrless k_2[\omega(p)]$ if and only if $k_1^*[\omega^*(p)] \gtrless k_2^*[\omega^*(p)]$.

1. SHORT-RUN EQUILIBRIUM

At any moment of time k and k^*, the factor endowment ratios of the home and foreign countries, respectively, are given. It follows that in each country the excess demand for any particular commodity can be viewed as depending on the terms of trade only. The equilibrium terms of trade may be obtained therefore as the solution to

$$Lz_2(p, k) + L^* z_2^*(p, k^*) = 0$$

or, defining the *constants* $\lambda \equiv L/(L + L^*)$ and $\lambda^* \equiv L^*/(L + L^*) = 1 - \lambda$, as the solution to

$$\lambda z_2(p, k) + \lambda^* z_2^*(p, k^*) = 0 \tag{10.1}$$

As we have seen in Chap. 3, we cannot in general say anything about the number of solutions to Eq. (10.1). The assumption of constant savings propensities, however, so restricts the shapes of the curves that the equilibrium terms of trade are unique. Thus

$$z_2(p, k) = sq_2 - y_2$$

$$= s\left(\frac{l_1 f_1}{p} + l_2 f_2\right) - l_2 f_2$$

$$= s\frac{l_1 f_1}{p} - (1 - s)l_2 f_2 \tag{10.2}$$

It follows that if $p \leq \underline{p}^s(k)$, so that the home country is completely specialized in the production of the first commodity, $l_2 = 0$ and

$$z_2\,(p, k) = s\,\frac{f_1 k}{p} > 0 \tag{10.2'}$$

For $p \leq \underline{p}^s(k)$, therefore, the excess demand function for the second commodity forms part of a rectangular hyperbola. If, at the other extreme, $p \geq \bar{p}^s(k)$, so that the home country is specialized in the production of the second commodity, $l_1 = 0$ and

$$z_2(p, k) = -(1 - s)f_2(k) < 0 \tag{10.2''}$$

For $p \geq \bar{p}^s(k)$, then, the excess demand is a negative constant. Thus for either extreme of complete specialization the excess demand function is nonincreasing. We now show that for $\underline{p}^s(k) < p < \bar{p}^s(k)$, that is, in the range of incomplete specialization, it is strictly increasing. For this purpose, we rewrite Eq. (10.2), first solving Eqs. (2.9) for l_1 and l_2 and then making use of Eqs. (1.11) and (1.11'):

$$z_2(p, k) = s\frac{l_1 f_1}{p} - (1 - s)l_2 f_2$$

$$= f_2'\left[s\frac{k_2 - k}{k_2 - k_1 f_1'}\frac{f_1}{f_1'} + (1 - s)\frac{k_1 - k}{k_2 - k_1 f_2'}\frac{f_2}{f_2'}\right]$$

$$= \frac{f_2'}{k_2 - k_1}\,[s(k_2 - k)(k_1 + \omega) + (1 - s)(k_1 - k)(k_2 + \omega)]$$

Differentiating with respect to ω, bearing in mind Eq. (1.4),

$$\frac{dz_2}{d\omega} = \frac{f_2'}{(k_2 - k_1)^2}\Bigg[(k_1 + \omega)(k - k_1)k_2'$$

$$+ (k_2 + \omega)(k_2 - k)k_1' + s\frac{(k_2 - k_1)^2(k_2 - k)}{k_2 + \omega}\Bigg] \tag{10.3}$$

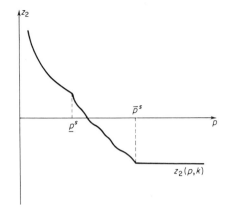

FIGURE 10.1

where $k'_i \equiv dk_i/d\omega$ is positive. Now k is a positively weighted average of k_1 and k_2; hence $dz_2/d\omega$ is positive or negative as $k_1(\omega)$ is less or greater than $k_2(\omega)$. On the other hand, from Eq. (1.22), $d\omega/dp$ is positive or negative as $k_1(\omega)$ is greater or less than $k_2(\omega)$. Hence

$$\frac{dz_2}{dp} = \frac{dz_2}{d\omega} \cdot \frac{d\omega}{dp} < 0$$

and the z_2-curve has the monotonic form depicted in Fig. 10.1. (In the very special case in which the R_i-curves of Fig. 1.2 touch or intersect at $k_i = k$, so

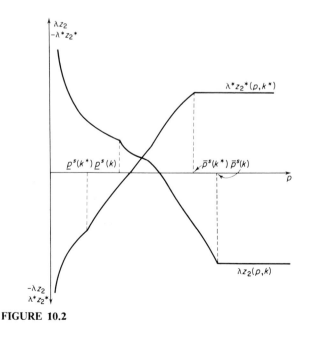

FIGURE 10.2

that $\underline{p}^s(k) = \bar{p}^s(k)$, the first and third segments of the curve are linked by a vertical line.)

Figure 10.2 provides a graphical counterpart to Eq. (10.1). (Cf. Fig. 3.1.) The equilibrium terms of trade are obtained as the intersection point of the two curves. It is obvious that the equilibrium exists and is unique. Without additional information about k and k^*, however, it is impossible to rule out any of the seven possible patterns of specialization: Either country, neither, or both countries may be completely specialized in production. Figure 10.2 illustrates the possibility that both countries are incompletely specialized.

Suppose that k or k^* undergoes a small once-over increase or decrease. Is it possible to determine the direction in which the equilibrium terms of trade will change? The answer is: Yes, provided we know the initial pattern of specialization and the relative capital intensities of the two industries in the country in which the disturbance is assumed to take place. Thus, from Eq. (10.1),

$$\frac{\partial p}{\partial k} = -\lambda \frac{\partial z_2}{\partial k} \bigg/ \left(\lambda \frac{\partial z_2}{\partial p} + \lambda^* \frac{\partial z_2^*}{\partial p} \right)$$

$$\frac{\partial p}{\partial k^*} = -\lambda^* \frac{\partial z_2^*}{\partial k^*} \bigg/ \left(\lambda \frac{\partial z_2}{\partial p} + \lambda^* \frac{\partial z_2^*}{\partial p} \right)$$

(10.4)

We know that the denominator is negative. Everything depends, therefore, on the signs of $\partial z_2/\partial k$ and $\partial z_2^*/\partial k^*$. Consider $\partial z_2/\partial k$. It is not difficult to see that the pattern of signs displayed in Table 10.1 must hold. The sign of $\partial z_2^*/\partial k^*$ follows a similar pattern. The signs of $\partial p/\partial k$ and $\partial p/\partial k^*$, for each of the seven possible patterns of specialization, must therefore be as displayed in Table 10.2.

TABLE 10.1: Sign of $\partial z_2/\partial k$

	$k_1 > k_2$	$k_2 > k_1$
Only commodity 1 produced	+	+
Only commodity 2 produced	−	−
Both commodities produced	+	−

Inspection of Table 10.2 brings up the following proposition: *If the ith industry is relatively capital-intensive in the country the capital:labor ratio of which has increased then the relative price of the ith product falls if and only if that country is not specialized in the production of the other commodity.*

2. LONG-RUN EQUILIBRIUM

As time passes, capital accumulates in each country. As a result, the two offer curves shift, as do the equilibrium terms of trade and the pattern of

TABLE 10.2

		$k_1 > k_2, k_1^* > k_2^*$		$k_1 < k_2, k_1^* < k_2^*$	
1.	Home country produces only commodity 1 Foreign country produces only commodity 2	$\dfrac{\partial p}{\partial k} > 0$	$\dfrac{\partial p}{\partial k^*} < 0$	$\dfrac{\partial p}{\partial k} > 0$	$\dfrac{\partial p}{\partial k^*} < 0$
2.	Home country produces only commodity 1 Foreign country produces both commodities	$\dfrac{\partial p}{\partial k} > 0$	$\dfrac{\partial p}{\partial k^*} > 0$	$\dfrac{\partial p}{\partial k} > 0$	$\dfrac{\partial p}{\partial k^*} < 0$
3.	Home country produces both commodities Foreign country produces only commodity 1	$\dfrac{\partial p}{\partial k} > 0$	$\dfrac{\partial p}{\partial k^*} > 0$	$\dfrac{\partial p}{\partial k} < 0$	$\dfrac{\partial p}{\partial k^*} > 0$
4.	Home country produces both commodities Foreign country produces only commodity 2	$\dfrac{\partial p}{\partial k} > 0$	$\dfrac{\partial p}{\partial k^*} < 0$	$\dfrac{\partial p}{\partial k} < 0$	$\dfrac{\partial p}{\partial k^*} < 0$
5.	Home country produces both commodities Foreign country produces both commodities	$\dfrac{\partial p}{\partial k} > 0$	$\dfrac{\partial p}{\partial k^*} > 0$	$\dfrac{\partial p}{\partial k} < 0$	$\dfrac{\partial p}{\partial k^*} < 0$
6.	Home country produces only commodity 2 Foreign country produces only commodity 1	$\dfrac{\partial p}{\partial k} < 0$	$\dfrac{\partial p}{\partial k^*} > 0$	$\dfrac{\partial p}{\partial k} < 0$	$\dfrac{\partial p}{\partial k^*} > 0$
7.	Home country produces only commodity 2 Foreign country produces both commodities	$\dfrac{\partial p}{\partial k} < 0$	$\dfrac{\partial p}{\partial k^*} > 0$	$\dfrac{\partial p}{\partial k} < 0$	$\dfrac{\partial p}{\partial k^*} < 0$

world specialization. In the present section we describe possible time paths of the terms of trade and the pattern of production and trade.

As a first, formal step, we add equations which describe the process of capital accumulation in each country. As we have seen in Sec. 1, the home demand for the second or investment good is $Ls[(l_1 f_1/p) + l_2 f_2]$. Hence

$$\frac{\dot{k}}{k} = \frac{s}{k}\left[\frac{l_1 f_1(k_1)}{p} + l_2 f_2(k_2)\right] - n \qquad (10.5a)$$

Similarly,

$$\frac{\dot{k}^*}{k^*} = \frac{s^*}{k^*}\left[\frac{l_1^* f_1^*(k_1^*)}{p} + l_2^* f_2^*(k_2^*)\right] - n^* \qquad (10.5b)$$

These are our basic differential equations. It is obvious, however, that the form of these equations, and therefore the dynamic behavior of our system, depends on the prevailing pattern of specialization.

As our second step, therefore, we try to divide the (k, k^*)-plane into areas each with its peculiar pattern of specialization. With this purpose in mind, we return to Fig. 10.1. For any given k, there is a $\underline{p}^s(k)$ and a $\bar{p}^s(k)$ which mark the boundaries between complete and incomplete specialization; and, corresponding to $\underline{p}^s(k)$ and $\bar{p}^s(k)$, there are excess demands $z_2[\underline{p}^s(k), k]$ and $z_2[\bar{p}^s(k), k]$, respectively. Now we define

$$\underline{P}(k) \equiv \{\underline{p}^s(k), \lambda z_2[\underline{p}^s(k), k]\}$$

and

$$\bar{P}(k) \equiv \{\bar{p}^s(k), \lambda z_2[\bar{p}^s(k), k]\}$$

and trace their paths on the $(p, \lambda z_2)$-plane as the parameter k is allowed to vary. Consider first the components of $\underline{P}(k)$. From Fig. (1.2) we know that $\underline{p}^s(k)$ is an increasing or decreasing function as $k_1(\omega)$ is greater or less than $k_2(\omega)$. The behavior of

$$z_2[\underline{p}^s(k), k] = s\,\frac{f_1(k)}{\underline{p}^s(k)}$$

is richer in possibilities. If $k_2(\omega) > k_1(\omega)$, z_2 obviously increases with k; hence the $\underline{P}$-curve is negatively sloped, as in Fig. 10.3(b). If $k_1(\omega) > k_2(\omega)$,

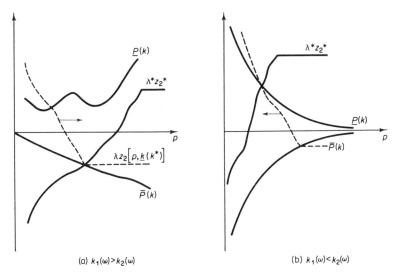

(a) $k_1(\omega) > k_2(\omega)$ (b) $k_1(\omega) < k_2(\omega)$

FIGURE 10.3

however, z_2 eventually increases with k but may be non-monotonic for small k; hence the $\underline{P}$-curve may have the shape displayed in Fig. 10.3(a). Turning to $\bar{P}(k)$, we note that

$$z_2[\bar{p}^s(k), k] = -(1 - s)f_2(k)$$

which decreases with k. It follows that if $k_1(\omega) > k_2(\omega)$ the $\bar{P}$-curve is negatively sloped, as in Fig. 10.3(a); and that if $k_1(\omega) < k_2(\omega)$ the curve is positively sloped, as in Fig. 10.3(b).

    A. Suppose for the time being that $k_1(\omega) > k_2(\omega)$ and imagine that k^*, and therefore the foreign offer curve, is fixed. Then, as Fig. 10.3(a) makes clear, there exists a $k = \underline{k}(k^*)$ such that for all $k \leq \underline{k}(k^*)$ the home country will completely specialize in producing the second commodity. If k^* is increased, so that the foreign offer curve shifts to the right, then the critical

$k = \underline{k}(k^*)$ increases too. Thus, in the (k, k^*)-plane we may draw a positively sloped curve corresponding to $k = \underline{k}(k^*)$. See Fig. 10.4. All points to the left of that curve correspond to the complete specialization of the home country in the production of the second commodity. A similar relationship, $k^* = \underline{k}^*(k)$, exists for the foreign country; it also is graphed in Fig. 10.4. Clearly the graph of $k^* = \underline{k}^*(k)$ must lie below that of $k = \underline{k}(k^*)$; otherwise, there would exist (k, k^*) such that only the second commodity would be produced in both countries, which is inconsistent with the assumptions made about saving.

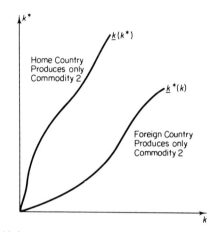

FIGURE 10.4

Equipped with Fig. 10.4 we can return to Eqs. (10.5). As already indicated, the dynamic behavior of the system depends on the prevailing pattern of specialization. We must now patiently examine each of the seven possible patterns.

Pattern (i): Each country produces both commodities. Total home output is equal to the sum of factor payments; that is, $(l_1 f_1/p) + l_2 f_2 = (k + \omega)f_2'$. Hence Eq. (10.5a) can be written in the alternative form

$$\frac{\dot{k}}{k} = s\,\frac{k + \omega}{k}\,f_2'[k_2(\omega)] - n \equiv \varphi(k, k^*) \qquad (10.6a)$$

Similarly, we may rewrite Eq. (10.5b) as

$$\frac{\dot{k}^*}{k^*} = s^*\,\frac{k^* + \omega^*}{k^*}\,f_2^{*\prime}[k_2^*(\omega^*)] - n^* \equiv \varphi^*(k, k^*) \qquad (10.6b)$$

Differentiating φ with respect to k, and recalling Eq. (1.4),

$$\frac{1}{\varphi + n} \cdot \frac{\partial \varphi}{\partial k} = \left(\frac{1}{k + \omega} - \frac{1}{k_2 + \omega}\right) \frac{d\omega}{dk} + \left(\frac{1}{k + \omega} - \frac{1}{k}\right)$$

$$= \left(\frac{1}{k + \omega} - \frac{1}{k_2 + \omega}\right) \left(\frac{\dfrac{\partial p}{\partial k}}{\dfrac{dp}{d\omega}}\right) + \left(\frac{1}{k + \omega} - \frac{1}{k}\right) \quad (10.7)$$

Hence, referring to Eqs. (1.6) and Table 10.2,

$$\frac{\partial \varphi}{\partial k} < 0 \qquad (10.8a)$$

Similarly,

$$\frac{\partial \varphi}{\partial k^*} < 0, \quad \frac{\partial \varphi^*}{\partial k} < 0, \quad \frac{\partial \varphi^*}{\partial k^*} < 0 \qquad (10.8b)$$

Moreover,

$$\left(\frac{dk^*}{dk}\right)_{\varphi=0} < \left(\frac{dk^*}{dk}\right)_{\varphi^*=0} < 0 \qquad (10.8c)$$

Pattern (ii): The home country produces both commodities, the foreign country produces only the second commodity. We retain Eq. (10.6a), but Eq. (10.6b) is replaced by a simple special form of Eq. (10.5b):

$$\frac{k^*}{k^*} = s^* \frac{f_2^*(k^*)}{k^*} - n^* \equiv \varphi^*(k, k^*) \qquad (10.9)$$

Again applying Eqs. (1.4) and (1.6), and Table 10.2,

$$\frac{\partial \varphi}{\partial k} < 0, \quad \frac{\partial \varphi}{\partial k^*} < 0, \quad \frac{\partial \varphi^*}{\partial k} = 0, \quad \frac{\partial \varphi^*}{\partial k^*} < 0 \qquad (10.10a)$$

$$\left(\frac{dk^*}{dk}\right)_{\varphi=0} > 0, \quad \left(\frac{dk^*}{dk}\right)_{\varphi^*=0} = 0 \qquad (10.10b)$$

Pattern (iii): The home country produces both commodities, the foreign country produces only the first commodity. We again retain Eq. (10.6a), but

Eq. (10.9) is replaced by a second special form of Eq. (10.5b):

$$\frac{k^*}{k^*} = \frac{s^*}{p} \frac{f_1^*(k^*)}{k^*} - n^* \equiv \varphi^*(k, k^*) \tag{10.11}$$

Hence

$$\frac{\partial \varphi}{\partial k} < 0, \quad \frac{\partial \varphi}{\partial k^*} < 0, \quad \frac{\partial \varphi^*}{\partial k} < 0, \quad \frac{\partial \varphi^*}{\partial k^*} < 0 \tag{10.12a}$$

and

$$\left(\frac{dk^*}{dk}\right)_{\varphi=0} < 0, \quad \left(\frac{dk^*}{dk}\right)_{\varphi^*=0} < 0 \tag{10.12b}$$

Pattern (iv): The home country produces only the second commodity, the foreign country produces only the first commodity. This time we retain Eq. (10.11) but replace Eq. (10.6a) by the appropriate special form of Eq. (10.5a):

$$\frac{k}{k} = s \frac{f_2(k)}{k} - n \equiv \varphi(k, k^*) \tag{10.13}$$

Thus

$$\frac{\partial \varphi}{\partial k} < 0, \quad \frac{\partial \varphi}{\partial k^*} = 0, \quad \frac{\partial \varphi^*}{\partial k} > 0, \quad \frac{\partial \varphi^*}{\partial k^*} < 0 \tag{10.14a}$$

and

$$0 < \left(\frac{dk^*}{dk}\right)_{\varphi^*=0} < \left(\frac{dk^*}{dk}\right)_{\varphi=0} = \infty \tag{10.14b}$$

The behavior of the system under each of the remaining three possible patterns of specialization may be inferred from the discussion of the preceding paragraph by appropriately shifting the asterisk.

Careful study of the inequalities (10.8), (10.10), (10.12), and (10.14) reveals that the slope of the curve defined by $\varphi(k, k^*) = 0$ depends critically

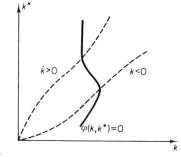

FIGURE 10.5

on whether either country is specialized in the production of the second or investment good. Whether either country is specialized in the production of the consumption good is immaterial. Figure 10.5 illustrates.

By drawing in the same figure the curves corresponding to $\varphi = \varphi^* = 0$, we are able to display the full variety of dynamic paths that may be generated by Eqs. (10.5). It is not difficult to see that, whatever their initial values, k and k^* converge on the uniquely determined stationary values $\hat{k}$ and $\hat{k}^*$ defined by

$$\varphi(\hat{k}, \hat{k}^*) = 0 = \varphi^*(\hat{k}, \hat{k}^*)$$

Figure 10.6 illustrates a case in which, on the long-run path of steady growth, the foreign country is completely specialized in the production of the investment good. For other values of s and s^*, however, different patterns of long-run specialization emerge.

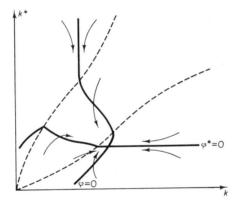

FIGURE 10.6

We have shown that if $k_1(\omega) > k_2(\omega)$ and if $k_1^*(\omega^*) > k_2^*(\omega^*)$ then k and k^* asymptotically approach stationary values $\hat{k}$ and $\hat{k}^*$, respectively. When $n = n^*$ this conclusion is easy to accept. Suppose, however, that $n \neq n^*$. From Eq. (10.1),

$$\frac{dz_2}{z_2} = \frac{dz_2^*}{z_2^*}$$

In steady growth, however,

$$\frac{dz_2}{z_2} = n, \quad \frac{dz_2^*}{z_2^*} = n^*$$

That is, for steady growth it is necessary that $n = n^*$. Thus we find that if $n \neq n^*$, long-run steady growth is impossible but that nevertheless each country asymptotically approaches a path of steady growth. It will be obvious that, mathematically, these two propositions are quite compatible. The economist's suspicions may be lulled perhaps by observing that, if $n \neq n^*$, eventually one country will dominate the other. If $n > n^*$, for example, both $L(t)/L^*(t)$ and $K(t)/K^*(t)$ go to infinity. After a certain point trade becomes an increasingly insignificant activity for the home country, which approximates ever more closely to a closed economy. For the foreign country the terms of trade approximate even more closely to a given parameter over which it has no control and to which it passively adjusts. The home country asymptotically approaches a closed-economy steady-growth path; and the foreign country asymptotically approaches a steady-growth path appropriate to a small open economy.

In the special case in which technology is the same everywhere, some of the conclusions just reached can be considerably sharpened. If then one country is completely specialized in the production of the labor-intensive investment good we can infer that that country has the lower savings ratio. Similarly, if one country is completely specialized in the production of the consumption good that country must have the higher savings ratio. Finally, if $s = s^*$ both countries must eventually be incompletely specialized; indeed, they must become completely self-sufficient, because then not only preferences and technologies but also factor endowments are the same everywhere. These conclusions are independent of the relative values of n and n^*.

Nothing has been said so far about the dynamic behavior of imports, exports, and the terms of trade. These, however, can be easily inferred from the behavior of k and k^*. For example, suppose that the dynamic process begins at Q_0 in Fig. 10.7. At that point the home country is relatively less well endowed with capital than is the foreign country; it specializes in the production of the second or relatively *labor*-intensive good, and imports the consumption good. The world moves from Q_0 to Q_1 with k increasing, k^* decreasing. The relative world output of the second commodity increases and therefore p falls. Moreover, home exports increase. (These propositions may be illustrated by shifts in the curves of Fig. 10.2.) From Q_1 to Q_3 the capital:labor ratios of both countries increase. During the first part of the journey (that is, from Q_1 to Q_2) the behavior of relative outputs, and therefore of the terms of trade, is ambiguous. At Q_2, however, the home country begins to produce something of the first commodity. From Q_2 to Q_3, therefore, the relative world output of the first or relatively capital-intensive good increases; hence p increases. From Q_3 to Q_5 (or Q_6), k increases and k^* decreases. The behavior of relative world outputs and terms of trade is indeterminate. *En route* to Q_5 (or Q_6) the foreign country ceases to produce the relatively capital-intensive consumption good. At Q_5, k too begins to fall. From Q_5 to Q_6, therefore, we can be sure that relative world output of the second good increases and p falls.

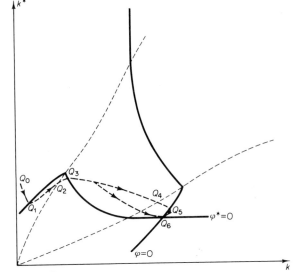

FIGURE 10.7

B. The preceding analysis of stability has been based on the assumption that the first or consumption goods industry is relatively capital-intensive. We now reverse that assumption and retrace our steps on the understanding that $k_2[\omega(p)] > k_1[\omega(p)]$ and $k_2^*[\omega^*(p)] > k_1^*[\omega^*(p)]$. It will be shown that in this case stability is not assured.

Suppose again that k^*, and therefore the foreign excess demand curve, is fixed. We wish to know whether there then exists a $k = \underline{k}(k^*)$ such that for all $k \geq \underline{k}(k^*)$ the home country will completely specialize in the production of the second or investment good. To help us answer this question, we draw both the $\bar{P}(k)$-curve and the $\underline{P}^*(k^*)$-curve in the lower quadrant of Fig. 10.8.

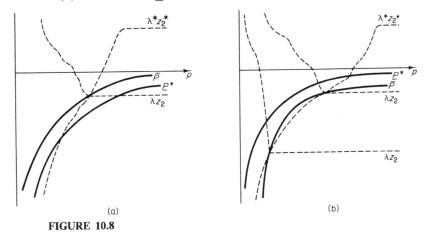

(a)   (b)

FIGURE 10.8

Then as is clear from Fig. 10.8(a), if the $\bar{P}$-curve lies uniformly above the $\underline{P}^*$-curve, $k = \underline{k}(k^*)$ exists. Moreover, if k^* is raised, so that the foreign offer curve moves to the *left*, the critical $\underline{k}$ increases too. Thus in the (k, k^*)-plane we may draw a positively sloped curve corresponding to the relation $k = \underline{k}(k^*)$. Figure 10.9(a) illustrates. If, however, the $\bar{P}$-curve either lies uniformly below the $\underline{P}^*$-curve [as in Fig. 10.8(b)], or intersects it, the critical $\underline{k}$ may not exist. To any particular k^* either there may correspond no k such that the home country specializes completely in the production of the second commodity, or there may correspond one or more k-intervals one of which may be infinite and each point in which involves complete specialization. Thus the graph of $k = \underline{k}(k^*)$ may be non-monotonic, as in Fig. 10.9(b).

We also mark out on the (k, k^*)-plane those areas in which the home country is completely specialized in producing the first or consumption good. As Fig. 10.3(b) makes clear, to every k^* there corresponds a $k = \bar{k}(k^*)$ such that for all $k \leq \bar{k}(k^*)$ the home country will completely specialize in the production of the consumption good. If k^* is increased, so that the foreign offer curve shifts to the left, then the critical k increases too. Thus in the (k, k^*)-plane we may draw a positively sloped curve all points to the left of which correspond to complete specialization by the home country in the production of the first commodity. Figure 10.9 illustrates.

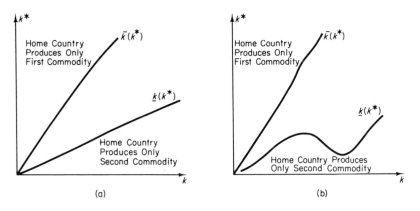

FIGURE 10.9

Graphs of the corresponding relationships for the foreign country, $k^* = \underline{k}^*(k)$ and $k^* = \bar{k}^*(k)$, are obtained in the same way. If the foreign curves are superimposed on Fig. 10.9 there is defined a possibly large number of areas each with its own distinctive pattern of specialization. The same pattern of specialization may emerge in several disconnected regions. Each of these patterns must be separately studied. We assume for the time being that $\underline{k}(k^*)$ and $\underline{k}^*(k)$ are monotonic.

Pattern (i): Each country produces both commodities. In this case Eq. (10.7) is relevant. From Table 10.2, $\partial p/\partial k < 0$; from Eqs. (1.6), $\partial p/\partial\omega < 0$; hence $d\omega/dk > 0$. The coefficient of $d\omega/dk$ is positive; but $[1/(k+\omega)-1/k]$ is negative. Thus the sign of $\partial\varphi/\partial k$ is ambiguous. It follows that the sign of $(dk^*/dk)_{\varphi=0}$ also is ambiguous. This inability to pin down the sign of $(dk^*/dk)_{\varphi=0}$ applies also to $(dk^*/dk)_{\varphi^*=0}$. The complete inventory of information about φ and φ^* is as follows:

$$\frac{\partial\varphi}{\partial k} \gtrless 0, \quad \frac{\partial\varphi}{\partial k^*} > 0, \quad \frac{\partial\varphi^*}{\partial k} > 0, \quad \frac{\partial\varphi^*}{\partial k^*} \gtrless 0 \tag{10.15a}$$

$$\left(\frac{dk^*}{dk}\right)_{\varphi=0} \gtrless 0, \quad \left(\frac{dk^*}{dk}\right)_{\varphi^*=0} \gtrless 0 \tag{10.15b}$$

Moreover it is easy to show that

$$\left(\frac{dk^*}{dk}\right)_{\varphi=0} \gtrless \left(\frac{dk^*}{dk}\right)_{\varphi^*=0} \tag{10.15c}$$

From Eqs. (10.15) we infer that, if the curves $\varphi = 0$ and $\varphi^* = 0$ intersect in an area where neither country is completely specialized, the long-run equilibrium thus defined will in most cases be unstable. Figure 10.10 displays the possible types of intersection, only the last of them being stable.

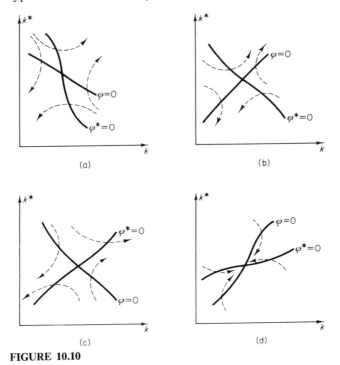

FIGURE 10.10

Pattern (ii): The home country produces both commodities, the foreign country produces only the second commodity. In this case our basic differential equations are Eqs. (10.6a) and (10.9), whence

$$\frac{\partial \varphi}{\partial k} \gtreqless 0, \quad \frac{\partial \varphi}{\partial k^*} > 0, \quad \frac{\partial \varphi^*}{\partial k} = 0, \quad \frac{\partial \varphi^*}{\partial k^*} < 0 \qquad (10.16a)$$

$$\left(\frac{dk^*}{dk}\right)_{\varphi=0} \gtreqless 0, \quad \left(\frac{dk^*}{dk}\right)_{\varphi^*=0} = 0 \qquad (10.16b)$$

We infer that if there exists a long-run equilibrium with this particular pattern of specialization, the equilibrium is stable or unstable as $\partial \varphi / \partial k$ is negative or positive. Figure 10.11 illustrates the two possibilities.

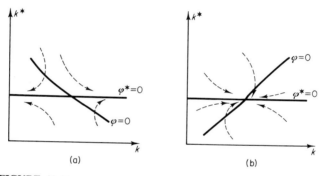

(a)   (b)

FIGURE 10.11

Pattern (iii): The home country produces both commodities, the foreign country produces only the first commodity. Our differential equations are Eqs. (10.6a) and (10.11), whence

$$\frac{\partial \varphi}{\partial k} \gtreqless 0, \quad \frac{\partial \varphi}{\partial k^*} < 0, \quad \frac{\partial \varphi^*}{\partial k} > 0, \quad \frac{\partial \varphi^*}{\partial k^*} < 0$$

$$\left(\frac{dk^*}{dk}\right)_{\varphi=0} \gtreqless 0, \quad \left(\frac{dk^*}{dk}\right)_{\varphi^*=0} > 0 \qquad (10.17a)$$

Once again we find that, if there exists a long-run steady growth path with this particular pattern of specialization, the path may either stable or unstable. Figure 10.12 displays some possibilities.

Pattern (iv): The home country produces only the second commodity, the foreign country produces only the first commodity. From Eqs. (10.11)

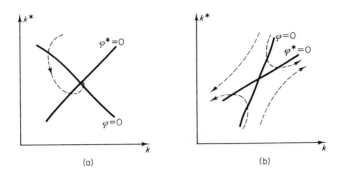

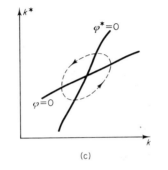

FIGURE 10.12

and (10.13)

$$\frac{\partial \varphi}{\partial k} < 0, \quad \frac{\partial \varphi}{\partial k^*} = 0, \quad \frac{\partial \varphi^*}{\partial k} > 0, \quad \frac{\partial \varphi^*}{\partial k^*} < 0 \qquad (10.18a)$$

$$\left(\frac{dk^*}{dk}\right)_{\varphi=0} = \infty, \quad \left(\frac{dk^*}{dk}\right)_{\varphi^*=0} > 0 \qquad (10.18b)$$

It is not difficult to see that in this case any steady growth equilibrium is stable. Figure 10.13 illustrates.

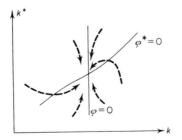

FIGURE 10.13

The dynamic behavior of the system in the remaining three possible patterns of specialization can be inferred from the above discussion. In view of the special intricacy of the analysis when the second commodity is relatively capital-intensive, however, that behavior is spelled out in detail.

Pattern (v): The home country produces only the first commodity, the foreign country produces only the second commodity. In this case our differential equations are

$$\frac{\dot{k}}{k} = \frac{sf_1(k)}{kp} - n \tag{10.19}$$

$$\frac{\dot{k}^*}{k^*} = \frac{s^* f_2^*(k^*)}{k^*} - n^* \tag{10.9}$$

We then calculate that

$$\frac{\partial\varphi}{\partial k} < 0, \quad \frac{\partial\varphi}{\partial k^*} > 0, \quad \frac{\partial\varphi^*}{\partial k} = 0, \quad \frac{\partial\varphi^*}{\partial k^*} < 0 \tag{10.20a}$$

$$\left(\frac{dk^*}{dk}\right)_{\varphi=0} > 0, \quad \left(\frac{dk^*}{dk}\right)_{\varphi^*=0} = 0 \tag{10.20b}$$

and deduce that any path of steady growth with this pattern of specialization is stable. Figure 10.13, with the asterisks changed about, illustrates.

Pattern (vi): The home country produces only the second commodity, the foreign country produces both commodities. From Eqs. (10.6b) and (10.13)

$$\frac{\partial\varphi}{\partial k} < 0, \quad \frac{\partial\varphi}{\partial k^*} = 0, \quad \frac{\partial\varphi^*}{\partial k} > 0, \quad \frac{\partial\varphi^*}{\partial k^*} \gtrless 0 \tag{10.21a}$$

$$\left(\frac{dk^*}{dk}\right)_{\varphi=0} = \infty, \quad \left(\frac{dk^*}{dk}\right)_{\varphi^*=0} \gtrless 0 \tag{10.21b}$$

Steady growth equilibrium, if it exists, is stable or unstable as $\partial\varphi^*/\partial k^*$ is positive or negative. Figure 10.11, with the asterisks changed about, illustrates.

Pattern (vii): The home country produces only the first commodity, the foreign country produces both commodities. From Eqs. (10.6b) and (10.19)

$$\frac{\partial\varphi}{\partial k} < 0, \quad \frac{\partial\varphi}{\partial k^*} > 0, \quad \frac{\partial\varphi^*}{\partial k} < 0, \quad \frac{\partial\varphi^*}{\partial k^*} \gtrless 0 \tag{10.22a}$$

$$\left(\frac{dk^*}{dk}\right)_{\varphi=0} > 0, \quad \left(\frac{dk^*}{dk}\right)_{\varphi^*=0} \gtrless 0 \tag{10.22b}$$

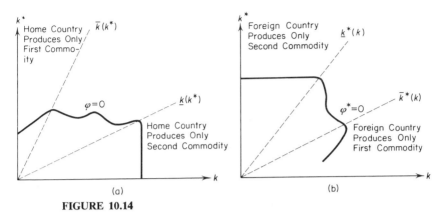

FIGURE 10.14

We infer that any steady-growth equilibrium may be stable or unstable. Figure 10.12, with the asterisks changed about, provides three illustrations.

Pulling together our information about the curves $\varphi = 0$ and $\varphi^* = 0$ we find that their shapes are as displayed in Figs. 10.14(a) and 10.14(b) respectively. Superimposing Fig. 10.14(a) on Fig. 10.14(b), and referring to the preceding stability analysis, one easily sees that

- (i) steady-growth equilibrium may not exist, may be unique, or may be multiple;
- (ii) any steady-growth equilibrium with both countries completely specialized is stable;
- (iii) steady-growth equilibrium with either country incompletely specialized may be stable or unstable.

    Similar conclusions emerge when $\underline{k}(k^*)$ and/or $\underline{k}^*(k)$ are nonmonotonic.

In subsection (A) it was assumed that the first industry is relatively capital-intensive. We found there that if $n \neq n^*$ one country eventually would dominate the other. This was easy to understand since it was shown that growth in both countries is asymptotically exponential. In the present sub-section, on the other hand, it has been assumed that the second industry is relatively capital-intensive; and we have found that growth may be unstable. It can be shown, however, that if $n \neq n^*$ one country eventually will dominate the other even though growth is unstable. For concreteness, let us suppose that $n > n^* \geqq 0$.

The essence of the proof consists in showing that (i) k, the capital:labor ratio of the home country, is bounded above and below by positive numbers, and that (ii) k^* is bounded above. The conclusion then follows easily. For from (i) and (ii) and the assumption that $n > n^*$ it follows that, by taking sufficiently large t, K/K^* can be made as large as need be; and, of course, the same is true of L/L^*.

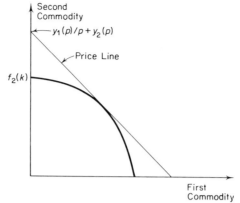

FIGURE 10.15

First we show that k is bounded below by a positive number. (It is assumed that initially both k and k^* are positive and finite; otherwise, production is impossible in one or both of the two countries.) It follows from the convexity of the production set that at any moment the value of competitive output in terms of the investment good is not less than the maximum possible output of the investment good: $[y_1(p)/p] + y_2(p) \geq f_2(k)$. See Figure 10.15.

Hence
$$\dot{K} = sL\left[\frac{y_1}{p} + y_2\right] \geq sLf_2(k)$$

From the restrictions placed on f_2 in Chap. 1, Sec. 1, however, $sf_2(k) > nk$ if k is sufficiently small and positive. It follows that

$$\dot{K} \geq sLf_2(k) > Lnk > 0$$

for k sufficiently small and positive. Hence k is bounded below by a positive number.

Next we show that k is bounded above. Suppose that the contrary is true. Then, clearly, $(K + K^*)/L = k + (K^*/L)$ also is unbounded, so that there exists an infinite sequence of time points $(t_1, t_2, \ldots, t_i, \ldots)$ such that

$$\lim_{i \to \infty} \frac{K(t_i) + K^*(t_i)}{L(t_i)} = \infty$$

In particular, the sequence can be chosen so that[1]

$$\left(\frac{d}{dt}(K + K^*)/L\right)_{t=t_i} > 0 \tag{10.23}$$

[1] For a proof, see Inada [5], Appendix C.

On the other hand

$$\frac{\dot{K} + \dot{K}^*}{L} \leq f_2(k) + \frac{L^*}{L} f_2^*(k^*) \tag{10.24}$$

that is, world output of the investment good cannot exceed its maximum possible value. If we define

$$\bar{k} \equiv \frac{K + K^*}{L + L^*} \equiv \lambda k + (1 - \lambda)k^*$$

where

$$\lambda \equiv L/(L + L^*),$$

we may use the concavity of f_2 and f_2^* to write

$$f_2(\bar{k}) \geq \lambda f_2(k) + (1 - \lambda)f_2(k^*)$$
$$f_2^*(\bar{k}) \geq \lambda f_2^*(k) + (1 - \lambda)f_2^*(k^*)$$

whence, returning to inequality (10.24),

$$\frac{\dot{K} + \dot{K}^*}{L} \leq \frac{1}{\lambda} \{ f_2(\bar{k}) - (1 - \lambda)f_2(k^*) + \frac{L^*}{L} [f_2^*(\bar{k}) - (1 - \lambda)f_2^*(k^*)] \}$$

$$< \frac{1}{\lambda} [f_2(\bar{k}) + \frac{1 - \lambda}{\lambda} f_2^*(\bar{k})]$$

$$< n\bar{k} \text{ for sufficiently large } \bar{k} \tag{10.25}$$

The final inequality follows from the restriction imposed on the functions f_2 and f_2^* in Chap. 1, Sec. 2: $\lim_{\bar{k} \to \infty} f_2'(\bar{k}) = \infty = \lim_{\bar{k} \to \infty} f_2^{*\prime}(\bar{k})$. Next, we notice that

$$\frac{d}{dt} \left(\frac{K + K^*}{L} \right) \equiv \frac{\dot{K} + \dot{K}^*}{L} - n \left(\frac{K + K^*}{L} \right) \tag{10.26}$$

From inequality (10.25) and Eq. (10.26),

$$\frac{d}{dt} \left(\frac{K + K^*}{L} \right) < 0$$

for sufficiently large $(K + K^*)/L$, in contradiction of inequality (10.23). It follows that $(K + K^*)/L$, and therefore k, is bounded above.

By similar reasoning, k^* is bounded above. That completes the proof.

PROBLEMS

10.1 Show that if $s = s^*$, if production functions are the same everywhere, and if the first commodity is relatively capital-intensive, neither country will be completely specialized in long-run, steady-growth equilibrium.

10.2 Under the same assumptions, show that in long-run equilibrium the home country is completely specialized in the production of the first or consumption good if and only if $s > s^*$.

10.3 Under the same assumptions, show that for each s^*, $0 < s^* < 1$,

(a) there exists an s, $0 < s < 1$, such that in long-run equilibrium the home country is completely specialized in the production of the consumption good,

(b) there exists an s, $0 < s < 1$, such that in long-run equilibrium the home country is completely specialized in the production of the investment good.

10.4 Do propositions (a) and (b) of Prob. 10.3 continue to hold if the assumptions are weakened to allow production functions to differ between countries?

REFERENCES

[1] Bardhan, P. K., *Economic Growth and the Pattern of International Trade and Investment: a Study in Pure Theory.* Unpublished doctoral thesis, University of Cambridge, June 1965.

[2] Bardhan, P. K., "Equilibrium Growth in the International Economy," *Quarterly Journal of Economics*, LXXIX, No. 3 (August 1965), 455–64.

[3] Bardhan, P. K., "On Factor Accumulation and the Pattern of International Specialization," *Review of Economic Studies*, XXXIII (1), No. 93 (January 1966), 39–44.

[4] Herberg, Horst, *Wirtschaftswachstum, Aussenhandel und Transportkosten.* Göttingen: Vandenhoeck und Rupprecht, 1966.

†[5] Inada, Ken-ichi, "International Trade, Capital Accumulation and Factor Price Equalization," *Economic Record*, XLIV, No. 107 (September 1968), 322–41.

†[6] Inada, Ken-ichi, "International Trade, Capital Accumulation and Factor Price Equalization," *Keizai to Keizaigachu* (Economies and Economics), No. 10–11 (February 1963), 13–28.

†[7] Oniki, H. and H. Uzawa, "Patterns of Trade and Investment in a Dynamic Model of International Trade," *Review of Economic Studies*, XXXII (1), No. 89 (January 1965), 15–38.

chapter 11

Trade,

International Investment

and Growth

In Chap. 10 we examined the interactions of trade and growth, abstracting throughout from international investment. In the present chapter, on the other hand, it is assumed that at each moment of time the world's stock of capital is so allocated between the two trading countries that the marginal return is everywhere the same.

1. THE MODEL

To keep complication to a minimum it will be assumed that the two countries enjoy a common technology and that the labor force grows at the same rate in each country: $n = n^*$. Otherwise, we shall employ the same assumptions as in Chap. 10; in particular, savings propensities may differ between countries. For concreteness, it is assumed that $s \leq s^*$.

From the assumptions that technology and the marginal product of capital are everywhere the same it follows that each country produces both commodities, or is on the verge of producing both. On the production side, therefore, our international economy behaves like a closed economy and we may take over from Chap. 1 the two production functions

$$y_i = l_i f_i(k_i) \quad i = 1, 2 \tag{11.1}$$

237

the two marginal conditions

$$\omega = \frac{f_i}{f'_i} - k_i \quad i = 1, 2 \tag{11.2}$$

and the two full employment conditions

$$l_1 k_1 + l_2 k_2 = \kappa \tag{11.3a}$$

$$l_1 + l_2 = 1 \tag{11.3b}$$

Now, however, y_i must be interpreted as the *world* per capita output of the *i*th commodity and l_i as the proportion of the *world's* labor force allocated to the *i*th industry; and where κ is the *world* capital:labor ratio $[= (K + K^*)/(L + L^*)]$.

Turning to the demand side, we note that the income of the home country, in terms of the capital good, is the sum of its wage income $L(f_2 - k_2 f'_2)$ and its interest income $K f'_2$. Total home demand for newly produced capital goods is, therefore,

$$s[L(f_2 - k_2 f'_2) + K f'_2] = s(L + L^*)[\lambda(f_2 - k_2 f'_2) + \delta \kappa f'_2]$$

where $\delta \equiv K/(K + K^*)$ is the proportion of the world's capital stock owned by the home country and λ is, of course, the home population as a proportion of world population. Similarly, the total foreign demand for newly produced capital goods is $s^*(L + L^*)[(1 - \lambda)(f_2 - k_2 f'_2) + (1 - \delta)\kappa f'_2]$. Thus, introducing the labor-weighted and capital-weighted averages of the marginal propensities to save, $s^L \equiv \lambda s + (1 - \lambda)s^*$ and $s^K \equiv \delta s + (1 - \delta)s^*$, respectively, we may express the world demand for newly produced capital goods as $(L + L^*)[s^L(f_2 - k_2 f'_2) + s^K \kappa f'_2]$ and the equilibrium in the market for newly produced capital goods as

$$l_2 f_2(k_2) = s^L(f_2 - k_2 f'_2) + s^K \kappa f'_2 \tag{11.4}$$

It follows from Eqs. (11.2)–(11.4) that

$$l_1 = \frac{(1 - s^K)\kappa + (1 - s^L)\omega}{k_1 + \omega} \tag{11.5a}$$

$$l_2 = \frac{s^K \kappa + s^L \omega}{k_2 + \omega} \tag{11.5b}$$

and, therefore, that

$$\kappa = l_1 k_1 + l_2 k_2$$

$$= \frac{k_1 k_2 + [s^L k_2 + (1 - s^L)k_1]\omega}{s^K k_1 + (1 - s^K)k_2 + \omega} \tag{11.6}$$

$$= \psi(\omega, \delta)$$

Equations (11.1)–(11.6) comprise a complete static model of the world economy. Given κ and δ, we may hope to solve Eq. (11.6) for ω. The equilibrium values of the k_i may then be sought from Eq. (11.2) and, finally, the equilibrium l_i's from Eq. (11.3). Whether such equilibrium values exist and, if they exist, whether they are unique, will be considered in Sec. 2.

To set the model in motion we append formal descriptions of the process of capital accumulation. As we have noted, the rate at which the home country accumulates capital is $s[L(f_2 - k_2 f_2') + Kf_2']$; hence

$$\frac{\dot{K}}{K} = s\left[f_2' + \frac{\lambda}{\delta\kappa}(f_2 - k_2 f_2') \right] \tag{11.7a}$$

Similarly,

$$\frac{\dot{K}^*}{K^*} = s^*\left[f_2' + \frac{1 - \lambda}{\kappa(1 - \delta)}(f_2 - k_2 f_2') \right] \tag{11.7b}$$

From Eqs. (11.7a) and (11.7b),

$$\frac{\dot{\kappa}}{\kappa} = \delta\frac{\dot{K}}{K} + (1 - \delta)\frac{\dot{K}^*}{K^*}$$

$$= \left(s^K + \frac{\omega}{\kappa} s^L \right) f_2'$$

However, from the definition of κ,

$$\frac{\dot{\kappa}}{\kappa} = \frac{1}{K + K^*}\frac{d}{dt}(K + K^*) - n$$

Hence

$$\frac{\dot{\kappa}}{\kappa} = \left[s^K + s^L \frac{\omega(\kappa, \delta)}{\kappa} \right] f_2'(k_2(\omega(\kappa, \delta))) - n \tag{11.8a}$$

$$= F(\kappa, \delta)$$

Finally, from the definition of δ,

$$\frac{\dot{\delta}}{\delta} = \frac{\dot{K}}{K} - \frac{\dot{\kappa}}{\kappa}$$

$$= \left\{ s\left[1 + \frac{\lambda}{\delta} \frac{\omega(\kappa, \delta)}{\kappa} \right] - s^*\left[1 + \frac{1 - \lambda}{1 - \delta} \frac{\omega(\kappa, \delta)}{\kappa} \right] \right\} \quad (11.8b)$$

$$\times (1 - \delta) f_2'\{k_2[\omega(\kappa, \delta)]\}$$

$$= G(\kappa, \delta)$$

Eqs. (11.8a) and (11.8b) set our model economy in motion. The properties of these equations are examined in Sec. 3.

2. EXISTENCE AND STABILITY OF SHORT-RUN EQUILIBRIUM

The restrictions placed on the production functions (in Chap. 1, Sec. 1) ensure that $\lim_{\omega \to 0} \psi(\omega, \delta) = 0$ and $\lim_{\omega \to \infty} \psi(\omega, \delta) = \infty$. It follows that a solution $\omega(\kappa, \delta)$ always exists. However, $\psi(\omega, \delta)$ need not be monotonic in ω; hence $\omega(\kappa, \delta)$ need not be unique. (Cf. Fig. 11.1.) And if ω is not uniquely determined, neither are the k_i and l_i.

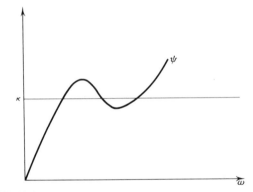

FIGURE 11.1

Multiplicity of short-run equilibria seriously complicates the long-run dynamic analysis to be attempted in Sec. 3. It is therefore important to know whether there exist plausible sufficient conditions for the monotonicity of $\psi(\omega, \delta)$ in ω. It is not difficult to see that ψ is monotonic when $s = s^*$; but that is a very special case indeed. A more convincing sufficient condition may be obtained by considering the short-run dynamic behavior of the economy. We now describe a simple model of market adjustment and show that $\partial\psi/\partial\omega > 0$ is a necessary condition of its stability.

It is assumed that in both countries firms in each industry adjust their capital:labor ratios instantaneously to the prevailing ratio of factor rewards, but that the allocation of factors between industries, and therefore relative outputs, adjust sluggishly to demand. The ratio of factor rewards is assumed to respond through time to the excess demand for capital and the allocation of labor between industries is supposed to respond to the excess demand for the producers' good.[1] We begin with some arbitrary allocation l_2 of labor between the two industries. Then the excess demand for the producers' good, per capita, is

$$E_2 = \frac{1}{L + L^*} [(sK + s^*K^*)f_2' + (sL + s^*L^*)(f_2 - k_2 f_2') - L_2 f_2]$$

$$= [\kappa s^K + \omega s^L - l_2(k_2 + \omega)]f_2' \qquad \text{[from Eq. (11.2)]}$$

$$= \{s^K k_1 + s^L \omega - l_2[(1 - s^K)k_2 + s^K k_1 + \omega]\}f_2' \qquad \text{[from Eq. (11.3a)]}$$

$$= E_2(l_2, \omega)$$

since k_1 and k_2 are both functions of ω. Similarly, the excess demand for capital, per capita, is

$$E_K = \frac{1}{L + L^*} (K_1 + K_2 - K - K^*)$$

$$= l_2 k_2 + (1 + l_2)k_1 - \kappa$$

$$= E_K(l_2, \omega, \kappa)$$

For given κ, the equilibrium values of l_2 and ω, say $\bar{l}_2$ and $\bar{\omega}$, are obtained as the solutions of

$$E_2(l_2, \omega) = 0 = E_K(l_2, \omega, \kappa) \tag{11.9}$$

and our dynamic assumptions may be expressed formally as

$$\dot{l}_2 = g_2(E_2) \qquad g_2(0) = 0 \qquad g_2' > 0 \tag{11.10a}$$
$$\dot{\omega} = g_K(E_K) \qquad g_K(0) = 0 \qquad g_K' < 0 \tag{11.10b}$$

or, expanding g_2 and g_K around $\bar{l}_2$ and $\bar{\omega}$ and choosing quantity units so that $g_2'(0) = 1$ and $g_K'(0) = -1$, as

$$\dot{l}_2 = \frac{\partial E_2}{\partial l_2}(l_2 - \bar{l}_2) + \frac{\partial E_2}{\partial \omega}(\omega - \bar{\omega}) \tag{11.11a}$$

$$\dot{\omega} = -\left[\frac{\partial E_K}{\partial l_2}(l_2 - \bar{l}_2) + \frac{\partial E_K}{\partial \omega}(\omega - \bar{\omega})\right] \tag{11.11b}$$

[1] Walras' Law makes it unnecessary to separately consider the market for the consumption good.

The necessary and sufficient conditions for the stability of Eqs. (11.11) are[2]

$$\frac{\partial E_2}{\partial l_2} - \frac{\partial E_K}{\partial \omega} < 0 \tag{11.12a}$$

$$\frac{\partial E_2}{\partial l_2}\frac{\partial E_K}{\partial \omega} - \frac{\partial E_2}{\partial \omega}\frac{\partial E_K}{\partial l_2} < 0 \tag{11.12b}$$

These conditions are also sufficient for the local stability of Eqs. (11.10).[3] It is easy to see that Eq. (11.12a) is always satisfied. We now show that if in addition Eq. (11.12b) is satisfied then $\partial \psi / \partial \omega$ is positive. From Eq. (11.9) we calculate that

$$\frac{1}{\partial \psi / \partial \omega} = \frac{\partial \omega}{\partial \kappa} = -\frac{\partial E_2}{\partial l_2} \cdot \frac{\partial E_K}{\partial \kappa} \left/ \left(\frac{\partial E_2}{\partial l_2}\frac{\partial E_K}{\partial \omega} - \frac{\partial E_2}{\partial \omega} \cdot \frac{\partial E_K}{\partial l_2} \right) \right.$$

which, in view of Eq. (11.12b), is positive. Thus if we are prepared to assume that all equilibria are locally stable we can be sure that the solution $\omega(\kappa, \delta)$ is unique.

Alternative sufficient conditions may be obtained from the literature on neoclassical growth[4] by noting that $\psi(\omega, \delta)$ has the same general form as the corresponding expression for closed two-sector models. In particular $\partial \psi / \partial \omega > 0$ if at least one of the following conditions is satisfied:

(i) $s^L = s^K$;
(ii) $k_1(\omega) = k_2(\omega)$
(iii) $k_1(\omega) < k_2(\omega)$ and $s^L > s^K$;
(iv) $k_1(\omega) > k_2(\omega)$ and $s^L < s^K$;
(v) $\sigma_1(\omega) + \sigma_2(\omega) \geq 1$

[$\sigma_i = (\omega / k_i)(dk_i / d\omega)$ is the elasticity of factor substitution in the ith industry].

In what follows it will be assumed that $\partial \psi / \partial \omega$ is positive and $\omega(\kappa, \delta)$ unique.

[2] These conditions correspond to the Marshall–Samuelson and related conditions for the stability of barter trade with both factors internationally immobile. For references, see Kemp [6], Chap. 5.

[3] If the characteristic roots of

$$\begin{pmatrix} \partial E_2 / \partial l_2 & \partial E_2 / \partial \omega \\ -\partial E_K / \partial l_2 & -\partial E_K / \partial \omega \end{pmatrix}$$

are neither purely imaginary nor zero, and if there are no multiple roots, conditions (11.12) are also necessary.

[4] See, for example, Drandakis [2].

3. EXISTENCE AND STABILITY OF LONG-RUN EQUILIBRIUM

We begin by considering whether balanced growth, with $\dot{\delta}/\delta = \dot{\kappa}/\kappa = 0$, is possible. That is, we seek the solution to

$$F(\kappa, \delta) = G(\kappa, \delta) = 0 \tag{11.13}$$

The Curve $F = 0$

We have assumed that $\lim_{k_2 \to 0} f_2'(k_2) = \infty$. It follows that $\lim_{\kappa \to 0} F(\kappa, \delta) > 0$; that is, the graph of $F = 0$ does not cut the δ-axis. Moreover, for any δ, it is possible to make F positive by selecting a sufficiently small (but positive) κ. For, from Eq. (11.6), ω can be made as small as need be by choosing a sufficiently small κ; $k_2(\omega)$ can be made as small as need be, and therefore $f_2'(k_2)$ as large as need be, by choosing a sufficiently small ω; and ω/κ is always finite. Finally we note that, for any δ, it is possible to make F negative by selecting a sufficiently large κ. For, from Eq. (11.6), ω can be made as large as need be by choosing a sufficiently large κ; $k_2(\omega)$ can be made as large as need be, and therefore $f_2'(k_2)$ as small as need be, by choosing a sufficiently large ω; and ω/κ is always finite. We may conclude, therefore, that the graph of $F = 0$ runs from $(\kappa, \delta) = (+, 0)$ to $(\kappa, \delta) = (+, 1)$.

The Curve $G = 0$

From Eq. (11.8b)

$$\frac{\omega}{\kappa} = -\frac{s - s^*}{\dfrac{\lambda}{\delta}s - \dfrac{1 - \lambda}{1 - \delta}s^*} \equiv g(\delta)$$

which is comparatively easy to graph.

Suppose that $s < s^*$ and consider $g(\delta)$. It is not difficult to see that $g(0) = 0 = g(1)$, $g(\lambda) = -1$ and $g(\bar{\delta}) = \infty$, where $\bar{\delta} = \lambda s/s^L$. Moreover,

$$\frac{dg}{d\delta} = -(s - s^*)\left[\frac{\lambda s}{\delta^2} + \frac{(1 - \lambda)s^*}{(1 - \delta)^2}\right]$$

which is positive. It follows that the graph of $g(\delta)$ is as shown in Fig. 11.2. If now (ω/κ) is superimposed, with κ fixed, we find the solution for δ. Let

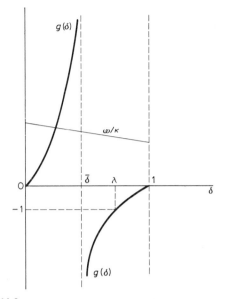

FIGURE 11.2

us define the *macro*-elasticity of substitution[5] $\sigma \equiv (\omega/\psi)(\partial\psi/\partial\omega)$. Then from Eq. (11.6) the slope of the curve (ω/κ) is

$$\frac{1}{\kappa} \cdot \frac{\partial\omega}{\partial\delta} = -\frac{1}{\kappa}\left(\frac{\partial\psi}{\partial\delta}\bigg/\frac{\partial\psi}{\partial\omega}\right)$$

$$= -\frac{\omega}{\sigma\kappa^2} \cdot \frac{\partial\psi}{\partial\delta}$$

$$= \frac{\omega}{\sigma\kappa}(s - s^*)(k_1 - k_2)[(1 - s^K)(k_2 + \omega) + s^K(k_1 + \omega)]^{-1} \quad (11.14)$$

and has the sign of $(k_2 - k_1)$; in Fig. 11.2 the curve (ω/κ) is drawn on the assumption that the first industry is relatively capital-intensive $(k_1 > k_2)$. Finally, by varying κ we may trace out the curve $G = 0$.

[5] From Eq. (11.6),

$$\sigma - 1 = \mu_1(\sigma_1 - 1) + \mu_2(\sigma_2 - 1)$$

where

$$\mu_1 = \frac{k_1(k_2 + \omega)(s^K k_2 + s^L\omega)}{\{k_1k_2 + \omega[s^Lk_1 + (1 - s^L)k_2]\}\{(1 - s^K)k_1 + s^Kk_2 + \omega\}}$$

and

$$\mu_2 = \frac{k_2(k_1 + \omega)[(1 - s^K)k_1 + (1 - s^L)\omega]}{\{k_1k_2 + \omega[s^Lk_1 + (1 - s^L)k_2]\}\{(1 - s^K)k_1 + s^Kk_2 + \omega\}}$$

are both positive.

The precise shape of the curve $G = 0$ depends on the relationship between κ and ω/κ. It can be shown[6] that, under the assumptions we have imposed on the production functions,

$$\lim_{\omega \to 0} \sigma_i = 1$$

It follows that

$$\lim_{\omega \to 0} \sigma = 1$$

so that $\lim_{\omega \to 0} (\omega/\kappa)$ is positive and finite. When $s < s^*$, therefore, the curve $G = 0$ must leave the δ-axis between $\bar{\delta}$ and 0. The behavior of ω/κ as κ increases from zero cannot be pinned down without assumptions about the production function even more stringent than those made so far. As a purely formal matter, one can say that

$$\lim_{\kappa \to \infty} \left(\frac{\omega}{\kappa}\right) = 0, \quad d \quad \text{or} \quad \infty \quad \text{if} \quad \sigma < 1, \quad \sigma = 1, \quad \text{or} \quad \sigma > 1$$

where d is positive and finite. However, σ is a variable quantity which may cross and recross the critical value of unity. The curve $G = 0$ is therefore in general a wavy line which begins on the δ-axis and is bounded by $\delta = 0$ and $\delta = \bar{\delta}$ [as in Fig. 11.3(a)].

From Eq. (11.8b), with $\delta \neq 0$,

$$\left[s^K + s^L \left(\frac{\omega}{\kappa}\right) - s\left(1 + \frac{\lambda}{\delta} \cdot \frac{\omega}{\kappa}\right) \right] f_2' = 0$$

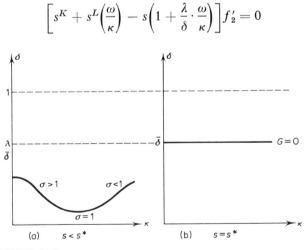

FIGURE 11.3

[6] See [5], Appendix.

whence[7]

$$s^K + s^L \frac{\omega}{\kappa} = s\left[\delta + \lambda \frac{\omega}{\kappa}\right]/\delta \quad \text{for} \quad k_2 < \infty$$

It follows that, when $s = s^*$, $\delta = \lambda$ [as in Fig. (11.3b)].

Having plotted the curve $G = 0$, it remains to indicate the behavior of δ off the curve. From Eq. (11.8b), for finite κ,

$$\dot{\delta} = \delta G(\delta, \kappa)$$

$$= \begin{cases} -s^*(1-\lambda)\dfrac{\omega}{\kappa}f_2' < 0 \\[2em] s\lambda\dfrac{\omega}{\kappa}f_2' > 0 \end{cases} \quad \text{at} \quad \delta = \begin{cases} 1 \\[2em] 0 \end{cases}$$

Moreover, $\delta G(\delta, \kappa)$ is a continuous function of δ. Hence

$$\frac{\partial G}{\partial \delta} < 0 \quad \text{at} \quad G = 0$$

From the above discussion we may conclude that Eqs. (11.13) have at least one solution, that is, a steady growth path always exists. We notice also that Eqs. (11.8) satisfy the conditions of a well-known lemma of Arrow, Block, and Hurwicz,[8] so that the global stability of Eqs. (11.8) is assured. It follows that if the solution of Eqs. (11.13) is unique it is locally stable. However, it does not seem possible to rule out multiple solutions and local instability without imposing further restrictions on the production functions.

Finally, we note from Figs. 11.2 and 11.3(b) that on a path of steady growth $\delta \leq \lambda$ as $s \leq s^*$, so that the thriftier country has the higher overall capital:labor ratio.

4. LONG-RUN TRADE AND INVESTMENT

It is noteworthy that nowhere in the above analysis was it necessary to mention international trade or investment. This is fortunate, perhaps, for at any point of time the level and direction of each is, within calculable bounds, indeterminate. The bounds, however, are of some interest.

[7] The left-hand expression is the ratio of total saving to total profit (interest), while the right-hand expression is the ratio of home saving to home profit.
[8] Arrow, Block and Hurwicz [1], p. 100.

Thus suppose that the world is moving along a path of steady growth, with the aggregate stock of capital and the aggregate labor force growing exponentially at rate n. And, for concreteness, let us suppose that $s < s^*$, so that $k < k^*$.

Case 1: $\min (k_1, k_2) < k < k^* < \max (k_1, k_2)$. Evidently both the direction and extent of international indebtedness are, within bounds, indeterminate; the direction and volume of trade are also indeterminate. In establishing those bounds it will be necessary to refer to the *installed* capital:labor ratio in the home country

$$v = \frac{K + J^*}{L} = k^* + \frac{J^*}{L}$$

where J^* is the home country's net indebtedness. Similarly

$$v^* = \frac{K^* - J^*}{L^*} = k^* - \frac{J^*}{L}$$

Evidently

$$\min (k_1, k_2) \leq v, v^* \leq \max (k_1, k_2) \tag{11.15}$$

for, otherwise, at least one country would be completely specialized in production.[9] It follows from the inequalities (11.15) that

$$\max J^* = \min \{[\max (k_1, k_2) - k]L, [k^* - \min (k_1, k_2)]L^*\} > 0$$

and

$$\min J^* = \max \{[\min (k_1, k_2) - k]L, [k^* - \max (k_1, k_2)]L^*\} < 0$$

Evidently both $\max J^*$ and $\min J^*$ grow in magnitude at rate n.

Case 2: $k < \min (k_1, k_2) < \max (k_1, k_2) < k^*$. In this case international investment is inevitable and the home country must be the debtor. Only the extent of the indebtedness is indeterminate. From the inequalities (11.15),

$$\max J^* = \min \{[\max (k_1, k_2) - k]L, [k^* - \min (k_1, k_2)]L^*\} > 0$$

and

$$\min J^* = \max \{[\min (k_1, k_2) - k]L, [k^* - \max (k_1, k_2)]L^*\} > 0$$

Case 3: $k < \min (k_1, k_2) < k^* < \max (k_1, k_2)$. International investment is inevitable and the home country must be the debtor. From the inequalities (11.15),

$$\max J^* = \min \{[\max (k_1, k_2) - k]L, [k^* - \min (k_1, k_2)]L^*\} > 0$$

[9] Incipient specialization is admitted.

and

$$\min J^* = [\min (k_1, k_2) - k]L > 0$$

Case 4: $\min (k_1, k_2) < k < \max (k_1, k_2) < k^*$. Again international investment is inevitable and the home country must be the debtor. From (11.15),

$$\min J^* = [k^* - \max (k_1, k_2)]L^* > 0$$

and

$$\max J^* = \min \{[\max (k_1, k_2) - k]L, \quad [k^* - \min (k_1, k_2)]L^*\} > 0$$

Bounds (on $J^* = -J$) when $s < s^*$ may be obtained from the above expressions by interchanging starred and unstarred symbols.

5. COMPARATIVE DYNAMICS

It remains to investigate briefly some of the comparative steady-growth properties of the model. The investigation makes sense, of course, only if paths of steady growth are locally stable.

It is easy to see that, under these assumptions, an increase in the common rate of population growth n moves the F-curve to the right and thus increases the equilibrium value of the world capital:labor ratio κ. Whether the equilibrium value of δ rises or falls depends on the slope of the curve $G = 0$.

Straightforward calculation from Eq. (11.8) reveals that an increase in the home saving ratio results in an increase in δ and, provided $s < s^*$, an increase in κ.

These conclusions are easy to digest. If $s > s^*$, however, it is possible (but not inevitable) that κ will fall. This is a paradox. The explanation seems to lie in the fact that, if $s > s^*$, the increase in δ with κ constant will be associated with an increase in the wage:rental ratio ω and, therefore, with a redistribution of world income in favor of the *low*-saving foreign country. It is paradoxical perhaps that the increase in the foreign saving ratio may (not must) give rise to a decrease in κ. The explanation seems to lie in the fact that, if $s < s^*$, the decrease in δ with κ constant will be associated with a decline in the wage:rental ratio ω and, therefore, with a redistribution of world income in favor of the low-saving home country.

6. CAUTIONARY REMARKS

The above discussion has been based on several quite severe assumptions. In particular, it has been assumed (a) that trade and investment are free, unhindered by tariffs or other taxes, and (b) that conditions of production are the same everywhere. A more general analysis is bound to be more complex. As partial compensation, however, the relaxation of (a) and (b) will remove the elements of indeterminancy encountered in Sec. 4.

REFERENCES

[1] Arrow, Kenneth J., H. D. Block and Leonid Hurwicz, "On the Stability of the Competitive Equilibrium, II," *Econometrica*, XXVII, No. 1 (January 1959), 92–109.

[2] Drandakis, Emanuel M., "Factor Substitution in the Two-Sector Growth Model," *Review of Economic Studies*, XXX (4), No. 84 (October 1963), 217–28.

[3] Hamada, Koichi, "Economic Growth and Long-Term International Capital Movements," *Yale Economic Essays*, VI, No. 2 (Spring 1966), 49–96.

†[4] Inada, Ken-Ichi, "International Trade, Capital Accumulation and Factor Price Equalization," *Economic Record*, XLIV, No. 107 (September 1968), 322–41.

[5] Kemp, Murray C., "International Trade and Investment in a Context of Growth," *Economic Record*, XLIV, No. 106 (June 1968), 211–23.

[6] Kemp, Murray C., *The Pure Theory of International Trade*. Englewood Cliffs, N.J.: Prentice Hall, Inc., 1964.

†[7] Sato, Kazuo, "Neo-classical Economic Growth and Saving: An Extension of Uzawa's Model," *Economic Studies Quarterly*, XIV No. 2 (February 1964), 51–67, and No. 3 (June 1964), 69–75.

part 3

The Appraisal of International Trade and Investment

The Gain from Trade and
Investment Statically Considered

We commonly take it for granted, in public debate over commercial policy, that countries do benefit from their participation in international specialization and trade: Countries are not obliged to trade; they *do* trade; therefore, they must gain from trade. This kind of argument does not, however, survive close inspection. For we know[1] that, in general, the opening up of trade makes some people worse off than under autarky. In what sense, then can we say that a country benefits from trade? One could, of course, engage in interpersonal comparisons of the utilities of gainers and losers, but then no two observers could be counted on to agree that a country had received benefit (or had suffered) from trade.

That some people are hurt by trade is indeed a substantial obstacle in the way of any evaluation of trade, free or otherwise. And it can scarcely be claimed that a way has been found around the difficulty. Nevertheless, some small progress has been made, with the aid of that characteristically modern device, the compensation principle. In particular it is possible to demonstrate, under certain familiar assumptions concerning market conditions, the nature of returns to scale, and so on, that free trade or any kind of restricted trade is better than

---

[1] See Chap. 2, Sec. 3.

no trade, in the sense that there exists a system of lump-sum money transfers which would ensure that every individual could improve upon the position he enjoyed in the absence of international trade (and in the absence of transfers). "In other words, if a unanimous decision were required in order for trade to be permitted, it would always be possible for those who desired trade to buy off those opposed to trade, with the result that all could be made better off."[2]

It is the main purpose of this chapter to construct a rigorous proof of this theorem and to show how it breaks down when certain of the assumptions are relaxed. Before embarking upon the proof, however, one possible misunderstanding may be forestalled. It will not be proved that the *collection of goods* that would be consumed in the pretransfer but post-trading situation could be redistributed in such a manner that every individual is better off than in the closed economy. In general such a redistribution is impossible. It would be ruled out, for example, if those who (in the absence of redistribution) gained from trade spent their entire incomes on commodities which had no utility at all for the rest of the community. It is held only that, given the opportunity to revise its consumption pattern after the transfer payments, a country would in the indicated sense be better off with trade than without.

1. STATEMENT AND PROOF OF THE THEOREM

The theorem will be proved in detail under the assumptions of perfect competition in all industries and the complete absence of local commodity taxes and of nonpecuniary external economies and diseconomies, both of consumption and of production. The stock and distribution of technological knowledge, and therefore the form of all production functions, are assumed constant. To ensure the possibility of perfect competition, production functions are assumed to show constant returns to scale and diminishing returns to proportions. The number of commodities is quite arbitrary, as is the number of productive factors; in this respect we depart from the assumptions of earlier chapters. Productive factors are not necessarily in completely inelastic supply but may respond to changes in factor rentals and product prices. Nor need factor owners be indifferent concerning the industry in which the factors are employed; if they are not indifferent, different rental and quantity symbols will be introduced for each employment, that is, if members of the same factor class are employed in different industries they will be treated as though they were members of different "factor" classes. Finally, abstraction is made from international capital movements and from trade in raw materials. As will be indicated in later sections, proofs can be constructed under less restrictive assumptions.

[2] Samuelson [12], p. 204.

The following notation will be adopted. The amount consumed of the ith commodity is denoted by D_i, the amount produced by X_i. The consumption vector is then

$$D = (D_1, D_2, \ldots, D_n)$$

and the production vector is

$$X = (X_1, X_2, \ldots, X_n)$$

The vector of domestic commodity prices, in terms of money or a commodity *numéraire*, is

$$p = (p_1, p_2, \ldots, p_n)$$

The vector of factor inputs is

$$A = (A_1, A_2, \ldots, A_s)$$

and the vector of factor rentals is

$$w = (w_1, w_2, \ldots, w_s)$$

Values of the variables under autarky are indicated by the superscript "0," free trade values by primes.

In the absence of trade, domestic demand equals domestic supply:

$$D^0 - X^0 = 0 \qquad (12.1)$$

But under balanced free trade the amount consumed of any particular commodity need not equal the amount produced. It is necessary only that the value of imports be equal to the value of exports or, what is the same thing, that the value of consumption equal the value of production:[3]

$$p'(X' - D') = 0 \qquad (12.2)$$

Turning to the keystone of the proof, we observe that, given constant returns to scale and the possibility of independently carrying on production in separate processes, the set S of production possibilities is convex (in fact, a convex cone). Under perfect competition and free trade S will be supported by the price plane

$$p'(X - X') - w'(A - A') = 0 \qquad (12.3)$$

[3] $p'X'$ is to be understood as the inner product $\sum_{i=1}^{n} p_i'X_i'$, $p'D'$ as $\sum_{i=1}^{n} p_i'D_i'$.

at the free trade production point $(X'; A')$. It follows that $p'X - w'A$, considered as a linear function defined on S, reaches a maximum at $(X'; A')$. This means that *at the free trade prices* the competitive quantities of commodities and factor services maximize for the economy as a whole the algebraic difference between the total value of output and total factor cost, as compared to any other commodity and factor combination in S, in particular the autarkic combination.[4] This result may be written

$$p'X' - w'A' \geq p'X^0 - w'A^0 \qquad (12.4)$$

and is illustrated, for the special two-commodities, fixed-factors case, by Fig. 12.1. Substituting from Eqs. (12.1) and (12.2) in Eq. (12.4), we obtain the basic inequality

$$p'D' - w'A' \geq p'D^0 - w'A^0 \qquad (12.5)$$

At free trade prices, the community's autarkic consumption pattern would have cost not more than the actual free trade consumption pattern.

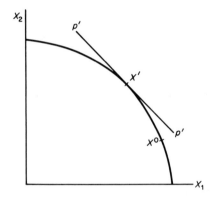

FIGURE 12.1

What can be inferred from the inequality (12.5)? Not very much, but enough for our purposes: That it is impossible, by simply redistributing the collection of goods actually chosen under autarky, to make everyone better off than in the chosen free trade position.

To see that this is so, let us define V_i, the set of consumption bundles which the ith individual regards as not inferior to the bundle he actually chooses under free trade. It is assumed that V_i is strictly convex; it is, of course, supported by the free-trade price hyperplane. Let us now define $V = \sum V_i$, the set of consumption bundles each of which could be so distributed among individual members of the community as to leave none worse off than in the

[4] Samuelson [12], p. 197.

actual free-trade equilibrium. Thus V may be described as the set of consumption bundles each of which the *community* regards as not inferior to the bundle (X', A') actually chosen under free trade. Like the individual V_i, V is a strictly convex set and is supported by the (p', w')-plane. From inequality (12.5), the bundle (X', A') is separated from V by the price plane; hence, if $(S', A') \neq (X^0, A^0)$ then $(X^0, A^0) \in V$ and it is impossible by simply redistributing the bundle (X^0, A^0) to make everybody as well off as they are under free trade.[5] This is readily illustrated, for the two-persons case, by means of Samuelson's utility possibility curves.[6] In Fig. 12.2 the point u^0 indicates the distribution of utilities which actually emerges under autarky, and the dotted curve g^0g^0 is the utility possibility curve corresponding to the collection of goods actually chosen under autarky. g^0g^0 passes southwest of u', the utility mixture of free trade.

[5] The proof is illustrated for the two-commodities, two-persons case in which

$$p'_1 D'_1 + p'_2 D'_2 > p'_1 D^0_1 + p'_2 D^0_2$$

The dimensions of the accompanying Edgeworthian box diagram are D^0_1 and D^0_2. The point P^0 indicates the autarkic distribution of consumptions between the two individuals: The first individual's consumption is measured from origin 0_1, the second individual's from origin 0_2. Aggregate consumption under free trade, on the other hand, is indicated by P' (referred to 0_1). The free-trade distribution of consumption must then be represented within the box by the pair of points, P'_1 and P'_2. (The vectors $P'_1P'_2$ and $P'0_2$ are, of course, equal.) The box illustrates the possibility that the first individual is harmed by trade, the second benefited. It is clear from this construction that, since the contract locus traverses the shaded band, it must be possible to *efficiently* redistribute the autarkic basket of goods in a manner calculated to leave both individuals worse off than under free trade. It follows that it is impossible by redistributing the autarkic basket, to make both individuals better off than in the chosen free trade position. The foregoing illustration was constructed by Samuelson. ([39], p. 8, note.)

Notice that it *cannot* be inferred from inequality (12.5) that it is possible, by simply redistributing the collection of goods actually chosen under free trade, to make everyone better off than in the chosen autarkic position.

[6] Samuelson [39].

Imagine that under autarky some other distribution of income had prevailed. Corresponding to it would be a new set of demands, a new production mixture, and hence a new utility possibility curve, say h^0h^0 in Fig. 12.2. If trade is opened up and if, simultaneously, appropriate lump-sum taxes and subsidies are introduced, D' will reappear and, with it, u'. Evidently h^0h^0, like g^0g^0, passes southwest of u'.

Consider now the envelope PP of all *point* utility possibility curves like g^0g^0 and h^0h^0. This envelope is the utility possibility curve of the autarkic

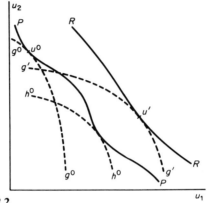

FIGURE 12.2

situation.[7] It too must pass southwest of u'. Thus it is impossible under autarky to make everyone better off than at the particular free trade point D' (or u'). Put otherwise, it would be impossible for those who expect to be hurt by the introduction of trade to bribe the rest of the community into foregoing the free trade point D' (or u').

But evidently a similar statement can be made with respect to *any* free trade point attainable by means of appropriate lump-sum taxes and transfers. In other words, the utility possibility locus of the free trade *situation*, say RR, cannot lie inside PP, the utility possibility locus of the autarkic situation.[8]

Thus we have proved that, for some systems of taxes and subsidies, inequality (12.5) would hold for every individual. (D^0, D', A^0, and A' must now

[7] Samuelson [39], pp. 12ff.

[8] PP and RR may possibly touch at one or more points. Note that $g'g'$, the *point* utility possibility curve corresponding to the collection of goods actually chosen under free trade, not only may cut PP but may pass southwest of u^0. (Cf. footnote 7.) This point has been emphasized by Erling Olsen who, mistakenly however, regards it as inconsistent with Samuelson's 1939 results. See Olsen [11].

That RR cannot lie inside PP is denied by Stephen Enke who holds that, given individual indifference curves of "extreme curvature," a change to *free* trade from no trade will lessen welfare for all after compensation. (Enke [3], p. 252.) Enke's mistake is in supposing that the compensated and uncompensated free trade consumption mixtures (represented by Z' in his Fig. 1) are identical and, by implication, in denying the necessity of the compensated free trade consumption mixture lying "above" the autarkic community indifference curve.

be interpreted as vectors of quantities of commodities bought and supplied by *individuals*.) Every individual would be revealed as better off (in the limiting case in which $D^0 = D'$ and $A^0 = A'$, not worse off) under compensated free trade than under autarky.

Note that nowhere in the above proof was it assumed that the trading country has no influence on world prices; nowhere was it necessary to assume that each point on the $p'p'$-curve of Fig. 12.1 is a possible trading point.

Note also that nowhere were purely "domestic" commodities ruled out. For such commodities it is only necessary to write $X_i = D_i$.

Note finally that while inputs and outputs are permitted to vary in response to changes in world prices, the proof does not *require* that such adjustments take place. Specifically, the theorem holds even for fixed, totally unresponsive inputs and outputs, whether the fixity be imposed by Nature or Government. The gain is greater if Nature's freedom is not impaired by governmental regulation. This suggests the possibility of decomposing the gain from trade into three components:

(i) the consumption gain, or the gain from international exchange, defined as the gain which accrues when both aggregate factor supplies and outputs are frozen by governmental regulation;

(ii) the production gain, or the gain from specialization, defined as the additional gain (over and above the consumption gain) resulting from the adjustment of the pattern of production to changing commodity and factor prices, with aggregate factor supplies unchanged;

(iii) the gain from revising aggregate factor supplies, especially labor, defined as the additional gain (over and above the consumption and production gains) resulting from the adjustment of aggregate factor supplies to changing commodity and factor prices. It is possible to regard (*iii*) as a special case of (*i*).

For the limiting case in which world prices are beyond the control of the country under consideration, this decomposition is illustrated by Fig. 12.3. One may imagine a three-dimensional production possibility surface (similar to that depicted in Fig. 5.2) to which the autarkic price plane ABC is tangential at P_0, the autarkic production-consumption point. One also may imagine a community indifference surface tangential to the price plane at P_0. Now trade is opened and the price plane changes slope. If both the labor supply and the output mixture are frozen at P_0, only the consumption point moves. Trade takes place from P_0 along the new price plane to a new consumption point which, if appropriate lump-sum transfers are effected, is superior to P_0. If, alternatively, the labor supply is frozen but outputs are free to respond to the price changes, the equilibrium production point moves, say to P_1. In view of the convexity of the production set, the free-trade price plane through P_0 passes above P_1; the community's income therefore increases and, with it, the community's welfare. If, finally, the labor supply is free to respond to the

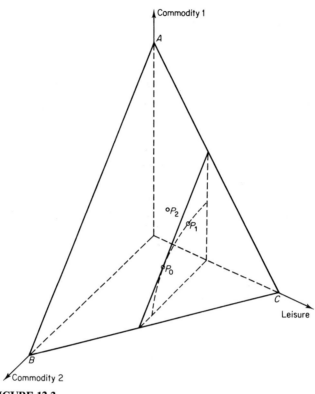

FIGURE 12.3

change in prices, production moves to P_2. If leisure is valued at the free-trade wage rate, we may again infer from the convexity of the production set that income and welfare increase.

2. EXTENSION OF THE PROOF TO COVER IMPORTED RAW MATERIALS

In the above proof it has been assumed implicitly that the trading country makes no use of imported raw materials. This is, of course, a blatantly unrealistic assumption. Fortunately, as must be intuitively obvious, the proofs can be easily modified to accommodate the possibility of imported raw materials.

Let

$$\hat{A} = (\hat{A}_1, \hat{A}_2, \ldots, \hat{A}_t)$$

represent the vector of imported raw materials, and

$$\hat{w} = (\hat{w}_1, \hat{w}_2, \ldots, \hat{w}_t)$$

the corresponding vector of raw material prices. Then Eq. (12.2) must be rewritten as

$$p'(X' - D') - \hat{w}'\hat{A}' = 0 \tag{12.2a}$$

and inequality (12.4) as

$$p'X' - w'A' - \hat{w}'\hat{A}' \geq p'X^0 - w'A^0 \tag{12.4a}$$

Substituting in inequality (12.4d) from Eqs. (12.1) and (12.2a), we obtain

$$p'D' - w'A' \geq p'D^0 - w'A^0 \tag{12.5}$$

and the proof proceeds as above.

The borrowing and lending of capital can be viewed as the purchase and sale of capital services (cf. Chap. 9, Sec. 1); and capital services are raw materials. It emerges then that free international trade *and investment* is gainful.

3. THE ACCOMMODATION OF UNILATERAL TRANSFERS

In the proofs furnished so far, balanced trade has been assumed. In the present section the implications of unilateral transfers are explored. Attention is confined to the case of net *receipts;* the extension of the argument to cover net payments is straightforward.

In the special and very simple case in which the thing to be transferred can be viewed as a constant vector of commodities,[9]

$$K = (K_1, K_2, \ldots, K_n) \geq 0,$$

Eqs. (12.1) and (12.2) become, respectively,

$$X^0 - D^0 + K = 0 \tag{12.1a}$$

and

$$p'(X' - D' + K) = 0 \tag{12.2b}$$

Substitution into inequality (12.4) from Eqs. (12.1a) and (12.2b) yields inequality (12.5) as before.

When the thing to be transferred is a sum of money, however, the proof becomes slightly more complicated. "Autarky" must be redefined to permit imports equal in value to the sum to be transferred, say T. Imagine that, under autarky thus defined, the last $(n - v)$ commodities are imported. Then we

---

[9] As it can, for example, when reparations are assessed and paid in kind.

may write

$$D = (D_1, \ldots, D_v; D_{v+1}, \ldots, D_n)$$

$$= (D_x; D_m)$$

Similarly,

$$X = (X_1, \ldots, X_v; \quad X_{v+1}, \ldots, X_n)$$

$$= (X_x; \quad X_m)$$

and

$$p = (p_1, \ldots, p_v; \quad p_{v+1}, \ldots, p_n)$$

$$= (p_x; \quad p_m)$$

Under autarky exports are, of course, prohibited, so that imports,

$$D_m^0 - X_m^0,$$

are limited in value to T:

$$p_m^0(D_m^0 - X_m^0) = T \qquad (12.1b)$$

As in Secs. 1 and 2,

$$X_x^0 - D_x^0 = 0 \qquad (12.1c)$$

Eq. (12.2) takes the revised form[10]

$$p_x'D_x' + p_m'D_m' = p_x'X_x' + p_m'X_m' + T \qquad (12.2c)$$

If with the introduction of free trade import prices rise, so that

$$p_m' > p_m^0$$

then, from Eq. (12.1b)

$$p_m'(D_m^0 - X_m^0) > T \qquad (12.1d)$$

Rewriting inequality (12.4) as

$$p_x'X_x' + p_m'X_m' - w'A' \geq p_x'X_x^0 + p_m'X_m^0 - w'A^0 \qquad (12.4a)$$

and substituting for X_x^0 from Eq. (12.1c), for $p_m'X_m^0$ from Eq. (12.1d), and for $(p_x'X_x' + p_m'X_m')$ from Eq. (12.2b), we obtain

$$p'D' - w'A' \geq p'D^0 - w'A^0 \qquad (12.5)$$

as before.

4. WELFARE AND THE TERMS OF TRADE

It has been proved in the preceding sections that exposure to world prices which differ from those which would prevail under autarky carries with it a

[10] That when free trade is introduced the list of imports may expand is of no importance here.

clearly defined benefit. Consider now the special case in which it is beyond the power of the individual country to influence world prices. Then the following question arises: Is it possible to show that the benefit increases with an improvement of the terms of trade? In our discussion of this question we again abstract from capital movements and imported raw materials.

Evidently a prerequisite of any analysis of the question is agreement on the sense in which in a world of many commodities the terms of trade can be said to improve or deteriorate. Let p' and p'' be two vectors of world commodity prices, w' and w'' the corresponding vectors of domestic factor rewards. Then we shall say that a change from p' to p'' involves an improvement in the terms of trade if and only if

$$p''(X' - D') > 0 \qquad (12.6)$$

Now it is clearly impossible to show that everyone is necessarily better off at the actually chosen position D'' than at the actually chosen position D'. The analysis of Sec. 1 suggests, however, that the utility possibility curve of the p''-situation might be shown to lie "outside" that of the p'-situation. This is indeed the case.

We wish to show that, if inequality (12.6) is satisfied, then

$$p''D'' - w''A'' \geq p''D' - w''A' \qquad (12.7)$$

From the discussion of Sec. 1

$$p''X'' - w''A'' \geq p''X' - w''A' \qquad (12.8)$$

$$p''(D'' - X'') = 0 \qquad (12.9)$$

From these materials the proof may be pieced together:

$$
\begin{aligned}
p''D'' - w''A'' &= p''X'' - w''A'' &&\text{[from (12.9)]} \\
&\geq p''X' - w''A' &&\text{[from (12.8)]} \\
&= p''D' + p''(X' - D') - w''A' \\
&\geq p''D' - w''A' &&\text{[from (12.6)]}
\end{aligned}
$$

Hence (12.7).

Figure 12.4 illustrates the theorem for the simple two-commodities, fixed-factors case. Inequality (12.6) means that the chosen point D' cannot lie on the heavy part of the p'-line in Fig. 12.4(a). Restricted in this way, the utility possibility curve of the p'-situation must lie inside the utility possibility curve of the p''-situation [as in Fig. 12.4(b)].

Notice that nowhere in the above proof was it assumed that each commodity is either imported or exported: Purely domestic goods, for which $X_i = D_i$, are admitted.

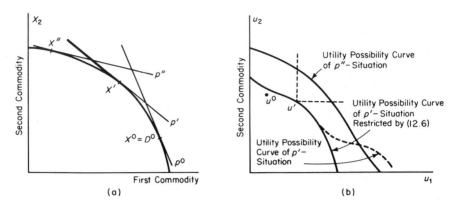

FIGURE 12.4

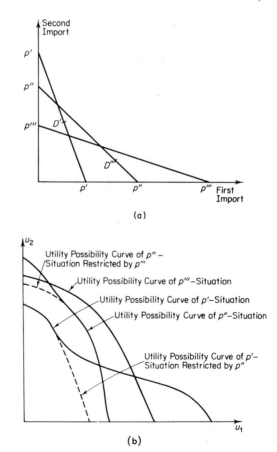

FIGURE 12.5

Notice also, however, that in defining an improvement in the terms of trade we have introduced quantity weights proportional to the actual imports and exports of one of the two situations compared. It follows that the theorem just proved does not establish transitivity: If p'' represents an improvement in the terms of trade in relation to p', and if p''' represents an improvement in relation to p'', then we may infer that the restricted p'-utility possibility curve lies inside the (unrestricted) p''-curve and that the restricted p''-curve lies inside the (unrestricted) p'''-curve; but we cannot infer that p''' represents an improvement of the terms of trade in relation to p'. As a simple counter example, consider a small country which produces a single commodity in fixed amount. Suppose also that a constant amount (possibly zero) is consumed at home, the balance being exported in exchange for two imports. At world prices p' imports (and consumption of the imported commodities) are indicated by point D' in Fig. 12.5(a). In the double primed situation the first import is cheaper in terms of the exported commodity, the second more expensive; imports and consumption are indicated by point D''. Evidently p'' represents an improvement in the terms of trade in relation to p'. In the triple primed situation the first import is even cheaper, the second even more expensive. p''' represents an improvement in the terms of trade in relation to p'' *but it does not represent an improvement in relation to p'.* Figure 12.5(b) corresponds to Fig. 12.5(a).

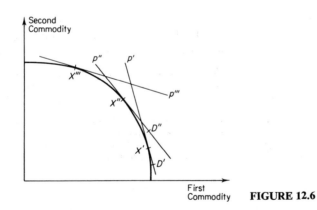

FIGURE 12.6

While it does not hold in general, transitivity does hold in the simplest textbook world of two commodities and fixed factor supplies. Figure 12.6 illustrates.

5. A FOOTNOTE TO THE PRECEDING SECTIONS

If exposure to prices which differ from those which would have prevailed under autarky is beneficial, one might have supposed that the benefit would be greater the more prices "deviate" from those of the autarkic state. Unfortunately, this attractive speculation is false.

Let p' and p'' be two vectors of world commodity prices. p'' will be said to deviate from p^0, the autarkic price vector, by more than does p' if p' can be expressed as a convex linear combination of p^0 and p'':[11]

$$p' = \alpha p^0 + (1 - \alpha)p'' \qquad (0 < \alpha < 1)$$

This condition is satisfied by the price vectors of Fig. 12.7.

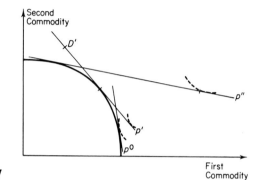

FIGURE 12.7

As is suggested by Fig. 12.7, and can be proved, the speculation is valid if factor supplies are inelastic and if for any reason the community behaves as though it were trying to maximize a single concave utility function.[12] The

[11] This definition should suffice to dispel the doubts expressed by Richard Caves ([2], p. 226): "The danger of circularity in reasoning becomes great unless some way of expressing 'greater deviation of world from autarkic prices' can be found which does not *define* an increase in welfare." Note that preliminary normalization of the price vector is unnecessary. The only weakness of the definition that I can detect is its failure to rank all p' and p'': For some p' and p'' it may not be possible to say that p' deviates from p^0 more than does p'', or that p'' deviates more than p', or that p' and p'' deviate equally.

[12] In fact the weak axiom of revealed preference suffices. Thus suppose that factor supplies are given and define

$$X(p) \equiv \{X \in S \mid p.X \text{ is a maximum}\}$$

Since S is a convex set, $p.X(p)$ is a convex function. (For a proof, see Fenchel [38], p. 60.) Hence

$$\alpha p^0 + (1 - \alpha)p'' \geq p'X'$$

or, since $p(X - D) = 0$,

$$\alpha p^0 D^0 + (1 - \alpha)p''D'' \geq p'D'$$

But $p' = \alpha p^0 + (1 - \alpha)p''$; hence

$$\alpha p^0 D^0 + (1 - \alpha)p''D'' \geq \alpha p^0 D' + (1 - \alpha)p''D'$$

Finally, from the weak axiom of revealed preference, $p^0 D' \geq p^0 D^0$, so that

$$p''D'' \geq p''D' \qquad \text{Q.E.D.}$$

assumption is, of course, extremely restrictive. If it is relaxed, D' may be as in Fig. 12.7, in which case it may be impossible to make everybody better off in the p''-situation than at D'.

6. RESTRICTED TRADE IS SUPERIOR TO NO TRADE

It has been proved that for any country compensated free trade is better than no trade. In the present section we shall argue the more general proposition that compensated free trade or compensated restricted trade is better than no trade. (It is understood, of course, that the restrictions are not prohibitive.) The manner in which trade is restricted is unimportant; the same conclusions hold for tariffs, quantitative commodity controls, or exchange restrictions. Attention is confined to the case in which imports are restricted. The assumption of perfect competition is retained, as is the assumption that internal commodity taxes are zero.

If imports are restricted, it is necessary to distinguish the domestic and world prices of imports. Imagine that, for any assigned set of trade restrictions and for any assigned system of lump-sum taxes and subsidies, the first v commodities are exported, and that the remaining $(n-v)$ commodities are imported.[13] If, as before, p denotes the vector of domestic prices, the vector of world prices is

$$p^* = (p_1^*, p_2^*, \ldots, p_v^*; p_{v+1}^*, p_{v+2}^*, \ldots, p_n^*) = (p_x^*; p_m^*) = (p_x; p_m^*)$$

where

$$p_m^* \leq p_m \tag{12.10}$$

Primes now indicate the magnitudes of the restricted trade situation.

With the aid of this extended notation, Eq. (12.1) may be expanded as

$$X_x^0 - D_x^0 = 0$$
$$X_m^0 - D_m^0 = 0 \tag{12.1e}$$

and Eq. (12.2) may be expanded as

$$p_x'(X_x' - D_x') + p_m^{*\prime}(X_m' - D_m') = 0$$

or

$$p_x' D_x' + p_m^{*\prime} D_m' = p_x' X_x' + p_m^{*\prime} X_m' \tag{12.2d}$$

Now it follows from Eq. (12.2d), inequality (12.10) and the fact that $D_m' > X_m'$, that

$$p_x' D_x' + p_m' D_m' \geq p_x' X_x' + p_m' X_m' \tag{12.2e}$$

[13] The proof could be modified to accommodate nontraded goods.

Substituting from Eq. (12.1e) and inequality (12.2e) in inequality (12.4a)

$$p_x' D_x' + p_m' D_m' - w'A' \geq p_x' D_x^0 + p_m' D_m^0 - w'A^0$$

that is,

$$p'D' - w'A' \geq p'D^0 - w'A^0 \tag{12.5}$$

From this point the proof progresses along familiar lines.

 If exports rather than imports are restricted the proof must be modified but follows essentially the same lines. The vector of world prices is now

$$p^* = (p_x^*; p_m^*) = (p_x^*; p_m)$$

where

$$p_x^* \geq p_x \tag{12.10a}$$

Equation (12.2) may be expanded as

$$p_x^{*\prime}(X_x' - D_x') + p_m'(X_m' - D_m') = 0$$

or

$$p_x^{*\prime} D_x' + p_m' D_m' = p_x^{*\prime} X_x' + p_m' X_m' \tag{12.2f}$$

From Eq. (12.2f), inequality (12.10a), and the fact that $X_x' \geq D_x'$ we may infer inequality (12.2e) again. From this point the proof proceeds as for the case of restricted imports.

 Note that in constructing the above proofs it has not been found necessary to refer to the tariff proceeds (if any), the profits derived from the sale of import or export licenses (if any), or the profits derived from exchange dealings (if any). The proofs can easily be expanded to cover imported raw material and capital movements.

7. WELFARE AND THE TERMS OF TRADE AGAIN

 In Sec. 4 it was shown that, under conditions of free trade, an autonomous improvement in a small country's terms of trade results in an improvement in its welfare. We now reconsider our earlier conclusions in a context of tariffs.

 It can be shown that an improvement in a tariff-ridden country's terms of trade may leave everyone worse off, that for this outcome it is necessary that at least one good be inferior in consumption, and that in any case it is always possible to find an equilibrium after the improvement in the terms of trade which is Pareto-superior to the initial equilibrium.

 The nature of the reasoning will be sufficiently indicated if we consider a very simple case: A small country with no appreciable influence on its terms of trade produces just one commodity, in constant amount; it exports part of

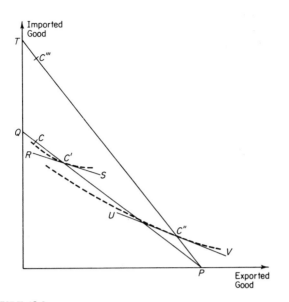

FIGURE 12.8

its production in exchange for a second commodity; and it levies a duty on imports at a constant *ad valorem* rate. In terms of Fig. 12.8, the country's output is *OP* and its trading and consumption opportunities are indicated by the straight line *PQ*. Under conditions of free trade, equilibrium would be reached at *C*, where a community indifference curve is tangential to the terms of trade line. But the effect of the tariff is to raise the internal relative price of imports above the world level. The internal price ratio is represented therefore by the slope of a line less steep than *PQ*, say *RS*, and the actual equilibrium is to be found on *PQ* at the point where the slope of the intersecting indifference curve is equal to that of *RS*. Suppose that *C'* is that point.

Now the terms of trade improve. The new trading possibilities are indicated by *PT* and the new internal price ratio by the slope of *UV*. The new consumption equilibrium is found on *PT* at that point *C''* where the slope of the intersecting indifference curve is equal to that of *UV*. The new indifference curve may imply either an improvement or a deterioration of welfare.

Figure 12.8 illustrates the possibility of deterioration. This anomalous result emerges, however, only when the export good is inferior (over the relevant range). This is clear from Fig. 12.8 if it is borne in mind that the slope of *RS* is *less* than that of *UV*. If neither good is inferior, an improvement in the terms of trade must increase welfare.

Moreover, even if a new equilibrium *C''* involves a deterioration of welfare, there exists an alternative final equilibrium *C'''* such that everyone is better off than at C'. To see this, consider the income-consumption curve corresponding to the new domestic price ratio. Evidently it passes through C'' and to the left of C'. It therefore must eventually cut PT a second time, possibly at T. It follows that an alternative final equilibrium exists and that welfare is greater than at C'.

8. INCREASING RETURNS TO SCALE

It was fundamental to the argument of Sec. 1 that the production set S be convex and supported by the price plane at the point of free-trade production. If either assumption is abandoned, the proof that free trade is gainful collapses. And if external economies are combined with constant returns for individual firms, so that the economy displays increasing returns, not only must the production set lose its convexity but the convenient tangency of price plane and production frontier may no longer hold in equilibrium.

The two complications are not inseparable. We know from Chap. 8 that there exist certain exceptionally well-behaved externalities such that production takes place on the production frontier and such that the slopes of the frontier reflect marginal private rates of substitution. Given such well-behaved externalities we can be sure that, in cases of incomplete specialization, the price plane is tangential to the production surface at the equilibrium point. In the present section we assume that externalities are of this convenient type; we are therefore able to study increasing returns without bothering about inessential complications. The cost-distorting effects of less well-behaved externalities are examined in Sec. 9. Both in the present section and in Sec. 9 attention will be confined to the simple and familiar case of two products, with two primary factors in fixed supply and with joint production ruled out.

We know[14] that if both industries display increasing returns then, in a neighborhood of each axis, the production frontier will be convex to the origin. If returns are increasing with sufficient severity, the frontier will be uniformly convex. We consider the latter case first.

In Fig. 12.9 the autarkic equilibrium is indicated by point X^0, where a community indifference curve I^0I^0 touches the production frontier $P_1 P_2$. If under free-trade specialization is incomplete, whether a gain or loss is incurred depends both on the curvatures of I^0I^0 and P_1P_2 and on the shape of the foreign import demand function. If, as in Fig. 12.9(a), I^0I^0 lies outside P_1P_2 everywhere except at X^0 free trade is necessarily harmful. (If I^0I^0 is permitted to touch P_1P_2 at points other than X^0, trade is necessarily non-beneficial.) In other cases of incomplete specialization, trade may be either harmful or beneficial, depending on the curvatures of I^0I^0 and P_1P_2, and on the equilibrium terms of trade. Figure 12.9(b) illustrates the possibility of

[14] See Herberg and Kemp [17].

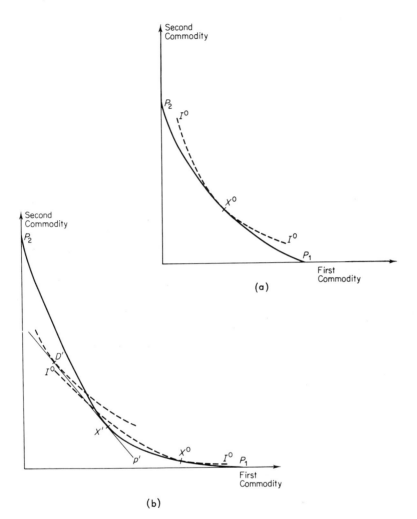

(a)

(b)

FIGURE 12.9

gain. Notice, however, that trade is gainful only if the autarkic equilibrium is sub-optimal. As a glance at Fig. 12.9(b) makes clear, there exists on P_1P_2, sufficiently far to the left of X^0, an alternative autarkic equilibrium which is preferable to X^0. If the initial autarkic equilibrium had been the most preferred of the several alternative equilibria, trade would have been inevitably harmful. We may conclude, then, that *if returns are increasing with sufficient severity to make the production frontier uniformly convex to the origin and if the autarkic equilibrium is optimal, then incompletely specialized free trade is necessarily harmful* (strictly, necessarily nonbeneficial). If under free trade production is completely specialized, either a gain or loss may accrue.

In cases of more mildly increasing returns the production frontier has at least one section which is concave to the origin, as in Fig. 12.10. In these cases our conclusions must be even less clear-cut. In particular, we must abandon our conclusion that incompletely specialized trade is necessarily harmful. Figure 12.10 provides a counter example. Clear conclusions emerge only if the autarkic and free-trade production points lie on the same section of P_1P_2: Either on the concave section defined by the inflexion points T_1 and T_2, or on one of the two convex sections P_2T_2 and T_1P_1. If both production points lie on the concave section T_1T_2 the conclusions of Sec. 1 carry over: Trade is inevitably gainful; if both production points lie on the same convex section the conclusions of the preceding paragraph are preserved.

Thus increasing returns are fatal to the sweeping conclusions of Sec. 1. In only two special cases can one be sure of the outcome: (a) if both the autarkic and free-trade production points lie on the same concave section of the production frontier, trade is necessarily gainful; (b) if both points lie on the same convex section, if the autarkic equilibrium is optimal, and if under free trade production is incompletely specialized, trade is necessarily harmful. In general, one must be prepared to admit that some autarkic positions can be bettered under free trade (in the sense that, by resort to appropriate lump-sum transfers, at least one person could be made better off, with none worse off, than in the state of autarky); and that some free-trade positions can be bettered under autarky. In short, the utility possibility loci of the free-trade and autarkic situations intersect. This is unfortunate, but unavoidable.

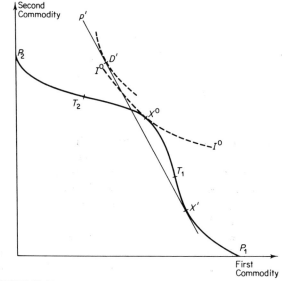

FIGURE 12.10

9. INCREASING RETURNS WITH DISTORTING EXTERNALITIES

It was assumed in Sec. 8 that externalities are well-behaved, so that in all nonspecialized equilibria the price plane is tangential to the production frontier. We now cast away the crutch and suppose that the external economies are produced by a single product, say the first. From the community's point of view, therefore, one industry displays increasing returns, the other constant returns. It follows that the production possibility curve may have the shape displayed in Fig. 12.11. It follows also that if production is

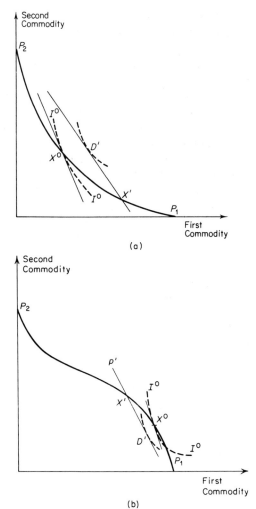

(a)

(b)

FIGURE 12.11

incompletely specialized the two marginal rates of substitution must be equal, so that production will take place on the frontier. On the other hand, the equilibrium marginal rate of transformation is no longer equal to the price ratio or, therefore, to the marginal rate of substitution in consumption. In terms of Fig. 12.11, autarkic consumption and production might be indicated by point X^0; free-trade production might be indicated by X', free-trade consumption by D'.

It is immediately obvious that we must abandon even the weak conclusions summarized in the last paragraph of Sec. 8. Figure 12.11(a) provides a counter example to proposition (*a*); Fig. 12.11(b) provides a counter example to proposition (*b*). However something can be salvaged. Figure 12.11(b) is based on the twin assumptions that the economies are generated by the *first* industry and that output expands in the *second* industry. It is easy to show that if instead the first industry expands (or even fails to contract) trade is necessarily gainful—provided only that, in the case of multiple trading equilibria, the community trades to its greatest advantage. What is more important, and less easy to prove, this proposition is valid *even when the two production points lie on different sections of the production frontier.*

The proposition is proved by first supposing that trade is harmful and then showing that the supposition is inconsistent with other assumptions made in the present section.[15] The proof runs in terms of two products and two factors but can be easily generalized to n factors and m industries (some of which display constant returns, others increasing returns).

If the autarkic equilibrium is preferred to the free-trade equilibrium,

$$p_1' D_1^0 + p_2' D_2^0 > p_1' D_1' + p_2' D_2'$$

or, using Eqs. (12.1) and (12.2),

$$p_1' X_1^0 + p_2' D_2^0 > p_1' X_1' + p_2' X_2' \qquad (12.12)$$

Let A_{ij} be the amount of the ith factor employed in the jth industry. Then, since factors are in inelastic supply,

$$\sum_j w_i' A_{ij}' = \sum_j w_i' A_{ij}^0 \qquad i = 1, 2$$

and the inequality may be written

$$\left(p_1' X_1^0 - \sum_i w_i' A_{i1}^0 \right) + \left(p_2' X_2^0 - \sum_i x_i' A_{i2}^0 \right) > \left(p_1' X_1' - \sum_i w_i' A_{i1}' \right)$$

$$+ \left(p_2' X_2' - \sum_i w_i' A_{i2}' \right) \quad (12.13)$$

[15] See Negishi [20].

However, with constant or decreasing returns in the second industry

$$p_2'X_2^0 - \sum_i w_i'A_{i2}^0 \leq p_2'X_2' - \sum_i w_i'A_{i2}' = 0;$$

and, with increasing returns in the first industry,

$$p_1'X_1' - \sum_i w_i'A_{i1}' \geq p_1'X_1^0 - \sum w_i'A_{i1}^0 \qquad \text{if } X_1' \geq X_1^0$$

Thus if the opening of trade stimulates the increasing-returns industry or leaves outputs unchanged, inequality (12.13) cannot hold and we may conclude that a trading loss is impossible.

It is tempting to conjecture the more general proposition that trade is never harmful if it stimulates the industry with more sharply increasing returns or leaves outputs unchanged. Such a proposition would cover the case just studied, in which returns are increasing in one industry and non-increasing in the other; it would be consistent with the basic proposition of Sec. 1, that if constant returns prevail in both industries, trade is never harmful. Unfortunately, the conjecture appears to be false; at any rate it cannot be proved by the methods employed above.

10. THE GAINS FROM TRADE FOR TAX-RIDDEN ECONOMIES

To this point local commodity taxes have been ignored. In the present section we consider the trade gains of a small tax-ridden country with no influence on world prices. It will be shown that even against a background of consumption taxes or (subject to a mild qualification) production taxes free trade is potentially gainful.

Suppose first that in the home country, *consumption* taxes (subsidies) are levied on (paid to) some or all commodities. Free trade prices as seen by producers are given by $p^{*\prime}$, so that Eq. (12.2) becomes

$$p^{*\prime}(X' - D') = 0$$

and Eq. (12.5) becomes

$$p^{*\prime}D' - w'A' \geq p^{*\prime}D^0 - w'A^0$$

This shows that at world prices the community's autarkic consumption pattern would cost not more than the free-trade consumption pattern. Since $p^{*\prime}$ is given, we may infer that the consumption possibility plane of the free-trade situation cuts (in an extreme case, touches) the autarkic indifference surface, so that the community conceivably could consume more (not less) of every commodity than in the autarkic state. It only remains to show that there exists a competitive equilibrium on an indifference surface lying above the autarkic surface. Suppose that there does not exist such an equilibrium but that there exists an equilibrium on a lower indifference surface. Figure 12.12 illustrates the possibility for the two-commodity case in which a tax is imposed on the consumption of the first commodity. Since world prices are the same as producers' prices, trade takes place along the *producers'* price line $p^{*'}$. The free-trade consumption equilibrium is represented by point D', on an indifference surface below I^0I^0. Notice, however, that the Engel curve passing through D' must cut I^0I^0 to the right of X^0, say in D'', so that over the relevant range the second commodity is inferior. The Engel curve therefore must eventually cut the line $p^{*'}$ a second time, above I^0I^0, possibly on the horizontal axis. Thus there must exist at least one additional consumption equilibrium superior to the initial autarkic equilibrium. The argument can be adjusted to cope with a tax on the consumption of the second commodity. The same conclusion (that trade is necessarily gainful) emerges. Moreover, the geometric argument can be extended algebraically to cover an arbitrary number of commodities.

When we turn our attention to *production* taxes the picture proves to be a little less tidy. Consider the simplest two-commodity world. Without further loss of generality we may suppose that a tax is imposed on the production of the first commodity. (Equivalently, we might suppose that the production of the second commodity is subsidized.) An initial pre-trade equilibrium is

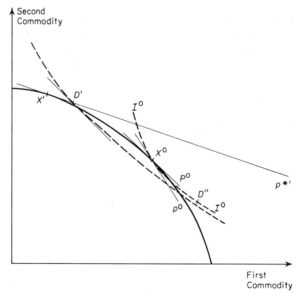

FIGURE 12.12

indicated by point X^0 in Fig. 12.13. The price ratio as seen by consumers is indicated by the slope of the line p^0, the producers' price ratio by the slope of P^0. The dotted Scitovsky indifference curve I^0I^0 is based on the distribution of earned incomes in the initial equilibrium. Suppose now that trade is opened and that, as a result, both price ratios move in favor of the first or taxed commodity. Then, as Fig. 12.13(a) makes clear, trade is inevitably gainful.

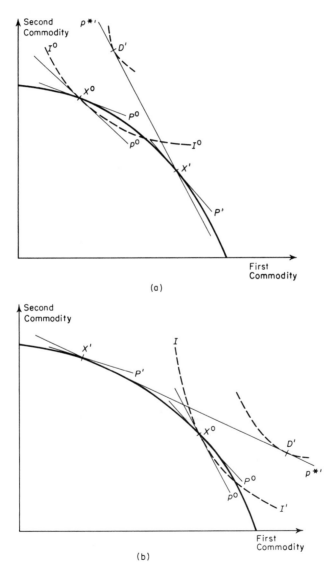

FIGURE 12.13

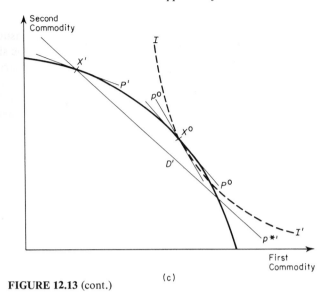

FIGURE 12.13 (cont.)

(c)

If, however, the opening of trade moves the two price ratios in favor of the second or untaxed commodity, the welfare outcome does not emerge so clearly. In this case trade shifts resources to the overproducing tax-protected industry. The implicit subsidy to that industry is passed on to foreign as well as to local consumers, suggesting that sometimes the subsidization of the foreigner may outweigh any gain from international exchange. The precise condition for this outcome is easy to find. If, as in Fig. 12.13(b), the rate of tax is small enough to ensure that the $p^{*'}$-line intersects I^0I^0, trade is inevitably gainful. If, as in Fig. 12.13(c), the rate of tax is large enough to ensure that the $p^{*'}$-line does not intersect or touch I^0I^0, trade is inevitably harmful. The critical rate of tax, for which trade is neither harmful nor gainful, depends on the difference between the world and autarkic consumers' price ratios and on the curvatures of the production frontier and I^0I^0.

From our discussion of production taxes, then, we may conclude that tax-distorted trade is necessarily gainful (a) if the opening of trade moves prices in favor of the relatively heavily taxed commodity, or (b) if the opening of trade moves prices in favor of the untaxed commodity and the rate of tax is sufficiently small. Since the critical tax rate depends on other things, however, only in case (a) can one infer from observable price changes alone that a gain has accrued. In all cases other than (a) and (b), trade either is harmful or carries neither gain nor loss.

11. THE GAINS FROM TRADE FOR ECONOMIES SUFFERING FROM OTHER DOMESTIC DISTORTIONS

It was assumed by most classical and neoclassical international trade theorists that factor rewards are perfectly flexible, that between occupations factors of production are perfectly mobile, and that the owners of factors are indifferent to the nonpecuniary advantages of hiring their factors to one industry rather than the other. From these assumptions it could be inferred that each homogeneous factor earns the same reward in every occupation. However, one can easily imagine circumstances in which a factor's reward varies from occupation to occupation. For example, minimum wage laws may apply to (or be enforced in) some occupations only. Or trades unions may restrict entry more severely in some industries than in others, and thus pry open a permanent wage differential. Or, finally, factory acts, by outlawing juvenile labor in city factories, may create an incipient discrepancy between average family incomes in urban and rural areas, a discrepancy which remains incipient only because the urban *wage rate* stands permanently above its rural counterpart.

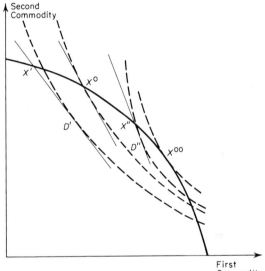

FIGURE 12.14

Suppose first that both labor and capital receive higher rewards in the first industry, and that the percentage interindustry differential is the same for each factor. Such a pattern of differentials leaves the productive efficiency of the economy unimpaired, for in competitive equilibria the marginal rate of substitution between factors must still be the same for each industry. In competitive equilibria, however, marginal private costs (and therefore prices) no longer reflect social opportunity costs. Equilibrium must be represented by a point on the curve of production possibilities at which the curve is cut by the price line. Thus point X^0 in Fig. 12.14 represents a closed economy equilibrium with higher factor rewards in the first industry. Point X^{00}, on the other hand, represents a hypothetical equilibrium with zero differentials in factor rewards. It is obvious that, as the result of the differentials, too little is produced by the first or high-wage (and high-rental) industry and too much is produced by the second industry.

If trade is opened, the price ratio will, save in a singular case, increase or decrease; as a result, both production and consumption will change. Now it can be shown that under the conditions assumed the commodity price ratio (or ratio of marginal costs) must bear a constant relation to the marginal rate of transformation.[16] Specifically, the relative price of the first commodity must equal the marginal rate of transformation $(-dX_2/dX_1)$ *times* one plus the percentage differential in factor rewards. In terms of Fig. 12.14, therefore, production moves to X' or X'', and consumption to D' or D'', depending on whether the relative price of the first commodity is, respectively, lower or higher abroad than at home under autarky. A country may produce too much and import too little of a low-wage (and low-rental) commodity. It is even possible, as X'' and D'' illustrate, that a country may export the commodity which, on a Laplacean calculation of marginal comparative advantages, it should import. What, then, of the gain from trade? The answer is straightforward. If the opening of trade increases the relative price of the low-wage, low-rental commodity, the gain may be positive or negative. (Points X' and D' in Fig. 12.14 illustrate the possibility of negative gain.) If, on the other hand, the relative price of the high-wage commodity increases, the gain from trade is inevitably positive—even when the "wrong" commodity is exported. (Points X'' and D'' of Fig. 12.14 illustrate.)

Let us consider, as our second case, a situation in which the wage rate, but not the rental of capital, differs from industry to industry.[17] Then, clearly

---

[16] From the production functions $X_i = F_i(K_i, L_i)$ and the full employment conditions we calculate that

$$-\frac{dX_2}{dX_1} = \left[\frac{\partial X_2}{\partial K_2} dK_2 + \frac{\partial X_2}{\partial L_2} dL_2\right] \Big/ \left[\frac{\partial X_1}{\partial K_1} dK_2 + \frac{\partial X_1}{\partial L_1} dL_2\right]$$

But, from the marginal conditions,

$$\frac{p_1}{p_2} = \rho\left[\frac{\partial X_2}{\partial K_2}\Big/\frac{\partial X_1}{\partial K_1}\right] = \rho\left[\frac{\partial X_2}{\partial L_2}\Big/\frac{\partial X_1}{\partial L_1}\right]$$

where $\rho > 1$ is the ratio of factor rewards in the first industry to those in the second. It follows that

$$\frac{p_1}{p_2} = \rho\left[\frac{\partial X_2}{\partial K_2} dK_2 + \frac{\partial X_2}{\partial L_2} dL_2\right] \Big/ \left[\frac{\partial X_1}{\partial K_1} dK_2 + \frac{\partial X_1}{\partial L_1} dL_2\right] = \rho\left(-\frac{\partial X_2}{\partial X_1}\right) > -\frac{\partial X_2}{\partial X_1}$$

Notice that this does *not* imply that the angle formed by the price line and the tangent to the curve of production possibilities is constant.

[17] This is, of course, a special case of nonuniform percentage differentials in factor rewards. It is a trivial matter to extend the discussion to cover the more general case.

the two marginal rates of factor substitution will be different and production will be inefficient. Except at its boundaries, the locus of competitive equilibrium outputs swept out by the price ratio will lie inside the locus of production possibilities. It is even possible that the locus of competitive outputs may be "bowed in" to the origin.[18] In either case simple diagrammatic methods of the type employed in the preceding paragraph do not suffice to establish the welfare effect of opening trade. The reason is that the angle formed by the price line and the tangent to the locus of competitive outputs is not pinned down.[19] Nevertheless it is possible to prove a proposition for this case just as sweeping as that established in the preceding paragraph: *If the opening of trade stimulates the employment of labor in the first or high-wage industry, trade cannot possibly be harmful.* To establish this proposition we revert to an algebraic form of analysis.[20]

Suppose that the wage rate paid by the first industry is λ times that paid by the second industry $(\lambda > 1)$ and let the first factor be identified as labor. Since factors are in inelastic supply,

$$A'_{i1} + A'_{i2} = A^0_{i1} + A^0_{i2} \qquad i = 1, 2 \tag{12.14}$$

and

$$\lambda w'_1 A'_{11} + w'_1 A'_{12} \geq \lambda w'_1 A^0_{11} + w'_1 A^0_{12} \quad \text{if} \quad A'_{11} \geq A^0_{11} \tag{12.15}$$

Applying Eq. (12.14) and inequality (12.15) to inequality (12.12), we obtain

$$(p'_1 X'_1 - \lambda w'_1 A'_{11} - w'_2 A'_{21}) + (p'_2 X'_2 - w'_1 A'_{12} - w'_2 A'_{22})$$
$$< (p'_1 X^0_1 - \lambda w'_1 A^0_{11} - w'_2 A^0_{21}) + (p'_2 X^0_2 - w'_1 A^0_{12} - w'_2 A^0_{22}) \tag{12.16}$$

---

[18] To see this, one need only suppose that factor proportions are the same in each industry, so that the locus of production possibilities is a straight line, and then inject a wage differential, however small. Cf. Fishlow and David [23], p. 541, n. 29; Johnson [26].

[19] While it is still true (cf. footnote 16 above) that

$$-\frac{dX_2}{dX_1} = \left[\frac{\partial X_2}{\partial K_2} dK_2 + \frac{\partial X_2}{\partial L_2} dL_2\right] \bigg/ \left[\frac{\partial X_1}{\partial K_1} dK_2 + \frac{\partial X_1}{\partial L_1} dL_2\right]$$

we must now write

$$\frac{p_1}{p_2} = \left[\frac{\partial X_2}{\partial K_2} dK_2 + \rho \frac{\partial X_2}{\partial L_2} dL_2\right] \bigg/ \left[\frac{\partial X_1}{\partial K_1} dK_2 + \frac{\partial X_1}{\partial L_2} dL_2\right]$$

which is greater than $(-dX_2/dX_1)$ but not equal to $\rho(-dX_2/dX_1)$. Fishlow and David state that "Hagen has shown that equilibrium occurs along inefficient transformation loci at points where price lines intersecting them at a constant angle (determined by the factor price differential) are tangent to indifference curves." ([23], pp. 534–35.) Both the imputation to Hagen and the statement imputed seem to be incorrect.

[20] Cf. Negishi [20].

However,

and

$$0 = p_1' X_1' - \lambda w_1' A_{11}' - w_2' A_{21}' \geq p_1' X_1^0 - \lambda w_1' A_{11}^0 - w_2' A_{21}^0 \quad (12.17a)$$

$$0 = p_2' X_2' - w_1' A_{12}' - w_2' A_{22}' \geq p_2' X_2^0 - w_1' A_{12}^0 - w_2' A_{22}^0 \quad (12.17b)$$

The two inequalities are obviously inconsistent with each other and we may conclude that if $A_{11}' \geq A_{11}^0$ trade cannot be harmful.

It remains only to note what must have been apparent to the reader for some time: That external economies and interindustrial differences in factor rewards pose problems which are formally identical, succumb to the same analysis, and can be corrected by similar policy devices.

12. WELFARE AND TECHNICAL IMPROVEMENTS

For a country *free of tariffs, taxes, and other domestic distortions* and *with negligible influence on world prices*, any technical improvement raises potential welfare. Both the locus of production possibilities and (therefore) the locus of consumption possibilities move out from the origin.

The italicized qualifications, however, are crucial. Thus it has already been shown (in Chap. 4, Sec. 4) that a technical improvement in the export industry may so depress the terms of trade that the country ends up less well off than before the "improvement."

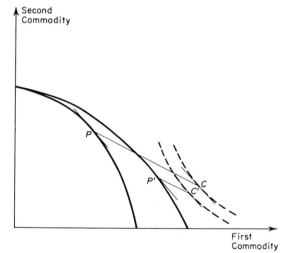

FIGURE 12.15

Nor are small countries immune from paradoxes of this sort.[21] Consider the position of a small tariff-ridden country for which the terms of trade are constant. Initially the country trades from the production point P to the consumption point C on terms indicated by the slope of PC in Fig. 12.15. A neutral improvement confined to the first or import-competing industry shifts out the curve of production possibilities and generates new equilibria at P' and C'. If P' lies below the terms of trade line PC and if inferiority is ruled out, the country will be worse off than before the "improvement." That P' may indeed lie below PC is easy to show.[22]

These examples of damnifying improvements are members of a large class.[23] It is common to the two examples that neither in the initial nor in the final equilibrium was the country in a full Paretian optimum: In the Mill–Edgeworth case examined in Chap. 4 the country was a free trader and therefore failed to maximize its trading gain; in the case examined above the country was *not* a free trader and therefore failed to maximize its trading gain. Without much trouble one could construct further examples involving commodity taxes, externalities, interindustrial differentials in factor rewards and other distortions. It seems to be the rule that in any suboptimal (or "second best") situation one can find a type of growth disturbance which is damnifying (a growth disturbance being one which would be beneficial if after the disturbance all Paretian conditions were satisfied).

We conclude with an amusing paradox involving a disturbance which does not fall into the class of growth disturbances just described.[24] Suppose that

---

[21] The following example was provided by Johnson [35].

[22] It was shown in Chap. 4, Sec. 4, that

$$\frac{\partial Q_1}{\partial \lambda} = \frac{\partial X_1}{\partial \lambda} + p \frac{\partial X_2}{\partial p}$$

and that

$$\frac{\partial X_1}{\partial \lambda} = \frac{1}{p} \frac{\partial X_1}{\partial (1/p)} = X_1 e_1$$

where e_1 is the "general equilibrium" elasticity of supply of the first commodity and p is, of course, the internal price ratio. It follows that the slope of PP' is, for small improvements,

$$\frac{dX_1}{dX_2} = \frac{\partial X_1}{\partial \lambda} \Big/ \frac{\partial X_2}{\partial \lambda} = \frac{p e_1}{1 - e_1}$$

Clearly P' will lie below PC if and only if $dX_1/dX_2 > -p(1 + \tau)$, where τ is the rate of duty; that is, if

$$e_1 > \frac{1 + \tau}{\tau}$$

Now e_1 is greater than one and otherwise unrestricted. Thus one can imagine cases in which the inequality is satisfied.

[23] Cf. Bhagwati [32].

[24] I owe this paradox to Maurice McManus.

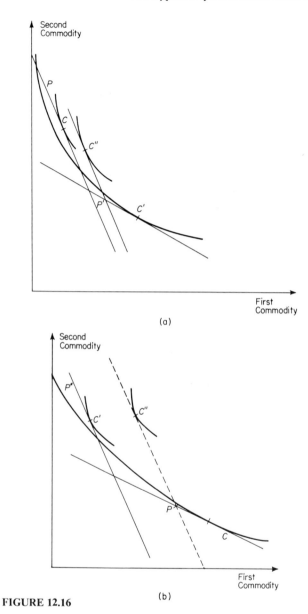

FIGURE 12.16

a trading equilibrium is disturbed by a shift in the production frontier of the home country, the nature of the shift being unspecified except that it must produce an increase in income at the initial terms of trade. Suppose further that, at the initial terms of trade, import demand falls so that in the new equilibrium the terms of trade have improved. Thus the home country experiences both an increase in real income and an improvement in the terms of trade. One might be forgiven for supposing that the net effect is an improvement in welfare.

In fact this outcome is not at all necessary. Figure 12.16(a) provides a counter example. P and C represent initial production and consumption, P' and C' the new production and consumption. (For simplicity the production frontiers are assumed to be rectangular.)

To obtain this paradoxical outcome it is necessary that the new production frontier passes SW of the old consumption point (and therefore of the old production point). It is also necessary that at the old terms of trade net demand for the good initially imported should become negative (cf. point C''); that, in other words, the home country wishes to interchange its import and export goods.

The second of these two conditions provides the key to the paradox. The change in the terms of trade is, from the viewpoint of either the initial or final equilibrium, an improvement. But from the viewpoint of the half-way point, at which the production set has changed but the terms of trade have not changed, the subsequent change in the terms of trade is *detrimental* to welfare. And, if the switch in import demand is sufficiently large, the terms of trade effect will outweigh the pure income effect of the shift in the production frontier.

A sort of dual paradox, according to which a *deterioration* of the terms of trade and a *decline* in income combine to produce an *increase* in welfare, can be constructed, and resolved. Figure 12.16(b) provides an illustration. Note, however, that in this case the change in income is evaluated at the *new* terms of trade; similarly the interchange of import and export commodity occurs at the *new* terms of trade and *old* production point.

13. FINAL COMMENTS

It is well in conclusion to emphasize that the entire preceding discussion has been conducted under some fairly severe assumptions. The assumption of stable ordinal preference scales for individuals has ruled out of consideration what Mill considered to be the greatest of the benefits imparted by trade: The destruction of old preferences and their replacement by new.[25]

[25] "A people may be in a quiescent, indolent, uncultivated state, with all their tastes either fully satisfied or entirely undeveloped, and they may fail to put forth the whole of their productive energies for want of any sufficient object of desire. The opening of a foreign trade, by making them acquainted with new objects, or tempting them by the easier acquisition of things which they had not previously thought attainable, sometimes works a sort of industrial revolution in a country whose resources were previously undeveloped for want of energy and ambition in the people: inducing those who were satisfied with scanty comforts and little work, to work harder for the gratification of their new tastes, and even to save, and accumulate capital, for the still more complete satisfaction of their tastes at a future time."
(Mill [10], Book III, Chap. XVII, Sec. 5.)

Similarly, no attention has been paid to the possible impact of trade on the state of technical knowledge and the rate of its accumulation. Finally, it has been assumed throughout that lump-sum taxes and subsidies are feasible. If the only kinds of taxes and subsidies available are those which carry with them a dead weight loss of allocative efficiency, then the theorems of this chapter are true but irrelevant. The utility *feasibility* locus[26] of the trade situation may well cut inside the no-trade feasibility locus.[27]

PROBLEMS

12.1 Comment on the following statement: "Countries trade with each other because this enables them to participate in and profit from the international division of labor." (Leontief [40], p. 9.)

12.2 "The National Dividend is, however, the sum of the private dividends of the members of the nation. Hence it follows that the dividend of the whole community is, *prima facie*, larger when exchange is free than when exchange is not free." (Pigou [41], p. 8.) Is the *prima facie* argument acceptable?

12.3 Prove that if all individuals are alike in preferences and assets the gain from trade increases as world prices deviate more from those of the autarkic situation. [Cf. Samuelson [12], p. 203.]

12.4 Suppose that each of three countries A, B, and C is initially in a state of autarky. Consider A's gain from trade in each of the following contingencies:

(i) A and B eliminate all barriers to mutual trade,

(ii) A and C eliminate all barriers to mutual trade,

(iii) both (i) and (ii).

Construct two-commodity examples to show that any ranking of the three gains is possible. Show that the gain from (iii) must be less than the larger of the gains from (i) and (ii) if A's export commodity in (i) is its import commodity in (ii).

12.5 Consider a world of one factor (labor), two countries, and two products. Suppose that in both countries the wage rates are twice as high in the first industry as in the second and that the nonpecuniary conditions of employment are equally attractive in the two industries. Taussig has argued that, in these circumstances, the volume and terms of trade will be the same as when wage rates are uniform within each country. What do you think? (Taussig [29], pp. 43–60; Ohlin [28]; Haberler [24], pp. 196–98; Viner [30], pp. 495–500.)

12.6 Suppose that initially trade is free in every commodity but one, in which trade is prohibited. Now the prohibition is removed. Show (a) that some

[26] Samuelson [38].

[27] One is reminded in this connection of Malthus' defense of the corn laws on the ground that they were a feasible means of redistributing income in favor of the wealthy, high-saving landlords.

countries may benefit, others suffer, (b) that those countries which benefit could overcompensate the losers, (c) that a particular country benefits if the terms on which it trades *in the initially traded goods* improve, and (d) that propositions (a)–(c) are true whether the newly traded good is a consumer good or a raw material (e.g., the services of capital).

REFERENCES

General References

[1] Baldwin, R. E., "The New Welfare Economics and Gains in International Trade," *Quarterly Journal of Economics*, LXVI, No. 1 (February 1952), 91–101.

[2] Caves, Richard E., *Trade and Economic Structure: Models and Methods*, Chap. VIII. Cambridge, Mass.: Harvard University Press, 1960.

[3] Enke, Stephen, "Trade Gains in the Short Run: a Reply to Mr. Kemp," *Canadian Journal of Economics and Political Science*, XXIII, No. 4 (November 1961), 522–26.

[4] Kemp, Murray C., "Gains and Losses from Trade," *Canadian Journal of Economics and Political Science*, XXVII, No. 3 (August 1961), 382–83.

[5] Kemp, Murray C., "The Gain from International Trade," *Economic Journal*, LXXII, No. 288 (December 1962), 303–19.

†[6] Krueger, Anne O. and Hugo Sonnenschein, "The Terms of Trade, the Gains from Trade and Price Divergence," *International Economic Review*, VIII, No. 1 (February 1967), 121–27.

[7] Krueger, Anne O. and Hugo Sonnenschein, "On Measures of Trading Gain and Maximum Bonus," unpublished.

[8] Marshall, Alfred, *Money Credit and Commerce*. London: Macmillan and Company Ltd., 1923.

[9] Mill, John Stuart, *Essays on Some Unsettled Questions of Political Economy*. London: The London School of Economics and Political Science, 1948.

[10] Mill, John Stuart, *Principles of Political Economy*, ed. Sir W. J. Ashley. London: Longmans, Green and Company, 1909.

[11] Olsen, Erling, "Udenrigshandelens Gevinst," *Nationalokonomisk Tidsskrift*, XCVI, Haefte 1–2 (Argang 1958), 76–79.

†[12] Samuelson, Paul A., "The Gains from International Trade," *Canadian Journal of Economics and Political Science*, V, No. 2 (May 1939), 195–205. Reprinted in *Readings in the Theory of International Trade*, eds. Howard S. Ellis and Lloyd A. Metzler, pp. 239–52. Philadelphia: The Blakiston Company, 1949. Page references are to the original article.

†[13] Samuelson, Paul A., "The Gains from International Trade Once Again," *Economic Journal*, LXXII, No. 4 (December 1962), 820–29.

[14] Viner, Jacob, *Studies in the Theory of International Trade*. New York: Harper and Brothers, n.d.

[15] Wan, Henry Y., Tr., "Maximum Bonus—an Alternative Measure for Trading Gains," *Review of Economic Studies*, XXXII (1), No. 89 (January 1965), 49–58.

Increasing Returns and the Gain from Trade

[16] Haberler, Gottfried, "Some Problems in the Pure Theory of Foreign Trade," *Economic Journal*, LX, No. 238 (June 1950), 223–40.

[17] Herberg, Horst and Murray C. Kemp, "Some Implications of Variable Returns to Scale," *Canadian Journal of Economics*, to be published.

[18] Kemp, Murray C., "The Efficiency of Competition as an Allocator of Resources," *Canadian Journal of Economics and Political Science*, XXI, Nos. 1 and 2 (February and May 1955), 30–42, 217–27.

†[19] Matthews, R. C. O., "Reciprocal Demand and Increasing Returns," *Review of Economic Studies*, XVII (2), No. 43 (1949-50), 149–58.

†[20] Negishi, Takashi, "Increasing Returns, Factor Market Distortions and Trade," unpublished.

Factor Reward Differentials and the Gain from Trade

[21] Bhagwati, Jagdish and V. K. Ramaswami, "Domestic Distortions, Tariffs and the Theory of Optimum Subsidy," *Journal of Political Economy*, LXXI, No. 1 (February 1963), 44–50.

[22] Cairnes, J. E., *Some Principles of Political Economy Newly Expounded*. New York: Harper and Brothers Limited, 1874.

†[23] Fishlow, Albert and Paul A. David, "Optimal Resource Allocation in an Imperfect Market Setting," *Journal of Political Economy*, LXIX, No. 6 (December 1961), 529–46.

[24] Haberler, Gottfried, *The Theory of International Trade with its Applications to Commerical Policy*, trans. Alfred Stonier and Frederic Benham. London: William Hodge and Company, Limited, 1936.

[25] Hagen, Everett E., "An Economic Justification of Protectionism," *Quarterly Journal of Economics*, LXXII, No. 4 (November 1958), 496–514.

[26] Johnson, Harry G., "Factor Market Distortions and the Shape of the Transformation Curve," *Econometrica*, 34, No. 3 (July 1966), 686–98.

[27] Manoilesco, Mihael, *The Theory of Protection and International Trade*. London: P. S. King and Son, 1931. French ed. 1929.

[28] Ohlin, Bertil, "Protection and Non-Competing Groups," *Weltwirtschaftliches Archiv*, XXXIII, Heft 1 (1931), 30–45.

[29] Taussig, F. W., *International Trade*. New York: Macmillan and Company, Ltd., 1927.

[30] Viner, Jacob, *Studies in the Theory of International Trade*. London: George Allen and Unwin Ltd., n.d.

Welfare and Technical Improvements

[31] Bhagwati, Jagdish, "International Trade and Economic Expansion," *American Economic Review*, LXVIII, No. 5 (December 1958), 941–53.

[32] Bhagwati, Jagdish, "Distortions and Immiserizing Growth," *Review of Economic Studies*, XXXV (4), No. 104 (October 1968), 481–85.

†[33] Edgeworth, F. Y., "The Theory of International Values. I," *Economic Journal*, IV, No. 1 (March 1894), 35–50.

†[34] Edgeworth, F. Y., "On a Point in the Pure Theory of International Trade," *Economic Journal*, IX, No. 1 (March 1899), 125–28.

[35] Johnson, Harry G., "The Possibility of Income Losses from Increased Efficiency or Factor Accumulation in the Presence of Tariffs," *Economic Journal*, LXXVII, No. 305 (March 1967), 151–54.

[36] Kemp, Murray C., "Technological Change, the Terms of Trade and Welfare," *Economic Journal*, LXV, No. 3 (September 1955), 457–74.

†[37] Mill, J. S., *Principles of Political Economy*, ed. Sir W. J. Ashley, Book III, Chap. XVIII, Sec. 5. London: Longmans, Green & Company, 1909.

Technical Equipment

[38] Fenchel, W., *Convex Sets, Cones and Functions*. Princeton: Department of Mathematics, Princeton University, 1953.

[39] Samuelson, Paul A., "Evaluation of Real National Income," *Oxford Economic Papers*, New Series, II, No. 1 (January 1950), 1–29.

Miscellaneous

[40] Leontief, Wassily, "Domestic Production and Foreign Trade: the American Capital Position Re-examined," *Economia Internazionale*, VII, No. 1 (February 1954), 9–45.

[41] Pigou, A C., *Protective and Preferential Import Duties*. London: Macmillan and Company Ltd., 1906.

chapter 13

Optimal Trade and Investment Statically Considered

It has been shown in Chap. 12, Secs. 1–3 and 6, that free or restricted trade is better than no trade—provided one can ignore local commodity taxes, market imperfections, increasing returns, and externalities. This leaves open the question whether the various trading situations can be ranked. What can be said of the relative desirabilities of the free trading situation, the trading situation characterized by a uniform 5 per cent import duty, that characterized by a uniform 10 per cent duty, and so on?

1. WORLD PRICES GIVEN

In the special, limiting case in which world prices are independent of the volume of a country's imports and exports, a particularly simple answer can be given: The free trade situation is superior to the 5 per cent situation, which in turn is superior to the 10 per cent situation, and so on. Note carefully, however, that the ranking is of alternative *situations*, each defined by its rate of duty, not of alternative *equilibria*. In tariff-ridden situations competitive equilibrium may not be unique; and when multiple equilibria exist it is *not* true that each 5 per cent equilibrium is necessarily superior to every 10 per cent equilibrium. It can be shown only that for every

290

high-tariff equilibrium there exists at least one superior low-tariff equilibrium, so that the maximum feasible utility of any randomly or arbitrarily chosen individual, given random or arbitrary minimum feasible utilities of all other individuals, is greater in the low-tariff than in the high-tariff situation.

As a first step in proving this proposition, let us consider the simple two-commodities case. A competitive economy produces two commodities and trades one for the other at constant world prices. In Fig. 13.1 the terms of trade are indicated by the slope of *PC*, and the free-trade production equi-

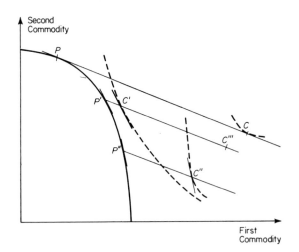

FIGURE 13.1

librium by *P*. Since we are interested in the effects of compensated tariff changes, with no two individual utilities moving in opposite directions, it is possible to associate the consumption equilibrium with the point of tangency of a price line and one of a family of (nonintersecting) Scitovsky indifference curves. Thus the free-trade consumption equilibrium is indicated by *C* in Fig. 13.1.

If an import duty is imposed, the internal price ratio turns in favor of the imported commodity. Production now takes place at *P'*; and let us suppose that consumption takes place at *C'*, a point on the new trading line *P'C'''* at which the slope of the intersecting community indifference curve is equal to the slope of the internal or domestic price line.

If the import duty is raised, the internal price ratio moves even further in favor of the imported commodity; production moves to *P''* and (let us suppose) consumption to *C''*. As Fig. 13.1 makes clear, high-tariff welfare may be greater than low-tariff welfare. The figure also makes clear that for the paradoxical outcome it is necessary (but not by itself sufficient) that the exported commodity be inferior in consumption, at least over the relevant range of prices.

In terms of utility feasibilities (Fig. 13.2), we have shown that U', a point attainable in the low-tariff situation, may lie inside or south-west of U'', a point attainable in the high-tariff situation.

It is not difficult to see, however, that there also exists a feasible low-tariff point U''' north-east of U''. Thus, in terms of Fig. 13.1, the income-consumption or Engel curve of the low-tariff situation passes south of C''.

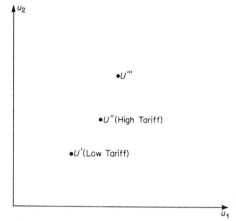

FIGURE 13.2

It therefore must intersect $P'C'$ extended, possibly on the horizontal axis. The point of intersection, say C''', corresponds to U'''. A similar argument applies to each feasible high-tariff point. Thus every high-tariff equilibrium is dominated by at least one low-tariff equilibrium.

Let us define the utility feasibility locus as the locus of possible equilibrium utilities, given the rate of import duty. If inferiority is present, this locus may incorporate several positively-sloped stretches; it may even include one or more disconnected loops. Fig. 13.3(a) illustrates.[1]

From this locus we may derive two further loci. The first of these tells us the maximum attainable values of u_2 for given minimum values of u_1: It is illustrated by Fig. 13.3(b). The second locus is defined analogously. From it we may read off the maximum attainable values of u_1 for given minimum values of u_2; it is illustrated by Fig. 13.3(c). We call these derived loci the *optimal loci*. In general the two optimal loci possess discontinuities and are not identical. If and only if the utility feasibility locus is monotonic are the optimal loci continuous and coincident.

---

[1] The construction of the utility feasibility locus is described in the first appendix to this chapter.

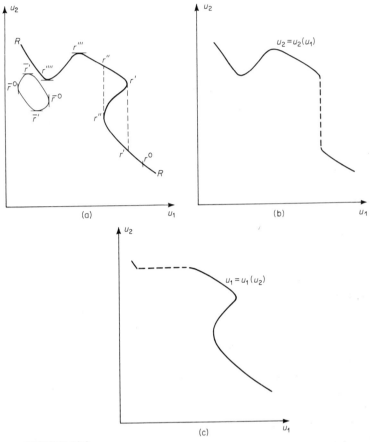

FIGURE 13.3

In terms of these constructions, and for the two-commodity case, we may paraphrase our main conclusion by saying that each low-tariff optimal locus lies uniformly outside both high-tariff optimal loci.

Does that conclusion carry over to a world of many traded commodities? The answer is: Yes, provided the tariff is not prohibitive for any nonexported commodity. For when tariffs are raised uniformly, the domestic prices of imported goods all rise in the same proportion, with the prices of exported goods unchanged. Within each commodity group relative prices are constant, leaving only one relative price free to change—the price of imports in terms of exports. In effect we are back in a world of just two commodities to which the preceding analysis applies unchanged.[2]

---

[2] This paragraph contains a particular application of the Leontief–Wold–Hicks theorem on composite commodities. See Leontief [58], Wold [61], pp. 108–110, and Hicks [57], p. 312.

If purely domestic goods are introduced, the outcome is not so clear, for in that case a change in the rate of duty affects at least two relative prices. One may conjecture that our proposition carries over to this case; strictly speaking, however, it is an open question.

With minor qualifications, we have shown that, up to the point at which all trade ceases, welfare is a decreasing function of the rate of import duty. We have, however, been concerned only with positive tariffs. For completeness we should also describe the effects of negative tariffs, that is, import subsidies.

By arguments quite similar to those set out above, it can be shown that, if satiety is ruled out, welfare falls with increases in the rate of subsidy until a point is reached, with a rate of subsidy $-\underline{\tau}$ not greater than 100 per cent, at which specialization in the production of the exported commodity and in the consumption of the imported commodity are complete. This is especially easy to see if we suppose that each member of the relevant family of Scitovsky indifference curves reaches the horizontal axis. Figures 13.4(a) and 13.4(b) illustrate the equilibrium with $\tau = \underline{\tau}$ for that case. [In both figures the international terms of trade are represented by the slope of PC, the domestic price ratio by the slopes of TC and PD.] Further increases in the rate of subsidy beyond $-\underline{\tau}$ change only the internal price ratio. The level of welfare reached at $\tau = \underline{\tau}$ may be greater or less than the autarkic level. [Figures 13.4(a) and 13.4(b) illustrate the possibility that the level of welfare at $\underline{\tau}$ is less than the autarkic level.] On the way from zero to $\underline{\tau}$ the rate of subsidy may assume values at which equilibrium is not unique. We suppose that in such cases the equilibrium with highest welfare prevails. Then we may be sure that increases in the rate of subsidy are associated with decreases in welfare.

To illustrate these conclusions, consider any particular distributive policy, constrained only by the requirement that no two individual utilities should be allowed to move in opposite directions. Knowing that policy we may

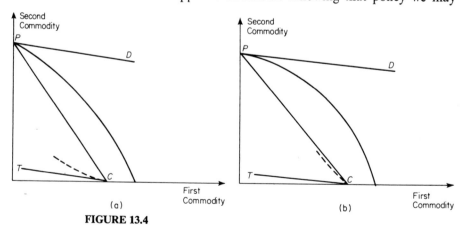

FIGURE 13.4

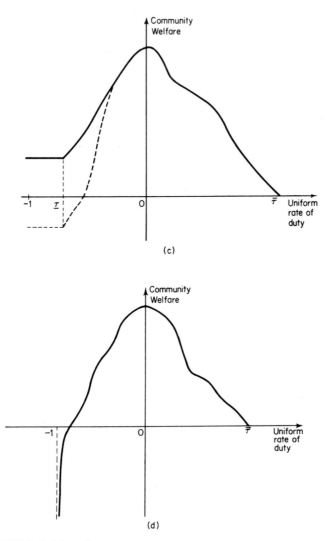

FIGURE 13.4 (cont.)

construct a map of nonintersecting (Scitovsky) community indifference contours. Let us now choose one of the many cardinal utility functions which generate that map, and let us choose the autarkic level of utility as zero. Figure 13.4(c) graphs cardinal utility against the (uniform) rate of duty. It shows utility declining as the rate of duty rises from zero to the minimum prohibitive level $\bar{\tau}$, and declining as the rate of duty falls from zero to $\underline{\tau}$. Two alternative left-hand branches of the curve are shown, the unbroken.

curve illustrating the possibility that welfare at $\underline{\tau}$ is greater than in a state of autarky, the broken branch illustrating the opposite possibility. Of course, the precise shape of the curve depends on the government's distributive policy and on the choice of utility function. But whatever the policy and whatever the choice of function the curve will reach its maximum height under free trade. Moreover, for any particular distributive policy, both $\underline{\tau}$ and $\bar{\tau}$ are invariant under the choice of cardinal utility function.

If the community indifference curves are asymptotic to the horizontal axis, our conclusions must be modified slightly. In that case, complete speciali-zation in production is inevitable, $\underline{\tau} = -1$, and the level of welfare corre-sponding to any τ sufficiently close to -1 is less than the autarkic level. Figure 13.4(d) illustrates.

The problems posed by the possibility that, in the relevant domain, the community can be sated by the first commodity are left to the reader. (See Prob. 13.10.)

2. WORLD PRICES VARIABLE

It has been shown in Sec. 1 that when a country has no influence on world prices it is possible to rank uniform tariff schedules on welfare grounds, with the null or free-trade schedule emerging at the top of the list and all pro-hibitive schedules together at the bottom.

When, however, world prices depend upon the amounts offered and demanded by the tariff-imposing country, this ranking is no longer valid. For then the average and marginal rates of transformation through trade diverge; and it is to the average rates or price ratios that under free trade the marginal rates of substitution and transformation through domestic produc-tion are equated. Hence a single-country Paretian optimum is not necessarily reached under free trade. The possibility emerges that an appropriate system of duties and subsidies on imports and exports, combined with lump-sum redistributive transfers between individuals, would leave everyone in the tariff-ridden country better off than in any particular free-trade position. We consider this possibility in some generality.

Optimal Tariff Structures

Suppose that there are n traded commodities, with foreign excess demand functions

$$Z_i^* = Z_i^*(p_1^*, \ldots, p_n^*) \qquad i = 1, \ldots, n$$

The constraint of international payments equilibrium is expressed by

$$\sum_{i=1}^{n} p_i^* Z_i^*(p_1^*, \ldots, p_n^*) = 0 \qquad (13.1a)$$

and the boundary of the convex set S of home production possibilities is

defined by
$$T(X_1, \ldots, X_n) = 0 \tag{13.1b}$$

We may formulate the policy problem, then, as that of maximizing a Scitovsky social welfare function U of the aggregate consumption vector $(X_1 - Z_1^*, \ldots, X_n - Z_n^*)$, subject to the constraints (13.1a) and (13.1b). The control variables are home outputs and world prices (which the home country manipulates indirectly, by means of its commercial policy). If we introduce Lagrange multipliers λ_1 and λ_2 the problem becomes that of maximizing

$$U[X_1 - Z_1^*(p_1^*, \ldots, p_n^*), \ldots, X_n - Z_n^*(p_1^*, \ldots, p_n^*)]$$
$$+ \lambda_1 \sum p_i^* Z_i^*(p_1^*, \ldots, p_n^*) + \lambda_2 T(X_1, \ldots, X_n)$$

with respect to X_i, p_i^* and λ_i. Among the necessary first-order conditions we find

$$-\sum_i U_i \frac{\partial Z_i^*}{\partial p_j^*} + \lambda_1 \left(Z_j^* + \sum p_i^* \frac{\partial Z_i^*}{\partial p_j^*} \right) = 0 \qquad j = 1, \ldots, n \tag{13.2}$$

where $U_i \equiv \partial U / \partial (X_i - Z_i^*)$. From the "budget" constraint (13.1a), however, the bracketed expression vanishes. Moreover, in competitive equilibrium $U_i = \mu p_i$ and $p_i = \pi_i p_i^*$, where π_i is one plus the rate of import duty if the ith commodity is imported and the inverse of one plus the rate of export duty if the ith commodity is exported. (Alternatively, in the latter case one may view π_i as one plus the rate of export duty with the duty applicable to the *foreign* price.) Thus Eqs. (13.2) reduce to[3]

$$\sum_i \pi_i p_i^* \frac{\partial Z_i^*}{\partial p_j^*} = 0 \qquad j = 1, \ldots, n$$

[3] Throughout the foregoing analysis it has been assumed that all goods are final goods and enter the utility function U in a nontrivial way. However, the assumption is quite inessential; in particular, the analysis carries over with only minor changes to the case of trade in purely intermediate goods which do not enter U. Thus suppose that goods $1, \ldots, N$ are final goods and that goods $N+1, \ldots, n$ are purely intermediate goods. Then X_i $(i = N+1, \ldots, n)$ must be interpreted as the home country's net output, over and above the home demand for the ith good as a factor of production. Clearly X_i may be of either sign—only *gross* output need be non-negative. Moreover, $X_i \equiv Z_i^*$ $(i = N+1, \ldots, n)$. The welfare problem therefore is to maximize
$$U[X_1 - Z_1^*(p_1^*, \ldots, p_n^*), \ldots, X_N - Z_N^*(p_1^*, \ldots, p_n^*)$$
with respect to $X_1, \ldots, X_N, p_1^*, \ldots, p_n^*$, subject to Eq. (13.1a) and to
$$T[X_1, \ldots, X_N, Z_{N+1}^*(p_1^*, \ldots, p_n^*), \ldots, Z_n^*(p_1^*, \ldots, p_n^*)] = 0$$
Among the necessary first-order conditions we find
$$U_i + \lambda_2 T_i = 0 \qquad i = 1, \ldots, N$$
$$-\sum_{i=1}^{N} U_i \frac{\partial Z_i^*}{\partial p_j^*} + \lambda_2 \sum_{i=N+1}^{n} T_i \frac{\partial Z_i^*}{\partial p_j^*} = 0 \qquad j = 1, \ldots, n$$

(Footnote continued at bottom of page 298.)

or, if we choose commodity units so that in an optimum $p_i^* = 1$ and adopt the matrix notation $\pi = (\pi_1, \ldots, \pi_n)$ and $Z^* = (\partial Z_i^* / \partial p_j^*)$, to

$$\pi Z^* = 0 \qquad\qquad (13.2')$$

Now the Z_i^*-functions are homogeneous of degree zero in money prices; hence Z^* is of rank less than n and we can be sure that a solution exists. The solution is, however, not unique: If π^0 is a solution, so is $\theta\pi^0$ where θ is any scalar. Since the rank of Z^* is $(n-1)$, it is possible to assign an arbitrary value to any π_i and then solve Eqs. (13.2') for the remaining π_j's. In particular, it is possible to choose π_i so that the corresponding rate of tax τ_i is zero; in other words, the home country may (but need not) choose to tax just $(n-1)$ commodities as they cross its frontier.

Besides its one-dimensional indeterminacy, what can we learn about the optimal tariff vector $(\tau_1, \ldots, \tau_n)$? We note first that it is always possible to choose an optimal vector containing both positive and negative terms. To see this, imagine the contrary and consider a particular nonnegative optimal vector $(\tau_1^0, \ldots, \tau_n^0)$. Since $\pi_i^0 = 1 + \tau_i^0$ if the ith commodity is imported and $\pi_i^0 = 1/(1 + \tau_i^0)$ if it is exported, we may infer that π^0 is positive. Let θ be a positive fraction small enough to ensure that at least one optimal import duty $\tau_i(\theta) = \theta\pi_i^0 - 1$ is negative, and note that the corresponding optimal export duties, $\tau_i(\theta) = (1 - \theta\pi_i^0)/\theta\pi_i^0$, are necessarily positive. Thus we emerge with an optimal tariff vector containing both positive and negative elements. In similar fashion, any nonpositive optimal tariff vector can be transformed into an optimal vector containing both positive and negative elements.

A question of greater interest concerns the possibility of finding a nonnegative optimal tariff vector (or a nonpositive vector). Simple examples will

---

(Footnote (3) continued from page 297.)

Substituting from the first equation into the second, we obtain

$$\lambda_2 \sum_{i=1}^{n} T_i \frac{\partial Z_i^*}{\partial p_j^*} = 0, \qquad j = 1, \ldots, n$$

Moreover, in competitive equilibrium, $T_i = \mu' p_i$ and $p_i = \pi_i p_i^*$; hence the conditions can be expressed as

$$\sum \pi_i p_i^* \frac{\partial Z_i^*}{\partial p_j^*} = 0 \qquad j = 1, \ldots, n$$

as above.

The significance of this finding lies in the fact that international borrowing and lending can be viewed as the purchase and sale of the services of capital. The problem of finding the optimal pattern of trade *and investment* therefore involves no fundamentally new issues. For an elaboration of these remarks, see Appendix 2. The reader may also refer back to Chap. 12, Sec. 2.

be produced below to show that it is not always possible to find a non-negative solution and that it is not always possible to find a nonpositive solution.

The special two-commodities case has been intensively studied. In that case a single tax suffices[4] and it can be levied indifferently on the exported or imported commodity. Suppose, for example, that the tax is levied on the first or imported commodity, so that Eq. (13.2') reduces to

$$(1 + \tau_1 \quad 1) \begin{pmatrix} \dfrac{\partial Z_1^*}{\partial p_1^*} & \dfrac{\partial Z_1^*}{\partial p_2^*} \\ \dfrac{\partial Z_2^*}{\partial p_1^*} & \dfrac{\partial Z_2^*}{\partial p_2^*} \end{pmatrix} = 0 \qquad (13.2'')$$

Solving for τ_1 and noting from Eq. (13.1a) that

$$Z_i^* = - \left(\frac{\partial Z_1^*}{\partial p_i^*} + \frac{\partial Z_2^*}{\partial p_i^*} \right) \qquad i = 1, 2$$

we find that

$$\tau_1 = \frac{-1}{1 + \xi^*}$$

If, on the other hand, the tax had been levied on the second or exported commodity, Eq. (13.2') would have reduced to

$$\left(1 \quad \frac{1}{1 + \tau_2} \right) \begin{pmatrix} \dfrac{\partial Z_1^*}{\partial p_1^*} & \dfrac{\partial Z_1^*}{\partial p_2^*} \\ \dfrac{\partial Z_2^*}{\partial p_1^*} & \dfrac{\partial Z_2^*}{\partial p_2^*} \end{pmatrix} = 0$$

that is, multiplying by $(1 + \tau_2)$, to

$$(1 + \tau_2 \quad 1) \begin{pmatrix} \dfrac{\partial Z_1^*}{\partial p_1^*} & \dfrac{\partial Z_1^*}{\partial p_2^*} \\ \dfrac{\partial Z_2^*}{\partial p_1^*} & \dfrac{\partial Z_2^*}{\partial p_2^*} \end{pmatrix} = 0$$

[4] This was recognized by Bickerdike at the outset of the discussion of optimal tariffs. ([7], pp. 100–101.)

which has the same form as Eq. (13.2″). It follows that

$$\tau = \tau_1 = \tau_2 = \frac{-1}{1 + \xi^*} \qquad (13.3)$$

Much attention has been lavished on this formula.[5] But it provides scant assistance in the search for the optimal τ since it involves two, not one, unknowns. The value of ξ^* depends on the point on the foreign demand curve at which it is evaluated; the point on the foreign demand curve depends on the import demand of the tariff-imposing country; that, in turn, depends on the internal distribution of income; but, finally, the post-tariff distribution of income depends on the arbitrary pattern of lump-sum taxes and subsidies. There is, then, not a single optimal tariff but an infinity.[6] A given τ, say 5 per cent, may be optimal for one distribution of income but in general will be either greater or smaller than the optimal τ for any other distribution. For the distribution represented by point u'' in Fig. 13.5, for example, a 5 per cent tariff is optimal, whereas the distribution represented by u''' calls for a 10 per cent tariff. (Note that the utility possibility curves corresponding to the two tariff levels may intersect;[7] if, as was assumed in drawing Fig.

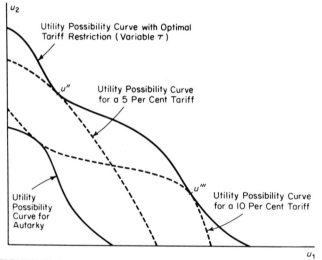

FIGURE 13.5

[5] Torrens, Mill, and Sidgwick early drew attention to the possibility, open to a single country, of gaining by imposing a tariff. It was left for Edgeworth and Bickerdike to clinch the matter. See Torrens [54], pp. 281–82, and [55], Postscript to Letter IX, especially pp. 329–38; Mill [39], pp. 21ff., and [40], Book V, Chap. IV, Sec. 6; Sidgwick [50], pp. 493ff.; Edgeworth [9], p. 15; Bickerdike [6]. For a more detailed account of the early history of optimal tariff theory, see Kemp [28], p. 788, n. 1.

[6] The same difficulty is present, of course, in the many-commodities case.

[7] For intersection it is necessary that world prices depend on the country's imports and exports. The possibility does not arise if, as was assumed in Sec. 1, world prices are given.

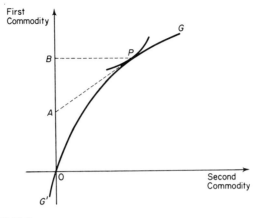

FIGURE 13.6

13.5, each rate is optimal for *some* distribution of income, they *must* intersect. About all one can be sure of is that neither curve will loop inside the
autarky curve—though they may touch it.) The utility possibility curve for
tariff-restricted trade is then the envelope of the set of all utility possibility
curves for specific τ's. These ideas are illustrated by Fig. 13.5.

It was asserted earlier that there may not exist a nonnegative optimal
tariff vector and that there may not exist a nonpositive optimal tariff vector.
We now seek to make good that assertion with simple examples involving
just two commodities. Suppose that in the optimum the home country
imports the first commodity; and, for the time being, suppose also that only
the first commodity is taxed (or subsidized). In Fig. 13.6 the foreign country's
offer curve is $G'OG$. The optimal tax or subsidy guides trade to the point
where the marginal rate of transformation through trade (indicated by the
slope of $G'OG$) is equal to the marginal rate of transformation through home
production and to the marginal social rate of substitution in home consumption. Suppose that the optimal trading point is P, with the home country
exporting the second commodity and importing the first. The home price of
exports in terms of imports, p, is indicated by the ratio AB/BP. The foreign
price ratio, p^*, is, on the other hand, indicated by OB/BP. But $p(1 + \tau_1) =
p^*$, where τ_1 is the *ad valorem* rate of import duty. Hence the optimal rate of
duty is

$$\tau_1 = \frac{p^*}{p} - 1$$

$$= \frac{OA}{OB}$$

which, necessarily, is positive.

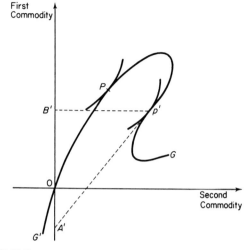

FIGURE 13.7

It is easy to see that, if instead of setting $\tau_2 = 0$ we had subsidized the export of the second commodity, the optimal import duty would have been even larger. We may conclude therefore that in the circumstances depicted by Fig. 13.6 a nonpositive optimal tariff vector is impossible.

It remains to find conditions under which a nonnegative optimal tariff vector does not exist. We know that the foreign offer curve need not possess the conventional shape displayed in Fig. 13.6. Two alternatives are displayed in Figs. 13.7 and 13.8, both of them consistent with the requirement that only

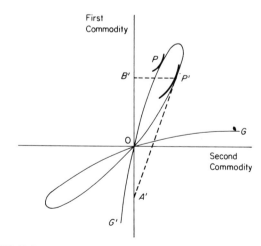

FIGURE 13.8

one offer should be forthcoming at given terms of trade.[8] In each case it is possible to find a trading point P' which *locally* maximizes the home country's welfare and to which there corresponds a "normalized" optimal tariff vector $(\tau_1, \tau_2) = (-, 0)$; in each case, therefore, a nonnegative optimal tariff vector is impossible. Also in each case, however, the trading point P which provides a *global* maximum can be reached with the aid of a nonnegative tariff vector.

The foreign offer curves of Figs. 13.6–13.8 have two features in common: They pass through the origin, and their northern silhouettes are, except possibly at the origin, concave down. It is obvious on reflection that whenever the foreign curve possesses these two features a nonnegative optimal tariff vector must exist. In our search for conditions which preclude nonnegative optimal tariff vectors therefore we must be prepared to sacrifice at least one of these features.

We now describe three alternative sets of circumstances in which there exists a normalized optimal tariff vector $(\tau_1, \tau_2) = (-, 0)$ and in which therefore there does not exist a nonnegative optimal vector.

Case 1: Foreign country imposes a tariff. If the foreign country itself imposes an import duty, its (tariff-distorted) offer curve need not be single valued. To see this, consider Fig. 13.9. The terms of trade are indicated by the slope of QQ''', the internal price ratio abroad by the steeper slope of the other straight lines. Q is the foreign production point, EE' is part of that foreign Engel curve which corresponds to the foreign internal price ratio, and Q', Q'', and Q''' are three possible consumption equilibria. Thus the possibility of multiple offers is established. (Note that inferiority of the imported

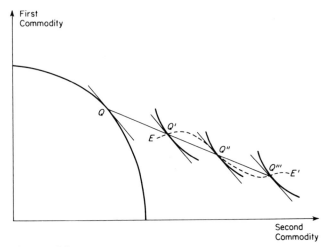

FIGURE 13.9

[8] That the foreign offer curve can take on these odd shapes is explained in Johnson [19] and in Kemp and Jones [31]. See also Chap. 2, Sec. 2 and Chap. 5, Sec. 4 above.

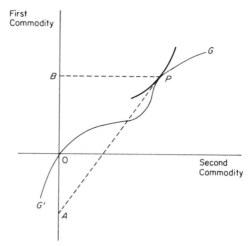

FIGURE 13.10

commodity is necessary, though not sufficient.) If, however, the foreign offer is multivalued, the offer curve may have the shape displayed in Fig. 13.10, with normalized optimal tariff vector $(\tau_1, \tau_2) = (-, 0)$. In such a case a nonnegative optimal tariff vector is impossible.

It is something of a paradox, perhaps, that the imposition of a tariff by the foreign country might change from semipositive to seminegative the normalized optimal tariff vector of the home country.

Case 2: Strongly increasing returns abroad. It is well-known that if returns are increasing, both the production possibility curve and the offer curve will depart from uniform convexity.[9] In that case, as Fig. 13.11 makes clear, the normalized optimal tariff vector may be seminegative and a nonnegative optimal vector impossible. Only if the optimum lies at the corner P', which corresponds to complete foreign specialization, may the normalized optimal

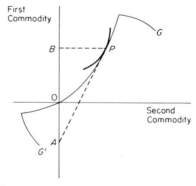

FIGURE 13.11

[9] See Matthews [38], also Chap. 9 above.

tariff be semipositive; then everything depends on the slope of the relevant home indifference curve.

Case 3: Factor market imperfections abroad. A related case is that in which, as the result of convention or law, a foreign factor receives a higher reward in one industry than in another. The *constrained* curve of production possibilities may then be convex to the origin[10] and give rise to an offer curve with the shape displayed in Fig. 13.11.

It is even possible that a seminegative normalized optimal tariff vector may be associated with a lower wage in the foreign export industry. It is amusing to compare this possibility with the pauper labor argument for tariff protection.

That concludes our demonstration that there may not exist a nonnegative or nonpositive optimal tariff vector.[11] Before passing to other matters, however, we note that, in each of the three situations discussed, the movement from free trade to optimal trade may involve the interchange of the import good and the export good. This is so even when there exists a nonnegative (nonpositive) optimal tariff vector and even though the welfare-maximizing equilibrium is chosen (from among possibly multiple free-trade equilibria) as the basis of the comparison. The demonstration is left to the reader (Prob. 13.13).

Ranking of uniform tariffs. Suppose that the home country has adopted a distributional policy which makes it impossible for two individual utilities to move in opposite directions. Then the community's preferences may be summarized by a consistent family of Scitovsky indifference surfaces. Consider $\lambda \tau^0$ where τ^0 is an optimal tariff vector corresponding to those preferences and λ is a scalar. Is it possible to show that the community's welfare, considered as a function of λ, increases steadily to a maximum when $\lambda = 1$, and thereafter declines steadily, at least until λ reaches some critical value? Does a similar progression emerge if we begin with an arbitrarily chosen tariff vector? If these questions could be answered affirmatively we should have a very satisfying generalization of the proposition established in Sec. 1 for the limiting case in which world prices are constant. I do not know the answer to either question. However, in the simple two-commodities case, with a tax on the imported commodity only, the two questions reduce to one, and it can be shown that in spite of the necessity of ranking suboptimal policies, the answer is: Yes, at least when the foreign offer curve has the

[10] Cf. Chap. 12, footnote 18.

[11] Since this was written I have been privileged to see a paper by D. J. Horwell and I. F. Pearce [15] in which it is shown that, even in the absence of foreign tariffs, market imperfections and increasing returns, a non-negative optimal tariff vector may not exist. Their demonstration requires, however, that there be more than two traded goods. Under the same conditions it can be shown that the transition from free to optimal trade may involve a change in the status of a commodity from import to export or from export to import. [See Prob. 13.14.]

conventional shape and passes through the origin, so that the optimal tariff is positive.

Consider Fig. 13.12, which shows the foreign offer curve OG and the trade indifference curves $u(\tau^0)$, $u(0)$, and $u(\bar{\tau})$ reached by the home or tariff-imposing country when it imposes an optimal tariff, a zero tariff and a prohibitive tariff, respectively. It is clear that as the rate of duty rises to the prohibitive level welfare steadily rises, reaches a peak, then falls *if and only if*

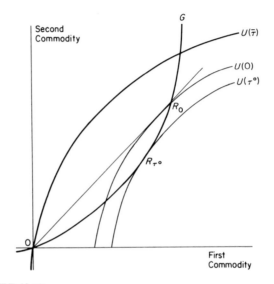

FIGURE 13.12

with given terms of trade an increase in the rate of duty is associated with a reduction in the demand for imports. For then, and only then, successive increases in the rate of duty, starting from a zero rate at R_0, will take the economy through higher and higher trade-indifference curves until it reaches R_{τ^0} and then through successively lower curves to 0 and $u(\bar{\tau})$.

Exceptions to the proposition therefore must constitute exceptions to the rule that an increase in the rate of duty is associated with a reduction in the demand for imports. It will now be shown that this rule admits of exceptions only when the exportable commodity is inferior.

Hold the terms of trade constant at unity. Suppose that the first commodity is imported and that the second is the *numéraire*. The internal price ratio is, therefore, $(1 + \tau)$ where τ is the rate of duty. The demand for imports is $Z_1(1 + \tau, Q_2)$, where

$$Q_2 = (1 + \tau)X_1 + X_2 + \tau Z_1$$

is income in terms of the *numéraire* and τZ_1 is the tariff revenue. We have

$$\frac{dZ_1}{d\tau} = \frac{\partial Z_1}{\partial \tau} + \frac{\partial Z_1}{\partial Q_2} \cdot \frac{dQ_2}{d\tau}$$

and, since

$$\frac{d[(1 + \tau)X_1 + X_2]}{d\tau} = X_1$$

$$\frac{dQ_2}{d\tau} = X_1 + Z_1 + \tau \frac{dZ_1}{d\tau}$$

Hence

$$\frac{dZ_1}{d\tau} = \frac{\partial Z_1}{\partial \tau} + \frac{m_1}{1 + \tau}\left(X_1 + Z_1 + \tau \frac{dZ_1}{d\tau}\right)$$

$$= \frac{\dfrac{\partial Z_1}{\partial \tau} + \dfrac{m_1}{1 + \tau} D_1}{1 - \dfrac{\tau}{1 + \tau} m_1}$$

Introducing the Slutzky decomposition,

$$\frac{\partial Z_1}{\partial \tau} = \left.\frac{\partial Z_1}{\partial \tau}\right| - \frac{m_1}{1 + \tau} D_1,$$

where

$$\left.\frac{\partial Z_1}{\partial \tau}\right|$$

is the pure substitution slope, we obtain, finally,

$$\frac{dZ_1}{d\tau} = \frac{\left.\dfrac{\partial Z_1}{\partial \tau}\right|}{1 - \dfrac{\tau}{1 + \tau} m_1}$$

which is negative unless the export is very inferior.

Figure 13.13 illustrates the possibility, ruled out by our restrictions on consumption inferiority, that an increase in the rate of duty may give rise both to an increase in import demand and to a deterioration in the terms of trade of the tariff-imposing country. With the lower tariff, production takes place at P, consumption at C; and the terms of trade are indicated by the slope of PC. With the higher rate of duty, production takes place at P', consumption at C'; and the (worsened) terms of trade are indicated by the slope of $P'C'$.

The possibility illustrated by Fig. 13.13 can be ruled out if very modest restrictions are imposed on the community's preferences. We now offer two observations designed to emphasize just how modest those restrictions are. First, we note that the reciprocal demand curve traced out by a higher tariff

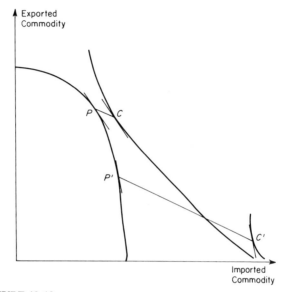

FIGURE 13.13

rate will always lie inside the curve traced out by a lower tariff rate.[12] It follows that the possibility illustrated by Fig. 13.13 requires offer curves which yield multiple equilibria at given terms of trade, as in Fig. 13.14. [Points W and W' of Fig. 13.14 correspond respectively to points C and C' of Fig. 13.13.] Second, it follows from our mathematical analysis that $dZ_1/d\tau$ is positive if and only if $1 - [\tau m_1/(1 + \tau)]$ is negative, that is, if and only if

$$1 + \tau(1 - m_1) < 0$$

Under plausible dynamic assumptions, however, this is precisely the condition for market *in*stability when the terms of trade are given.[13]

For our purposes, however, whether or not the possibility illustrated by Fig. 13.13 can be ruled out is irrelevant. For, even when an increase in the

[12] See Johnson [20], p. 34, n. 7.
[13] See Kemp [30].

rate of duty may be associated with an increase in the demand for imports and a deterioration of the terms of trade, nevertheless there exists an alternative high-tariff equilibrium characterized by reduced import demand and improved terms of trade. [Point W'' in Fig. 13.14 illustrates.] It follows that by choosing carefully from alternative equilibria one can ensure that increases in the rate of duty are associated with reductions in the demand for

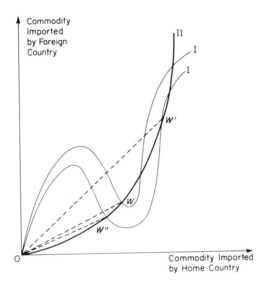

OI is the low-tariff offer curve of the home country
OI' is the high-tariff offer curve of the home country
OII is the offer curve of the foreign country

FIGURE 13.14

imports, so that as the rate of duty is raised welfare rises steadily, reaches a maximum, then declines until the duty is prohibitive.

If the possibility of satiety is ruled out, it can be shown also that, as the rate of duty declines from zero, through negative values, welfare declines until a point is reached, with a rate of import subsidy $-\tau$ not greater than 100 per cent, at which specialization in the production of the exported commodity and specialization in the consumption of the imported commodity is complete. The level of welfare at τ may be greater or less than in the autarkic state. Thus for a particular distributional policy and choice of cardinal utility function (zero in autarky) we may draw the curve C in Figs. 13.15(a) and (b), which correspond to Figs. 13.4(c) and 13.4(d) respectively. In Fig. 13.4(c) two alternative left-hand branches of C are shown, the unbroken curve illustrating the possibility that welfare at τ is greater than in a state of autarky, the dotted branch illustrating the opposite possibility. The

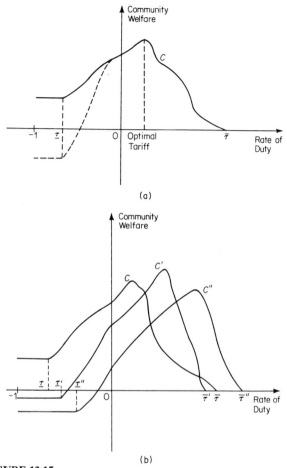

FIGURE 13.15

shape of the curve varies with the government's distributive policy and with the choice of cardinal utility function. In particular, the optimal rate of duty as well as both τ and $\bar{\tau}$ may depend on the choice of distributive policy. Thus the curves $C, C', C'', \ldots$ of Fig. 13.15(b) correspond to distributive policies $\mathscr{P}, \mathscr{P}', \mathscr{P}'', \ldots$

It is left to the reader to explore the implications of unconventionally shaped foreign offer curves and of import satiety. (See Problems 13.11 and 13.12.)

3. SUB-OPTIMAL TARIFF POLICY

In Secs. 1 and 2 we assumed away local taxes, market imperfections, price rigidities, and externalities. Each of these, if present, is capable of distorting the allocation of resources and the country's foreign offer; each therefore affects the calculation of the optimal tariff vector. In the present section we illustrate how the calculation may be affected by considering the particular case of a tax on the production of the exported commodity. The common-sense expectation—that sufficiently high rates of tax may rule out non-negative optimal tariff vectors—is confirmed.

Before launching into detailed analysis we emphasize one respect in which the problem here considered differs from that considered in Secs. 1 and 2.

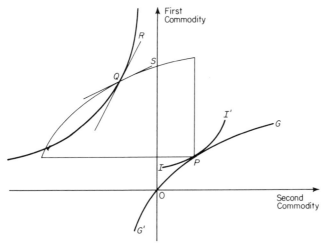

FIGURE 13.16

There we sought a full Paretian optimum in which all marginal conditions are satisfied. Since the production tax is a wedge between the marginal rates of substitution is production and consumption, it makes impossible the attainment of full optimum. Our present problem is therefore that of finding a suboptimum.[14] To attain a full optimum it would be necessary to first remove the local tax.

Figure 13.16 illustrates the argument. In the second quadrant are drawn a single consumption indifference curve and the familiar "production block." At point Q, the marginal rate of substitution in consumption R is minus the slope of the tangent to the indifference curve; and the marginal rate of transformation S is minus the slope of the tangent to the production possibility curve. Because of the excise tax $R > S$:

$$R = S(1 + t) \qquad (13.4)$$

where t is the rate of tax on the second commodity. If now we slide the

[14] Bhagwati and Ramaswami [5] deny the existence of a suboptimum. See, however, Kemp and Negishi [32].

production block round the indifference curve, maintaining the relation (13.4) between R and S, we trace out the *constrained* trade indifference curve II'.[15] To find the optimal tariff vector we need the slope of II'. Consider point P, which corresponds to point Q on the consumption indifference curve. If we change slightly the consumption C_1 of the first commodity, the consumption of the second commodity must change by $dC_2 = dC_1/R$. Moreover, from Eq. (13.4), the production X_1 of the first commodity must change by $dX_1 = R'dC_1/S'(1 + t)$ and the production of the second commodity by $dX_2 = dX_1/S = R'dC_1/SS'(1 + t)$, where primes indicate differentiation with respect to the consumption or production of the first commodity. The slope of II' is therefore

$$-\frac{dC_1 - dX_1}{dC_2 - dX_2} = -\left[1 - \frac{R'}{S'(1 + t)}\right] \bigg/ \left[\frac{1}{R} - \frac{R'}{SS'(1 + t)}\right]$$

Now in equilibrium $R = p$, which now represents the home price ratio as seen by consumers; and $S = p/(1 + t)$, the home price ratio as seen by producers. Hence the slope of II' reduces to

$$\frac{p\left[1 - \dfrac{R'}{S'(1 + t)}\right]}{\left(1 - \dfrac{R'}{S'}\right)} \tag{13.5}$$

In a trade optimum a trade indifference curve must be tangent to the foreign offer curve $G'OG$. Suppose that the optimum occurs at P, where II' and $G'OG$ touch. The slope of $G'OG$ is[16]

$$p^*\left(\frac{1}{\xi^*} + 1\right) \tag{13.6}$$

where ξ^* is, of course, the total price elasticity of foreign import demand. Equating expressions (13.5) and (13.6), and recalling that when imports only are subject to duty $p^* = p(1 + \tau)$, we obtain

$$1 + \tau^0 = \frac{\left[1 - \dfrac{R'}{S'(1 + t)}\right]}{\left[1 - \dfrac{R'}{S'}\right]} \bigg/ \left(\frac{1}{\xi^*} + 1\right) \tag{13.7}$$

---

[15] In general the trade indifference curves need not possess the usual curvature. (In the face of consumption distortions the same is true of the ordinary Scitovsky indifference curves.) In a neighborhood of the equilibrium point, however, the usual curvature must prevail.

[16] See Appendix on Price Elasticities.

where τ^0 is the optimal rate of duty. Now R' is negative, S' positive; hence $-R'/S'$ is positive. It follows that the numerator of (13.7) is a positive fraction which approaches $1 \Big/ \left(1 - \dfrac{R'}{S'}\right)$ as t goes to infinity. In an optimum $\xi^* < -1$; hence the denominator of (13.7) also is a positive fraction and approaches one as ξ^* goes to minus infinity. Clearly the optimal tariff τ^0 is negative for a sufficiently high rate of production tax or for sufficiently elastic foreign import demand; and whenever τ^0 is negative a nonnegative optimal tariff vector does not exist. If foreign demand is perfectly elastic, τ^0 must be negative if $t > 0$.

It will be obvious that if the home country were to subsidize the production of the imported commodity, the optimal tariff might again be negative.

PROBLEMS

13.1 Consider a two-commodities, two-factors world. A country imposes a small import duty. If we neglect the tariff proceeds, one factor will be benefited, the other harmed. Is it possible that the harmed factor could be fully compensated from the tariff proceeds alone? Formulate the demand conditions for the border-line case in which compensation is barely possible.

13.2 For a two-commodities, two-factors world obtain an expression for the revenue-maximizing tariff. Is it greater or smaller than the optimal tariff?

13.3 Suppose that a country wishes to raise a *given* tariff revenue. Subject to that restriction, what is the optimal set of tariffs?

13.4 What happens to the vector of optimal tariffs if the production and sale of all export commodities are in the hands of a monopolist? (See Kemp [25], pp. 172–73, and Polak [45].)

13.5 Can all optimal tariff rates be zero—that is, can free trade be optimal—even when foreign demands and supplies are imperfectly elastic? (See Graaff [11], p. 53 and [12], pp. 127, 130.)

13.6 Can net tariff revenue be negative in an optimum if more than two commodities are traded?

13.7 Can all optimal tariff rates be negative when more than two commodities are traded?

13.8

(a) Suppose that all tariff rates are pegged by international agreement but that a country is free to vary its local taxes on production and consumption. On the assumption that production taxes are zero, derive expressions for the optimal consumption taxes. On the assumption that consumption taxes are zero, derive expressions for the optimal production taxes.

(b) Consider the special case in which all tariff rates are pegged at zero, and suppose that world prices depend on the purchases and sales of the country under study. Does a nonzero vector of optimal production taxes always exist? Does a nonzero vector of optimal consumption taxes always exist? If either answer is *no*, construct a two-commodity counter example.

13.9 Suppose that just two countries trade in just two commodities. The home country imposes an optimal tariff, the foreign country trades freely. The foreign country considers the possibility that it might be able to persuade the home country to forego its tariff by undertaking to subsidize its own exports and thus forcing the terms of trade to move in favor of the home country. Is it ever possible for the foreign country to move the terms of trade far enough to make the (free-trading) home country as well off as with an optimal tariff? Is it *always* possible? When it is possible, does it ever pay the foreign country to do so? Does it always pay the foreign country?

13.10 Draw the counterpart to Figs. 13.4(c) and 13.4(d) for the case in which, in the relevant domain, the community can be sated by the imported commodity.

13.11 Draw the counterpart to Fig. 13.15(a) for the case in which, in the relevant domain, the community can be sated by the imported commodity.

13.12 Draw the counterpart to Fig. 13.15(a) under the assumption that the foreign curve has the shape shown in Fig. 13.7. Repeat the exercise with Fig. 13.11 before you.

13.13 Consider a two-commodity world and suppose either that the foreign country imposes an import duty or that the foreign factor market is distorted or that foreign industry is subject to increasing returns, so that the foreign offer curve has the shape displayed in Fig. 13.10 or that displayed in Fig. 13.11. Show that the transition from free home trade to optimal home trade may involve the interchange of the import and export goods and that this is so even when there exists a non-negative (non-positive) optimal tariff vector and even though the welfare-maximizing free-trade equilibrium is chosen (from among possibly multiple free-trade equilibria) as the basis of the comparison.

13.14 Consider a three-commodity world which is free of factor market distortions, in which returns to scale are constant, and in which the foreign country trades freely. Show that, for the home country, the transition from free to optimal trade may involve a change in the status of a commodity from import to export. Is it possible for all traded commodities to change status?

13.15 Derive expressions for the "second best" optimal tariff on the assumption that t is pegged by law or custom at some arbitrary level $\bar{t}$. Consider the special case in which $\bar{t} = 0$.

13.16 Derive expressions for the "second best" optimal tax on the assumption that τ is pegged by law or custom at some arbitrary level $\bar{\tau}$. Consider the special case in which $\bar{\tau} = 0$.

13.17 Derive expressions for the "second best" optimal tax and tariff on the assumption that $\tau + t$ is pegged at some arbitrary level.

REFERENCES

[1] Baldwin, R. E., "The New Welfare Economics and Gains in International Trade," *Quarterly Journal of Economics*, LXVI, No. 1 (February 1952), 91–101.

[2] Balogh, T. and P. P. Streeton, "Domestic Versus Foreign Investment," *Bulletin of the Oxford University Institute of Statistics*, XXII, No. 3 (August 1960), 213–24. A revised version appears in Paul Streeton, *Economic Integration*, Chap. 4. Leyden: A. W. Sythoff, 1961.

[3] Bhagwati, Jagdish, "The Gains from Trade Once Again," *Oxford Economic Papers*, New Series, XX, No. 2 (July 1968), 137–48.

[4] Bhagwati, Jagdish and Murray C. Kemp, "Ranking of Tariffs under Monopoly Power in Trade," *Quarterly Journal of Economics*, LXXXIII, No. 2 (May 1969).

[5] Bhagwati, Jagdish and V. K. Ramaswami, "Domestic Distortions, Tariffs and the Theory of Optimum Subsidy," *Journal of Political Economy*, LXXI, No. 1 (February 1963), 44–50.

[6] Bickerdike, C. F., "The Theory of Incipient Taxes," *Economic Journal*, XVI, No. 64 (December 1906), 529–35.

†[7] Bickerdike, C. F., review of A. C. Pigou, *Preferential and Protective Import Duties*, in *Economic Journal*, XVII, No. 65 (March 1907), 98–102.

[8] Cairncross, A. K., *Home and Foreign Investment* 1807–1913, Chap. IX. Cambridge: Cambridge University Press, 1953. Reprinted from *Review of Economic Studies*, III (1), No. 7 (October 1935), 67–78.

†[9] Edgeworth, F. Y., *Papers Relating to Political Economy*, Vol. II. London: Macmillan and Company, Ltd., 1925.

†[10] Fishlow, Albert and Paul A. David, "Optimal Resource Allocation in an Imperfect Market Setting," *Journal of Political Economy*, LXIX, No. 6 (December 1961), 529–46.

†[11] Graaff, J. de V., "On Optimal Tariff Structures," *Review of Economic Studies*, XVII (1), No. 42 (1949–50), 47–59.

[12] Graaff, J. de V., *Theoretical Welfare Economics*. Cambridge: Cambridge University Press, 1957.

[13] Hamada, Koichi, "Strategic Aspects of Taxation of Foreign Investment Income," *Quarterly Journal of Economics*, LXXX, No. 3 (August 1966), 361–75.

[14] Hamada, Koichi, "On the Optimal Level of Risky Foreign Investment," *The Economic Studies Quarterly*, XVI, No. 1 (November 1965), 62–68.

†[15] Horwell, D. J. and I. F. Pearce, "A Look at the Structure of Optimal Tariff Rates," *International Economic Review*, to be published.

[16] Inada, Ken-ichi and Murray C. Kemp, "International Capital Movements and the Theory of International Trade," *Quarterly Journal of Economics*, LXXXIII, No. 2 (May 1969).

[17] Iversen, Carl, *Aspects of the Theory of International Capital Movements*, pp. 160–70. London: Oxford University Press, 1936.

[18] Jasay, A. E., "The Social Choice between Home and Overseas Investments," *Economic Journal*, LXX, No. 277 (March 1960), 105–13.

[19] Johnson, Harry G., "International Trade, Income Distribution, and the Offer Curve," *Manchester School*, XXVII, No. 2 (September 1959), 241–60.

[20] Johnson, Harry G., *International Trade and Economic Growth*. London: George Allen and Unwin Ltd., 1958.

[21] Jones, Ronald W., "International Capital Movements and the Theory of Tariffs and Trade," *Quarterly Journal of Economics*, LXXXI, No. 1 (February 1967), 1–38.

[22] Kemp, Murray C., "Foreign Investment and National Advantage," *Economic Record*, XXVIII, No. 1 (March 1962), 56–62.

[23] Kemp, Murray C., "The Benefits and Cost of Private Investment from Abroad: Comment," *Economic Record*, XXVIII, No. 1 (March 1962), 108–10.

[24] Kemp, Murray C., "The Gain from International Trade," *Economic Journal*, LXXII, No. 4 (December 1962), 803–19.

[25] Kemp, Murray C., *The Pure Theory of International Trade*. Englewood Cliffs., N.J.: Prentice–Hall, Inc., 1964.

[26] Kemp, Murray C., "A Guide to Negishi," *Economic Record*, XXI, No. 4 (December 1965), 632–33.

[27] Kemp, Murray C., "Note on a Marshallian Conjecture," *Quarterly Journal of Economics*, LXXX, No. 3 (August 1966), 481–84.

[28] Kemp, Murray C., "The Gain from International Trade and Investment: a Neo-Heckscher–Ohlin Approach," *American Economic Review*, LVI, No. 4, Part 1 (September 1966), 188–909.

[29] Kemp, Murray C., "Notes on the Theory of Optimal Tariffs," *Economic Record*, XLIII, No. 103 (September 1967), 395–404.

[30] Kemp, Murray C., "Some Issues in the Analysis of Trade Gains," *Oxford Economic Papers*, New Series, XX, No. 2 (July 1968), 149–61.

[31] Kemp, Murray C. and Ronald W. Jones, "Variable Labor Supply and the Theory of International Trade," *Journal of Political Economy*, LXX, No. 1 (February 1962), 30–36.

[32] Kemp, Murray C. and Takashi Negishi, "Domestic Distortions, Tariffs and the Theory of Optimum Subsidy," *Journal of Political Economy*, LXXVII, to be published.

[33] Keynes, J. M., "Foreign Investment and National Advantage," *The Nation and Athenaeum*, XXXV (August 9, 1924), 584–87.

[34] Keynes, J. M., "Some Tests for Loans to Foreign and Colonial Governments," *The Nation and Athenaeum*, XXXVI, No. 16 (January 17, 1925), 564–65.

[35] Keynes, J. M., *Treatise on Money*, Vol. I, pp. 343–46. London: Macmillan and Company, Ltd., 1930.

[36] MacDougall, G. D. A., "The Benefits and Costs of Private Investment from Abroad: a Theoretical Approach," *Economic Record*, XXVI, No. 1 (March 1960), 13–35. Reprinted in *Bulletin of the Oxford University Institute of Statistics*, XXII, No. 3 (August 1960), 187–212.

[37] Marshall, Alfred, *Memorandum on the Fiscal Policy of International Trade*. House of Commons No. 321, 1908. Reprinted in J. M. Keynes, ed., *Official Papers by Alfred Marshall*. London: Macmillan, for the Royal Economic Society, 1926.

[38] Matthews, R. C. O., "Reciprocal Demand and Increasing Returns," *Review of Economic Studies*, XVII, No. 2 (February 1950), 149–58.

[39] Mill, John Stuart, *Essays on Some Unsettled Questions of Political Economy*. London: The London School of Economics and Political Science, 1948.

[40] Mill, John Stuart, *Principles of Political Economy*, ed. Sir William J. Ashley. London: Longmans, Green and Company, 1909.

[41] Negishi, Takashi, "Foreign Investment and the Long-Run National Advantage," *Economic Record*, XXI, No. 4 (December 1965), 628–32.

[42] Negishi, Takashi, "Optimal Capital Movements Revisited," *American Economic Review*, to be published.

[43] Nurkse, Ragnar, "The Problem of International Investment Today in the Light of Nineteenth-Century Experience," *Economic Journal*, LXIV, No. 256 (December 1954), 744–58.

[44] Pearce, I. F. and D. G. Rowan, "A Framework for Research into the Real Effects of International Capital Movements," in Tullio Bagiotti, ed., *Essays in Honour of Marco Fanno*, pp. 505–35. Padova: Cedam, 1966.

[45] Polak, J. J., " 'The Optimal Tariff' and the Cost of Imports," *Review of Economic Studies*, XIX (1), No. 48 (1951–52), 36–41.

[46] Samuelson, Paul A., "Welfare Economics and International Trade," *American Economic Review*, XXVIII, No. 2 (June 1938), 261–66.

[47] Samuelson, Paul A., "The Gains from International Trade Once Again," *Economic Journal*, LXXII, No. 288 (December 1962), 820–29.

[48] Schonfield, Andrew, *British Economic Policy Since the War*, rev. ed., pp. 108–22. London: Penguin Books Ltd., 1959.

[49] Scitovsky, Tibor, "A Reconsideration of the Theory of Tariffs," *Review of Economic Studies*, IX, No. 2 (Summer 1941), 89–110. Reprinted in *Readings in the Theory of International Trade*, eds. Howard S. Ellis and Lloyd A. Metzler, pp. 358–89. Philadelphia: The Blakiston Company, 1949.

[50] Sidgwick, Henry, *The Principles of Political Economy*, 2nd ed. London: Macmillan and Company Ltd., 1887.

[51] Simpson, Paul B., "Foreign Investment and the National Economic Advantage: a Theoretical Analysis," Chapter XVIII of Raymond F. Mikesell, ed., *U.S. Private and Government Investment Abroad.* Eugene, Oregon: University of Oregon Books, 1962.

[52] Singer, H. W., "The Distribution of Gains between Investing and Borrowing Countries," *American Economic Review, Papers and Proceedings*, XL, No. 2 (May 1950), 473–85.

[53] Smith, Adam, *An Inquiry into the Nature and Causes of the Wealth of Nations.* London: Oxford University Press, 1928.

[54] Torrens, R., *An Essay on the Production of Wealth.* London: Longman, Hurst, Rees, Orme, and Brown, 1821.

[55] Torrens, R., *The Budget. On Commerical and Colonial Policy*, London: Smith, Elder, and Co., 1844.

[56] Vanek, Jaroslav, *General Equilibrium of International Discrimination. The Case of Customs Unions.* Cambridge, Mass.: Harvard University Press, 1965.

[57] Hicks, J. R., *Value and Capital*, 2nd ed. Oxford: The Clarendon Press, 1946.

[58] Leontief, W., "Composite Commodities and the Problem of Index Numbers," *Econometrica*, IV, No. 1 (January 1936), 39–59.

[59] Samuelson, Paul A., "Evaluation of Real National Income," *Oxford Economic Papers*, New Series, II, No. 1 (January 1950), 1–29.

[60] Samuelson, Paul A., "Social Indifference Curves," *Quarterly Journal of Economics*, LXX, No. 1 (February 1956), 1–22.

[61] Wold, Herman in association with Lars Juréen, *Demand Analysis.* New York: John Wiley and Sons, 1953.

APPENDIX I:

Derivation of the Utility Feasibility Locus

Consider an economy with just two individuals and with a fixed output of each of two commodities. Trade with the rest of the world takes place at fixed terms of trade $p = p_2^*/p_1^*$. Let τ_i be the rate of import duty on the ith commodity. Then the internal price ratio is

$$p = \frac{p^*}{1 + \tau_1} \quad \text{if the first commodity is imported}$$

$$p = p^*(1 + \tau_2) \quad \text{if the second commodity is imported}$$

$$\frac{p^*}{1 + \tau_1} \leq p \leq p^*(1 + \tau_2) \quad \text{otherwise}$$

For such an economy we may construct a box diagram with dimensions given by the fixed outputs. Within this box we may draw four Engel curves, one for each individual for each of the two extreme price ratios, $p^*/(1 + \tau_1)$ and $p^*(1 + \tau_2)$. In Figure 13A.1 are drawn the curves corresponding to $p^*/(1 + \tau_1)$. $E_i^1 E_i^1$ is the Engel-curve of the ith individual. The internal price ratio is represented by the slope of QQ; the international terms of trade are indicated by the common slope of the other straight lines.

Consider r_1^0 and r_2^0 in Fig. 13A.1. These represent a possible trading equilibrium with $r_1^0 r_2^0$, the net foreign trade vector, revealing that the first

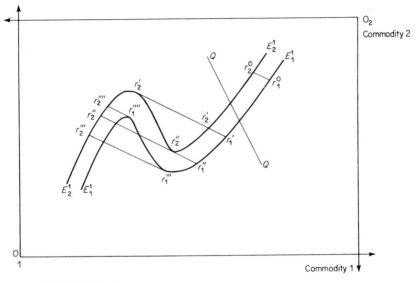

FIGURE 13A.1

commodity is imported, the second exported. Corresponding to r_1^0 and r_2^0 in Fig. 13A.1 is r^0 on the utility feasibility curve of Fig. 13.3(a). Now let r_1 move in a southwesterly direction along $E_1^1 E_1^1$, beginning at r_1^0, and let us trace out the corresponding equilibrium r_2-points on $E_2^1 E_2^1$. Until r_1 reaches r_1' this is a simple matter; the utility of the first individual steadily declines and that of the second individual steadily grows. To r_1', however, there correspond not one but two r_2-points; and to r_1-points between r_1' and r_1'' there correspond three equilibrium r_2-points, each with its associated trading vector and level of utility for the second individual. Continuing in this way we eventually trace out the RR-curve of Fig. 13.3(a).

The above construction was based on the assumption that the first commodity is imported. It is possible, however, that for some income distributions the second commodity will be imported. To explore this possibility we need the remaining pair of Engel curves, corresponding to an internal price ratio of $p^*(1 + \tau_2)$. These are drawn in Fig. 13A.2 and labelled $E_i^2 E_i^2$, with the old $E_i^1 E_i^1$-curves included for comparison. It is not difficult to see that only those r_1-points which lie between $\bar{r}_1^0$ and $\bar{r}_1^0$, and the corresponding r_2-points, represent possible trading equilibria, with net imports of the second commodity. As we allow r_1 to run through this restricted range, r_2 moves between the two $\bar{r}_2'$-points and traces out in Fig. 13.3(a) a closed loop of

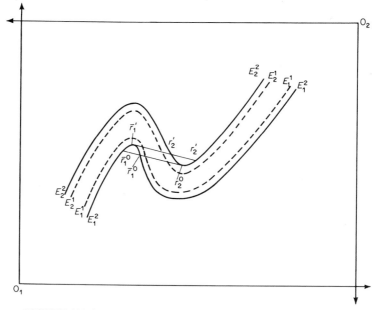

FIGURE 13A.2

utility possibilities. When added to the RR-curve this loop gives us our complete set of feasible utility combinations. In the case illustrated the set is not connected.

That completes the derivation. It is to be emphasized that inferiority is necessary but not by itself sufficient to produce positively sloped stretches in the utility feasibility locus. And even when inferiority is sufficiently strong to produce positive slopes it may not be strong enough, or may not prevail over a sufficiently wide range of incomes, to produce a closed loop. Finally, even if the loop exists, it is disconnected only if $E_1^2 E_1^2$ and $E_2^2 E_2^2$ do not intersect. If $E_1^1 E_1^1$ and $E_2^1 E_2^1$ intersect, and if $E_1^2 E_1^2$ and $E_2^2 E_2^2$ intersect, the loop and RR can be connected by movements along the contract locus, with net foreign trade zero.

APPENDIX II:

Optimal Trade and Investment in a Special Case

It has been noted (in footnote 3) that our analysis of optimal tariff structures is sufficiently general to cover trade in intermediate goods, including the services of primary factors such as capital. That a country may gain by curbing its net international borrowing and lending is, however, not well-known[17] and the notion that there may exist an optimal degree of restriction is fairly new.[18] Moreover, the discussion of Sec. 2 was quite abstract. The purpose of this appendix therefore is to examine in detail the special case in which two countries trade in two finished goods and also borrow and lend a homogeneous physical capital stock.

The specific assumptions underlying the analysis will for the most part be familiar from Chap. 9. Both factors are assumed to be in fixed world supply, with capital internationally mobile, labor immobile. It is assumed that markets are perfectly competitive, all participants being well informed about world trading and investing opportunities. It is assumed also that, if it is a net creditor, the home country either exports the second commodity or exports nothing and that, if it is a net debtor, the home country exports the second commodity or exports both commodities. The second commodity is, in this sense, the "natural" export of the home country.

1. GEOMETRIC STATEMENT OF THE PROBLEM

Putting aside net new borrowing, grants, indemnities and remittances every country is subject to a budget constraint of the form

(Quantity of Exports) *minus* (Quantity of Imports) × (Terms of Trade)

minus (Net International Indebtedness) ×

(Average Earnings on Debt)

$= 0$

The desired imports and exports of a country depend both on the terms of trade and on its net indebtedness. Suppose the latter is given. Then for each

---

[17] See, however, Keynes [33]–[35], Iversen [17], Cairncross [8], Singer [52], Nurkse [43], Schonfield [48]. It is worth looking also at Smith [53], Book II, Chap. V.

[18] MacDougall [36].

hypothetical value of the terms of trade we can plot desired imports and exports. By varying the terms of trade we can trace a locus of import-export combinations, each of which represents a potential international equilibrium. [Cf. Fig. 13A.3.] This locus is a straightforward generalization of the familiar foreign trade offer curve. Note, however, that only when net indebtedness is zero does the curve pass through the origin and that, except in that special case, it is not possible to read off the terms of trade corresponding to a particular point on the locus by simply connecting that point

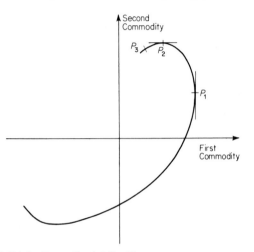

FIGURE 13A.3: Generalized Offer Curve.

by a straight line to the origin—the capital item in our equation complicates things. Note also that an equilibrium is possible in which the debtor country imports neither commodity; such an equilibrium would be located in the fourth quadrant of Fig. 13A.3.

Now take the foreign country's offer curve thus defined and slide it round the home country's production-possibilities curve in the manner made familiar by Baldwin and Samuelson.[19] In this way is generated an envelope— the home country's consumption-possibilities curve (*cc′* in Fig. 13A.4). Throughout this exercise, however, the net indebtedness of each of the two countries has been held constant. Suppose now that the home country invests a little more or less in the foreign country and that this is accomplished by shipping equipment from one country to the other. Evidently both the home country's production frontier and the foreign country's (generalized) offer curve will shift, and there will emerge a new envelope. Consider the envelope of all such envelopes (*CC′* in Fig. 13A.4). This truly describes the consumption possibilities facing the home country.

[19] Baldwin [1] and Samuelson [47].

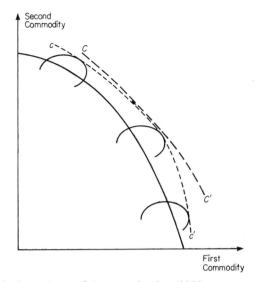

FIGURE 13A.4: Curve of Consumption Possibilities.

The problem is to find that combination of tariffs which will move the home country to the favored point on its generalized consumption-possibilities curve.

2. SOLUTION OF THE PROBLEM: INCOMPLETE FOREIGN SPECIALIZATION

For the time being it will be assumed that each country produces something of both commodities.

An Interior Optimum

As in Chap. 9 we let r_i stand for the return on one unit of capital in terms of the ith commodity and J for the net amount of capital invested abroad by the home country. Finally, U is a concave Scitovsky[20] index of the home country's welfare, a function of the aggregate amounts consumed by the home country of each of the two commodities, and of nothing else:

$$U = U(D_1; D_2) = U(X_1 + Z_1; X_2 + Z_2)$$

[20] Scitovsky [49]. See also Samuelson [60].

The foreign country, however, is subject to the budget constraint

$$Z_1^* + p^* Z_2^* + J r_1^* = 0 \qquad (14A.1)$$

Moreover, in market equilibrium

$$Z_i + Z_i^* = 0 \qquad i = 1, 2$$

Hence the index may be written as

$$U(X_1 + p^* Z_2^* + J r_1^*; \, X_2 - Z_2^*)$$

Now foreign excess demand depends on the world terms of trade, on real income and on the amount of capital invested abroad by the home country. However, real income is itself related to the terms of trade and to the level of net international indebtedness; hence we may simply write $Z_2^* = Z_2^*(p^*, J)$. We note also that, since the foreign country is assumed to be incompletely specialized, r_1^* depends on p^*, but not on J.[21] We therefore may write $r_1^* = r_1^*(p^*)$, with $\partial r_1^* / \partial p^* \gtrless 0$ if the second commodity is relatively capital-intensive, the two commodities are equally capital-intensive, or the first commodity is relatively capital-intensive. Finally, we note that the home output of the second commodity depends on the output of the first commodity and on the amount of capital invested abroad; that is $X_2 = \varphi(X_1, J)$. [$\partial \varphi / \partial X_1$ is the slope of the production possibilities curve; $-\partial \varphi / \partial J$ is the marginal productivity of capital in terms of the second commodity, r_2.] It follows from all this that the welfare index can be written as a function of the three parameters X_1, p^* and J:

$$U[X_1 + p^* Z_2^*(p^*, J) + r_1^*(p^*)J; \, \varphi(X_1, J) - Z_2^*(p^*, J)]$$

Each of the three parameters can be varied as an act of policy. The problem is to find those values of X_1, p^* and J which maximize U.

It is worth noting, perhaps, that in this formulation of the problem the proceeds of the tariff and income tax are not explicitly recognized. This does not mean, of course, that matters of public finance and income distribution are overlooked. The disposition of revenue is implicit in the selection of a social welfare function.

[21] With constant returns technology, a given price ratio and incomplete specialization, changes in the factor endowment give rise to changes in outputs but not to changes in factor proportions and (therefore) not to changes in marginal products. Cf. Chap. 1, Sec. 2.

The first order conditions of an interior maximum[22] may be written[23]

$$\frac{U_2}{U_1} = -\frac{1}{\dfrac{\partial \varphi}{\partial X_1}} \tag{13A.2a}$$

$$\frac{U_2}{U_1} = \frac{p^*}{\xi_2^*}\left(1 + \xi_2^* + \frac{J}{Z_2^*}\cdot\frac{\partial X_2^*}{\partial J}\right) \tag{13A.2b}$$

$$\frac{U_2}{U_1} = p^*\left(\frac{\partial X_2^*}{\partial J} - \frac{r_1^*}{p^*}\right)\bigg/\left(\frac{\partial X_2^*}{\partial J} - \frac{r_1}{p}\right) \tag{13A.2c}$$

where $U_i \equiv \partial U/\partial D_i$, $\xi_2^* \equiv (p^*/Z_2^*)(\partial Z_2^*/\partial p^*)$ is the total price elasticity of foreign import demand, and $\partial X_2^*/\partial J$ is the rate at which the foreign output of the second commodity responds to a unit change in the capital endowment, given the price ratio but assuming equilibrating adjustments in both industries.

The first of these three conditions states simply that the marginal social rate of substitution between the two commodities must equal the slope of the production frontier. This condition will be met under competitive conditions, when both are equal to the home price ratio.

The second condition may be interpreted as defining the optimal rate of duty. As we have just noted, $U_2/U_1 = p$; also, $p = \bar{p}/(1+\tau)$, where τ is the *ad valorem* rate of import (or export) duty. The second condition may be written, therefore, as

$$\frac{1}{1+\tau} = \frac{1 + \xi_2^* + \rho_2^*}{\xi_2^*}$$

where $\rho_2^* \equiv (J/Z_2^*)(\partial X_2^*/\partial J)$. It follows that the optimal rate of duty is

$$\tau = -\frac{1 + \rho_2^*}{1 + \xi_2^* + \rho_2^*} \tag{13A.3}$$

Of special interest is the zero-indebtedness case, in which $J = 0$. For then $\rho_2^* = 0$ and the optimal rate of duty takes its familiar value:

$$\tau = -\frac{1}{1 + \xi_2^*} \tag{13A.4}$$

[22] Those boundary cases in which the *home* country is completely specialized will be considered later.

[23] In writing Eq. (13A.2b) use has been made of the fact that $\partial X_2^*/\partial J = dr_1^*/dp^*$. This remarkable equality was proved in Chap. 1 (See Eq. (1.24)). In writing Eq. (13A.2c) use has been made of the fact that, given p^*, changes in J have no effect on net foreign real income and hence no effect on foreign demand. Changes in J therefore affect $Z_2^*(\equiv D_2^* - X_2^*)$ solely through X_2^*: $\partial Z_2^*/\partial J = -\partial X_2^*/\partial J$. Use has been made also of the relation: $\partial \varphi/\partial J = r_1/p$.

It is not surprising perhaps that free trade is optimal if the foreign import demand is perfectly elastic ($\xi_2^* = -\infty$) or, when the home country is a net creditor and imports *both* final goods, if the foreign supply of the second commodity is perfectly elastic ($\xi_2^* = +\infty$).

The interpretation of the third condition, contained in Eq. (13A.2c), is a little more intricate. We recall that in competitive equilibrium the earnings of foreign capital must be the same in both countries:

$$r_1(1 - t)(1 + \tau) = r_1^* \qquad (9.11b)$$

From Eqs. (13A.2b), (13A.2c), and (13A.3), on the other hand,

$$r_1 = r_1^*\left[1 + \frac{\rho_2^*(1 + \rho_2^*)}{\mu_2 \xi_2^*}\right] \qquad (13A.5)$$

where $\mu_2 \equiv r_1^* J / p^* Z_2^*$. It follows from Eqs. (13A.5) and (9.11b) that the optimal rate of tax is

$$t = (\rho_2^* - \mu_2)\frac{1 + \rho_2^*}{\mu_2 \xi_2^* + \rho_2^*(1 + \rho_2^*)} \qquad (13A.6)$$

Note that when $|\xi_2^*| = \infty$, so that free trade is optimal, it also is optimal to refrain from tinkering with the international allocation of capital. When $J = 0$, so that $\mu_2 = \rho_2^* = 0$, the optimal tax rates are, as one might have expected, indeterminate.

Boundary Optima

So far we have confined our attention to interior optima. Specifically, we have put aside both the possibility that it is optimal for the home country to specialize completely and the possibility that the optimal J assumes one or other of the two extreme values determined by national capital endowments.

Fortunately our conclusions, with minor modifications, cover also the possibility of complete home specialization. For then $X_1 = 0$ and the welfare index becomes

$$U\{0 + p^* Z_2^*(p^*, J) + r_1^*(p^*)J; \varphi(0, J) - Z_2^*(p_\bullet^*, J)\},$$

a function of two parameters only, p^* and J. The first order conditions are identical with those contained in Eqs. (13A.2b) and (13A.2c), hence the optimal tariff and tax are set out in Eqs. (13A.3) and (13A.6). Equation (13A.2a) no longer holds, and must be replaced by a suitable inequality.

The possibility that J assumes an extreme value is ruled out by the restrictions placed on production functions in Chap. 1, Sec. 2.

3. SOLUTION OF THE PROBLEM: COMPLETE FOREIGN SPECIALIZATION

The discussion of Sec. 2 was limited to the case of incomplete foreign specialization. The same general approach can be applied to the Classical case in which the foreign country produces one commodity only. The cases differ, however, in two important respects. In the first place, the return on foreign investment, r_1^*, now depends on the level of net foreign indebtedness, J, but not on the terms of trade, p^*; specifically, $\partial r_1^*/\partial p^* = \partial X_2^*/\partial J = p_2^* = 0$ and $\partial r_1^*/\partial J < 0$. Second, it is no longer true that net foreign real income is, for given terms of trade, invariant under changes in J. Thus, if the foreign country is completely specialized in the production of the first commodity, we have

$$\frac{\partial Z_2^*}{\partial J} = \frac{\partial D_2^*}{\partial J} = \frac{\partial D_2^*}{\partial Q_1^*} \cdot \frac{\partial Q_1^*}{\partial J}$$

$$= \frac{m_2^*}{p^*}\left(-J\frac{\partial r_1^*}{\partial J}\right)$$

$$= -\frac{m_2^*}{p^*}r_1^*\delta_1$$

where $\delta_1 \equiv (J/r_1^*)(\partial r_1^*/\partial J)$ is the elasticity of the foreign rate of return with respect to foreign investment, and $Q_1^* = X_1^* - Jr_1^*$ is the income of the foreign country in terms of the first commodity.

In view of these differences, Eq. (13A.3) must be replaced by

$$\tau = -\frac{1}{1 + \xi_2^*} \tag{13A.3'}$$

Equation (13A.2c) becomes

$$\frac{U_2}{U_1} = r_1^* \frac{1 + \delta_1 m_1^*}{\dfrac{r_1}{p} - \dfrac{m_2^* r_1^* \delta_1}{p^*}} \tag{13A.2c'}$$

Equation (13A.5) is replaced by

$$r_1 = r_1^*\left\{1 + \delta_1\left[m_1^* + m_2^* \cdot \frac{1 + \xi_2^*}{\xi_2^*}\right]\right\} \tag{13A.5'}$$

and Eq. (13A.6) becomes

$$t = \frac{\delta_1(\xi_2^* + m_2^*) - 1}{\delta_1(\xi_2^* + m_2^*) + \xi_2^*}$$

$$= \frac{\delta_1\bar{\xi}_2^* - 1}{(1 + \delta_1)\bar{\xi}_2^* - m_2^*} \tag{13A.6'}$$

part 4

The Introduction of Money and Other Securities

chapter 14

The Rate of Exchange, the Terms of Trade, and the Balance of Payments

Throughout Parts II and III it was pretended that trade is conducted in barter fashion, without the mediation of money. It was found convenient to adopt one commodity as the unit of account, but it was not assumed at any stage that the *numéraire* was also a medium of exchange or store of value.

The pretense has served us well. Many of the important questions of international economics can be posed without reference to national currencies. But not all. It is now time to consider those questions which can be posed only against a background of specific monetary assumptions. In the present chapter we shall be especially interested in the relationships which prevail between the rate of exchange, national price levels, the terms of trade, and the balance of payments. More specifically, we shall explore the implications of a change in the rate of exchange for money prices, the terms of trade, and the balance of payments.

Such a change may take place within either of two institutional arrangements. On one hand, we may imagine that the rate of exchange is determined in a competitive world money market, free of all interference by agencies of government, and that it *floats* at whatever level will equate monetary demand and supply. Changes in the rate may in this case occur only in response to changes in private demand or supply. On the other hand, we may imagine that the rate is pegged by agreement between the two governments, and maintained at the agreed level by continuous intervention in the market by governmental agencies. Changes in the rate occur, under these arrangements, only as the result of changes in official policy. Under the auxiliary assumptions which we shall make in this chapter, the analysis of exchange rate variations proceeds along very similar lines, whatever the institutional arrangements. To avoid needless repetition, therefore, attention will be focused on one possibility only: That the rate of exchange is set, and varied, as a matter of official policy. But a few remarks about floating rates of exchange may be found in Sec. 5.

Throughout the present chapter we continue to assume that the full employment of resources is maintained by the flexibility of commodity prices and factor rewards. Until Sec. 5, international borrowing and lending, other than that implicit in the exchange operations of government agencies, is ignored. In particular, it is assumed that the current rate of exchange is expected to prevail indefinitely; we thus rule out of consideration the analysis of traders' responses to uncertainty.

1. THE INTRODUCTION OF FIAT CURRENCIES—PEGGED RATE OF EXCHANGE

An essential preliminary is the formal extension of our earlier barter model [Eqs. (3.1)] to incorporate fiat currencies, money prices, and the possibility of unbalanced international payments.

Let us suppose, then, that the rate of exchange is pegged by the operations of an Exchange Stabilization Fund, which undertakes to buy and sell the two national currencies at a fixed rate of exchange. Suppose, further, that the Fund is sponsored jointly by the two governments, so that it runs no risk of exhausting its supply of either currency. Then the activities of the Fund will ensure that for each currency, aggregate demand (private demand *plus* the Fund's demand) is equal to aggregate supply. The balance of payments, B, may be defined as the difference between the home country's exports and imports, each valued in terms of the *foreign* currency. Thus if we represent by R the rate of exchange, defined as the price of foreign currency in terms of home currency, we may write

$$B = \frac{1}{R}(p_2 Z_2^* - p_1 Z_1)$$

Next we must reconsider the determinants of the excess demands, Z_i and Z_i^*. Under barter assumptions they have been shown to depend on the price ratio, p_2/p_1, alone. But this simple resolution of the problem is no longer available. In particular, the demand for each commodity must now be supposed to depend on the aggregate privately-held stock of money. Moreover, we must distinguish Z_3, the excess demand for home money, and Z_4^*, the excess demand for foreign money. Let us suppose that individuals wish to hold only the currency of their country of residence, so that the two currencies serve as purely domestic or nontraded goods. Then if we denote by A the privately held stock of home money, and by Q the money income of the home country, we may write

$$D_i = \varphi[p_1, p_2; Q(p_1, p_2); A]$$
$$= D_i(p_1, p_2; A) \qquad\qquad i = 1, 2, 3 \qquad\qquad (14.1)$$

The output of each commodity depends on the two money prices only: Hence the excess demand functions may be written

$$Z_i = D_i(p_1, p_2; A) - X_i(p_1, p_2)$$
$$= Z_i(p_1, p_2; A) \qquad\qquad i = 1, 2, 3 \qquad\qquad (14.2)$$

where $Z_3 \equiv A$.

We may now write down a system of equations appropriate to the study of the short-run or "impact" effects of devaluation:

$$Z_i(p_1, p_2; A) + Z_i^*\left(\frac{p_1}{R}, \frac{p_2}{R}; A^*\right) = 0 \qquad i = 1, 2$$

$$B - \frac{p_2}{R} Z_2^*\left(\frac{p_1}{R}, \frac{p_2}{R}; A^*\right) + \frac{p_1}{R} Z_1(p_1, p_2; A) = 0 \qquad\qquad (14.2)$$

The first pair of equations expresses the requirement that both commodity markets be in equilibrium; the third equation defines the balance of payments. Commodity and currency units are so chosen that, in the initial equilibrium,

$$p_i = R = 1 \qquad\qquad (14.4a)$$

and it will be assumed that initially international payments are in balance:

$$B = 0 \qquad\qquad (14.4b)$$

It will be assumed throughout the chapter that the commodity excess demand functions are homogeneous of degree zero in the p_i and A, and that the excess demand for money is homogeneous of degree one:

$$p_1 \frac{\partial Z_i}{\partial p_1} + p_2 \frac{\partial Z_i}{\partial p_2} + A \frac{\partial Z_i}{\partial A} = 0 \qquad i = 1, 2 \qquad (14.5a)$$

$$p_1 \frac{\partial Z_3}{\partial p_1} + p_2 \frac{\partial Z_3}{\partial p_2} + A \frac{\partial Z_3}{\partial A} = Z_3 \qquad (14.5b)$$

It will be assumed also that an increase in A results in an increase in the demand for each commodity:

$$\frac{\partial Z_i}{\partial A} > 0 \qquad i = 1, 2 \qquad (14.6)$$

Frequently we shall resort to the less plausible assumption that the two commodities are gross substitutes:[1]

$$\frac{\partial Z_i}{\partial p_j} > 0 \qquad i, j = 1, 2; \quad j \neq i \qquad (14.7a)$$

From Eqs. (14.5a), (14.6), and (14.7a)

$$\frac{\partial Z_i}{\partial p_i} < 0 \qquad i = 1, 2 \qquad 14.7b)$$

and

$$-\frac{\partial Z_i}{\partial p_i} > \frac{\partial Z_i}{\partial p_j} \qquad i = 1, 2; \quad j \neq i \qquad (14.7c)$$

Finally, it will be assumed occasionally that each commodity is a gross substitute for money:

$$\frac{\partial Z_3}{\partial p_i} > 0 \qquad i = 1, 2 \qquad (14.8)$$

Similar restrictions will be placed on the excess demand functions of the foreign country. These may be written

$$Z_i^* = Z_i^* \left(\frac{p_1}{R}, \frac{p_2}{R} ; A^* \right) \qquad i = 1, 2, 4$$

[1] We shall not in the present chapter pay much attention to questions of stability. It may be noted, however, that the assumption of gross substitutability guarantees the stability of the system of differential equations, $\dot{p}_i = E_i + E_i^*$ $(i = 1, 2)$, based on the familiar "law of supply and demand." See Negishi [25] for relevant references to the work of Arrow and Hurwicz, Hahn and Negishi.

It will be convenient, sometimes, to be able to refer to the budget constraint of the home country:

$$p_1 Z_1 + p_2 Z_2 + Z_3 = 0 \tag{14.9}$$

5. THE SHORT-RUN EFFECTS OF DEVALUATION

As our first exercise, we study the implications of a small devaluation of the home currency with a time reference so brief that the effects of payments imbalance on A and A^* can be ignored. In particular, we seek to pin down the directions in which the money prices of both countries, the terms of trade and the balance of payments change.

Differentiating Eqs. (14.3) with respect to R, and recalling Eqs. (14.4), we obtain

$$
\begin{bmatrix}
\dfrac{\partial Z_1}{\partial p_1} + \dfrac{\partial Z_1^*}{\partial p_1} & \dfrac{\partial Z_1}{\partial p_2} + \dfrac{\partial Z_1^*}{\partial p_2} & 0 \\[2ex]
\dfrac{\partial Z_2}{\partial p_1} + \dfrac{\partial Z_2^*}{\partial p_1} & \dfrac{\partial Z_2}{\partial p_2} + \dfrac{\partial Z_2^*}{\partial p_2} & 0 \\[2ex]
Z_1 + \dfrac{\partial Z_1}{\partial p_1} - \dfrac{\partial Z_2^*}{\partial p_1} & -Z_2^* - \dfrac{\partial Z_2^*}{\partial p_2} + \dfrac{\partial Z_1}{\partial p_2} & 1
\end{bmatrix}
\begin{bmatrix}
\dfrac{dp_1}{dR} \\[2ex]
\dfrac{dp_2}{dR} \\[2ex]
\dfrac{dB}{dR}
\end{bmatrix}
=
\begin{bmatrix}
-\dfrac{\partial Z_1^*}{\partial R} \\[2ex]
-\dfrac{\partial Z_2^*}{\partial R} \\[2ex]
\dfrac{\partial Z_2^*}{\partial R}
\end{bmatrix}
\tag{14.10}
$$

Solving, and recalling Eqs. (14.5), (14.6), and (14.9),

$$\frac{dp_1}{dR} = -\frac{A^*}{\Delta}\left[m_1^*\left(\frac{\partial Z_2}{\partial p_2} + \frac{\partial Z_2^*}{\partial p_2}\right) - m_2^*\left(\frac{\partial Z_1}{\partial p_2} + \frac{\partial Z_1^*}{\partial p_2}\right) \right] \tag{14.11a}$$

$$\frac{dp_2}{dR} = \frac{A^*}{\Delta}\left[m_1^*\left(\frac{\partial Z_2}{\partial p_1} + \frac{\partial Z_2^*}{\partial p_1}\right) - m_2^*\left(\frac{\partial Z_1}{\partial p_1} + \frac{\partial Z_1^*}{\partial p_1}\right) \right] \tag{14.11b}$$

$$\frac{d}{dR}\left(\frac{p_2}{p_1}\right) = \frac{AA^*}{\Delta}(m_1 m_2^* - m_1^* m_2) \tag{14.11c}$$

$$\frac{dB}{dR} = -\frac{A^*}{\Delta}\left\{ m_1^*\left[\frac{\partial Z_3}{\partial p_1}\left(\frac{\partial Z_2}{\partial p_2} + \frac{\partial Z_2^*}{\partial p_2}\right) - \frac{\partial Z_3}{\partial p_2}\left(\frac{\partial Z_2}{\partial p_1} + \frac{\partial Z_2^*}{\partial p_1}\right) \right] \right.$$

$$\left. + m_2^*\left[\frac{\partial Z_3}{\partial p_2}\left(\frac{\partial Z_1}{\partial p_1} + \frac{\partial Z_1^*}{\partial p_1}\right) - \frac{\partial Z_3}{\partial p_1}\left(\frac{\partial Z_1}{\partial p_2} + \frac{\partial Z_1^*}{\partial p_2}\right) \right] \right\} \tag{14.11d}$$

where $m_i = p_i(\partial Z_i/\partial A)$ is the home marginal propensity to consume the ith commodity and

$$\Delta \equiv \left(\frac{\partial Z_1}{\partial p_1} + \frac{\partial Z_1^*}{\partial p_1}\right)\left(\frac{\partial Z_2}{\partial p_2} + \frac{\partial Z_2^*}{\partial p_2}\right) - \left(\frac{\partial Z_1}{\partial p_2} + \frac{\partial Z_1^*}{\partial p_2}\right)\left(\frac{\partial Z_2}{\partial p_1} + \frac{\partial Z_2^*}{\partial p_1}\right) \quad (14.11c)$$

is the Jacobian determinant of the system.

If now we introduce the assumption that commodities are gross substitutes for each other, so that inequalities (14.7) hold,

$$\Delta > 0 \quad\quad\quad\quad\quad\quad (14.12a)$$

$$0 < \frac{R}{p_i} \cdot \frac{dp_i}{dR} < 1 \quad\quad\quad\quad\quad\quad (14.12b)$$

$$0 > \frac{R}{p_i/R} \cdot \frac{d(p_i/R)}{dR} > -1 \quad\quad\quad\quad\quad\quad (14.12c)$$

That is, both commodity prices (and therefore any price index[2]) must rise at home, but in smaller proportion than the price of foreign exchange; hence both commodity prices (and therefore any price index) must fall abroad, but in smaller proportion than the price of home currency in terms of foreign. If it is assumed in addition that each commodity is a gross substitute for money, so that (14.8) and similar inequalities for the foreign country hold, we find that

$$\frac{dB}{dR} > 0 \quad\quad\quad\quad\quad\quad (14.13)$$

That is, devaluation must improve the home country's balance of trade, even if the terms of trade move adversely.

So much for the bare mathematical proofs. We turn now to the task of reconciling the several propositions with our intuitive expectations. Imagine first that home prices, p_1 and p_2, remain unchanged, with foreign prices, p_1/R and p_2/R, bearing the full burden of adjustment (downwards) to the change in the exchange rate. The residents of the foreign country would benefit from a windfall increase in the real value of their cash balances. This in turn would give rise to an increase in foreign demand for both commodities and, hence, to a rise in both home prices. Thus, by a *reductio ad absurdum*, the assumption of constant home prices must be abandoned. The rise in home prices, however, must, in percentage terms, fall short of the devaluation. For suppose that home commodity prices were to rise in the same proportion as the price of foreign exchange, with foreign prices (and real balances) constant. Then the loss of real balances at home would result in a

[2] For our purposes a price index may be defined as any function f of money prices, homogeneous of degree one and such that $\partial f/\partial p_i > 0$.

curtailment of demand and a reduction of prices. Thus the assumption that the full burden of adjustment falls on home prices cannot be sustained either. *A fortiori*, neither home nor foreign prices could "over adjust." It follows that the burden of adjustment must be shared by the two sets of money prices, home and foreign.

We have just seen that home prices will rise, foreign prices fall. It follows that the real value of cash balances will fall at home, rise abroad and, further, that home demand for both commodities will fall and foreign demand for both commodities rise. What will happen to the terms of trade depends on the relative magnitudes of the four marginal propensities involved, m_i and m_i^* ($i = 1, 2$). In particular, if the ratio of the home country's marginal propensity to buy the first commodity (its import) to its marginal propensity to buy the second commodity (its export) should exceed the corresponding ratio for the foreign country, that is, if

$$\frac{m_1}{m_2} > \frac{m_1^*}{m_2^*} \tag{14.14}$$

then the terms of trade would move in favor of the home, or depreciating country. Criterion (14.14) is reminiscent of a well-known result in the theory of international transfers:[3] If the home country transfers a sum of money to the foreign country, the terms of trade will move in favor of the home country if $(m_1/m_2) > (m_1^*/m_2^*)$. That similar criteria should apply in the two situations is reconciled with common sense by noting that, *via* the real balance effects of price changes, devaluation imposes a loss of purchasing power on the devaluing country and throws up a windfall gain to the rest of the world analogous to the increments of purchasing power associated with a transfer.

The balance of payments is

$$B = \frac{1}{R}(p_2 Z_2^* - p_1 Z_1)$$

$$= -\frac{1}{R}(p_1 Z_1 + p_2 Z_2) \qquad \text{[from Eqs. (14.3)]}$$

Hence, making use of Eqs. (14.9) and (14.4),

$$\frac{dB}{dR} = \sum_{i=1}^{2} \frac{\partial Z_3}{\partial p_i} \cdot \frac{dp_i}{dR}$$

But $\partial Z_3/\partial p_i > 0$, from Eqs. (14.8); and we have just shown that $dp_i/dR > 0$. Hence dB/dR is positive.

[3] Cf. Chap. 4, Sec. 3.

An interesting limiting case is that in which the devaluing country is *small*, in the sense that world prices p_i/R are beyond its control Then, clearly, home prices must change in the same proportion as the exchange rate: $(R/p_i) \times (dp_i/dR) = 1$. The increase in home prices reduces real cash balances. This in turn gives rise to hoarding and, therefore, to a change in the balance of payments favorable to the home country. Thus, in this special case, the home balance of payments necessarily improves, with or without gross substitutability. In confirmation:

$$\frac{dB}{dR} = -\left(\sum \frac{\partial Z_1}{\partial p_i} + \sum \frac{\partial Z_2}{\partial p_i}\right) \qquad \text{since } B = 0$$

$$= A\left(\frac{\partial Z_1}{\partial A} + \frac{\partial Z_2}{\partial A}\right) \qquad \text{from Eq. (14.5a)}$$

$$= -A\frac{\partial Z_3}{\partial A} \qquad \text{from Eq. (14.9)}$$

$$> 0 \qquad \text{from Eqs. (14.6) and (14.9)}$$

Finally, we note the very special but historically interesting case in which all "cross" price slopes are zero:

$$\frac{\partial Z_i}{\partial p_j} = 0 \qquad i, j = 1, 2; \ i \neq j$$

Then, from Eqs. (14.4a) and (14.9),

$$\frac{\partial Z_i}{\partial p_i} = -A\frac{\partial Z_i}{\partial A} = -Am_i$$

$$\frac{\partial Z_3}{\partial p_i} = -\left(Z_i + \frac{\partial Z_i}{\partial p_i}\right) \qquad i = 1, 2$$

Applying these relationships to Eqs. (14.11), we obtain

$$\frac{dp_1}{dR} = \frac{A_1^* m_1^*}{Am_1 + A^* m_1^*} = \frac{\eta_s^*}{\eta_D + \eta_s^*}$$

$$\frac{dp_2}{dR} = \frac{A^* m_2^*}{Am_2 + A^* m_2^*} = \frac{\eta_D^*}{\eta_s + \eta_D^*} \qquad (14.11)$$

$$\frac{d}{dR}\left(\frac{p_2}{p_1}\right) = \frac{AA^*(m_1 m_2^* - m_1^* m_2)}{(Am_1 + A^* m_1^*)(Am_2 + A^* m_2^*)}$$

$$= \frac{\eta_D \eta_D^* - \eta_s \eta_s^*}{(\eta_D + \eta_s^*)(\eta_s + \eta_D^*)}$$

$$\frac{dB}{dR} = -E_1\left[\frac{\eta_s^*(1 - \eta_D)}{\eta_D + \eta_s^*} - \frac{\eta_D^*(1 + \eta_s)}{\eta_s + \eta_D^*}\right]$$

where $\eta_D \equiv -(p_1/Z_1)(\partial Z_1/\partial p_1)$, $\eta_s \equiv (p_2/Z_2)(\partial Z_2/\partial p_2)$, $\eta_D^* \equiv -(p_2/Z_2^*) \times (\partial Z_2^*/\partial p_2)$, and $\eta_s^* \equiv (p_1/Z_1^*)(\partial Z_1^*/\partial p_1)$. The third and fourth of these expressions derive from Mrs. Robinson[4] and Bickerdike,[5] respectively, and figure prominently in textbook discussions of devaluation.[6]

3. THE LONG-RUN EFFECTS OF DEVALUATION

Except in a singular case, devaluation destroys the initial balance of international payments and thus causes A and A^* to change.[7] If, for example, $dB/dR > 0$ (as when goods and currencies are gross substitutes), private holdings of home currency increase and private holdings of foreign currency decrease, at least for a time. But these changes in turn disturb world excess demands; and the secondary changes are stabilizing, for [from Eq. (14.6)] the increase in home balances stimulates home demand for commodities and the decline in foreign balances damps foreign demand. Two questions arise: Is the dynamic process stable, in the sense that international payments return (at least asymptotically) to their initial balance? And, supposing that a new stationary equilibrium is attained, what relation does it bear to the initial equilibrium?

Both questions are easy to answer, though the answers may be obscured by our asymmetric and inessential practice of expressing prices in terms of the home country's currency. Suppose that instead we express all nominal prices, including the prices of the two currencies, in terms of an arbitrary international unit of account. Devaluation of the home currency in terms of the foreign can then be represented as an increase in the price of the home currency in terms of the unit of account, accompanied by a decline in the

[4] Robinson [30], p. 163, n. 1. See also Haberler [7].

[5] Bickerdike [3]. See also Robinson [30], p. 142, n. 1; Metzler [22], pp. 225–33; Haberler [6]; Hirschman [10]; and Bronfenbrenner [4].

[6] The formulae of Bickerdike and Robinson lend themselves to an alternative, partial-equilibrium interpretation. Thus the formulae would be perfectly acceptable (a) if in each country there were at least one nontraded commodity; (b) if the nontraded commodities dominated the budgets of consumers; and (c) if in each country both the cross-elasticity of excess demand for the imported commodity with respect to the price of the exported commodity, and the cross-elasticity of excess demand for the exported commodity with respect to the price of the imported commodity were zero. Note, however, that on this interpretation the several price elasticities are of the *ceteris paribus* or constant-money-income kind, not the *mutatis mutandis* or variable-money-income variety of the text. The interpretation of the formulae provided in the text is Negishi's [26]. For the partial-equilibrium interpretation, see Kemp [14], pp. 323–24.

[7] It is assumed that the amount of money in private hands is allowed to vary. This seems to be the most natural assumption. One could imagine, however, that in each country offsetting fiscal policy ensures that private monetary holdings do not change. Then, clearly, the short-run and long-run effects of devaluation would be the same.

The process of adjustment we are contemplating is, of course, essentially that of the international gold specie standard. Any conclusions we reach therefore apply to the gold standard or to any monetary system obeying the rules of the gold standard.

price of the foreign currency. To maintain symmetry, we may suppose that the two price changes are in the same proportion. It is now clear that, in real terms, devaluation is equivalent to a decrease in the value of the home country's cash balances and an equiproportionate increase in the value of foreign balances. It follows that if devaluation of the home currency improves the home balance of payments then the changes in A and A^* referred to in the preceding paragraph must cause the home balance of payments to deteriorate: If $(dB/dR) > 0$, international payments must asymptotically return to complete balance.

That in real terms the new and old equilibria are identical is easily shown. Taking advantage of the homogeneity of the excess demand functions, we may rewrite Eqs. (15.3) as

$$Z_i\left(1, \frac{p_2}{p_1}; \frac{A}{p_1}\right) + Z_1^*\left(1, \frac{p_2}{p_1}; \frac{RA^*}{p_1}\right) = 0 \qquad i = 1, 2$$

$$\frac{RB}{p_1} - \frac{p_2}{p_1} Z_2^*\left(1, \frac{p_2}{p_1}; \frac{RA^*}{p_1}\right) - Z_1\left(1, \frac{p_2}{p_1}; \frac{A}{p_1}\right) = 0 \qquad (14.15)$$

(14.15) may be treated as a system of three equations in the terms of trade (p_2/p_1) and the two real cash balances, (A/p_1), and (RA^*/p_1). The solutions are obviously independent of R.

Finally, we seek to pin down the changes in money prices. We may assume that $dB/dR > 0$; otherwise, the investigation is pointless. We may be sure, then, that A must be greater and A^* smaller in the new equilibrium than in the old. But if A has increased, p_1 also must have increased (for A/p_1 has not changed); and if A^* has declined, p_1/R also must have declined (for RA^*/p_1 has not changed). Thus home prices must have risen, but in smaller proportion than R; and foreign prices must have fallen, but in smaller proportion than $1/R$.

4. RELATED COMPARATIVE STATICAL PROBLEMS

A variation of the exchange rate is only one of many disturbances to which the system (14.3) might have been subjected. We might have explored instead the implications of a shift in demand, or of a unilateral transfer, or of a technological improvement, or of an autonomous change in the money supply. To plod through all comparative statical exercises of this kind would invite boredom. Let us consider, then, very briefly, just two additional problems.

Consider first the implications of a small transfer from the home country to the foreign. As an aid to our analysis we rewrite the system (14.3) as

$$Z_i(p_1, p_2; A - \alpha) + Z_i^*(p_1, p_2; A^* + \alpha) = 0 \qquad i = 1, 2$$

$$B - p_2 Z_2^*(p_1, p_2; A^* + \alpha) + p_1 Z_1(p_1, p_2; A + \alpha) + \alpha = 0 \qquad (14.3a)$$

where α, the amount transferred, is initially zero and where the balance of payments B has been redefined to include α. Differentiating Eqs. (14.3a) with respect to α we obtain

$$
\begin{bmatrix}
\dfrac{\partial Z_1}{\partial p_1} + \dfrac{\partial Z_1^*}{\partial p_1} & \dfrac{\partial Z_1}{\partial p_2} + \dfrac{\partial Z_1^*}{\partial p_2} & 0 \\[3mm]
\dfrac{\partial Z_2}{\partial p_1} + \dfrac{\partial Z_2^*}{\partial p_1} & \dfrac{\partial Z_2}{\partial p_2} + \dfrac{\partial Z_2^*}{\partial p_2} & 0 \\[3mm]
Z_1 + \dfrac{\partial Z_1}{\partial p_1} - \dfrac{\partial Z_2^*}{\partial p_1} & -Z_2^* - \dfrac{\partial Z_2^*}{\partial p_2} + \dfrac{\partial Z_1}{\partial p_2} & 1
\end{bmatrix}
\begin{bmatrix}
\dfrac{dp_1}{d\alpha} \\[3mm]
\dfrac{dp_2}{d\alpha} \\[3mm]
\dfrac{dB}{d\alpha}
\end{bmatrix}
=
\begin{bmatrix}
m_1 - m_1^* \\[3mm]
m_2 - m_2^* \\[3mm]
m_1 + m_2^* - 1
\end{bmatrix}
$$

$$(14.16)$$

whence, recalling Eqs. (14.5a), which merely summarize the homogeneity properties of the excess demand functions for commodities,

$$\frac{dp_1}{d\alpha} = \frac{1}{\Delta}\left[(m_1 - m_1^*)\left(\frac{\partial Z_2}{\partial p_2} + \frac{\partial Z_2^*}{\partial p_2}\right) - (m_2 - m_2^*)\left(\frac{\partial Z_1}{\partial p_2} + \frac{\partial Z_1^*}{\partial p_2}\right)\right]$$

$$\frac{dp_2}{d\alpha} = -\frac{1}{\Delta}\left[(m_1 - m_1^*)\left(\frac{\partial Z_2}{\partial p_1} + \frac{\partial Z_2^*}{\partial p_1}\right) - (m_2 - m_2^*)\left(\frac{\partial Z_1}{\partial p_1} + \frac{\partial Z_1^*}{\partial p_1}\right)\right]$$

$$\frac{d}{d\alpha}\left(\frac{p_2}{p_1}\right) = \frac{A + A^*}{\Delta}(m_1 m_2^* - m_1^* m_2) \qquad (14.17)$$

$$\frac{dB}{d\alpha} = (m_1 + m_2^* - 1)$$

$$+ (m_1 - m_1^*)\left[\left(\frac{\partial Z_2}{\partial p_2} + \frac{\partial Z_2^*}{\partial p_2}\right)\frac{\partial Z_3}{\partial p_1} - \left(\frac{\partial Z_2}{\partial p_1} + \frac{\partial Z_2^*}{\partial p_1}\right)\frac{\partial Z_3}{\partial p_2}\right]$$

$$+ (m_2 - m_2^*)\left[\left(\frac{\partial Z_1}{\partial p_2} + \frac{\partial Z_1^*}{\partial p_2}\right)\frac{\partial Z_4^*}{\partial p_1} - \left(\frac{\partial Z_1}{\partial p_1} + \frac{\partial Z_1^*}{\partial p_1}\right)\frac{\partial Z_4^*}{\partial p_2}\right]$$

The most interesting feature of these calculations is the reappearance, in the third equation, of the simple terms of trade criterion $(m_1 m_2^* - m_1^* m_2)$. To simplify the first pair of equations we apply Eqs. (14.7), which give expression to the assumption of gross substitutability. Then it emerges that

$$\frac{dp_j}{d\alpha} \text{ is } \begin{cases} >0 & \text{if } m_i < m_i^* \quad i = 1, 2 \\ <0 & \text{if } m_i > m_i^* \quad j = 1, 2 \end{cases} \qquad (14.18)$$

If income is taken from a country with a low marginal propensity to spend and given to a country with a high propensity, world prices rise; if the transfer is in the opposite direction, prices fall.

Suppose next that there is a shift in home demand away from cash in favor of the first or imported commodity. Our system (14.3) must be rewritten as

$$Z_1(p_1, p_2; A; \beta) + Z_1^*(p_1, p_2; A^*) = 0$$

$$Z_2(p_1, p_2; A) + Z_2^*(p_1, p_2; A^*) = 0 \qquad (14.3')$$

$$B - p_2 Z_2^*(p_1, p_2, A^*) + p_1 Z_1(p_1, p_2; A; \beta) = 0$$

where β is a shift parameter of demand with $\partial Z_1/\partial \beta \equiv 1$. Differentiating with respect to β, and solving for $dp_i/d\beta$ and $dB/d\beta$:

$$\frac{dp_1}{d\beta} = -\frac{1}{\Delta}\left(\frac{\partial Z_2}{\partial p_2} + \frac{\partial Z_2^*}{\partial p_2}\right)$$

$$\frac{dp_2}{d\beta} = \frac{1}{\Delta}\left(\frac{\partial Z_2}{\partial p_1} + \frac{\partial Z_2^*}{\partial p_1}\right)$$

$$\frac{d}{d\beta}\left(\frac{p_2}{p_1}\right) = \frac{1}{\Delta}\left(\frac{\partial Z_2}{\partial p_1} + \frac{\partial Z_2}{\partial p_2} + \frac{\partial Z_2^*}{\partial p_1} + \frac{\partial Z_2^*}{\partial p_2}\right) = -\frac{1}{\Delta}(Am_2 + A^* m_2^*) \qquad (14.19)$$

$$\frac{dB}{d\beta} = -1 - \frac{1}{\Delta}\left[\left(\frac{\partial Z_2}{\partial p_2} + \frac{\partial Z_2^*}{\partial p_2}\right)\frac{\partial Z_3}{\partial p_1} - \left(\frac{\partial Z_2}{\partial p_1} + \frac{\partial Z_2^*}{\partial p_1}\right)\frac{\partial Z_3}{\partial p_2}\right]$$

Thus, given the assumption of gross substitutability, the price of the first commodity must rise, that of the second fall, so that the terms of trade move against the home country. This might have been expected. More surprising is the possibility that the balance of payments might move in favor of the home country: For this paradoxical outcome it is necessary that the increase in the price of the first commodity gives rise to a very substantial increase in the foreign demand for the second commodity and, therefore, for the home country's exports.

In similar fashion we may calculate the effects of a shift in home demand away from cash in favor of the second or exported commodity:

$$\frac{dp_1}{d\beta'} = \frac{1}{\Delta}\left(\frac{\partial Z_1}{\partial p_2} + \frac{\partial Z_1^*}{\partial p_2}\right)$$

$$\frac{dp_2}{\partial \beta'} = -\frac{1}{\Delta}\left(\frac{\partial Z_1}{\partial p_1} + \frac{\partial Z_1^*}{\partial p_1}\right)$$

$$\frac{d}{d\beta'}\left(\frac{p_2}{p_1}\right) = -\frac{1}{\Delta}\left(\frac{\partial Z_1}{\partial p_1} + \frac{\partial Z_1}{\partial p_2} + \frac{\partial Z_1^*}{\partial p_1} + \frac{\partial Z_1^*}{\partial p_2}\right) = \frac{1}{\Delta}(Am_1 + A^* m_1^*)$$

(14.20)

$$\frac{dB}{d\beta'} = \frac{1}{\Delta}\left[\left(\frac{\partial Z_1}{\partial p_1} + \frac{\partial Z_1^*}{\partial p_1}\right)\frac{\partial Z_4^*}{\partial p_2} - \left(\frac{\partial Z_1}{\partial p_2} + \frac{\partial Z_1^*}{\partial p_2}\right)\frac{\partial Z_4^*}{\partial p_1}\right]$$

Thus if commodities and currencies are gross substitutes, both prices increase, the home terms of trade improve, and the balance of payments deteriorates.

Finally, we may use Eqs. (14.19) and (14.20) to calculate the effects of a shift in demand from the second commodity to the first:

$$\frac{dp_1}{d\beta} - \frac{dp_1}{d\beta'} = -\frac{1}{\Delta}\left(\frac{\partial Z_2}{\partial p_2} + \frac{\partial Z_2^*}{\partial p_2} + \frac{\partial Z_1}{\partial p_2} + \frac{\partial Z_1^*}{\partial p_2}\right)$$

$$= \frac{1}{\Delta}\left(\frac{\partial Z_3}{\partial p_2} + \frac{\partial Z_4^*}{\partial p_2}\right)$$

$$\frac{dp_2}{d\beta} - \frac{dp_2}{d\beta'} = \frac{1}{\Delta}\left(\frac{\partial Z_2}{\partial p_1} + \frac{\partial Z_2^*}{\partial p_1} + \frac{\partial Z_1}{\partial p_1} + \frac{\partial Z_1^*}{\partial p_1}\right)$$

$$= -\frac{1}{\Delta}\left(\frac{\partial Z_3}{\partial p_1} + \frac{\partial Z_4^*}{\partial p_1}\right)$$

(14.21)

$$\frac{d}{d\beta}\left(\frac{p_2}{p_1}\right) - \frac{d}{d\beta'}\left(\frac{p_2}{p_1}\right) = -\frac{1}{\Delta}[A(m_1 + m_2) + A^*(m_1^* + m_2^*)]$$

$$= -\frac{1}{\Delta}(Am_3 + A^* m_4^*)$$

$$\frac{dB}{d\beta} - \frac{dB}{d\beta'} = -1 - \frac{1}{\Delta}\left[\left(\frac{\partial Z_2}{\partial p_2} + \frac{\partial Z_2^*}{\partial p_2}\right)\frac{\partial Z_3}{\partial p_1} - \left(\frac{\partial Z_2}{\partial p_1} + \frac{\partial Z_2^*}{\partial p_1}\right)\frac{\partial Z_3}{\partial p_2}\right.$$

$$\left. + \left(\frac{\partial Z_1}{\partial p_1} + \frac{\partial Z_1^*}{\partial p_1}\right)\frac{\partial Z_4^*}{\partial p_2} - \left(\frac{\partial Z_1}{\partial p_2} + \frac{\partial Z_1^*}{\partial p_2}\right)\frac{\partial Z_4^*}{\partial p_1}\right]$$

Thus if commodities and currencies are gross substitutes, the price of the first commodity must increase, the price of the second decline, and the home terms of trade deteriorate. The response of the balance of payments remains undetermined.

5. THE ANALYSIS OF FLOATING EXCHANGE RATES

In Secs. 2–4 we have explored the implications of various disturbances for the balance of payments, on the assumption that the rate of exchange is pegged. Alternatively, it might have been assumed that the rate of exchange floats at whatever level is necessary to maintain balance of payments equilibrium $(B = 0)$, and we might then have explored the implications, for money prices, the terms of trade, and the rate of exchange, of disturbances of various kinds: Changes in demand, technical improvements, changes in the money supply, and so on. As will be made clear in the next two paragraphs, however, the problems encountered in this kind of exercise are closely related to those with which we have already grappled. They are, accordingly, banished to the collection of problems at the end of the chapter. Here we are content to indicate the general nature of the relationship.

Our formal model (14.3) is easily amended to accommodate a floating rate of exchange:

$$Z_i(p_1, p_2; A) + Z_i^*\left(\frac{p_1}{R}, \frac{p_2}{R}; A^*\right) = 0 \qquad i = 1, 2$$

$$p_1 Z_1(p_1, p_2; A) - p_2 Z_2^*\left(\frac{p_1}{R}, \frac{p_2}{R}; A^*\right) = 0$$

(14.22)

The third equation gives expression to the requirement that international payments be in balance. Since A and A^* are constants, we have a system of three equations in the three unknowns p_1, p_2, and R.

In view of the family relationship of systems (14.3) and (14.22) one would expect them to possess similar comparative statical properties. In fact, *all* of the comparative statical properties of Eqs. (14.22) can be inferred from the impact or short-run responses of the "parent" system (14.3). Suppose, for example, that one wishes to know the effect on the rate of exchange R of a change in some parameter γ. The answer may be obtained with the aid of the following simple bridge relationship between the two systems:

$$\left(\frac{dR}{d\gamma}\right)_{R\text{ floating}} = \left(\frac{dB}{d\gamma}\right)_{R\text{ pegged}} \div \left(\frac{dB}{dR}\right)_{R\text{ pegged}}$$

(14.23)

Or suppose that one wishes to know the effect on the ith price of a change in the same parameter. This is a more complicated problem; but it too may be solved by judicious deployment of the comparative statical properties of system (14.3). The appropriate bridging relationship in this case is

$$\left(\frac{dp_i}{d\gamma}\right)_{R\text{ floating}} = \left(\frac{dp_i}{d\gamma}\right)_{R\text{ pegged}} + \left[\left(\frac{dp_i}{dR}\right)_{R\text{ pegged}} \times \left(\frac{dR}{d\gamma}\right)_{R\text{ floating}}\right]$$

(14.24)

where the last term on the right-hand side is already known to us from Eq. (14.23).

6. THE INTRODUCTION OF BONDS AND THE RATE OF INTEREST

In the present section we indicate very briefly how our monetary model may be extended to embrace bonds and a money rate of interest. Much depends on the degree to which the bonds of each country are internationally tradable. We consider two extreme cases, that in which bonds are not tradable (so that private international lending is ruled out) and that in which bonds are freely tradable.

A. Suppose first that bonds are not tradable and must be held by residents of the country of issue. We define a home bond as a title to one unit of home currency per period indefinitely. The price of a bond, denoted by p_0, is then the reciprocal of the rate of interest. If the private holding of bonds at home is represented by G and the excess demand for bonds by Z_0, we may write the home excess demand functions as

$$Z_i(p_0; p_1, p_2; p_0 G, A) \qquad i = 0, 1, 2, 3$$

The foreign excess demand functions are written analogously as

$$Z_i^*\left(p_5^*; \frac{p_1}{R}, \frac{p_2}{R}; p_5^* G^*, A^*\right) \qquad i = 1, 2, 4, 5$$

where p_5^* is the foreign price of a foreign bond. The commodity excess demand functions may be assumed to be homogeneous of degree zero in commodity prices and the two financial assets:

$$p_1 \frac{\partial Z_i}{\partial p_1} + p_2 \frac{\partial Z_i}{\partial p_2} + p_0 G \frac{\partial Z_i}{\partial(p_0 G)} + A \frac{\partial Z_i}{\partial A} = 0 \qquad i = 1, 2$$

or, assuming that $\partial Z_i/\partial(p_0 G) \equiv \partial Z_i/\partial A \equiv m_i/p_i$,

$$p_1 \frac{\partial Z_i}{\partial p_1} + p_2 \frac{\partial Z_i}{\partial p_2} + (p_0 G + A) \frac{m_i}{p_i} = 0 \qquad i = 1, 2 \quad (14.25a)$$

The excess demand for money Z_3 and the excess demand for bonds Z_0 may be assumed to be homogeneous of the first degree in the same variables:

$$p_1 \frac{\partial Z_i}{\partial p_1} + p_2 \frac{\partial Z_i}{\partial p_2} + p_0 G\left[\frac{\partial Z_i}{\partial (p_0 G)}\right] + A \frac{\partial Z_i}{\partial A} = Z_i \qquad i = 0, 3 \quad (14.25b)$$

Similar homogeneity relations may be assumed to hold for the foreign country. Equations (14.7) and (14.8) carry over to our more complex system. It may be convenient to assume in addition that

$$\frac{\partial Z_0}{\partial p_i} > 0 \qquad i = 1, 2 \tag{14.26a}$$

$$\frac{\partial Z_0}{\partial p_0} < 0 \tag{14.26b}$$

$$\frac{\partial Z_i}{\partial p_0} > 0 \qquad i = 1, 2, 3 \tag{14.26c}$$

Finally, the budget constraint of the home country becomes

$$p_0 E_0 + p_1 E_1 + p_2 E_2 + E_3 = 0 \tag{14.9'}$$

Our basic system of equations is

$$Z_0(\cdot) = 0 \tag{14.27a}$$
$$Z_i(\cdot) + Z_i^*(\cdot) = 0 \qquad i = 1, 2 \tag{14.27b}$$
$$Z_5^*(\cdot) = 0 \tag{14.27c}$$

to which may be appended the definition of the balance of payments

$$B \equiv \frac{p_2 Z_2(\cdot) - p_1 Z_1(\cdot)}{R}$$

$$= \frac{Z_3}{R} \tag{14.27d}$$

The stage is now set for the usual comparative statical exercises. These are left to the reader.

B. If there is a perfect international market in bonds, the same rate of interest must prevail everywhere:

$$p_0 = p_5^*$$

Moreover, a distinction must now be drawn between $\bar{G}$, that part of the home bond issue held at home, and $(G - \bar{G})$, the portion held abroad. A similar distinction must be drawn between $\bar{G}^*$, that part of the foreign bond issue held by residents of the foreign country, and $(G^* - \bar{G}^*)$, the portion held by residents of the home country. The value of home bond holdings, in terms of home currency, is then $p_0\bar{G} + Rp_5^*(G^* - \bar{G}^*) = p_0[\bar{G} + R(G^* - \bar{G}^*)]$; and the value of foreign bond holdings, in terms of foreign currency, is $p_0(G - \bar{G})/R + p_5^*\bar{G}^* = p_0(G - \bar{G} + R\bar{G}^*)/R$. Home and foreign excess demand functions must be written therefore as

$$Z_i[p_0; p_1, p_2; p_0(\bar{G} + R(G^* - \bar{G}^*)), A] \qquad i = 0, 1, 2, 3, 5$$

and

$$Z_i^*\left[p_0; \frac{p_1}{R}, \frac{p_2}{R}; p_0 \frac{G - \bar{G} + R\bar{G}^*}{R}, A^*\right] \qquad i = 0, 1, 2, 4, 5$$

respectively. The interest paid by the home government to foreign holders of its bonds is, in terms of foreign currency, $(G - \bar{G})/R$; the interest paid by the foreign government to home holders of its bonds is $(G^* - \bar{G}^*)$. Hence the net interest receipts of the home country are

$$(G^* - \bar{G}^*) - (G - \bar{G})/R$$

and the budget constraint is

$$p_0Z_0 + p_1Z_1 + p_2Z_2 + Z_3 + p_0RZ_5 = R(G^* - \bar{G}^*) - (G - \bar{G}) \quad (14.9'')$$

The basic system of equations becomes

$$[Z_0(\cdot) + Z_0^*(\cdot)] + R[Z_5(\cdot) + Z_5^*(\cdot)] = 0 \qquad\qquad (14.28a)$$
$$Z_i(\cdot) + Z_i^*(\cdot) = 0 \qquad i = 1, 2 \quad (14.28b)$$

To this system we may append definitions of the balance of trade,

$$B_t \equiv \frac{p_2Z_2^*(\cdot) - p_1Z_1(\cdot)}{R}$$

the balance of payments on capital account (net interest receipts plus the value, in terms of foreign currency, of the home excess demand for bonds),

$$B_c \equiv \left[(G^* - \bar{G}^*) - \frac{G - \bar{G}}{R}\right] - p_0\left[\frac{Z_0}{R} + Z_5\right],$$

and the overall or cash balance of payments,

$$B \equiv B_t + B_c$$
$$= Z_3/R \qquad \text{[from Eq. (14.9'')]} \qquad (14.28c)$$

The comparative statics of the system are again left to the reader.

PROBLEMS

14.1 Given a pegged rate of exchange, what is the impact, for the p_i, for p_2/p_1 and for B, of a technical improvement at home with equal incidence in each industry?

14.2 Given a floating rate of exchange, what are the implications for p_1, p_2, p_2/p_1, and R of an increase in the foreign demand for the home country's exports?

14.3 Given a floating rate of exchange, what are the implications for $_1$, p_2, the terms of trade, and R of a tariff imposed by the home country?

14.4 It was assumed in Sec. 2 of the text that policy adjustments of the exchange rate are accommodated by allowing exchange reserves to vary. Suppose, instead, that reserves are maintained at a constant level by variations in the tariff. What is the impact of a devaluation of the home country's currency on money prices, the terms of trade, and the rate of duty? Assume that, initially, the rate of duty is zero, and that the proceeds of the duty are distributed to the public.

14.5 Show that, if the two commodities and money are gross substitutes for each other, $(p_1/E_1)(\partial E_1/\partial p_1) < 1$.

14.6 Show that if $1 - \eta_D - \eta_D^* < 0$ then $dB/dR > 0$ in Eq. (14.11a).

14.7 Show that devaluation of the home currency improves the home balance of payments if and only if an increase in the home money supply causes the balance to deteriorate and if and only if an expansion of the foreign money supply improves the home balance.

14.8 Introduce a purely domestic good both at home and abroad. Show that the proposition of Prob. 14.7 still holds.

14.9 Under the assumptions of Prob. 14.8 show that:

(a) If in each country commodities are weak gross substitutes for each other and if all marginal propensities to consume are positive, then (i) an increase in the home or foreign money supply gives rise to an increase in each commodity price, but in smaller (for the domestic good, not greater) proportion than the increase in the control variable; and (ii) devaluation of the home currency gives rise to an increase in each home commodity price and to a decrease in each foreign commodity price, the change being in smaller (for the domestic good, not greater) proportion than the devaluation.

(b) If in addition each commodity is a gross substitute for money then devaluation of the home currency, expansion of the foreign money supply, and curtailment of the home money supply all give rise to an improvement of the home country's balance of payments.

REFERENCES

[1] Alexander, S., "The Effects of Devaluation on a Trade Balance," *International Monetary Fund Staff Papers*, II, No. 2 (April 1952), 263–78.

[2] Alexander, S., "The Effects of Devaluation: a Simplified Synthesis of Elasticities and Absorption Approaches," *American Economic Review*, XLIX, No. 2 (March 1959), 22–42.

†[3] Bickerdike, C. F., "The Instability of Foreign Exchange," *Economic Journal*, XXX, No. 117 (March 1920), 118–22.

[4] Bronfenbrenner, M., "Exchange Rates and Exchange Stability: Mathematical Supplement," *Review of Economics and Statistics*, XXXII, No. 1 (February 1950), 12–16.

[5] Day, A. C. L., "Relative Prices, Expenditure, and the Trade Balance," *Economica*, New Series, XXI, No. 82 (May 1954), 64–69.

[6] Haberler, Gottfried, "The Market for Foreign Exchange and the Stability of the Balance of Payments," *Kyklos*, III, No. 3 (1949), 193–218.

[7] Haberler, Gottfried, "Currency Depreciation and the Terms of Trade," in *Wirtschaftliche Entwicklung und Soziale Ordnung*, eds. E. Lagler and J. Messner, 149–58. Vienna: Verlag Herold, 1952.

†[8] Hahn, F. H., "The Balance of Payments in a Monetary Economy," *Review of Economic Studies*, XXVI (2), No. 70 (February 1959), 110–25.

[9] Harberger, Arnold C., "Currency Depreciation, Income and the Balance of Trade," *Journal of Political Economy*, LVIII, No. 1 (February 1950), 47–60.

[10] Hirschman, A. O., "Devaluation and the Trade Balance—a Note," *Review of Economics and Statistics*, XXXI, No. 1 (February 1949), 50–53.

[11] Johnson, Harry G., *International Trade and Economic Growth*, Chaps. VI and VII. London: George Allen and Unwin Ltd., 1958.

[12] Jones, Ronald W., "Depreciation and the Dampening Effect of Income Changes," *Review of Economics and Statistics*, XLII, No. 1 (February 1960), 74–80.

[13] Jones, Ronald W., "Stability Conditions in International Trade: a General Equilibrium Analysis," *International Economic Review*, II, No. 2 (May 1961), 199–209.

[14] Kemp, Murray C., "The Rate of Exchange, the Terms of Trade and the Balance of Payments in Fully Employed Economies," *International Economic Review*, III, No. 3 (September 1962) 314–27.

[15] Kemp, Murray C., "The Balance of Payments and the Terms of Trade ṅn Relation to Financial Controls," *Review of Economic Studies*, to be published.

†[16] Komiya, Ryutaro, "Monetary Assumptions, Currency Depreciation and the Balance of Trade," *The Economic Studies Quarterly*, XVII, No. 2 (December 1966), 9–23.

[17] Laursen, Svend and Lloyd A. Metzler, "Flexible Exchange Rates and the Theory of Employment," *Review of Economics and Statistics*, XXXII, Xo. 4 (November 1950), 281–99.

[18] Machlup, Fritz, "The Theory of Foreign Exchanges," *Economica*, New Series, VI, No. 24 (November 1939), 275–97; and VII, No. 25 (February 1940), 23–49. Reprinted in *Readings in the Theory of International Trade*, eds. Howard S. Ellis and Lloyd A. Metzler, pp. 104–58. Philadelphia: The Blakiston Company, 1949.

[19] Machlup, Fritz, "Relative Prices and Aggregate Expenditure in the Analysis of Devaluation," *American Economic Review*, XLV, No. 3 (June 1955), 255–78.

[20] Machlup, Fritz, "The Terms of Trade Effects of Devaluation upon Real Income and the Balance of Trade," *Kyklos*, X, No. 4 (1956), 417–52.

[21] Meade, J. E., *The Theory of International Economic Policy. Volume One, The Balance of Payments*, Chap. XII. London: Oxford University Press, 1951.

[22] Metzler, Lloyd A., "The Theory of International Trade," in *A Survey of Contemporary Economics*, ed. Howard S. Ellis, pp. 210–54. Philadelphia: The Blakiston Company for The American Economic Association, 1948.

[23] Metzler, Lloyd A., "The Process of International Adjustment under Conditions of Full Employment: a Keynesian View," in Richard E. Caves and Harry G. Johnson, eds., *Readings in International Economics*, 465–86. London: George Allen and Unwin Ltd., 1968.

[24] Mosak, Jacob L., *General Equilibrium Theory in International Trade*. Bloomington, Indiana: The Principia Press, Inc., 1944.

[25] Negishi, Takashi, "The Stability of a Competitive Economy: a Survey Article," *Econometrica*, XXX, No. 4 (October 1962), 635–69.

†[26] Negishi, Takashi, "Approaches to the Analysis of Devaluation," *International Economic Review*, IX, No. 2 (June 1968), 218–27.

[27] Negishi, Takashi, "The Dichotomy of Real and Monetary Analyses in the International Trade Theory," unpublished.

[28] Pearce, I. F., "Note on Mr Spraos' Paper," *Economica*, New Series, XXII, No. 86 (May 1955), 147–51.

[29] Pearce, I. F., "The Problem of the Balance of Payments," *International Economic Review*, II, No. 1 (January 1961), 1–28.

[30] Robinson, Joan, *Essays in the Theory of Employment*, 2nd ed. Oxford: Basil Blackwell, 1947.

[31] Spraos, J., "Consumers' Behaviour and the Conditions for Exchange Stability," *Economica*, New Series, XXII, No. 86 (May 1955), 137–47.

[32] Spraos, J., "Stability in a Closed Economy and in the Foreign Exchange Market and the Redistributive Effects of Price Changes," *Review of Economic Studies*, XXIV (3), No. 65 (June 1957), 161–76.

[33] Spraos, J., "Devaluation under a Policy of Full Employment," *Economica*, New Series, No. 123 (August 1964), 270–78.

[34] Tsiang, S. C., "The Role of Money in Trade Balance Stability," *American Economic Review*, LI, No. 5 (December 1961), 921–36.

Appendix on Price Elasticities

It may be convenient to have listed in one place the definitions of the principal excess demand and supply elasticities employed, with an indication of some of the relationships which exist between them.

Two countries (the home country and the foreign country) trade in two commodities. Tariffs and taxes are assumed away, as in the possibility of international borrowing and lending.[1] An asterisk relates a variable to the foreign country.

1. DEFINITIONS

In the home country the gross demand for any commodity depends on the price ratio and on real income (in terms of the *numéraire*); the gross supply of the commodity depends on the price ratio alone; the excess demand for the commodity therefore depends on the price ratio and real income. But real income is itself a function of the price ratio. Hence excess demand can be written as a function of the price ratio p alone: $Z_1 = Z_1(1/p)$ and $Z_2 = Z_2(p)$.

Suppose that the home country imports the first commodity. *The total price elasticity of home import demand* is then defined as

$$\xi = \frac{1}{pZ_1} \frac{dZ_1}{d(1/p)} \tag{A.1}$$

[1] In Chap 9, Sec 1, some of the definitions are generalized to allow for international borrowing and lending.

We define also

$$\Delta = 1 + \xi + \xi^*, \tag{A.2}$$

one plus the sum of the two total price elasticities of import demand.

Since Z_i is the excess demand for the ith commodity, $-Z_i$ must be the excess supply. Accordingly, we may define the home country's *total price elasticity of export supply* as

$$\epsilon = \frac{p}{Z_2} \frac{dZ_2}{dp} \tag{A.3}$$

Let

$$Z_2 = G(Z_1)$$

be the equation of the home country's offer curve. Then

$$e = \frac{Z_1}{Z_2} \frac{dZ_2}{dZ_1} = \frac{Z_1}{Z_2} G_2' \tag{A.4}$$

is the *elasticity of the offer curve*.

2. RELATIONSHIPS BETWEEN ELASTICITIES

We have

$$
\begin{aligned}
&= \frac{Z_2}{Z_1^2}\left(dZ_1/d\,\frac{Z_2}{Z_1}\right) \qquad \text{Since } Z_1 = -pZ_2 \\
&= \left(\frac{Z_1}{Z_2}\frac{dZ_2}{dZ_1} - 1\right)^{-1} \\
&= \frac{1}{e-1}
\end{aligned}
\tag{A.5}
$$

We have also

$$
\begin{aligned}
&= \frac{Z_1}{Z_2^2}\left(dZ_2/d\,\frac{Z_1}{Z_2}\right) \\
&= \left(\frac{Z_2}{Z_1}\frac{dZ_1}{dZ_2} - 1\right)^{-1} \\
&= \frac{e}{1-e}
\end{aligned}
\tag{A.6}
$$

It follows from (A14.5) and (A14.6) that

$$1 + \xi + \epsilon = 0 \tag{A.7}$$

Finally, from (A14.7),

$$(1 + \xi + \epsilon) + (1 + \xi^* + \epsilon^*) = (1 + \xi + \xi^*) + (1 + \epsilon + \epsilon^*) = 0 \tag{A.8}$$

Index

Author Index *

Allen, R. G. D., 27
Arrow, Kenneth J., 246, 334

Baldwin, R. E., 322
Benham, Frederic, 21–22
Bhagwati, Jagdish, 283, 311
Bickerdike, C. F., 299, 300, 339
Block, H. D., 246
Bronfenbrenner, M., 339
Brown, A. J., 89

Caincross, A. K., 321
Caves, Richard E., 2, 266
Chipman, John S., 2, 32, 33, 79, 94

David, Paul A., 281
Drandakis, Emanuel M., 242

Edgeworth, F. Y., 53, 57, 107, 108, 113, 300
Eisenberg, E., 22
Enke, Stephen, 258

Findlay, Ronald, 57
Fishlow, Albert, 281

Graham, Frank D., 99, 115
Grubert, Harry, 57

Haberler, Gottfried, 286, 339
Hagen, Everett E., 281
Hahn, F. H., 334
Herberg, Horst, 166, 270
Hicks, J. R., 54, 293
Hirschman, A. O., 339
Horwell, D. J., 305
Hurwicz, Leonid, 246, 334

Inada, Ken-ichi, 33, 190
Iversen, Carl, 321

Johnson, Harry G., 21, 33, 127, 281, 283, 303, 308
Jones, Ronald W., 54, 303

Kemp, Murray C., 33, 37, 90, 98, 99, 107, 156, 175, 190, 239, 242, 270, 300, 303, 308, 311
Keynes, J. M., 321

Laing, N. F., 174

* Bibliographies at the end of each chapter are arranged according to the subject matter treated, each section in alphabetical order according to the last name of the author. Page references to works in these bibliographies are not included in this index.

355

Leontief, Wassily, 88–90, 286, 293
Lerner, Abba P., 77, 84, 96, 114

MacDougall, G. D. A., 321
McManus, Maurice, 283
Malthus, Thomas Robert, 286
Marshall, Alfred, 84, 89, 90, 98, 99, 114, 115
Matthews, R. C. O., 304
Metzler, Lloyd A., 339
Mills, John Stuart, 53, 57, 103, 113, 285, 300
Minabe, Nobuo, 33

Negishi, Takashi, 155, 274, 281, 311, 334, 339
Nurkse, Ragner, 321

Ohlin, Bertil, 286
Olsen, Erling, 258
Ostrowski, Alexander, 34

Pearce, I. F., 305
Pigou, A. C., 286

Ramaswami, V. K., 311
Robinson, Joan, 339
Rybczynski, T. N., 130

Samuelson, Paul A., 20, 22, 77, 84, 90, 130, 254, 256, 257, 258, 286, 322, 323
Schonfield, Andrew, 321
Scitovský, Tibor, 321
Sidgwick, Henry, 300
Singer, H. W., 321
Slutzky, Eugene E., 23, 25
Smith, Adam, 321

Taussig, F. W., 286
Torrens, R., 300

Uekawa, Yasuo, 33, 37

Viner, Jacob, 2, 286

Walsh, V. C., 129
Wegge, Leon L., 30, 33, 37
Wold, Herman, 293

Subject Index

Autarkic equilibria, 75–77

Balance of payments, 141–142
Bonds, 345–348

Cobb-Douglas production function, 54
Commodities, non-traded, 134–147
Commodity prices, 122–127
  equilibrium outputs and, 166–167
Constants:
  endowments, 162–164
  factor rewards, 164
  outputs, 161
  product prices, 165–166
Consumption taxes, 275–276
Corn Laws, 51

Damnification, 108, 110, 111–112
Demand shifts, 98–102, 114–115
  generalized, 102
  Grahamesque, 101
  Marshallian, 100–101
  of the third kind, 101–102
Devaluation:
  long-run effects, 339–340
  short-run effects, 335–339
Duality relations, 13–19

Economic expansion, 104–113

Economies:
  barter, 5, 212
  simple closed, 5–51
  simple open, 52–63
  tax ridden, 275–278
Edgeworth-Bowley box diagram, 15
Elasticities:
  impart demand, 190–191
  prices, 352–353
  relationships between, 353
  of substitution, 27
Endowments:
  changes in, 109–111, 144–146
  constant, 162–164
Equalization of factor rewards, 77–83,
    92–94
Equilibria:
  autarkic, 75–77
  equalization of factor rewards, 77–83,
    92–94
  of factor prices, 82–83
  free-trade, 75
  the Heckscher-Ohlin Theorem, 74–77
  international, 169–173
  long-run, 219–235, 243–246
  outputs, commodity prices and, 166–
    167
  properties, 74–87
  short-run, 216–219, 240–242

Equilibria (*cont.*)
stability, 83–87
Excess demands, 85
Exchange rates, floating, 344–345
Exchange Stabilization Fund, 332

Factor Prices Equalization Theorem, 154, 155
Factors:
changes in endowment, 109–111, 144–146
equal numbers, 32–44
equalization of prices, 82–83
equalization of rewards, 77–83, 92–94
partial correspondence, 44
prices, 122–127
of production, international migration, 181–182
real income and increase in supply, 111
relative rewards, 21–26, 28, 173–174
rewards constant, 164
unequal numbers, 45–51
variable supply, 119–133
Free trade, 182, 185–187
equilibria, 75

Geometric illustrations, 129–132
Grahamesque demand shifts, 101
Growth, 215–249
international trade and, 215–236
trade, international investment and, 237–249

Heckscher-Ohlin Theorem, 74–77
Hicksian stability, 126

Import demand, elasticity of, 190–191
Imported raw materials, 260–261
Increasing returns:
with distorting externalities, 273–275
to scale, 270–272
Interest, rate of, 345–348
Intermediate goods, 148–153
International equilibrium, 169–173
stability, 169–173
International investment:
appraisal, 253–327
trade, growth and, 237–249
International migration of factors of production, 181–212
International trade:
appraisal, 253–327
economic growth and, 215–236
investment and growth, 237–249
theory, 119–133

International transfers, 102–104, 116
Investment, 215–249
gain from, 253–289
international, 237–249
international, appraisal, 253–327
long-run, 246–248
statically considered, 290–327

Jacobi's theorem, 34, 36

Labor, migration of, 206–210
Leontief's paradox, 88–90
Leontief-Wold-Hicks Theorem, 293
Lerner-Metzler condition, 203
Lerner-Metzler possibility, 143
Long-run equilibrium, 219–235, 243–246
Long-run investment, 246–248
Long-run trade, 246–248

Market stability, 192–196
Marshallian demand shifts, 100–101
Marshallian model, 89
Marshall-Lerner condition, 84
Migration:
international, 181–212
of labor, 206–210
Minkowski matrices, 34, 35, 36

Non-traded commodities, 134–147

Offer curve, 63, 127–129, 138–141, 167–169
Optimal Loci, 292
Outputs, 122–127
constant, 161

Prices:
commodity, 122–127
commodity, equilibrium outputs and, 166–167
elasticities, 352–353
factor, 122–127
factor equalization, 82–83
product, 165–166
world, 290–310
Product prices constant, 165–166
Production:
Cobb-Douglas function, 54
international migration of factors, 181–212
taxes, 276–278
Products:
equal numbers, 32–44
partial correspondence, 44
unequal numbers, 45–51

Rate of exchange, pegged, 332–335
Rate of interest, 345–348
Raw materials, imported, 260–261
Real income, increase in factor supply and, 111

Samuelson-Rybczynski Theorem, 14–16, 43–44, 152, 154, 155, 164–166
Short-run equilibrium, 216–219, 240–242
Slutzky decompositions, 140
Stability, 83–87
  Hicksian, 126
  international equilibrium, 169–173
  long-run equilibrium, 243–246
  market, 192–196
  short-run equilibrium, 240–242
Stolper-Samuelson Theorem, 16–19, 30–32, 33, 43, 151, 152, 154, 155, 161–164

Tariffs:
  changes, 95–98, 113–114, 142–144, 196–203
  foreign country, 303–304
  optimal structures, 296–305
  ranking of uniform, 305–310
  -ridden trade, 183–184, 187–190
  sub-optimal policy, 310–313
Taxes:
  changes, 203–206
  consumption, 275–276
  production, 276–278
  relative factor rewards and, 21–26, 28
Tax-ridden economies, 275–278
Technical improvements, 282–285
  implications, 53–60
Technological improvements, 111–113
Trade, 215–249
  barter, 5, 212
  change in the terms, 60–63

Trade (*cont.*)
  free, 75, 182, 185–187
  gain from, 253–289
  international, appraisal, 253–327
  international, economic growth and, 215–236
  international, investment and growth, 237–249
  international, theory, 119–133
  long-run, 246–248
  optimal, 290–327
  restricted, 267–268
  tariff-ridden, 183–184, 187–190
  in tax-ridden economies, 275–278
  terms, 141–142
  welfare and, 262–265, 268–270
Trading world, 71–94
  comparative statics, 95–118
  demand shifts, 98–102, 114–115
  economic expansion, 104–113
  equalization of factor rewards, 77–83, 92–94
  the Heckscher-Ohlin Theorem, 74–77
  international transfers, 102–104, 116
  model, 71–73
  properties of equilibria, 74–87
  stability, 83–87
  tariff changes, 95–98, 113–114

Unilateral transfers, 141–142, 261–262

Variable returns to scale, 154–180

Wage rates, 279
Walras' Law, 241
Welfare:
  technical improvements and, 282–285
  terms of trade and, 262–265, 268–270
World prices, 290–296
  variable, 296–310